KU-131-618

# Hugh Johnson's *Wine*

# Hugh Johnson's *Wine*

Drawings by Owen Wood

MITCHELL BEAZLEY

0755697 A

Class φ 641 . 22 Joh

Hugh Johnson's Wine
First published in Great Britain in 1966 by Thomas Nelson
Limited, London

Revised edition 1974
Reprinted 1978, 1981, 1984, 1987, 1992, 1994
This edition reprinted 1997 by Mitchell Beazley,
an imprint of Reed International Books Limited,
Michelin House, 81 Fulham Road, London SW3 6RB and
Auckland and Melbourne

Copyright © Reed International Books Limited 1997
Text copyright © Hugh Johnson 1974, 1997

All rights reserved. No part of this work may be
reproduced or utilized in any form or by any means,
electronic or mechanical, including photocopying,
recording or by any information storage and retrieval
system, without the prior written permission of the
publisher.

ISBN 0 85533 039 2

A CIP catalogue record for this book is available from the
British Library.

Typesetting by Tradespools Ltd, Frome, Somerset
Produced by Mandarin Offset
Printed and bound in China

# Contents

*Wine* 9

How Wine is Made—Wine in the Past—Wine in Britain and
the United States—The Names of Wines—What is "Great"
Wine?—Wine and Time—Vintages—Choosing Wine—
Serving Wine—Food and Wine

*Aperitifs* 46

Sherry—Champagne—Other Sparkling Wines—Madeira—
Vermouths and Patent Aperitifs

*White Table Wines* 82

The White Wines of Burgundy—The White Wines of
Bordeaux—The White Wines of the Loire—The White
Wines of Alsace—The Rhône Valley—German White Wines—
Italian White Wines—Portuguese White Wines—Spanish
White Wines—Swiss and Austrian White Wines—Eastern
European White Wines—Californian White Wines—
Australian White Wines—South African White Wines—
White Wines of the Eastern Mediterranean—Rosé Wines

*Red Table Wines* 166

The Red Wines of Bordeaux—The Red Wines of Burgundy—
The Rhône Valley—Vins de Pays—Italian Red Wines—
Spanish Red Wines—Portuguese Red Wines—Eastern
European Red Wines—Californian Red Wines—Other Red
Wines

*After-Dinner Wines* 230

Port—Madeira—Other Strong Sweet Wines—Light Sweet
Wines—The Muscat Family—Passiti—Sparkling Wines after
Dinner

*Vintage Charts* 256

*Index* 258

*To the many lovers of wine who have helped*
*and instructed me, and particularly*
*to those who read the manuscript*
*of this book and suggested improvements*
*I offer my heartfelt thanks; to none more than*
TO MY WIFE JUDY

# Wine

Think, for a moment, of an almost paper-white glass of liquid, just shot with greeny-gold, just tart on your tongue, full of wild-flower scents and spring-water freshness. And think of a burnt-umber fluid, as smooth as syrup in the glass, as fat as butter to smell and sea-deep with strange flavours. Both are wine.

Wine is grape-juice. Every drop of liquid filling so many bottles has been drawn out of the ground by the roots of a vine. All these different drinks have at one time been sap in a stick. It is the first of many strange and some—despite modern research—mysterious circumstances which go to make wine not only the most delicious, but the most fascinating, drink in the world.

It would not be so fascinating if there were not so many different kinds. Although there are people who do not care for it, and who think it no more than a nuisance that a wine-list has so many names on it, the whole reason that wine is worth study is its variety.

From crushed grapes come an infinite number of scents and flavours, to some extent predictable, to some extent controllable—to some extent neither. The kind of vines, where they are planted, how they are pruned, when they are picked, how they are pressed and how long they are aged all bear on the eventual taste. And behind each of these factors there is a tradition or argument or set of reasons why it should be done this way rather than that, and a wonderful variety of ideas about the ideal in view.

Wine is the pleasantest subject in the world to discuss. All its associations are with occasions when people are at their best; with relaxation, contentment, leisurely meals and the free flow of ideas. The scope of the subject of wine is never-ending. To me its fascination is that so many other subjects lie within its boundaries. Without geography and topography it is incomprehensible; without history it is colourless; without taste it is meaningless; without travel it remains unreal. It embraces botany, chemistry, agriculture, carpentry, economics—and any number of sciences whose names I do not even know. It leads you up paths of knowledge and byways of expertise you would never glimpse without it. Best of all, it brings you into friendly contact with some of the most skilful and devoted craftsmen, the most generous and entertaining hosts you will find anywhere.

Wine has the most precious quality that art has: it makes ideas, people, incidents, places, sensations seem larger than life. It is, in Bernard Berenson's awkward but irreplaceable phrase, life-enhancing.

Unfortunately, one of the things which wine can make larger than life is a bore. A wine bore is a serious menace. Worse still is a wine snob. But boredom and snobbery lurk in every calling and every subject. They are no monopoly of wine. To me a car bore is far worse than a wine bore. I find even in an old droner's reminiscences about cobwebbed bottles a possible source of illumination.

There is, as I have already said, no end to what you can learn about wine. I know perfectly well that I have only just begun. Everybody will find some hole in this book. Some will find more holes than substance. But if this is the case I hope they will at least, like the holes in lace, make a pattern.

# How Wine is Made

The difference between grape-juice, simple and sweet, and wine with all its qualities of keeping, of maturing and finally of inspiring, is the process of fermentation. In fermentation sugar is transformed into alcohol: grape-juice becomes wine.

Fermentation comes naturally to grapes. Wine did not have to wait to be invented. A grape left alone could make wine if its skin were broken. Everything needed to make wine is there already when the grape has ripened on the vine.

In the final stages of ripening, yeast cells appear from somewhere—it is not clear where—on the skin of the grape and cling to it. As soon as its skin is broken they pounce on the sugar in its juice, which is their object, and turn it into alcohol. Only a grape has enough sugar for this to happen naturally. So-called wines are made from other fruit, but all need extra sugar. Something like 30 per cent of the juice of a ripe grape is sugar, and this the yeast cells set about converting.

*Pressing*

The way the grapes are broken and the container they ferment in are two of the most variable things about wine. On small farms in Chianti all the grapes, black and white, are bundled together in a large opening at the top of a barrel. They still have their stalks, even the mud from the fields on them. They have only been slightly broken up, in the big tub on an ox-cart into which they were gathered, by the farmer with a knotty club. He plunges it up and down a few times to see that a fair proportion of the grapes have been smashed, relying on the heat generated in the barrel when fermentation starts to swell and burst the rest.

On a few farms in France, Portugal, Spain and some parts of Italy the grapes are still trodden by bare feet, as they have been since wine was first made.

Larger wine-growers now all have presses or mechanical crushers to break the grapes, but even these vary from old hand-operated squeezers to huge revolving horizontal drums. The latest kind have a gigantic rubber balloon inside. When it is inflated it presses the grapes against the slatted sides and forces out their juice without crushing their pips, which contain unwanted and evil-tasting substances.

The biggest presses of all are those of Champagne, in which an enormous weight descends by scarcely perceptible degrees on an enclosure containing four tons of grapes at a time.

Usually the juice and broken grapes, or for white wine the juice alone, are pumped for fermentation into vats or barrels, traditionally of oak but now more and more of concrete, glass or stainless steel. Sometimes it is left to ferment where it has been crushed or trodden.

*Fermentation*

The process of fermentation, which is what happens when the yeast cells get to work, produces turbulent eruptions in the juice. Not only alcohol is made, but carbon dioxide gas is given off in large quantities. Its bubbles keep the mass of broken grapes moving. At the same time the heat given off by the reaction makes it warm.

Fermentation goes on until the sugar supply runs out, or until the yeast cells are asphyxiated by the growing concentration of alcohol, whichever happens sooner. Usually it is the sugar which gives out first. The liquid, then, instead of being a solution of sugar and water, is a solution of alcohol in water, with the same small quantities of the acids and oils which give it its peculiar flavour and scent. On average there will be about 10 per cent of alcohol in red wine, a little more—11 or so—in white. There is no sugar left at all and the resulting wine is completely dry.

If, on the other hand, the grapes were so ripe that there was still more sugar to ferment when a concentration of 15 per cent alcohol was reached, it would be the yeast cells which would give out first. In a solution of alcohol this strong they grow drowsy and cease to function. They are not dead, but they are completely under the table. When this happens there is still some sugar left unconverted into alcohol and the wine is more or less sweet to the taste.

This process is the basic one for the making of all wine and, come to that, of any other alcoholic drink.

*Table wine*

A wine made in this way, without any diversions from the natural processes, will be what we call a table wine. It will be mild in flavour, moderate in alcoholic strength; still, not sparkling. It will be red or white or pink according to whether the juice was separated from the skins before or after it was allowed to ferment, and according to what colour of grapes it was made from.

Diversions can be put in its way during the fermentation process, however, which can make it other things. It can be made to stay sweet, by keeping its natural sugar, or it can be made to sparkle, by keeping its natural gas. These two techniques together with the first make up the three main classes of wine: natural, fortified and sparkling.

*Sparkling wine*

Champagne is the greatest and best-known sparkling wine. All other makers of quality sparkling wines proceed on principles worked out in Champagne over the last three hundred years. It is a question of bottling the wine before the fermentation is quite finished, so that some of the natural carbon dioxide is trapped in the bottle. (This will be explained in the chapter on champagne in the Aperitifs section.)

*Fortified wine*

Port is the typical fortified wine. The object is to make it as sweet as possible. This is done by starting the fermentation in the usual way, with very ripe grapes capable of continuing to ferment until there is at least 15 per cent alcohol, and then suddenly, at the halfway point, emptying them out of the tank where they are fermenting into a barrel a quarter full of brandy. The alcohol level is immediately raised to the point where the yeast cells are stupefied and can do no more. Half the sugar from the grapes remains in the wine, which is hence very strong and very sweet at the same time.

Sherry, though a fortified wine, is made quite differently. Fermentation goes right on to the end, and no sugar whatsoever is left. Fortification comes afterwards; the brandy is used as a sort of preservative. Any sweetness which is required has to be added in a blend.

*Chaptalization*

In some northern wine-areas, notably in France and Germany, the sun often fails to produce enough sugar in the grapes. The growers then have to resort to adding sugar—a process known as chaptalization after M Chaptal, the French Minister for Agriculture who first authorized it—to get the fermentation going and to make the wine strong enough to keep. Originally this only happened in poor years: it made poor wine, but the wine would have been worse without it. Today, to the regret of many, the practice has spread, so that sugar is often added as a means of increasing the strength of perfectly sound wine. Wine which contains alcohol derived from cane- as opposed to grape-sugar can never be as good as the natural product—an argument the Californians are not slow to use against the French, who are increasingly prone to sugar their vats. For their part, the Germans today keep some sweet unfermented must or *süss-reserve*, handy to adjust the eventual sweetness of the wine. At least it is grape-sugar they are adding.

## The scientific revolution

What modern scientific knowledge has brought to wine-making is above all the power of control. Our ancestors who developed the time-hallowed ways of making our different wines—discovering, for instance, the use and value of barrels and cellars—were working in the dark. They had little or no notion of the reasons for the success of one approach and the failure of another.

Pasteur introduced the scientific approach to wine a hundred years ago. But still, until very recently, we had scarcely got further than druggists' remedies for the ills that wine is heir to. It is the last two decades, and above all the last ten years, which have perfected our understanding. Revolution is the only possible word for the changes in wine-technique which are coming into use today. In a nutshell, this revolution consists of a shift from chemical to physical techniques. Where, for example, germ-bludgeoning sulphur was universally used as wine's antiseptic, the modern wine-maker can keep his wine safe and sound by refrigeration, and by excluding the air from it with a blanket of carbon dioxide.

Such controls are daily being proved capable of making silk purses out of what used to be considered sows' ears. To some extent they are proving that the long-established superiority of the cooler vineyards of, for example, France, over the hotter ones of Spain or Italy or Australia, is a question of timings and temperatures perfectly susceptible to human control. If, let us say, what was wrong with Australian Riesling was that the grapes were too ripe, and fermented too hot, Australians have now learnt to pick them sooner and keep them cool.

Better still, having found that such controls work, growers have the incentive to plant the finer grape varieties to take advantage of them. Areas where quantity was the only aim (the South of France is the obvious example) are realizing that quality is within their reach—and they are grasping for it.

# Wine in the Past

It is not known who first discovered wine. *Vitis vinifera*, the species of vine which grows wine-grapes, is apparently a native of Persia. Certainly wine was drunk in ancient Persia, in ancient Egypt and in ancient Greece. It spread, as our civilization spread, from the East. At each move of civilizing influence—of the Phoenicians to Spain, the Greeks to Italy and Provence, the Romans through Gaul to Germany—the vine moved too. Wine lies at the roots of our civilization. It is an integral part of both the Christian and Jewish religions.

*The Romans*

There is no room here to trace its progress in detail. It came to many of what are now its most prosperous regions with the Romans. The routes the Romans took, and made their lines of communication, were the river valleys. In France and Germany they are still the centres of wine-growing, for nothing has challenged their old-established position, their accessibility and the convenience of their transport. At the start there were probably two considerations. The first was to clear the forests on the river banks to make guerrilla warfare and ambushes more difficult; where the ground was cleared would be the natural place to plant vines. The second was that transport of bulky wine-barrels was impossible except by water.

In the event it was found that nothing had such a pacifying and civilizing effect on the tribes as having their own vineyards. People whose previous life had been hunting and fighting became farmers for the sake of wine. The vine is as demanding as it is rewarding to grow. It needs constant care, so it required settling down. Out of the inspiration it gave, the arts of peace grew. In a very important way you can say that wine was responsible for the establishing of a stable society, and hence of civilization, in Europe.

So it is not surprising that the vine is an age-old symbol of peace and prosperity. As James Busby, the man who inspired the beginnings of the Australian wine industry, declared: "The man who could sit under the shade of his own vine with his wife and children about him, and the ripe clusters hanging within their reach, and not feel the highest enjoyment, is incapable of happiness . . ."

*The Church*

The decline and fall of the Roman Empire in continental Europe left the Church in power. It was the Church that kept alive the vital skills of civilization—agriculture, letters, the law—while the new races from the East came to take over the Empire. The knowledge of wine-making became almost a monopoly of the Church.

So it remained, by and large, for a thousand years. All over the vineyards of Europe the traces remain to this day. In France it was the Revolution which deprived the Church of her lands and auctioned them among the people. In Germany many of the monasteries were secularized by Napoleon. The Church has few vineyards of note now except in Germany, but to her we owe the whole of the long wine-making tradition which is continuous from the Romans to the twentieth century.

## Establishment of regional characters

Already in Roman times most of the vineyards we know in Europe today were planted and producing. The wines were different. Champagne was not sparkling; sherry was not fortified; we do not know where white wine was made and where red. None of the now familiar and long-established types of wine were known—but the ball had been set rolling. Each district would slowly discover for itself what its natural inclinations were, for white or red, for one kind of grape or another, for longer or shorter periods of ripening, of fermentation, of maturing. Nobody came to Burgundy and said, "Here we will make a rich, savoury, ruby-red table wine"; nobody planting a vine on the Mountain of Reims ever dreamt that its wine would one day be full of glittering foam. It was Burgundy which decided what burgundy would be like, and Champagne which put the first bubbles into champagne. After generations, centuries, of experiment the character of the region began to emerge and men began to see what had to be done to perfect it. In this sense the wines of Europe are direct expressions of the country they come from: natural, not designed; emerging, not induced.

Each of the vineyards of Europe now has one kind of wine and makes no other. The result of centuries of trial and error is complete specialization. One grape-variety and one method of making the wine has always established itself as the best for the district in the end.

## The New World

Wine has been a brilliantly successful transplantation from the Old World to the New. The first of the European settlements to have the vine were South America and South Africa. To South America it went with the Conquistadors. It was already well established at the Cape by the end of the seventeenth century. California and Australia, the two other chief New World vineyards, started their development simultaneously in the second quarter of the nineteenth century.

The New World settlers took over from Europe not only the vine but the ideas of what kinds of wine they wanted to make. The process of trial and error to establish the country's own kind of wine was never really allowed to happen. The principal difference between the wines of the New and Old Worlds results from this transplantation of ideas.

In California or Australia one winery often makes "champagne", "port", "claret" and "Chablis" from the grapes of one vineyard. It is only a matter, they tell you, of planting the right variety for the job and using the right techniques of vinification. Rather than give the country the chance to express itself through the wine it produces, by experimenting until a new personality emerges, wine-makers tried to get burgundy, for example, out of Australia, a task more difficult than getting blood out of a stone.

It is apparently better business for a wine-maker to be able to offer a complete range of products than to be famous for one; say, his sparkling wine or his dessert wine. The difference in philosophy is basic. There are still very few exceptions. It should always be borne in mind when comparing New World vintages with those of the Old.

## The phylloxera

It is curious that wine-making in North America had to wait until the developing of California. By that time the eastern States had been settled and civilized for two hundred years. Their climate was equally suited to the vine. Their people were good wine-drinkers. Why did Virginian wine not grow up in the seventeenth century?

The answer lies in the terrible little beetle-like creature called the phylloxera, a native of the eastern United States. Nothing was known about him until about a hundred years ago, but he had meanwhile been preventing the growing of grapes for wine anywhere in his domain. All that the farmers knew was that the European vines they planted withered and died. There is a kind of vine that is native to North America; it grew profusely—giving really terrible wine where anybody tried to tame it—and was immune to the attacks of the phylloxera. But the imported vines of Europe were no sooner planted than their roots were eaten up and they died.

The importance of this for Europe was not realized until too late. The little beetle found its way to France in the 1860s, probably on an American vine being imported for experimental grafting purposes. Its progeny swept through the country like the plague, doing the most appalling damage. Within twenty years they had killed virtually every vine in France—in Bordeaux, Burgundy, Champagne: nowhere was spared. The rest of Europe suffered the same fate. So, before long, did the European vines in California and Australia. For a while it looked like the end of European wine. But it was discovered that the roots of the American vines were immune to phylloxera. There was nothing else for it but to bring in millions of American vine-stocks and graft on to them the remaining cuttings of the old European vines. To everybody's infinite relief it worked. The roots resisted the scourge; the branches bore their old fruit. There will always be arguments about whether the wine is quite as good as it was before the disaster. But it was saved, that was the great thing. And to this day every European vine is grafted, before it is planted, on to an American root.

# Wine in Britain and the United States

An English autumn, though it hath no vines
Blushing with Bacchant coronals along
The paths, o'er which the far festoon entwines
The red grape in the sunny lands of song,
Hath yet a purchased choice of choicest wines;
The claret light and the Madeira strong.
If Britain mourn her bleakness, we can tell her,
The very best of vineyards is the cellar.                    Byron, *Don Juan*, 13, LXXVI

There is no reason why wine should not be grown in England. At the present time there are only a fistful of commercial vineyards of any size. But there are two dozen or more in small-scale production. The climate is no more unsuitable for the vine than it is in the northern Rhine vineyards of Germany. Indeed Britain's chief drawback as a vineyard seems to be the number of its birds which are fond of grapes. For the months before the harvest English wine growers have to be out in the vineyards at dawn and keep watch till nightfall to prevent their year's work from being gobbled.

## The Middle Ages

Wine used to be grown in England on a large scale, and might easily be a normal part of British agriculture today had it not been for the marriage of King Henry II of England to Queen Eleanor of Aquitaine in 1152. The Queen's lands included the vineyards of Bordeaux. There was a plentiful supply of the best red wine in the world, grown on an estuary within easy sailing distance of England. As Edward Hyams says in *Dionysus*, his history of the vine, "the infant English industry was overlaid at birth by its immensely vigorous Gallic mother"

*The rise of Bordeaux*

During the three hundred years that Bordeaux belonged to England its wine was the everyday English drink. The discovery of Bordeaux by the English made a tremendous difference to that quiet province. Nothing like today's vast acreage was planted with vines in those days. The whole of the Médoc, the district which is now the most important, was unplanted; production was, by present-day standards, minute. But the connection with England changed things completely. The English soon proved to have an unquenchable thirst for claret, which was what they christened the pale red wine that was Bordeaux's principal produce. New vineyards sprang up everywhere —even on the corn-lands, causing a serious shortage of bread.

It is astonishing to think that in the fourteenth century more claret was being drunk in England than is today. The population was not a twentieth of today's but the total gallonage of claret shipped was as high or higher. So important was the wine trade in medieval England that the size of all ships, whatever their cargo or purpose, was measured in the number of tuns of wine that they could carry.

*British consumption*

A tun was a cask which held about two hundred and fifty gallons. In Froissart's *Chronicle* there is a reference to the wine fleet of 1372 of ships from England, Wales and Scotland at Bordeaux. There were, he said, two hundred ships. According to Sir John Clapham, in his *Concise Economic History of Britain*, "the average tonnage of the time would be well over fifty, seeing that at Bristol rather later it was eighty-eight". Allowing sixty tuns to the ship, the total cargo of wine in 1372 was three million gallons; perhaps something in the region of six bottles of claret per head for every man, woman and child in England, Wales and Scotland. Today, of all table wines, claret included, we barely drink the same amount.

That claret was considered a part of the staple diet, even of the ordinary man, is clear from the fact that, again according to Clapham, in 1282 Edward I, providing for his Welsh war, ordered six hundred tuns of wine (a hundred and fifty thousand gallons) as an ordinary commissariat operation.

England lost Bordeaux in 1453. At an action which was nonetheless heroic—though a good deal less talked about in England—because we lost it, Marshal Talbot was killed defending the last of the dwindling English interests in Aquitaine. An apple tree grows today on the spot where the last English troops are said to have held the last piece of English Bordeaux. The place is called Castillon.

From that time on, claret supplies slowly became more difficult for the English. The people of Bordeaux, who were not necessarily any too pleased by their liberation, could not afford to stop selling their wine in its best market. Precautions had to be taken, though, to prevent the English wine fleet from singeing the King of France's beard. For a time the English ships were compelled to heave to at the fortress of Blaye on the way up the Gironde and land their guns on the quay, like gunfighters going into a Dodge City saloon. They then sailed up to Bordeaux unmolested, checking out at Blaye on the way back.

The story goes that the Scottish merchants took advantage of the friendly relations between Scotland and France to get the pick of the vintage each time. Not having to stop to surrender their guns, they managed to get the best wine at the best price. The taste for fine claret persists in Scotland to this day.

*The seventeenth century*

The English have never drunk so much claret as they did in the days when it was, as it were, native produce. They turned to Rhenish, the wine of the Rhine, and more and more to the sweet Mediterranean wines which the Genoese merchants brought. Sack was the best.

Nevertheless the claret habit never completely died in England. It is at the end of the seventeenth century that we find the first mention of a château of Bordeaux by name in English. It was Pepys who mentioned it, and the wine was "Ho Bryan [Haut-Brion]; that hath a good and most particular taste that I ever met with". The date was 10 April 1663.

*The beginning of port*

But that was the age of Louis XIV. With the fall of the royal house of Stuart, animosity between England and France grew from dark dealings to war, and then, as now, economic sanctions were a useful weapon. The trade in French wines was sharply discouraged by the English government, and England made a treaty with Portugal (whose wine she had first met when Charles II married a Portuguese princess) to ensure herself an alternative supply, as well as a market for her manufactured goods.

That the change from claret to port was not a change of taste is shown by the famous Scottish verse:

> Firm and erect the Highland chieftain stood
> Old was his mutton and his claret good.
> "Thou shalt drink Port" the English statesman cried.
> He drank the poison—and his spirit died.

To start with, certainly, the Portuguese wine which the English and (since the Parliamentary Union of England and Scotland in 1707) the Scots were obliged to drink instead of claret was a poor substitute. How merchants—it is interesting that some of the first were Scotsmen —went out to Portugal and invented port is another story. They made out of a bad substitute for claret one of the great, and completely different, wines of the world. It is noticeable how the torrent of protest died away as the eighteenth century wore on—and the port matured. During the eighteenth century it was port—and in America Madeira—which might have been called the favourite and most fashionable wine.

*A great invention*

But during this time also the vineyards of Bordeaux were taking on a new splendour. In the eighteenth century the great invention, the cork, changed the nature of claret—and indeed of every wine. It made its long ageing in bottle (instead of its rapid consumption from the barrel) a possibility. It brought new sensations into being, and changed wine from a mere healthy, pleasant, enlivening drink to something which was capable of real character, and hence of every level of enjoyment from the purely sensual to the purely aesthetic.

Claret changed, during the century when it was least drunk in England, from being a pale, short-lived, hand-to-mouth sort of drink —indeed the wine which had earned the name of claret—to a deep, brilliant, strong and incredibly long-lived, yet subtle, delicate and delicious wine.

In the cellar of Château Lafite there is to this day a bin of the vintage of 1797. When they last opened a bottle, not many years ago, it was still good wine. That was the difference the cork had made.

## The Golden Age

The nineteenth century is often called the Golden Age of wine. The great estates were making wine regardless of cost. It was bought by a discerning few who had time and space to lay it down for twenty or thirty years. A race of connoisseurs grew up (there had been no such things since ancient Rome, for there had not been wine worth tasting and discussing). Vintages of superb quality seemed to come with amazing regularity.

It was then that the blow of phylloxera fell. At the time, after an extraordinary run of fine vintages in Bordeaux in the 1870s, it must have seemed to wine-lovers like the end of the world. But, oddly enough, after the replanting the recovery was remarkably swift in the best vineyards. The years 1894, 1896, 1899 and 1900 were all famous vintages. The older generation who foretold that things would never be the same again were disappointed.

The return of claret as the everyday British wine, or indeed of wine as the everyday British drink, did not come quite so easily. High rates of duty were still very much against it for most of the nineteenth century. It was not until Gladstone, with understanding unique among politicians, realized that Britain was starving herself of exactly what she needed—a supply of cheap, healthy, nourishing wine—that duties on light (i.e. table) wines were lowered, and it began to be possible, after two hundred years of being forced to drink bad spirits or heavy, liverish, cheap, fortified wines, to go back to the old English habit of a glass of red wine at every meal as a matter of course.

## Prohibition in the United States

In the second and third decades of this century the United States were foolish enough to keep themselves out of the market for the wonderful wine which Europe offered—or which California could grow. Prohibition let Britain have it all her own way. It was not really until after the Second World War that the American influence began to be felt in the auction rooms of Beaune and Trier, and wherever it is that prices are decided in the dignified silence of Bordeaux.

As for prices in the Age of Inflation, they have little to do with the history of wine, reflecting nothing but the market-place, and above all the new concept of wine as an investment commodity.

## Wine today

Wine means more to the French than even beer to the British. It almost plays the part of tea as well in their lives. Workmen start with wine for breakfast, and never stop drinking it until they go to bed. There has been a great deal of talk recently about how wine consumption is on the increase in Britain and the United States. Certainly the percentage increases over the last few years have been impressive. But we have a long way to go before we can be called wine-drinking nations. Compared with the French the Anglo-Saxon countries still scarcely touch it. The following are the total wine-drinking figures for the United Kingdom and France:

Every man, woman and child in the United Kingdom—7 bottles a year.
Every man, woman and child in France—142 bottles a year.

The figures for the United States are slightly higher than those for Britain—owing, above all, to the cheap and excellent wines of California.

*Medicinal properties*

We still suffer from ancient puritanical misconceptions which run contrary to the evidence of medical science as well as the evidence of the senses of every citizen. I am told that the medical benefits of wine are many and its disadvantages few or none. It is an antiseptic, a stimulant to the appetite (which is especially valuable to old people), an aid to digestion. It can be a help in cases of diabetes, anaemia and heart trouble. On the undiscovered borders between physical and psychological disorders its morale-raising and soothing properties can literally save life. It is absorbed at a slow and steady rate by the blood, unlike spirits, which enter the bloodstream at a gallop and, for a shorter time, raise the blood alcohol to a higher level.

People of perfectly sound health are aware of how it helps to keep them so, how it helps the body and mind to relax after the strain of work and regain the fluidity and naturalness which tension destroys.

## The wine-trade

Being importers, seeing wine as a luxury, England and America have developed a highly specialized and immensely skilful wine-trade. With no commitment, save in frequent times of war, to or against any wine-growing country or district we have learnt how to bring home the best from everywhere. In Bordeaux no-one has burgundy; in Germany nobody drinks Sauternes. Each district is loyal to its own produce. So the French, if they are the greatest producers and drinkers of wine, are also the most hidebound. To find a connoisseur in the English sense is almost impossible in France. Even a Parisian gourmet who knows his Bordeaux and burgundy back to front ignores the Moselle, say, and certainly knows nothing of sherry. Nor has he ever tasted vintage port. But we have a unique opportunity. The whole world's wines are offered to us. A good London or New York wine-list is a compilation of the best that is made in every corner of the globe.

*The great importers*

The Londoner has, if anything, the advantage over the New Yorker for variety. With wine from the Commonwealth, Eastern Europe and South Africa (even, now, from China), and with regular and flourishing auctions at Christie's and Sotheby's, London is really the wine market of the world. The only wines Britain sees little of are those of California and South America.

*New opportunities*

We are lucky in time as well as in place. There is a greater variety of wine on our lists now than there has ever been before. Modern methods and knowledge are making the production of good wine possible in countless countries where it used to be out of the question. They are also making the moving of wine safe enough to be a sound business proposition. "Small" wines have always been hamstrung in the past by the fact that even a short journey altered them radically, even if it did not spoil them altogether. With our new knowledge of their physical needs they can be stabilized, and with stability there comes the possibility of a world market for every wine under the sun.

*Decline in quality*

On the debit side it may be true that Bordeaux and burgundy used to be even better than they are today, and that German wine is not what it was. Modern conditions have skimmed off the cream of the cream. During the Golden Age in the last century and at the beginning of this, demand was comparatively low, prices of the finest wines were low, and storage of a great red wine for the twenty years or more which it takes to reach maturity presented no problem. There was no urge to keep the relatively small amount of capital involved moving. The connoisseur had a fine cellar in his own house. The wine reached its maturity slowly and a few lucky people were more than satisfied.

This is virtually impossible today. First-growth clarets come on the market at £100, or $240, a case. The interest on the value of a good cellar of such wine over twenty years is enough to make anyone pause. Even the cheapest of fine clarets which are really worth cellaring involve tying up a fair sum of money for a long, financially unprofitable time.

*Changes to come*

What is happening, and is bound to happen more and more, is that the growers, knowing perfectly well that none of their wine will be allowed to reach its maturity in the old slow way, will make a quick-maturing wine. In doing so, however, they are narrowing the gap between the traditional great wines of the world and the ever-increasing field of good wines getting better.

We are lucky, therefore, to live at the time when the old world of wine is still functioning more or less intact alongside the new world. When we can still buy clarets and burgundies made in traditional ways to develop slowly to their full stature of complexity—and put on the same table wines with new names from new places which clearly have the seeds of comparable quality in them.

# The Names of Wines

It is not heredity so much as environment which shapes a wine's character. Where a vine is planted, far more than how or even what kind of vine it is, decides the kind of wine it will give. The importance of the exact spot is graphically illustrated by the classification of the wines of Bordeaux according to quality, which was done over a hundred years ago. Since that time everything in that country—the methods, the people, even the vines themselves—have changed radically, sometimes repeatedly, and yet most of the list still holds good. The same vineyards are the best today as were the best then. In fact the land, the one unchanging factor, has turned out to be the most important.

Logically enough, then, wines are named after their birthplaces. The better the wine the more specific it is about its origin. At one end of the scale there is the homeless *vin rouge* (or even lower perhaps the bottle simply labelled Le Bon Vin, which I saw a fisherman swigging from in Brittany). At the other end there is the exceptional German growth which puts all its cards on the table, telling you the village, the vineyard, the kind of grapes, when they were picked and even the number of the barrel the particular wine came from, where it was bottled and who was responsible for each stage of its history: the growing, the bottling and the shipping.

Even among the wines whose nature depends on blending, where more specific information about their birthplace would not be available or would be far too complicated to put on a label, the better the wine the more details we are given. Sherry, champagne and port are all blended wines; we buy them by the maker's name and not by their vineyard origins, but nonetheless the best champagne and port is the one which has specific information on the label about its vintage year, the best sherry always carries its exact description in the Spanish classification—fino, amontillado or oloroso.

As the wines of the New World come of age they follow the same pattern. From merely being "Australian burgundy", the specifications begin to creep in. First it is the grape-variety that is named, then the vintage; already, in some cases, it is the particular vineyard, as it is in France.

## Fraud

It is no secret that the names of wines which have turned out, over the years, to be best and most popular have been borrowed, not to say stolen, by competitors. In some cases it is a borrowing, admitted and outright. "Spanish Chablis" may be a regrettable way of describing a white wine which has nothing whatsoever to do with the famous town of France, but it can scarcely be said to be making a false claim. False claims are, however, often made. The art of faking has at various times been carried further with wine than with any other commodity. There is plenty of wine about which pretends to be real Chablis from Chablis (France) and is not. In everybody's interest the French government has taken a firm—if not totally effective—line about this. The result of its defence of the unique rights of places to use their own names on their wines are the laws of *Appellation Contrôlée*, which can be taken as representative of the efforts of all wine countries to regularize and protect their growers. As such they have become an integral part of the naming of wine. If we are to understand the meaning of modern wine-labels at all we must have some idea of what *Appellation Contrôlée* means.

## The laws of Appellation Contrôlée

The phylloxera disaster in the 1870s and 1880s, in which virtually every vine in France died and had to be replaced (an operation which cost France considerably more even than the disastrous Franco-Prussian War), started a wave of fraud in the wine industry. Phylloxera, more than anything else, brought the government into the affairs of the wine-grower and merchant to regulate their activities. Old vineyards were in many places abandoned and new ones planted in easier, but unsuitable, places where wine was plentiful but terrible. The wrong vines were planted. In the general uproar the forgers got to work as never before.

As a result, after years of discussion, the government evolved control systems for all the important wine-areas of France. There could be no standard formula. Variation in practice, in traditions, in land-holding and every other possible aspect of wine-making meant that each system had to be evolved for the particular place. A grape which was banned in one place might be exactly right for another. In Bordeaux it was enough to protect the names of villages; in Burgundy individual plots had to have their own protection. These are the laws of *Appellation Contrôlée*. They have long had their counterpart in Germany, and Italy has now initiated a similar system. In Portugal you can see the French words *Appellation d'Origine Contrôlée* on labels as though the French laws applied in that country—so wide has been their influence.

*Quality control*  The laws of *Appellation Contrôlée* have simplified the customer's life enormously. They have laid down a naming system for each wine-district which, once you have grasped it, is pretty well foolproof. But they have another object, too. Apart from laying down what a wine may be called, they do a great deal to control its quality. They only grant the right to a name to wine which is grown on the right vine of the right age, pruned in the right way, achieves the right degree of alcoholic strength and comes up to a standard of flavour which is tested by tasting. The requirements are admittedly minimal, but they prevent any serious lagging behind by the owners of fine land.

Perhaps most important of all, both from the customer's and the grower's point of view, the *Appellation* is only granted to a certain quantity of wine from each hectare of vines each year. For a very grand growth it can be as low as thirty hectolitres, or six hundred and sixty Imperial gallons, per hectare (which is two and a half acres). In a less exalted region, Beaujolais for example, it rises to about eleven hundred gallons per hectare. But any wine made above this quantity, however good, is denied the *Appellation* and the official papers that go with it. It cannot legally be sold with its own natural name. So it becomes available for blending or selling under a brand name.

Before Britain joined the EEC (or rather up to 1974 when this particular bit of legislation was given teeth in Britain) it was the accepted practice in the British wine-trade to buy the wine which was surplus to the *Appellation* maximum (at a lower price than fully approved wine), to ship it without papers and to sell it with its full name as though it were approved. Thus Britain had supplies of genuine Nuits St. Georges, Beaune and the rest which could be sold cheaper than any in France. It goes without saying that spurious wine was easily introduced into this system. But it is absurd to suggest, as people often do, that the whole thing was a wine-trade fraud. Many wine-merchants deal strictly honestly without bureaucratic supervision. On balance it was the customer who benefited most.

Only the best wines are dealt with under the *Appellation Contrôlée* laws. Among *vins de pays* there is always the possibility of improving enough to achieve an *Appellation*. The cadet branch, as it were, for wines which are better than *ordinaire* but not quite in the *A.C.* class, is known as *V.D.Q.S.—vins délimités de qualité supérieure*. *V.D.Q.S.* wines are often seen in France, but so far the initials have made little impact abroad.

*Château-bottling*  At more or less the same time as the government in France started to talk about State controls on wine-dealing, the best dealers and growers began to take their own action. The producer's or merchant's way of tackling the problem was to bottle his wine himself with his own branded cork and give his own guarantee that the wine his customer eventually drank was the wine he grew. The practice started in Bordeaux. This bottling of the wine at the château where it was grown adds to the cost, but it is the most complete guarantee of authenticity. The words *mis en bouteilles au château*, or alternatively *mise en bouteille au château*, appearing on the label, are the guarantee. Château-bottling was followed by its equivalents, estate-bottling in Germany and domaine-bottling in Burgundy, so that now the greater part of the finest wines of all these areas are bottled where they are grown and shipped abroad, with extra freight costs, in crates instead of barrels.

The German term for estate-bottled is *eigene abfüllung*. In Burgundy there is a variety of terms, of which the commonest and best is the forthright *mise au domaine*, *mise du domaine* or *mise en bouteille au domaine*. Alternative forms, *mis en bouteilles à la propriété*, or *mise en bouteille dans nos caves* (bottled in our cellars), are suspect. Even "bottled by the proprietor" is no real guarantee; the same man may be the proprietor of several widely different properties. His *caves*, come to that, may be anywhere and contain anything.

Despite the extra cost of shipping wine in bottle rather than bulk the practice gains ground every day. Apart from the question of authenticity there is a certain amount of snobbishness in it. Shippers hope that some of the glory of the great château-bottled clarets will rub off on the cheap wines if they can announce that these, too, were château-bottled. In places—Italy is the chief example—it also helps the grower to ship his wine in good condition; he can pasteurize it in its bottle. Again, there are some wines, like the Portuguese sparkling rosé, which can only be made to stay fizzy by shipping them in bottle. Champagne, which is made in its bottle, is another matter. It does not exist in bulk, so there is no question of shipping it except in bottles.

## What is "Great" Wine?

Anyone who has high claims for his wine, then, tends to be as specific as possible about it. He uses whatever cover the law of his country allows him—the most specific appellation he is entitled to. He often goes further and bottles it himself, adding his personal guarantee.

If these precautions seem over-elaborate, consider what danger there is in more generalized naming. It is the same with food. The statement "Yorkshire pudding is delicious" is of very limited value. The important thing is who cooks it.

*Ordinary*

The daily drink of real wine-drinking countries—not those for whom wine is a luxury—is ordinary wine. In France *vin ordinaire* has a definite connotation. It is not a vague term for anything which is not very exciting. Its price depends on its strength—nothing else. It is almost always red. In Germany it is called *Konsumwein*, in Spain *vino corriente* ("current", or running, wine), in Portugal *consumo*. We have no real term of our own for it in English. *Ordinaire* is the word most commonly used. In America, particularly, "ordinary" sounds more or less insulting.

*Vin de pays*

*Vin de pays*—wine of the country—is a cut above *ordinaire*. Though the wine in itself may be no better it has one added dignity; you know where it comes from. *Ordinaire* is completely anonymous. It is often a blend of the wine of France, Spain, North Africa, Italy or anywhere where the price per degree of alcohol is low at the time. *Vin de pays* at its worst is simply *ordinaire* with a birth-certificate. At its best, on the other hand, it can be one of those excellent regional specialities that are always referred to in a patronizing way as "little". A good hotel almost anywhere in the southern half of France should have quite a good *vin du pays* (switched from *de* to *du* because it is referring to the particular bit of *pays* in question). The *patron* gets it by knowing the grower. There is not enough to become a widespread marketable proposition, but it is none the worse for that.

*Good*

With "good" wine we are on trickier ground. What does a dealer mean when he says that a picture is good? What do you mean when you say that a dish is good? They are not quite the same thing. "Good" must be allowed to cover all wine from just plain well-made upwards to the top. But at the same time it has a field of its own, between ordinary and fine. Whereas ordinary is not worth tasting with any attention, has no scent or characteristics of its own, good wine begins to be worth thinking about. It is well made and has its own character, its own variation on the general character of its region. In this class come most of the wines of Bordeaux, for example, which are not Classed Growths and, come to that, a few that are; the wines of Burgundy which are known by their village-names alone, not the names of their individual vineyards; the blended German wines such as Liebfraumilch; the Chiantis and Orvietos of Italy—all the wines which carry the name of their type, when that name is one of the world's great wine-regions.

*Fine*     There is no general agreement on what is meant by the word "fine", often though it comes into discussions about wine. I would narrow it down to the field above Good and below Great. All wines which tell their full story—their vintage year, the particular vineyard and not just the village where they were grown, often the name of the owner—on their labels should come into this class. Most—though not all—estate-bottled wines deserve to be called fine wines. In France the annual production of fine wines (in the broadest sense) in a typical year is in the region of one seventh of the total (178 million Imperial gallons in a total of 1,170 million in 1971).

*Great*     Great wine is a different matter. There is no vineyard in the world which always produces great wine, however great and famous its name. Great wine is the rare and exquisite result of perfect conditions in a perfect vineyard, perfectly handled by the grower and carefully matured afterwards. Where the line comes between fine and great is always a matter for debate. But the word should not be used lightly. A great wine is a work of art, capable of providing aesthetic pleasure of the highest order to anyone who will be attentive. As an everyday drink it is as fitting as *Hamlet* is for cabaret in a night-club. Only five or six districts in the whole world have shown themselves to be capable of producing wine like this with any regularity. They are Bordeaux, Burgundy, Champagne, the Rhine and Moselle, the Douro river in Portugal and Jerez in Spain. At various times great wine has been made in Hungary, Italy, South Africa, California, Australia, central Portugal and maybe elsewhere. But it remains rare, and grows more and more expensive as more and more people want to taste it. Even a convinced ordinary-wine drinker should taste great wine sometimes. It is easy to get into a rut with wine and to wonder what all the fuss is about when anyone mentions the glory of the best growths. I hope nobody drinks them every day, because it is partly by comparison that their superlative qualities stand out.

It is hard to put a finger on the quality of greatness in wine. To me there is always something faintly sweet, but sweet in the sense of sweet-natured rather than sugary, about one. There is a definite tendency to reach a quintessential taste of fresh grapes, as even really fine cognac does although it has been distilled. But this they all have in common, whether they are clarets, delicate fino sherries, champagne or hock or burgundy: they provoke discussion. To drink a great wine alone is almost painful. There must be somebody to share the experience with, for it is an experience, and it needs discussing, analysing and gloating over just as a great play does; or, to put it more precisely, a great picture, for it is not dramatic—it is beautiful.

# The Work of the Vineyard

"Wine is grape-juice. Every drop of liquid filling so many bottles
has been drawn out of the ground by the roots of a vine. All
these different drinks have at one time been sap in a stick."
**Above:** at Bernkastel on the Moselle Riesling vines engulf the
headlong hills of slate. Their sap becomes one of the world's most
richly aromatic wines.

There is an infinity of different ways of growing vines, adapted to local conditions, different varieties, different climates and terrains, different cultural conditions. In the simplest vineyards the vines are grown among other plants and trees, as a low bush pruned back each year to a stout stump, like the ones (**below left**) in Roussillion, south-west France. The next stage is to banish the trees and grass altogether and train the best shoots on to wires. The most extreme examples of this method are the high pergolas that are traditional to the Italian Tyrol (**below**). These are becoming scientifically fashionable as giving a big leaf area while shading the bunches. But, however vines are grown, the vineyard is full of activity all the year round from winter ploughing (**top left**), in the Loire valley, to the vintage (in Bordeaux, **bottom**) in September and October. The hand-wound machine in the picture is a *fouloir*—an old device for crushing the grapes ready for fermentation.

The vintage takes many forms: from the jolly picking party (**above**) at a Bordeaux château to the latest mechanical harvester (**above left**), which straddles a row of vines and grinds noisily along it, slapping off the bunches with plastic paddles. But like many agricultural jobs the work is hard and dull and the loads are heavy. Two men (**below**) shoulder a tub weighing as much as both of them in a Beaujolais vineyard. There are compensations, however; notably the large quantities of good food and wine (**left**) that are traditionally provided for the pickers during the three weeks or so of harvest.

# Wine and Time

It is wrong to assume that because a wine is older it is better. Tales of wonderful cobwebby old bottles have led to a general belief that age is in itself a good thing for wine. It is only partially true. There are wines which need a long time to mature. But there are others which are ruined by being kept for even as much as a year or two.

To make a very broad—in fact overbroad—rule, red wine needs more time to mature and reach its best; white wine needs less. The making of red wine, which involves the skins and the pips as well as the juice of the grapes, leaves extra substances dissolved; above all, tannin. This gives the wine the special quality of hardness, of drying up your mouth.

These extras need time to resolve themselves, to carry out slow and obscure chemical changes which make all the difference in the world to the eventual glass of wine. The better the wine, the longer it takes.

*The process of maturing*

What actually happens to wine when it ages in the bottle is not precisely known. It is assumed that it is a slowed-down version of what happens when it ages in cask. The oak staves of a cask are porous; they allow a certain amount of oxygen through to the wine and this, together with the oxygen which it has already absorbed from its previous fleeting contacts with the air, feeds the wine and causes it, in some mysterious way, to grow.

Its life-cycle is very like that of man. It develops until it reaches maturity. It stays at its peak for longer or less long; it declines and grows feeble; it finally dies. When it is dead it corrupts and grows unpleasantly rotten.

When a wine is bottled it has time to take, so to speak, a deep breath of oxygen from the air on its way from cask to bottle. Once in the bottle the air supply is short but it still, apparently, exists. Oxygen finds its way either through the cork or through the tiny space between cork and glass.

On the oxygen dissolved in it and what it can get through the cork the wine lives and grows in the bottle, as it did in the cask but more slowly. But the difference in speed of development is vital. If it were left in cask its strength and nerves would be exhausted by the growing process and it would grow old before it even matured. Only in bottle can it reach maturity.

**The cork**    For this reason the invention of the cork is the most important event in the history of fine wine. Until the time of the cork the bottle was only a decanter. Wine was kept in barrels. When it was wanted it was poured into a bottle (which might have been made of leather, earthenware or glass) and brought to table. Some wine was shipped in bottles stoppered with twisted straw or even with a film of olive oil over the wine to protect it from the air. But no wine was stoppered up for the express purpose of improving it.

However well our ancestors may have been able to make their wine in those days, therefore, it could never have reached anything like the point of soft, sweet perfection which a claret or burgundy can, if it is given the chance, today. One vintage lasted until the next, and even by this time the wine in some of the barrels had started to turn into vinegar. Usually the safest, most stable wines were those with the most sugar in them, which acted as a preservative. For this reason sweet sack, Malmsey and the muscat family of wines were the luxuries of the late Middle Ages and the Renaissance; they did not "prick", as it was called, and need disguising with honey and herbs.

When, at the beginning of the eighteenth century, the cork arrived on the scene, the perfect method of not-quite-airtight sealing was invented. From that day on, probably with port before table wine, the possibility of a wine reaching superlative maturity began to be realized. In the course of the eighteenth century the technique evolved; first with corks, then with cork-screws (without them the cork could not be rammed right home; it would never be got out again), then with the shape of the bottle changing from the old decanter shape, which could only stand up, to the modern cylindrical shape which is stored lying down.

The latter was a vital part of it. If a corked bottle is left standing up the cork eventually dries out and shrinks, air gets in and the wine turns to vinegar. The way to keep the cork from shrinking is to keep the wine touching it, storing the bottle on its side.

A few old wine "bins" in country-houses bear the marks of an intermediate stage, when it was realized that the wine must touch the cork, but the bottle shape had not yet evolved. These bins are shelves with holes cut in them so that the necks of the bulbous bottles could go downwards.

By the middle of the eighteenth century the wine had begun to emerge which would benefit by this new kind of storage. A race of connoisseurs grew up to appreciate and discuss it. Then began the age of vintage wine which is still, after two hundred years, with us.

**Quick-maturing wines**    A good many wines are still made today in the way they were before bottle-ageing came on the scene. They are all light in colour, even when they are red. To this family belong the rosés and many white wines; particularly those with not very much alcohol—refreshing, often slightly sharp, like ordinary Moselles, Muscadet, Portuguese *vinho verde*.

The fermentation of these wines is quick. There is not very much sugar to turn into alcohol, and not very much of the other substances which give wine flavour and body.

Pink wine is made like this on purpose, quickly, drawing only a thin veil of red from the skins in the fermenting vat. Of red wines which are made this way the most famous is Beaujolais *en primeur*—in the form in which it is drunk in the restaurants of Lyons and Paris, and raced by helicopter and pillion to be the first of the year in New York. It is fruity but ephemeral, purple but translucent, above all light enough to drink in full-throated swallows.

All these wines should bear as a vintage date, if they bear one at all, the latest one. In France they are called *vin de l'année*—the wine of the year. The lightest of all, which you sometimes see in cafés, is called *vin d'une nuit*—wine which only took one night to make.

By far the greater part of wine in any part of the world, however, belongs to a middle category. It has nothing special—no lovely freshness—to lose by being kept. But it has nothing to gain either. It will be drunk, because it will be needed, within a year or two of being made. It could be stored longer, but it would get no better—so why tie up the capital in it?

*Slow-maturing wines*

But all the world's best wines, certainly all great wines, belong to the last class—those which are barely drinkable when they are new; which are drinkable but rather difficult, strong-tasting, harsh, when young; but which find balance, smoothness and the full flowering of their individual character when they have been carefully, patiently stored.

It may take six years; it may take sixteen; it may even take twenty or forty. I have tasted a wonderful old South African wine, Constantia, which after a hundred and thirty years was still showing no sign of declining, but had been getting slowly better and better all that time.

That was a very sweet after-dinner wine. But I have had a claret of 1870, over a hundred years old, which though it had no sugar left to support it, nevertheless, light as a feather as it was, was lovely, complete, barely faded.

*Steinwein 1540*

Most remarkable of all—indeed probably the only case of its kind there has ever been—was a bottle of Steinwein 1540 (everybody always thinks the second figure is a misprint), the wine of Würzburg on the river Main in Germany, which Ehrmann's, the wine-merchants of Grafton Street in London, had salvaged from the cellar of King Ludwig of Bavaria. Nobody who was there when it was opened expected the contents to be wine at all. They should have been too old to drink when Shakespeare was born. Bottles of Johannisberger 1820 and Rüdesheimer 1857 had been opened first, and had been far, far too old; not a trace of the taste of wine was left. But the Steinwein 1540 was still wine; Madeira-like, dark, feeble but quite definitely alive. There was a mouthful or two, still, somehow, with the smack of a German wine about it—before it turned to vinegar in the glass. The year 1540 was an utterly exceptional one. It is said that the Rhine dried up so that you could ride a horse across it. Water cost more than wine. There never were riper grapes or sweeter wine in Germany. A big tun, or cask, was built to hold the best of the vintage at Würzburg, and there it stayed until bottles were invented to put it in two hundred years later.

If, in fact, it had been left so long it would all have evaporated—if it had not been drunk—which rather spoils the story. What really happened in all probability was that it was kept topped up with the best and sweetest of the wine from subsequent vintages. It may have been run off into smaller and smaller casks as time went on. Another German habit is to fill up the space in the cask as wine evaporates by dropping pebbles through the bung-hole: as long as the cask is full to the top the danger of the wine going bad is minimized.

In any case the wine which was eventually bottled in the eighteenth century no doubt contained a proportion of that wonderful vintage, but rather in the way that a solera sherry is partly wine eighty or a hundred years old. Its character is handed down, as it were, to its successors in the same cask. What actual liquid is the original precious grape-juice of that far-off hot summer is anybody's guess.

What cannot be denied is that this wine, after a long time in cask, was still able to survive two hundred and more years in bottle. I doubt if it will ever have a challenger.

*Red table wine*

The wine which usually needs keeping most, and repays it best, is red table wine—and, of course, port. Vintage port is a subject in itself. No other wine demands laying down in such clear terms, being undrinkable until it is at least ten years old. The effects of time on port, and the comparatively tricky business of looking after it and decanting it are discussed in the After-Dinner Wines section (page 231).

Each red wine has its own optimum age for drinking. It varies from vintage to vintage of the same vineyard, and from vineyard to vineyard of the same vintage. In the vintage charts on pages 256 and 257 there are comments on the age to drink each of the classes of wine from each district. The very lightest and weakest of clarets and red burgundies (the kind of wines which are made in rainy years) need eighteen months in cask before bottling; stronger wines with a longer future ahead of them may be kept in wood for two and a half years.

This means that the newest claret you will ever find yourself drinking will be two years old, and that will be a wine with no pretensions to class. Better wines, which are made with a view to how good they can eventually become rather than how quickly they can be ready to drink, are offered for sale two and a half to three years after the vintage, with the idea that people will buy them to keep until they are ready.

*Fatal impatience*

The system tends to break down nowadays. Everything has speeded up to such an extent; cars, jets and telephones have produced such a state of mind that it is difficult to believe that it is really necessary to keep the bottle you buy for five, even ten, years before it is ready to drink. And since many of the people—and firms—who can now afford to buy the best and most expensive have no personal experience or tradition of great wines they do not know what they are missing when they drink fine clarets too young. The honest ones admit their disappointment at having to pay eight or nine pounds a bottle for something much less pleasant to drink than the Beaujolais of the same year that they can get for an eighth of the price. The snobs pretend they like it because the name Lafite or whatever it may be is known all over the world as a superlative wine. Certain unscrupulous firms in the wine-trade more or less encourage the drinking of wine too young because it means that their money turns round faster. I remember reading in 1964 the circular of a New York wine-merchant of high repute, which said that the finest of 1961 clarets could do with a few more years in bottle "though they are excellent for drinking now" The first part is a serious understatement; the first-growth 1961s are not ready to drink yet. They may not be at their best (if any of them still exist then) for another twenty years. The second part is, to anyone with experience of drinking fine claret, a palpable lie. Only a snob could pretend that Lafite 1961 was, in 1964, as good a drink as an ordinary red Bordeaux which had come quickly to its prime. This matter of age is vital. There is no short cut. Great clarets are glorious only when they are mature, never before. To try to find out what

Château Haut-Brion is like by drinking a bottle less than (at the very least) six years old is like trying to judge a painting by not even a photograph, but a sketch.

If this seems like flying in the face of the *status quo*, if restaurant wine-lists offer three- or four-year-old first-growth clarets for drinking now, there is only one thing to be said; it is a pity. They are throwing down the drain something excellent, of which there can never be more than a limited supply.

What, then, do you drink if there is no fine claret on the list old enough to be mature? The answer is that while you are restricted to that wine-merchant or that restaurant you drink cheap wine, which has no need to be old to be at its best. For your fine wine you go elsewhere, to a merchant who has a supply of the older vintages, for wine to drink presently. And you buy some young wine, with his good advice, to lay down and keep until it is ready to drink.

*White wines*    There is no agreement about the maturing of white wines. Some like them all young. Some think nothing of them until they have begun to deepen to gold. In general it is the traditional French taste to drink them up without waiting, the English to give them three or four years in their bottles.

The effect of time on a white wine is not quite the same as it is on a red one. Red wines start with a great knot of flavour which slowly unravels itself, becoming smoother and more harmonious, lighter and easier to drink. White wines tend to intensify their flavours. While red wines slowly fade towards brown, white wines slowly darken in the same direction. It is sometimes difficult with a very old wine to tell whether it started red or white; it reaches the centre of the spectrum.

So a Château d'Yquem, the greatest of Sauternes, or a Montrachet, the best of white burgundies, is not exactly unready to drink at four or five years old, but it will go a long way before it starts to deteriorate at all, and many think it is getting better all the time. The same is true of champagne, and of the best wines of the Rhine and the Moselle. With age the richness and depth of flavour grows, freshness gives place to mellowness, the flavour of spring to the flavour of autumn.

Opportunities for discovering how fine old white wines can be come rarely. Personally I lay down white wine as well as red, in smaller quantities and for less long. But far more wine is drunk too soon than too late—white or red.

# Vintages

Nancy Mitford once said "There is even a public for yesterday's weather." On the face of it whether or not it rained yesterday does seem the most barren of all topics. As far as most people are concerned once the clouds are gone they are gone. Only the wine-grower will have reason to reflect on it, to be glad or sad about it, two—or even ten—years later.

The weather in northern Europe is always uncertain. At any time of year it can have an effect for good or ill on the vine and its grapes. While the vine lies dormant in the winter there is the possibility of frosts, which can come, too, in the spring. If a frost comes after the vital budding time it can destroy the crop before it ever even appears.

*The hundred days*

In the hundred days that it takes a vine to bear ripe grapes from the time of flowering the weather is of the utmost importance. There must be sun, but not only sun. A little rain is needed—but at the right times. Some early morning mist is helpful—but not too much. Really heavy rain can be disastrous. Hail can destroy everything—even the vines themselves. There is nothing the grower can do about any of these things. He may see everything ripening to perfection with day after cloudless day of sunshine, and only rain on the days he has to stay indoors to do his accounts, or he may have to stand helpless, with tears in his eyes, as he sees hail tearing his beloved vines apart. The wine-grower is a farmer, and a farmer learns patience by bitter experience. But one must not be too sorrowful. Can there be any more satisfying, natural way of life than tending vines and making wine?

The actual weather pattern of those hundred days between flowering and ripening decides, if all has gone well up to that point, the nature and quality of the vintage. Not surprisingly, it is never the same two years running—or any two years. In Australia or California the weather follows a fairly predictable pattern. Vintages vary relatively little in quality, and the chief reason the drinker should want to know which vintage produced the wine is to tell its age. In France it is the character of the wine which changes completely from year to year. A knowledgeable wine-merchant cannot confuse 1961 and 1962 or 1969 and 1970.

*The vital years*

To anyone who is not particularly interested in wine it may seem just another nuisance that vintages matter. The fact is that they matter—where they matter at all—very much indeed. There is far less truly awful wine made today than there used to be. Yet three times in Bordeaux in the 1960s (which must be rated one of the luckier decades for weather) the vintage can be said to have been a disaster; in 1963, 1965 and 1968. Of the remaining vintages (speaking of red wine), two were excellent (1961 and 1966), two were pretty good (1962 and 1967), one (1964) was patchy and two (1960 and 1969) were passable.

In Burgundy in the same decade (again for red wine) the odds were a little better. The same three vintages were virtual washouts. Four, on the other hand, were excellent: 1961, 1962, 1966 and 1969. One (1964) was good; 1967 was moderate and 1960 was disappointing.

Curiously enough white burgundy has a much more consistent pattern than red: dud vintages are rare. 1960 was nothing special, but 1961, 1962, 1964, 1966, 1967, 1969, 1970, 1971, 1972 and 1973 have all been good, and some reasonable wine was made even in the three missing years.

One almost always can, in fact, find *some* good wine, even in a disastrous vintage. Either some grower has had exceptional luck, or taken exceptional trouble. In 1968, for example, at Château La Mission Haut-Brion they went through the vineyard twice at vintage-time; the first time cutting out all the mildewed grapes and simply letting them fall to the ground, the second time for the harvest. It may have cost the year's profit, but it made La Mission one of the three or four good Bordeaux of a memorably bad year. Wine-merchants, on the other hand, are given to finding exceptions suspiciously often. I have occasionally been encouraged to buy a wine of a notorious year only to find the notoriety well and truly justified.

Unfortunately one cannot always trust even the most illustrious names. Château Lafite published a booklet a few years ago in which Elie de Rothschild, the President, wrote "all good vineyards sell off their products of a poor year as ordinary wine". There must have been a change of policy in the house of Rothschild since he wrote that.

On the other hand (a phrase never far from one's lips when wine is the subject), some vineyards give of their very best in years of adverse weather. The Corton-Charlemagne of 1956 (a rotten year) was one of the best white burgundies I have drunk, while the 1959 ("vintage of the century") was overweight. The Rüdesheimer Berg in the Rheingau is another well-drained hill that needs a moderately rainy year to achieve perfection.

Such considerations as this are the life and soul of wine. They are the source of its endless fascination and the reason why there are more exceptions than rules.

*Micro-climates*    If anyone asks whether vintage charts are helpful or a pitfall the answer lies here. Of course some years are better than others, and of course it is possible to generalize about what happened in any given district as a whole. But it can rain in Hampstead while Chelsea basks in the sun. There is a micro-climate for each locality, as well as the overall climate of the area. The tilt of a hill; the depth of the subsoil, affecting drainage; a stream, which makes morning mist, or a dip in the ground which catches frost, are all factors which can give one field the edge over its neighbour in one year, and do the reverse in another. Vintage charts, therefore, like all quick-reference works, need a pinch of salt. But this does not disqualify them completely.

On pages 256 and 257 I have tried to characterize the recent vintages rather than classify them. The important thing is when the wine will be at its best. For poor years maturity comes quickly, for great years slowly. Similarly, for cheap wines age can do less than it can for good ones. Even such a chart as this is too broad a generalization to be defended in detail, but it may help.

*Individuality of*    Even given two vintages which everyone agrees in calling good, or
*a vintage*    even great, for a particular area, the wine, even from the same vineyard, will not be the same. The years 1949 and 1953 were great ones for Château Lafite, yet the characters of the two wines are different. Even discounting the difference in age, the fact remains that the 1949 was smooth and elegant, sleek and splendid, while the 1953 was more delicate and subtle, more feminine, more scented and possibly a shade less satisfying. Yet both were unmistakably Lafite.

## National tastes

So there are not only good and not-so-good vintages (not to mention downright bad vintages), there are vintages which appeal to different tastes. The British, for example, found 1959 a superlative vintage for German wine; it was rich, strong and every wine's individuality was brought out almost to the point of caricature. It was a school for studying the districts of Germany and their distinctions in itself. The glory of hock (to the British) is the sort of clear and concentrated flavour it can only achieve in this sort of year. And yet to the Germans the 1959s were out of balance. They were alcoholically too strong. The German likes to drink his wine in draughts and refill his glass often; the 1959s were for respectful sipping.

## Personal tastes

Apart from national tastes you will find that personal tastes, even among acknowledged experts, differ on a vintage. One famous English merchant was almost alone in seeing a great future for the

1957 burgundies. Others, who were in the majority, happy with their stocks of 1952, 1953 and 1955, gave it a miss. They thought it unripe, awkward and harsh. As it happened, they were right in the short run and wrong in the long one: 1957s were late in developing, but they finally found a finesse which is all too rare in burgundy today. Some of those that still exist are superb.

Vintages, therefore, cannot usefully be discussed without very particular references. To prophesy about them as soon as the grapes are gathered is folly. It is good to be told of a plentiful vintage, because of the effect it may—or at any rate should—have of stabilizing prices. About the quality of the vintage you must make up your own mind when you come round to tasting it.

*"Vintage"* A word must be said about champagne and port vintages. Here the word has a special meaning. In the normal way neither of these wines carries a vintage year, because the wine which is sold is a blend of those of many years, the whole being better than any of its parts. When an exceptional year comes along—which may happen perhaps three times in ten years—the shippers "declare a vintage". They announce that this wine is so good that there is no need to blend it; indeed that it would be a waste of its well-balanced natural character. Then you have a vintage port or champagne, which is always more expensive and usually better than non-vintage wine.

Before we finish with vintages, it is worth mentioning the misunderstanding that has made the word come into use as a term of praise. To qualify port or champagne with the word vintage is reasonable; you are referring to the best, or one of the best. But all claret is "vintage". To say "vintage claret", therefore, is not to add anything to just saying "claret"

# Choosing Wine

*The price* There are very few people whose choice of a wine is not guided, in the first instance, by the price. You know, when you look at a list, whether it is the bottom of the column, where the Great First-Growths grow, or the top, where the cheapest wines live, or somewhere in the middle reaches, which is your territory. I have been told time and again by restaurateurs and wine-merchants that the strategic place to put a wine to sell it is number three on the list. The undecided are apparently all in agreement that number one looks downright mean, number two perhaps a bit stingy, but that number three is safe. If only they knew it, the cheapest wine was probably much better value and the third one down a drug in the market which the restaurant was trying to get rid of. But so, apparently, buyers are guided.

Still, you know your price. The essential thing to do is to stick to it. If you are wondering what is the cheapest you can get a bottle of wine at all there is no sense in buying anything but the cheapest on the list. It is often very good. Restaurants usually find the carafe wine the wrong thing to save money on.

If, on the other hand, price is no object it is rash to head straight for the bottom and buy the most expensive. The most expensive white wine on many lists is the honey-sweet Château d'Yquem. It is glorious after dinner, and superb—occasionally—before. But the only-the-best-will-do technique has led people to drink it with steak, which is, to put it mildly, like having chocolate sauce on kippers.

There is, in short, an appropriate wine somewhere on the list for each dish, pocket and temperament. The business of finding it is very different in a wine-merchant's shop, where you have time and leisure to read and compare what he offers, and in a restaurant, where wine-waiters make some of their most (to them) satisfactory sales by using the feeling of pressure and hurry which is at their disposal. So different are the circumstances, in fact, that I will deal with them separately.

*In a wine-shop*

The best place to read a wine-list, to start with, is at home. Every wine-merchant has a list of what he offers, which he will willingly give to anyone who looks as though he might buy something. The first thing to do is to acquire one—or better, two or three from different merchants—and take it home. There, though you may not want a bottle at the moment at all, you can see what is available when the time comes, compare prices and values, and mark things to try for the future.

You can also look up in a reference book wines you are not sure about, so that you can approach the storeman with confidence the next day or whenever you are buying the wine. I put this plan forward humbly after having seen and felt the predicament of going into a shop whose range is unfamiliar and being quite overwhelmed by the choice. You are (I am, anyway) determined to come out with a bargain, something unspeakably delicious, and yet you do not know where to begin. Finally, the man behind the counter, who, as I suspect, knows next to nothing about what he is selling anyway, sells you the one thing he does know about, which is the wine with the biggest profit margin. All these difficulties are overcome if you ask for a list and take it home.

*The governing factors*

Are you choosing a wine to go with a particular dish or meal, or to be at hand whatever dish comes along? Are you looking at the thing as an investment in future pleasure or with the immediate moment on your mind? Can you think in terms of buying a dozen bottles rather than one at a time? These are the things which will influence you. To take the last first, there is every possible reason why buying wine a little at a time, just when you want it, is a bad idea. First, you have the trouble of remembering to go and get it or order it every time. Second, you never have the right thing if someone turns up out of the blue and you cannot go shopping. Third, the wine is never at its best if you open it just after a quick flight from the corner shop, any more than any of the food which goes with it is ready without preparation (of the preparation, which is simple but nonetheless necessary, we will speak in a moment). Fourth, which is worth considering, orders of a dozen at a time are often blessed by a discount. Fifth, it is a good feeling to have a rack of assorted wine bottles in the house—but I have said enough. Avoid buying the odd bottle when you want it if you possibly can. Carrying this way of thinking a little further is starting what is so impressively called a cellar.

Really long-term buying, laying down young wines to go through their essential stages of development under your roof, is fascinating and even profitable. Wine always costs less, naturally enough, when it first comes on the market, too young to drink, than when it has been stored, paying rent and interest charges, for several years. Nowadays, I know, very few people do lay down wine in the old-fashioned way, but this does not weaken the arguments for it. The principal one against it, in most cases, is lack of space.

## A cellar

Very few modern houses, even in France, are built with wine-cellars. The number of people who have the satisfaction of going down their short flight of stairs into their little vault of wine, therefore, must be declining all the time. Architects and builders who are so careful to provide utility-rooms for every other aspect of life might well consider changing this state of affairs, but I cannot see it happening. Most of us, then, must find a cellar-substitute. The cupboard under the stairs is often suggested. It is not ideal, because it is usually too small and stuffy, suffers the pounding of feet on the treads above it all day, and doubles as a broom-cupboard. But most houses and apartments have some accessible and otherwise wasted space. An unused fireplace is often well-insulated. And cupboards can easily be fitted with racks for bottles. All that is asked of the wine-store, then, is that it never freezes, never boils, but stays at a comfortable temperature (even central-heating temperature will probably do little harm so long as it stays constant). Constancy is the most important thing. It is the reason why underground storage is traditional and best for wine. But the combination of central heating and air-conditioning in modern apartments has almost the same effect.

## Constant temperature

Light and vibration are the other things which could harm wine, but they are comparatively easy to avoid. Finally, wine must be kept lying down. All wine-bottles which are going to be kept for longer than a week or two should stay horizontal. If you put the label uppermost it helps you remember where the sediment, if any, will be in the bottle—lying along the side opposite the label. The reason for keeping bottles lying down is perfectly simple; it keeps the corks wet, which prevents them shrinking and letting the air in.

## Laying down

There is more profit in laying down good red wines than any other kind. Vintage port, as we shall see in the chapter on port, demands it. It forms sediment in such a way that if it is not drunk where it has been resting, or at least decanted there, it will be stirred up and stay like mud for a long time. Almost all wines benefit by a little keeping. The improvement even in a bottle of the cheapest available red wine which I kept for a year was astonishing. Wine-merchants can save costs by bottling their cheap lines when they are called for, so that the wine you buy could have only a few days in bottle behind it. It is a well-known phenomenon that the transfer from barrel to bottle leaves wine in a shocked state for a while. It tastes as though there is something wrong with it for a month or so. The trade knows it as "bottle-sickness". A great deal of wine is drunk in this state with no great satisfaction by people who expect it to be drinkable when it is sold. Good wine-merchants avoid it by ageing their wine before putting it on the market, but it still pays to buy and keep all your wine for at least three months before drinking it. The one wine which I would except from this rule is new Beaujolais. It is best as young as you can get it.

I have discussed (in Wine and Time, page 25) the laying down of fine wine to mature. Clarets are the wines which demand this treatment most. Burgundies also benefit enormously, more or less depending on the vintage. In talking about wines as they occur later in this book I have named a number which an be laid down with profit, particularly the wines of the Rhône valley, Portugal, Spain, California and Italy.

## *Wine for immediate drinking*

The wine to choose for drinking straight away or in the near future is either wine which has, in effect, been laid down already because the merchant has had it for a long time, or wine which is better drunk quite young—or at least which would gain little with age. In the second category are the cheaper wines—rosés, whites, light reds and brand-named products. Cheap, sweet white wines always come into this class because they have been treated in such a way that age can do nothing to improve them. So does any wine which has been pasteurized, but there is unfortunately no way of telling in most cases if it has or not. All too many have. Aperitif and after-dinner wines—sherry, and tawny and ruby ports, for example—are always sold ready to drink and change little, if at all, with keeping.

Wine-merchants used to be able to keep a stock of good table wines until they were really ready to drink, and list clarets at ten or fifteen years old as a matter of course. Now they feel less and less inclined to invest the money in them for so long. A quick turnover is their theme, and to this end they will assure the public that a wine is at its best long before it really is. Four-year-old clarets are offered as ready for immediate drinking. They will do if there is no alternative, but it is worth finding a wine-merchant who can offer a choice of clarets at least seven or eight years old. With most other wines, in most stores, sad to say, there is rarely a choice of vintages at all: one German vintage comes on the market as the previous one is used up. To go to a specialist wine-merchant—or to buy the wines as they come on the market and keep them for yourself—is the only answer here.

The thing not to do at any price is to spend a lot of money on a bottle of a really fine wine which is not nearly old enough to drink—and drink it.

## *The food*

The food you are going to be eating will be your main consideration when you come to choose the wine for a particular meal. I will discuss this in the chapter on Food and Wine (page 41). But it is one of the charms of wine that there are other considerations as well.

*Other considerations*

Wine has a wonderfully personal and intimate character. A bottle of somebody's birth-year, or wedding-year, opened at a party specially for them is worth a tremendous amount of trouble. There is no more thoughtful way of reminding a friend of something pleasant in the past than by producing again the same wine as you drank then, or finding an association—the wine from a friend's favourite spot in Europe, for example. All these things take on a personal character and add to celebration in a way which may often be far beyond the wine's intrinsic merit. They are evidence of your foresight, thoughtfulness and imagination. Even just remembering somebody's particular favourite and making sure that you have a bottle of it when they come to see you is a compliment you can only pay with wine. So is the very simple device (which far too many people think of as an affectation of advanced gastronomy) of serving two bottles of similar and comparable wines—or very dissimilar wines—at the same time, so that your guests can notice the difference and say which they prefer. You can serve two clarets of the same château, for example, and consecutive vintages, or different châteaux of the same vintage. Unless you occasionally do these things you may well say with some justice that all the fuss that is made about the differences between wines is unimportant, and that differences are so slight as not to be worth taking your time. As far as your memory of one wine compares with the taste of another, you may be right. Yet one can be the success you want, live up to your expectation, make the food taste delicious and make the meal: the other can be disappointing and add nothing to the evening. That is the difference between vintage and vintage which, tasting them at different times, you may not notice. But seeing them side by side it comes into focus. It becomes all the more interesting if you have friends there to help you to decide.

*Two wines at a time*

## In a restaurant

Much as I love restaurants and the exotic experiences they offer without any effort on my part, I am always loath to buy expensive wines in them, unless they are restaurants I know very well, or which obviously make their wine-list a matter of particular pride and care.

The cost factor apart (and the restaurant's 100 per cent mark-up, though inevitable, is to me a strong disincentive to push the boat out), the main trouble is the vagueness of most wine-lists, which just say "Pommard" or "Gevrey-Chambertin" in an airy way as though anything with such an august name should be good enough for *you*. It is even quite common practice to leave the vintage year off the list, with the excuse that they don't want to have to keep reprinting it. Pigs in pokes *can* be bargains, but my inclination is try the carafe wine: if it's good, I'll be happy—and perhaps inspired to trust them further.

*Compromise*

The choosing of wine is usually also complicated by the different tastes of the party. One chooses a *tournedos*, another a Dover sole. At home, of course, the worst that happens is that the vegetarian of the party is eating his nut cutlet; the rest are unanimously eating whatever is on offer. You choose the wine which seems a good idea with the one dish (which, for that matter, you know about beforehand). But in a restaurant you are choosing a wine to go with a gastronomic Tower of Babel. Lobster on the one hand, chicken pancake on the other, and on the third Boeuf Strogonoff. It is too much to ask of any wine that it should be the perfect accompaniment to all these things. If there cannot be unanimity about the food there cannot be any about the wine. Even pink wine is a poor compromise; although it is rarely nasty (if you like it) with any food, it is even more rarely an aesthetic revelation. And champagne, which some people fall back on, has the same fault. The answer—I see no other—is to order two kinds of wine. If it is a party of two, have two half-bottles. If there are three or more, order two whole bottles, or two carafes—one of red and one of white.

I confess I even do this at home sometimes. With all kinds of informal meals there can be a division of opinion about which wine is ideal, so why not have a choice? A carafe of white wine and a carafe of red can go round together. People can have one or the other or both if they want. If there are enough people to drink it, there might be a bottle of pink as well.

*Ordering in advance*

The ideal host in a restaurant would go round there on the morning of the day and choose a dinner which would suit everybody, and the wine to go with it. There would be no fluttering over the menus when the party arrived. The chef would have a chance to get everything ready at the right moment. The performance would go off like clockwork. But that is a counsel of perfection, and hardly anyone ever does it. And it is true that some people feel cheated if they cannot see the menu for themselves. They feel that they are missing something, if it is only the prices.

But, as far as wine is concerned, if the host has not done this he is foolish to order a really fine one. The conditions of keeping wine in restaurants, with very few exceptions, are anything but ideal, and the handling of wine is worse. Whether you like it or not, the best wine, the kind that any restaurant prides itself on having in its cellar, takes a little time and care to be got ready for drinking. It cannot be at its best if it is just brought up from the cellar the moment you ordered it; nor, for that matter, if the alternative has happened and they have been keeping it in readiness over the last few months in the hot dining-room.

It is not elaborate precautions that are needed to see that a wine is at its best when you drink it (and is it not wasted if it is not at its best?) but a little gentleness and a little patience. If you realize that the wine has been cooped up in its bottle for five or perhaps ten years when suddenly, at the drop of a hat, you ask it to put on its best performance without warning, you can see that it may easily be a bit shy. And shy, despite the mockery that usually follows the use of words like this about wine, is just what it very often is. You open it, you drink it, and just as you are swallowing the last drop of what has been (at the price) a frankly disappointing bottle, you suddenly get a whiff of magic: the scent has begun to come out, the wine has begun to expand and show itself, like a peacock spreading its tail. But it is too late. You have finished the bottle.

*The sommelier routine*

What actually happens when you order wine in the majority of restaurants makes this only too likely. The *sommelier* (the wine-waiter, in the United States as often as not in an apron, hung about with bunches of keys and a silver tasting-cup) loses all his dignity as he moves through the service door. He rushes to the wine-bin, grabs the bottle (or gets a boy to go and grab it for him), waves it around as he weaves back through the milling *commis* waiters, slams it down in a basket, recomposes himself and arrives at your table triumphant, sedate, as slow and stony as the best of butlers. With infinite gravity he condescends to let you glimpse the still palpitating bottle before going into his routine with the corkscrew.

With ordinary, carafe-type wine it obviously does not matter how much he waves it around. His worst offence is pretentiousness in serving it in a cradle as though it were liquid gold. But with the sort of wine you sometimes go to restaurants specially for, because nobody else has such old vintages or such noble growths, it is a pitiful waste.

This pantomime and its sad consequences can be avoided to some extent by asking the restaurateur beforehand to decant the wine. But this means choosing it in advance, too. In short, as a general rule, it is wiser to keep to the kind of wine which cannot suffer much harm and needs no time to take the air before it reaches its best; not to buy the best unless you know all about the restaurant.

White wine is normally an easier case than red. All it needs is long enough in an ice-bucket to be well chilled, or if it has been kept in a refrigerator, long enough to warm up to a pleasant coolness. It is worth noting, though, that the ice-bucket should be full of water with ice in it, not just ice; it is far more quickly and evenly effective. The bottle will probably need five minutes' standing on its head in the ice, for few ice-buckets are deep enough for the water to reach the wine in the neck.

*Sending wine back*

The wine-waiter pours half an inch of wine into your glass before he sets off round the table with the bottle. The idea is both to see if there is anything wrong with this particular bottle and also to see if you like the wine in a general way. As to the first, the chances of a bottle being corky, which means smelling musty from having had a dud cork, are very slim. The corky smell is immediately obvious and very unpleasant. Any restaurant will take back a bottle afflicted with it. Occasionally, though, perfectly good bottles have an odd smell in the first minute after opening—with white wine there is often a smell of sulphur, with red sometimes a dank smell. This will go away almost at once. The trick, in fact, if you are not sure about the smell of the sample you have been given, is to swirl it round your glass for a minute and sniff it again. If it is as bad as ever you have a bad bottle; if the smell has gone you will not have risked a clash of opinions with the management.

Whether or not you can return a bottle which has no intrinsic faults depends, I suppose, on how certain you are that it is not what it claims to be, and also how wide of the mark it is. Some can do it with panache; others turn pale at the thought. It is, in fact, a matter of personality, which does not call for discussion here.

# Serving Wine

You can play stereophonic records on an ordinary record-player. Similarly with wine you can just pull the cork, pour it out and knock it back. But either is a waste of the potential you have paid for. It is worth taking the little extra trouble to see that all its qualities (neither ordinary records nor ordinary wine can be made wonderful by wonderful equipment) can be appreciated.

*Simple equipment*

Wine does not even need any special equipment. You have glasses. You have a corkscrew. That's it. The refrigerator will come in useful, and the next thing you will want will be a decanter or carafe—one of the most useful and decorative pieces of glassware anyway, whether you use it for wine or not.

*Wine-glasses*

Your glasses must be two things—large and clear. Small glasses not only look mean, they have to be filled to the top. There is no possibility of the wine's scent collecting in the top of the glass so that when you drink it comes to you all at once, scent and flavour. A wine-glass should never be more than half full. For half a glass to be a reasonable measure the glass has to be big.

As for clarity, one of the joys of wine—a minor one, but still a joy—is its colour. There are infinite variations between petal-white and gold, and between purple and tawny. Coloured, or even slightly shaded, glass ruins the colour of the wine.

A good wine-glass, in short, is a big one, clear and uncoloured, preferably with a stem and a round or roundish bowl, cupping in towards the top to embrace the wine's bouquet. A glass like this is perfect for any wine, French or German, Californian or Chilean, red or white, still or sparkling. Different wine-glasses for different wines can be a pretty sight, but as far as the wine is concerned there is no need for them. A glass which is good for one wine is good for all wines.

*Corkscrews*

There are better and less good corkscrews. The best kind, without question, is the one made of boxwood with two threads which turn in opposite directions. With the top handle you drive the screw into the cork in the usual way. When it is in and the wooden body of the corkscrew is resting against the rim of the bottle you turn the other handle. The cork is drawn steadily and easily into the body of the device. I have never known a cork, however tough, to resist it. Simple corkscrews can be helpless against a really solid cork. The kind which inject air are terrifying if the cork does not come out straight away. You feel as if you are holding a bomb.

## Preparing wine

The objects of preparing the wine beforehand, rather than just opening it and drinking it straight away, are three. It may have sediment; you must get this to the bottom of the bottle so that it does not get into the glasses. Its temperature probably needs adjusting. It will almost certainly be improved by contact with the air.

*Sediment*

It is remarkably hard to convince people, especially in the United States, that sediment in wine is harmless and natural. More than that, it is a good sign. It means that the wine is natural and untampered-with. But there is a fetish about a speck of deposit, or a single crystal appearing in a bottle. It is sometimes carried to well-meaning but absurd lengths. One of the best-known shippers of German wine to Britain and the United States told me how he once had a thousand cases of wine held up in Chicago because there was said to be broken glass in the bottles. In fact there were crystals of tartaric acid, which often form in white wine in cold weather. It was harmless, natural—indeed expected—but it caused a tremendous crisis.

If wine has been pasteurized, put through very fine filters or otherwise denatured it is possible to avoid sediment, either in the short run or the long. But it is no longer natural wine; it will no longer age properly and develop its potential. It seems too high a price to pay to avoid the chance of a speck in the bottom of the bottle.

*Red wine*

Red wine, especially, of any age should have a few black dregs in it. While it is lying in its rack they will lie along the bottom side of the bottle. The object of the cradle which restaurants use for serving wine which has been taken straight out of its rack is to keep them there. Once a bottle has been stood up and the sediment moved from the side there is no point in laying it down again in a cradle. I have often seen wine-waiters take bottles out of their cradles to pull the cork and then put them back on their sides again. The customer may be sure of a muddy glass of wine.

*Decanting*

The decanter or carafe is the answer (oddly enough, the French have no word for decanter; *carafe* is equally a water- and a wine-container). The ideal arrangement is to plan several days, or at least twenty-four hours, ahead which bottle you are going to open, and stand it up in the dining-room or the kitchen, wherever it is warm. The sediment will settle at the bottom. Well before you are going to drink the wine you pull the cork and pour it gently and steadily into the decanter. As you reach the bottom of the bottle, hold it against a light or a white surface. You will see the first of the dregs move in arrowhead formation towards the decanter. When they reach the neck of the bottle stop pouring. The wine is as clean as a whistle.

If you now leave it in the kitchen where it is warm—not near the fire, where it is hot—it will be in perfect condition for drinking. It will be clear, at room temperature, and in the full flow of its perfume. Its contact with the air will have livened it up and given it much more vigour than it had at the moment the bottle was opened.

How far in advance you should decant it depends on two things: its age and its strength—not just of alcohol, but of body and character. By and large the younger and/or bigger a red wine is, the more it will benefit from contact with the air before drinking, so the longer ahead you should decant it. Twenty-four hours is often none too long for wines with plenty of vigour and personality. To judge whether you are getting the best out of a wine try leaving a third or so of the bottle in the decanter, stoppered, until the next day. In many cases you will find you were only getting half the potential, at least of the wine's scent, by drinking it too soon after opening. In others, particularly with lighter wines or wines faded by age, the reverse is true. But more wine is drunk too quickly than too late, just as more is drunk too young than too old.

*Using a cradle*

If foresight has failed, and you must open the wine the moment you take it from the rack where it has been lying, a cradle or basket is useful. It keeps the wine in the nearest position to the horizontal which allows the cork to be taken out without the wine spilling. Bring the cradle to the rack and put the bottle straight in it without moving it more than you can help. Pull the cork as it lies in the cradle. A double-action corkscrew is essential for this; you cannot hold the cradle and tug at the end of it at the same time.

Decant the wine (this is what restaurants so rarely do) from the cradle. The cradle is not a substitute for a decanter. If you pour inter-mittently from a bottle at all, as you must if you are filling several glasses, the wine washes back on to its dregs each time you stop pour-ing. There is no way of preventing it getting mixed with them. Only by pouring in one continuous movement can this be avoided. So unless you are dining alone and filling one enormous glass the decanter is the only answer.

I hasten to say that all this business takes far less effort and time to do than it does to read—let alone write.

*White wines*

There is no reason why white wines should not be decanted, but less reason why they should. Very old ones have a deposit, but the great majority of bottles of white wine are clear to the last drop. With white wines the only problem is the temperature—and letting them have a little air. I find, indeed, that pouring white wine into the glass from enough height to make it splash about a bit (in the glass, that is), aerates it enough to bring out the flavour.

*Temperature*  I don't think there is a right temperature for white wines. It is certain that they are better cool, but some people like them icy, some just chilled. I think they are usually served much too cold in the United States, but then so is the water, the beer and even the salad. But at least I can wait until my glass warms up a bit, whereas no amount of waiting will cool down a glass served too warm. My favourite image to give the right idea for white wine is that of well-water. Freshness is the thing, not frostiness.

# Food and Wine

In general it is true that table wines are never better than when they are served with some suitable food. This much is almost a truism. But from here the schools of thought divide. One would have it that any wine goes with any food, the other that there is for each wine a dish pre-ordained by divine decree: that, for example, a Volnay Caillerets should be drunk with well-done lamb, and Volnay Clos des Chênes should be drunk with under-done lamb; that a little parsley with potatoes brings out the individuality of the Caillerets, particularly the 1961, to perfection; that the 1962 should never be served with green peas, and so on.

There is a good deal of private amusement to be had from this sort of talk, though it is double-Dutch to most people, just as discussion of British Honduras penny reds or uncancelled triangular blue two-pennies has meaning, and brings pleasure, to the initiated philatelist.

The difference with wine is that everybody thinks he ought to be one of the initiated. As somebody has said, wine is like sex; nobody will admit to not knowing all about it.

*Formal dinners*  There are dinners where the whole gamut of wines is gone through. They start, as it were, at the beginning of this book and go on until they reach the end, picking and choosing, but visiting each section.

There are dinners that begin with an aperitif glass of champagne; that have a glass of sherry with the soup; a glass of Rhine wine with the fish; a claret with the entrée. With the roast pheasant there is a glass of burgundy, and maybe another, a different one, with some cheese after it. Then there is a glass of Sauternes and a great gorgeous *bombe* of some kind or other; then port; then brandy. This is at least a dinner which I could eat, if I had room. But look at the following.

This is a dinner that was really given, and by George Saintsbury, the man who was considered to be one of the greatest English connoisseurs of his day, at about the turn of the century:

| The wines | The food |
|---|---|
| Montilla | Consommé aux pointes d'asperges |
| Johannisberg Klaus Auslese | John Dory, |
| 1874 | Sauce livournaise |
| Château Grillet 1865 | Filets de saumon à la gelée |
| | Cotelettes à la Joncourt |
| Champagne, Dragonet 1874 | Plovers' eggs |
| (a Jereboam) | |
| | Aspic de volaille à la reine |
| Romanée-Conti 1858 | Haunch of mutton |
| Château Margaux 1868 | Mayonnaise de homard |
| Port, 1853 | Soufflé glâcé au marasquin |
| Pedro Ximenes | Canapés de crevettes |

Tastes change. If this was the fashion in eating and drinking within the last seventy years, I have great doubts if there is anything so profound or unchanging about what we call the art of the table. If you produced a lobster mayonnaise today after a haunch of mutton and an aspic of chicken, not to mention soup, two kinds of fish, cutlets and plovers' eggs, everybody would think you were mad. At that moment the wines on the table were persumably burgundy (Romanée-Conti) and claret. The port appears to have been served with a maraschino soufflé and followed by a very sweet sherry with shrimp canapés (the fourth fishy manifestation of the meal).

We could, presumably, turn our meals inside out and very quickly believe that it was unnatural to start dinner with anything but roast meat, or end with anything but soup. We are, after all, only subject to the three-course habit because that is the way hoteliers set things up at the beginning of this century. What it boils down to is that far too much is written and said about what goes with what, what goes before or after what, or what to do and what to avoid.

## The enemies of wine

Wine has certain basic enemies, at table as in barrel or bottle. Its first enemy is vinegar. A vinegary salad will turn the wine to vinegar; this is a matter of science, not taste.

Its second enemy is acid—the acid of grapefruit, orange or lemon. You cannot taste a wine with any of these fruits. There is a third enemy, but I am not sure what it is. It is something which occurs in some oily kinds of fish. It makes wine, particularly red wine, taste steely—something like the taste of tin cans.

All these things positively spoil wine, so it is a waste to serve it with them. Beyond this, though, taste is an anarchy; all anyone can hope to do is suggest combinations which have appealed to him. This is the object of the following pages.

## Hors d'oeuvre

The typical mixed hors d'oeuvre leans heavily on vinegar for its savour, and thus becomes the enemy of wine. Most of the courses we start meals with—artichokes, avocadoes, tomato salad, radishes, little dishes of carrots and cucumbers, smoked fish or sausages, eggs, pâtés, melon—are happy with the remains of the glass of sherry which was an aperitif, or another glass of the same thing. Alternatively, a first glass of whatever is to be the main wine of the meal goes well with the hors d'oeuvre. The principal exceptions to this simple arrangement are shellfish, which are always best with a very dry white wine. The association of oysters and Chablis is no accident; *Oysters* the sharpness of the wine does something essential to an oyster. It has the effect of a squeeze of lemon. Champagne is equally effective, and so—much less expensive, too—is Muscadet. Some people find that the *Smoked salmon* rich oiliness of smoked salmon or eel is too much for a light white wine. Dry sherry in this case is ideal. All meaty and savoury hors d'oeuvre are fine with an ordinary red wine or rosé. If there are enough people to drink more than one bottle with the meal it makes things more interesting to have different wines with the hors d'oeuvre and. the main course.

*Soup*   There is no need for a special wine to go with the soup at an ordinary meal. Wine goes *in* a number of soups—particularly Madeira, Marsala or sherry in clear soup—to great effect. The same wines are good sipped with most soups. I would never choose a wine to go specifically with a soup, however, unless the soup were the main part of the meal —as, for example, in a snack lunch of soup, bread and cheese. Then it would be a cheap, light red wine.

*Pizza, pasta,*   The obvious thing is to drink Italian wine with pasta, although some *paella, etc.*   Italians drink water with it. It makes a difference whether pasta is the whole meal, or, as in Italy, merely the opening salvo. In any case, and whatever the sauce, I find red wine is usually best with pasta and related dishes—all those in which cereals of some kind play an important part, whether it be rice, pastry, bread-dough or noodle. There is a way out for a risotto made with prawns, of course—Soave is perfect for this—although it is worth noting that the Spanish usually drink red wine with paella, which should contain plenty of seafood. Pizza and Chianti are inseparable. Quiche Lorraine, on the other hand, is usually eaten with a white Alsace, if only for geographical reasons.

*Eggs*   Egg dishes are very comforting and satisfying, but they are not a good background, or foreground, for fine wines. A little egg dish at the beginning of a meal (baked egg, scrambled egg or egg in aspic) would make no difference to the wine which followed it. Allow the choice of wine, in fact, to be influenced by the other elements in the meal and treat the egg as neutral. For a simple omelette and salad a cheap red wine is perfect; say, a Côtes-du-Rhône.

*Picnics*   The pleasure of a picnic is the simple joy of refreshment in the open air. It is not the time for assertive or expensive wine, but for something thirst-quenching. If there is some way of making it cold (a stream will do very well), a white Loire wine, a cheap Moselle, an Alsace wine, or virtually any rosé is ideal. If conditions hardly allow this kind of refinement, drink plain good red Bordeaux, not old enough for any sediment to have formed to cloud it when it is shaken about en route. If you are in wine-country there is no hesitation—drink the *vin du pays*.

*Fish*   White wine tastes better than red with most fish because its acidity helps to cut out the fishy taste which red wine somehow emphasizes. There is a peculiar metallic quality about a fish eaten with red wine which spoils every other sensation. Fish dishes with considerable flavour, either in their flesh or in their sauce, are best matched by fairly rich-flavoured wines: the more expensive white burgundies, Rhine wines (though really good ones are wasted on fish) or any of the white wines of farther south. Very white and light-flavoured fish, unsauced, can easily be, as it were, overwined. A young Moselle or a Loire wine is best for the delicate flaky river-fish and the subtler creatures of the sea.

More depends, usually, on the way of cooking than the fish itself. A plain grilled sole, for example, is a much more subtle-flavoured dish than a *sole Deauvillaise*, which is smothered in onions and cream. A trout *au bleu* is a more delicate one than a trout from a hot buttery pan with brown butter poured over it. Along these lines, then, you would choose a younger, fresher, more northern wine for the grilled sole or the trout *au bleu*; a warmer-flavoured, more assertive wine with the fish *Deauvillaise* or *meunière*. The fish of the Mediterranean cooked with garlic are another matter again; they are better with the rather hard-tasting, strong and mellow wines of their own countries.

*Salmon*  Salmon needs a word of its own. Some like claret with it when it is served hot. I like it best with as good a white burgundy as I can afford. The earlier in the season, the better the fish, so the better the wine.

If the fish comes before a meat course, one, or at the most two, glasses of white wine is usually enough with it. A half-bottle for two people, therefore, or a whole bottle for three or four is plenty, if you are going to have a red wine afterwards.

*Meat*
*Pork and veal*  There is good sense in the old rule about white wine with white meat, red wine with red. Pork, veal and chicken are the principal white meats. Chicken we will come to in a minute, but both pork and veal are usually, depending on the sauce, excellent with a not-too-dry white wine. They will make a young Moselle, a Muscadet or cheap Chablis taste a bit thin, but a wine of any power or warmth of flavour —an Alsace wine, a hock, a good white burgundy or Chardonnay, a Graves or a Hungarian wine, or virtually any white wine from southern Europe—will go well with them. Light red or rosé will go equally well, but strong red wines of real character—all the best wines of France, for example—are better matched with beef or lamb.

*Beef and lamb*  With beef and lamb I personally much prefer red wine to white. Tender, expensive cuts of these meats are an ideal accompaniment to the world's best red wines—Bordeaux and burgundy. The cheaper cuts which take more cooking are best with their opposite numbers, as it were, among the wines of the same districts. If there is ever a question of opening a very fine bottle of wine it is as well to avoid any of the really pungent seasonings of meat—whether they be garlic, mint sauce or anything flavoured with herbs or onions. If the wine's flavour is overwhelmed there is little point in spending more money on specially good wine.

*Ham*  I would not have the very best wine with ham, either—much to my regret, as it is one of my favourite kinds of meat. But halfway between ordinary and great there are any number of good clarets and burgundies which would do a ham every kind of pleasure.

*Venison*  Really gamey meat, oddly enough, although the darkest of all in colour, can be as good with a rather sweet white wine as with a dark, strong red. I am thinking particularly of the venison and wild boar which is the best meat of all in Germany. The luxuriously full-flavoured white wine of the Rhineland Palatinate is perfect with it.

In meat's hinterland, as it were, the world of kidneys and sweetbreads and liver, tripe and brains, tongue and the more visceral kind of sausages, what are known as sound red wines, not fine ones, are called for. This, to me, means experimenting among the wines of Italy, Spain, California, Australia and Portugal.

*Birds*

The chicken is the most versatile of all dishes. It is a wonder to me how it has changed from being a luxury to being the cheapest of all forms of meat, and yet remained a luxury. Even roadside fried chicken has failed to give it a bad name. It remains the chef's favourite canvas for his more elegant flourishes. As far as wine is concerned everything depends, of course, on the way it is cooked. A *coq au vin* where the *vin* is Chambertin clearly calls for Chambertin in the glass beside it. A *coq au vin jaune* in the Jura, where it is cooked in the strange mellow white wine of the country, also dictates its own accompaniment. But you can cook chicken in a way to go perfectly with almost any wine under the sun. For a really good wine nothing is as good as a young bird plain roasted in butter.

*Game*

The guinea-fowl, the turkey and the capon are as adaptable as the chicken and are usually even better to eat. Game birds, on the other hand, even those which are eaten unhung—the partridge, the young grouse, the snipe and the quail—are all committed red-wine dishes. A simple rule is to drink (very) good red Bordeaux with unhung game, (very) good red burgundy with any game which has been hung, burgundy with game pie, and either Châteauneuf-du-Pape, strong and soft-flavoured, or rather sweet Rhine wine with duck or goose—birds which need their fat counterbalanced.

*Cheese*

It is a matter of faith among wine-lovers that cheese is the perfect accompaniment to any wine. I am a dissenter from this view, but I must record it. Cheese is always served after the meat in France to give you an opportunity of finishing your red wine with it, and to tempt you to open another bottle.

All except the milder cheeses, I find, have too strong a flavour for any except the strongest-tasting red wines. Roquefort, for example, is as pungent and salty a morsel as civilized man ever put in his mouth. Many of the soft French cheeses have either a goaty or an ammoniac reek. English cheese is frequently sharp. Italian cheese, curiously enough, is milder and goes very well with Italian wine; Parmesan in its sweet granular crumbs is one of wine's best friends. But for Stilton and most of the other cheeses which are offered in Britain I find the best wine is port, which is sweet enough to take care of itself.

*Sweet dishes and desserts*

You rarely find among sweet wines and sweet food the same kind of perfect match as you do among savoury things. Two different sweet tastes in the mouth at once seem to be too much of a good thing. It is hard, for example, to taste a Sauternes at all if you drink it with ice-cream or fruit salad. The more cake-like kind of sweet dishes, on the other hand, and the lovely diversions which good cooks make with strawberries and raspberries, peaches or apricots, and pastry and cream, are delicious with the heavier kind of sweet wine—Madeira, tawny port, the muscatels, Tokay.

Peaches and grapes, pears and apples do not call for any special wine, but it is worth remembering that any wine you do serve with them must be good; they show up the faults of a thin or phoney wine more than anything else.

# Aperitifs

Anything you drink before a meal, with the idea of getting into the right frame of mind for eating, is an aperitif. Aperitifs are a modern idea. By a significant coincidence, the word entered our language in the same year as the word motor-car. A hundred years ago it was not the custom to drink anything before sitting down at table. Our ancestors found no difficulty in setting about their food as single-mindedly as cats about milk. True, the awkward moments of meeting in the drawing-room before dinner were known as the Black Half-Hour. But no-one thought of having a drink to break the ice.

*The black half-hour*

Social drinking used to take place at the end of dinner. It was then that the champagne, if any, was drunk, and, of course, after dinner that the port went round. But the first glass of the evening was the Madeira with the soup. The unwinder before dinner was unknown.

In this century things have gone too far the other way. In the United States, especially, the custom is to spend an hour drinking cold hard liquor on an empty stomach, and then to go into dinner and drink nothing but water. The stomach has been primed all right—but too far. It has gone past the point of sharpened receptivity; it is numbed into insensibility. All food tastes alike. Wine is pointless because it cannot be tasted.

The word aperitif, after all, means appetizer. A small amount of the right kind of wine—sherry, any dry white wine, vermouth or champagne—can put you in the right state of mind to enjoy the food, the company and the whole occasion.

*Spirits*

I have a bias towards wine, rather than spirits, for drinking before meals, principally, I think, because I normally drink wine with the meal itself. Wine goes well after wine, after gin or whisky not so well. This is my experience, and everyone has his own. If I were asked to explain it I should say that spirits have a way of drying up your mouth which is the opposite of appetizing. The great sign of appetite is plenty of saliva. Spirits remove it. Worse, perhaps, they leave behind a flavour which interferes with the taste of the next thing that comes along. To me, spirits do not go with wine, so I go without spirits.

*The aperitif qualities*

The qualities which make a wine really appetizing, and hence good to drink before a meal, are cleanness of taste, coldness, strength, dryness, tartness or bitterness.

A sweet drink taken before lunch or dinner does the opposite of stimulating the appetite. It depresses it. Sugar produces a feeling of satisfaction, which is the last thing an aperitif should do. Sweetness cloys the appetite, which needs to be pointed up, balanced, set off with a tang and a hint of a shudder.

The same is true of a warm drink: ice brings it to life. It is also true of a long drink—say, a pint of beer. It fills you up—so it cannot be appetizing. For this reason an aperitif should be reasonably strong.

*Table wine as aperitif*

Very often a glass of the wine you are going to drink with the meal—white wine especially—is as good an aperitif as anything. Vermouths are stronger, champagne more stimulating, sherry more soothing, but the appetite-making qualities you want are all present in a glass of dry white wine. On a hot summer day, for that matter, a bottle does not go all that far.

A Moselle, an Alsace or Loire wine, a Graves or a Riesling from Hungary, California, Yugoslavia, Australia or any of its adopted lands makes an excellent aperitif. In Portugal the white *vinho verde*, slightly sparkling and almost cidery, is the natural choice. In any wine-growing district, in fact, the ordinary café white wine, brought to table in a jug or carafe from a barrel, is the one to have before eating.

If you prefer red, or only intend to open a red wine for the meal, a glass of this can be almost as good. It should be a light one, preferably —a Beaujolais rather than a burgundy. Claret, though, seems too austerely dry without food.

Of the wines which exist simply for the pleasure of a glass before eating, sherry is the universal champion. For sherry can be as dry as a lemon or as sweet as a date. It can be almost white or almost black. It is the most appetizing wine under the sun. Sherry's place is before a meal: its strength is too high, its flavour too forceful for a table wine. It is the wine to drink with the perfume from under the kitchen door.

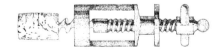

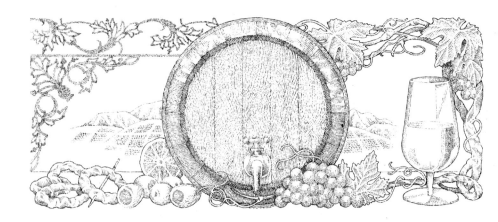

# Sherry

Sherry is the English name for a town in Spain. Its original Moorish name was Scheris. Its modern name is Jerez de la Frontera. The wine of Jerez belongs to a class that used to be known as sack, which was strong and sweet—a great luxury in the cold, sugarless days of the sixteenth century, when it first reached England. Falstaff drank "an intolerable deal" of it, and composed a superb canticle in its praise.

Sack came from all over the Mediterranean. Malmsey wine from Cyprus and Greece was sack. There was sack from Sicily and Canary sack from the Canary Islands. The sack from Jerez, though, soon came to be established as the best, partly as the result of the plundering of Cadiz, when Sir Francis Drake carried off shiploads of it from the burning town.

For a while the wine was known as sherris-sack. Then the word sack was dropped, and by the early seventeenth century the drink was sherry.

Sherry clearly means the wine of Jerez. As everyone knows, it has now been borrowed to such an extent by South Africa, Australia, California, Cyprus and even Surrey, where "British sherry" is made, that it seems unlikely that the Spanish will ever get it back. Some of these places make wine which is intended to be as near as they can get to the Spanish original, and is often very good. Others simply trade on the established name because it is less trouble than launching a new one.

*Jerez de la Frontera*

Jerez is the biggest of the three towns which produce sherry, and the capital of the industry. It is prosperous enough to be much less squalid than the majority of Spanish towns—though it has its share of mud streets and hovels. The other two sherry towns, Sanlucar de Barrameda and Puerto de Santa Maria (Port St Mary's to the British wine-trade), remain pretty much in their ancient squalor. The three lie in a triangle twenty miles north of Cadiz and eighty south of Seville, a hundred and twenty miles from Gibraltar. Sanlucar and Puerto are on the sea, Jerez fifteen miles inland.

It was here that the Moors conquered Spain. The site of the battle, which is said to have raged for four days, on the Guadalete river is just outside Jerez. Though it was not in this part of Spain that they held out longest against the reconquest, the Moorish influence is still strongly felt. Andalusia is the luxurious part of Spain, where every door offers a glimpse of a cool patio, green leaves and blue tiles. It is the country of flamenco dancing.

*The Feria*  Jerez should be seen at the time of its *Feria*, which starts each year on 8 September. It is the most spectacular, romantic and beautiful form of celebration imaginable.

The *Feria* begins with a ceremony for the blessing of the vintage. On the steps outside one of the great Baroque churches of the town a *lagar*—a treading press—is set up. The prettiest girls of Jerez, dressed in their Andalusian costumes, bring baskets of grapes to the press and, as the men begin to tread and the grape-juice begins to flow, a cloud of white doves is released, to rise above the belfry, wheel and soar into the dazzling sky, taking the good news of the new vintage to the neighbouring districts.

The afternoons are spent in bullfights—for the *Feria* goes on for four or five days—and the evenings in balls and parties. As night falls the whole town goes to the public gardens, which are closed to all traffic except horses and carriages. Flowing dresses and mantillas are everywhere, and the air is full of the music of guitars. Here and there in the crowd a girl breaks into a dance.

At intervals among the trees and side-shows in the park there are pavilions of wrought iron and soaring glass. Here the great families entertain, have supper, dance and pass the sultry evening. Many of them are sherry families, as proud of their olorosos and amontillados as they are of their horses and fighting bulls.

*The vineyards*  The grapes of sherry, all white, are grown within the small area bordered by the three sherry towns. The land rises and falls in low hills of startlingly white earth. Under the tremendous southern sun they are dazzling. It is chalk, the best soil for clean-tasting white wines.

It is all the more surprising, in this heat, that the vines covering the hills are so green. Even at vintage time, when in the vineyards much farther north the leaves are beginning to turn, they are as fresh-looking as in the spring. The secret of this is the first of the secrets of making good sherry—the deep and constant cultivation of the soil.

Before ever a sherry vineyard can be planted it has to be ploughed to a depth of three feet, in virgin, hard-baked earth. This used to be done by a team of twelve mules, using a winch. Now an eighty-five horse-power tractor can do it, at a crawling pace. All the moisture the vines can get in the summer, while they are fattening huge bunches of juicy grapes, is obtained from the sub-soil. There is no rain. The vines must be able to draw on the moisture below. The land has to be constantly worked and broken up all the year through to keep the moisture rising. Otherwise the vine would starve, its leaves flag and its grapes wither.

Sherry vines are not trained up on wires or on poles, but kept low on the ground. Their only support is a short stick under the grape-bearing branches. They are kept so low because of the searching wind, the *Levante*, which howls through the vineyards in winter.

*The vintage*  By vintage time the grapes are golden, very much the colour of the finished wine. Their juice is deliciously sweet. The sun, reflected by the white chalky soil, makes them as warm as pies from an oven. The great sherry grape is the Palomino, which has the alternative name—

as though there were not far too many grape varieties already—of Listan. It is used for all except the sweetest and darkest wines.

The grapes are picked by teams of men. In the most modern vineyards they are immediately put into shallow boxes, as carefully as if they were going straight to the market to be sold for eating.

What is needed for sherry is a high concentration of sugar, which will make strong wine. Ripe as they are, the grapes are not quite sweet enough. The practice is to lay them out in their boxes or on esparto-grass mats in the sun. If light wine is wanted they sometimes stay there only for a few hours, until they are almost imperceptibly withered and shrunk. For heavy, sweet wines they sometimes stay on the ground in the vineyard for a week or more, sun-scorched by day and by night protected from the dew by matting.

*Pressing*

The pressing of the grapes took place, until very recently, in the vineyards where the grapes were grown. It is still done like this in a few cases, although the biggest firms have nearly all set up modern pneumatic presses at their headquarters, and take the grapes there to extract the maximum from them under ideal conditions.

Jerez is one of the very few places, in fact, where part of the wine is still trodden by foot. Not by bare feet, however, as port is, or was, but by feet in heavy hide boots. The boots are patterned on the sole with rows of nail-heads sticking out to catch the pips and prevent them getting crushed and adding their tannin to the juice.

The treading takes place at night, in *lagares* in long white barns among the vines. The grapes are brought in from the yard outside where they have been sunning themselves and are tipped on to the platform. As soon as the men begin to tread, the juice (which is called *mosto* from this moment until months later, when it is finally declared *vino*) begins to run. It is channelled off into waiting butts.

But a large part of the juice has to be squeezed out. In the middle of each *lagar* there is a tall iron screw. The men pile the skins into a great toppling cake round the screw, and bandage it round with a long strip of esparto-grass matting. This they attach to the top of the screw and then turn it with bars like sailors round a capstan on an old sailing ship. The bandage acts as a tourniquet, squeezing the juice out without crushing the pips.

*Fermentation*

As soon as the *mosto* is in its butt it begins to ferment. The weather is warm and the sugar content high. The yeast cells lose no time. As fast as the butts of *mosto* are loaded on to lorries and carts and hurried into town to the cool bodegas some of them begin to ferment on the way.

Lorries rumble down the narrow streets with froth streaming from the bung-holes of the casks on top. In the bodega fountains of froth erupt as high as the ceiling in the first stages of what is graphically called the "tumultuous fermentation".

It is not so surprising that the sense of propriety of some of the senior shippers should make them prefer these things to happen in an orderly way under white-coated supervision. These dramas will be seen less and less in the future as the pale horizontal cylinders turn out impeccable must into unsullied casks. They are part of the wonderful variety of wine-lore which will soon only be in museums. They seem to be part of the essence of the wine itself. But no doubt sterile conditions will prove that they were not, and that they add nothing but a good anecdote.

*The bodega*

From this moment until the day it is shipped off to be drunk, the wine lives and grows in a bodega. The bodegas are the cellars and the factories of Jerez: colossal white-walled sheds, inevitably likened to cathedrals because of their long rows of tall arches. Until recently there was only one kind of building—one storey on ground level. But now the firm of Gonzales Byass has broken with even this tradition, and has built a three-storey bodega.

A bodega has a special kind of shade. It is unchanging, like the light in a painter's studio. A few windows high up near the roof throw bright shafts about far above, but the lines of butts, piled three high, remain in permanent half-light.

As long as it is fermenting violently, and later more gently, the new butt of sherry is left untasted. At this time of year, soon after the vintage, the sour smell of fermentation is inescapable in Jerez.

At the beginning of the new year the wine is ready to taste. This is the moment that decides each butt's future.

*Classification*

Sherry has this peculiarity: until you taste an individual butt of wine you do not know what it will be like. Perhaps this does not sound so surprising. But knowing that a cask came from a certain vineyard in France, for example, and knowing the vintage, its maker will be able to form a very good notion of the wine before he tastes it. Furthermore he will expect all the casks from one vineyard to be the same. But this is not so in Jerez. This cask and that cask were made at the same time from the same grapes from the same slope, and yet this one has delicacy, style, promise of beautiful wine in the future; that one has a flat, coarse, feeble taste, and will never be worth drinking unless something is done to liven it up.

This mystery about Jerez has been exaggerated. The shippers do know from experience to quite a large extent what style of wine each vineyard mainly produces. One area is more famous for finos, another for olorosos. But the element of chance remains. Until the wine is tasted nobody can say what its future is going to be.

The director in charge of the new wine and the *capataz* of the bodega will taste and classify as many as two hundred butts a day. They may have four or five thousand butts of the new vintage to get through. They record their findings—in a form of hieroglyphics that fascinates visitors—on the end of the butt. Wine which shows signs of being fino—the highest class—they mark with a tiny formalized palm, known as a *palma*. Wine with the recognizable oloroso character, which from the start is fuller in body, with a less fresh and fine scent, they mark with an O. Rayas; wines which lack the style to be anything much on their own account, and may even be such failures that they have to be disposed of outside the stocks or turned into vinegar, are marked with a stroke of the chalk. On the other hand many rayas make up the body of a medium-class blend of the sweeter kind. It is wonderful what a small addition of a really fine old wine will do.

*Flor and finos*

The distinguishing mark of a fino is its tendency to grow *flor*. *Flor* is a peculiar form of yeast which is native to Jerez and its area and practically nowhere else on earth. It is peculiar because it breaks most of the laws which govern the treatment of new—or indeed any—wine. The first thing to do to new wine is to keep the air away from it. Air carries all sorts of wild yeasts and bacteria which will inevitably, if allowed to get at the wine freely, turn it into vinegar. *Flor* is, indeed, one of the wild yeasts that the air carries, but once it has settled there is nothing to fear from the others. It grows and covers the wine in the cask with a thick white scum. To let it grow freely, the wine is left several inches below the top of the barrel.

The taste of *flor* is fresh and yeasty. It reminds one a little of new bread. This is the quality it imparts to the wine. A real fino has a delicate freshness which is extraordinary in such a strong wine.

Among the wines that grow *flor* there will always be some that are better than others, for sherry does not categorize itself as neatly as all that. Those that show all the characteristics of delicacy and finesse that make them seem almost drinkable at once, without further age, will be set aside in the *criadera*, or nursery, for finos. Those with a less perfect balance which seem to need more ageing will more probably go into the *criadera* for amontillados.

At this stage, when they are classified, put into clean casks and sorted out into their different nurseries, the wines are slightly fortified with pure alcohol. For a fino the fortification is very light; it brings the strength up from about fourteen and a half to about fifteen and a half degrees. Finos are sometimes sold as pale and dry as they naturally are. More often, though, they are slightly sweetened with sugar—which does not affect their taste and colour—or blended.

## Olorosos

The oloroso category is the basis of all sweet sherries. It lends itself perfectly to blending to make the sweet sherry known as cream. Olorosos are rarely—even more rarely than amontillados—drunk unsweetened. When they are, and when they are old, they can be superlative. The Spanish word *oloroso* means fragrant, although, curiously enough, the wine which is classed as fragrant is less scented than the wine which is classed as fine.

At the time of the classification it is quite easy to tell fino and oloroso apart. The fino is starting to grow *flor* freely; the oloroso shows little or no sign of it. In the sampling-glass the fino has the freshness which will still distinguish it when it is ready to be drunk; the oloroso has a rounder, flatter, less exciting smell. The clarity of scent is not there. It is almost as though it were muffled.

As oloroso ages it begins to acquire authority and definition. It seems to ripen almost like a cheese—the scent getting stronger and sharper and at the same time the body expanding into something which seems to explode in your mouth. But this is only at great age, and only in an unblended state. Olorosos like this are virtually never seen outside a bodega. They are nonetheless the basis of the personality of many of the most popular and finest sherries on the market.

## Palo cortado

A palo cortado is a rarity—and proof of the fact that nothing is easy and predictable in wine. Sometimes a wine is excellent at the classification, and yet it is neither fino of the lightest kind, nor the kind of fino which will develop into an amontillado, nor is it an oloroso. This wine may be a palo cortado. The best way to describe it is something between a fino and an oloroso; but not even extreme age will make it incline either way. It holds a middle course, developing along fairly predictable lines—for if this style appears at all it will be a good one—into a wine of lovely balance and distinction; dry, but soft, full-flavoured and rich. There are one or two on the market. The word Cortados will probably be part of the name. In any case they are some of the very finest sherries you can buy.

*The solera*
*system*

The sherry-shipper's objective is to have his own peculiar style of each category of wine always on tap, and never changing. The only way he is able to do this is, logically enough, to get it all out of one barrel. This is the basis of his way of blending, which is known as the solera system.

A solera is a group of barrels of wine, all of different ages. The only wine which is ever drawn off for bottling comes from the oldest barrel. To make good the deficit in the oldest barrel when some of it is drawn off, it is filled from the second oldest barrel, and so on down the line. Thus new wine is continually being added to the solera at one end, and old wine taken out at the other.

The new wine which is chosen to replenish the first barrel is the one from the nursery which is nearest to the rest of the solera in character. It will probably be eighteen months or two years old when it joins the line. By the time it reaches the end it may be three or four years old, perhaps ten or twelve. It depends how many stages there are in the solera.

In the course of the new wine's progress through the solera it is not only mixed with older wine, it takes on the older wine's character. An amazingly small proportion of older wine will affect an amazingly large proportion of younger. After successive drawings-off and toppings-up over a number of years the proportion of the original wine will naturally be minute—and yet its character will have been bequeathed to its successors in the same butt.

Each shipper has a large number of solera systems operating. One will be his most delicate and straw-pale fino, another a stronger fino from Chipiona or one of the outlying districts, another a gloriously pungent oloroso, another a lovely old fino becoming amontillado. There are also soleras of rayas—sound base-wines—and soleras of lesser and greater olorosos and amontillados of various ages. He has perhaps fifty of these unique essences of his own particular idea of what such a wine should be, and with these as his materials he can blend a wine for any taste under the sun.

*Blending*

Rarely is the final produce of the solera the exact sherry which is offered for sale. There are cases, and they are nearly always particularly expensive wines appealing to a limited public. The reason for this is that sherry is naturally completely dry. Even the dark olorosos are fermented to their natural finish, when all the sugar is turned into alcohol. Fortification does not, as it does with port, keep the wine sweet: it comes too late.

The public does not like completely dry sherry. It is an austere taste, which takes a bit of acquiring. It is an expensive taste, too, for only a first-class wine is good enough to enjoy in its natural state.

The shipper's resort, then, is blending. He follows either his own idea of what the public wants or the order of a wine-merchant who wants a brand of his own. Thus the name of an English wine-merchant can justifiably appear on a bottle of sherry, though he has no bodegas in Jerez. It is his sherry, because it is made to his specification, but in fact it comes from a shipper who also has his own ideas of what a popular sherry should be.

A blended sherry is a wine designed for a particular market. The first and easiest thing to calculate about that market is the price that it will be willing to pay. When the shipper knows that, he can see what can be done.

He is asked by a merchant to provide, say, an amontillado which will sell at a fairly low retail price. He looks at his soleras of amontillados. The best would cost far more than that. It is made of superb and long-aged finos. There is another which would almost do, except that it is also a bit expensive. It would, of course, need a good deal of sweetening to be what the English understand by amontillado. It is dry as a bone, and clear gold. It has the fine rich nutty scent that is needed, but almost too much flavour. Let us suppose, though, that he mixed this wine with another, much younger and less splendid—a raya. It would bring the price down and at the same time soften the penetrating flavour. Then perhaps a small measure of a youngish, rather strong fino to give it more freshness. Now he has a wine at the right price, already more to the English taste than the original amontillado. It is still dry, so he sweetens it with a little Pedro Ximenez, which also gives it colour. Not quite enough, in fact, so he adds a measure of a jet-black colouring wine. He has the perfect medium wine the market requires.

If this blend, which he has made in his sample-room in sample quantities, meets with approval from the merchant who is going to launch the brand, he goes ahead and makes it up. The right number of butts of the various wines are poured into a vat and stirred. When they are thoroughly mixed they are run back into butts and left to marry and mature together. Perhaps before they are actually shipped they will be fortified a little more with alcohol, one per cent or so, to make sure of their stability en route.

*Pedro Ximenez*

Three categories of wine are kept apart for blending alone. One is for sweetening, which is made of Pedro Ximenez (P.X.) grapes. These are left out in the sun to shrivel and become raisins before they are pressed. The wine they make is almost black, treacly, undrinkably sweet on its own. Its influence in a blend is immensely powerful.

*Very old sherry*

The other infinitely valuable additive in making a blend which is to have the depth of flavour and some of the value of a really fine wine is very old sherry. One or two soleras are established in any of the great shippers' houses simply to provide the oldest sherry possible. The wine is used with great discretion, for its influence is immense. An oloroso that has been in the solera for forty years is so strong in taste that it is almost painful to hold a sip of it in your mouth. It is another of sherry's peculiarities that age concentrates it, in strength and flavour, until it is the very quintessence of the wine it once was. A small quantity of such a wine will go a long way in a blend.

*Vino de color*

Finally there is the colouring wine. This is made by boiling and reducing *mosto* until it is almost black. Its taste is a little caramelly, but almost neutral. With this the colour of the blend can be adjusted to whatever the market requires. Paxarete, a mixture of this wine and sherry, is bought by whisky-blenders and shipped to Scotland for colouring their blends in exactly the same way.

*The finished wine*

When the wine is ready to be shipped it is no longer necessarily described in the way it was when it was first classified. The trade in each country has its own terms, which the customers know better than the Spanish names. In English the principal terms which appear on labels are "fino", which keeps its name, "amontillado", whose name has come to mean something different in English, "cream", "old full pale", "dry", "golden", "brown" and other words that are purely descriptive.

Besides these universally understood type-names there are also blends which sell on their brand-name alone, without any description. The choice of sherry by its name is complicated by this practice more than any other. The following are some of the words which occur most often on sherry labels.

*Dry*

The word dry has lost most of its original meaning. It used to denote without any, or much, sugar. Thus all sherry is dry until it has been sweetened. But "dry" is now used either to mean comparatively dry, as in Dry Sack (which justifies itself by saying, quite rightly, that for a sack—a sweet kind of wine—it is fairly dry), where it means medium; or just as part of the name, as in Dry Fly, where it does not mean dry at all. The word is also used to mean the driest of a range, as in Regency Dry or Bristol Dry, where its meaning is fairly clear, although it still does not mean without sugar, by any means. It is more certain, if you want a really dry sherry, to look for one labelled "fino".

*Fino*

All—or nearly all—finos are sweetened slightly for the British and American markets. It has been quite rightly observed that a wine which tastes perfectly dry in Spain is hard to drink without a shudder in England: the farther north you go the more a little sugar is needed to keep a balance. Finos are nonetheless the driest, palest and perhaps least blended of all sherries. They are comparatively young, and (for sherry) delicate. A brown sherry can be left in an open bottle for weeks without coming to harm, but a fino loses the freshness which is its principal charm after a few hours. A bottle of Fino ought to be opened and drunk up straight away, like any white wine; six months on a shelf in a shop has often been enough to ruin it. A good fino is intensely appetizing. It is never so good as it is before a meal. It goes excellently with olives and almonds, or crumbled dry cheese. In Spain it is never drunk without tapas, little morsels of some kind. They range from a few shrimps to a young banquet of steak and onions or lobster claws and mayonnaise.

The perfect glass for a fino is the Spanish wine-taster's *copita*. It is slim, elegant, tall; a narrow rose-bud in shape. The wine can be swirled in it with magnificent panache without a drop going astray. There is just room for your nose at the top.

Williams & Humbert's Pando, Gonzales Byass's Tio Pepe, Valdespino's Inocente, Pedro Domecq's La Ina, Garvey's San Patricio, Dry Lustau Fino, Avery's Elizabetha, La Riva's Tres Palmas and Sandeman's Apitif are some of the best finos to be had.

*Manzanilla*

The manzanilla characteristic is something that a fino can acquire or lose. It is found in the very tart, pale finos made in the distinct area of Sanlucar de Barrameda, which starts some fifteen miles from Jerez. Sanlucar is on the sea, or rather the broad estuary of the Guadalquivir. The local fino has a style which can only be described as salty, as though the sea air somehow impregnates it. But take it to Jerez and store it there and the peculiar taste goes; it becomes just a plain, very elegant fino. Conversely, a plain fino taken from Jerez to Sanlucar and stored there takes on, after a while, the manzanilla character. The thing is a mystery.

Manzanillas are shipped abroad, but they run the risk of losing the very thing that makes them manzanillas and not just finos en route, and very often lose it they do. Moreover, this particular style of wine is light in alcohol for sherry, and always needs fortifying, which changes its character, before it can travel.

Sad to say, therefore, to taste a real manzanilla there is no alternative but to go to Sanlucar. It is no hardship, for it has one of the best fish restaurants in the world, Casa Juan, which serves its food on a wooden platform out over the beach with the fishing boats all around. If you should ever be there in bad weather the restaurant on the beach will be out of action. You can still eat just as well in the bar, but it is just a fisherman's bar, and the odd tables they set up do nothing to subdue the fishermen. There, and I believe only there, you may taste a rare and superb thing, a manzanilla amontillado—a wine which has been in cask, in the sea air, for ten or fifteen years and has acquired, with quite a dark colour, the most clean, full, salty, savoury taste it is possible to imagine. Half a bottle of this, with dishes of *langostinos* and grilled red mullet and herbs, is the finest eating and drinking in Spain.

*Amontillados*    Strictly speaking, an amontillado is a fino which has become, with age, heavier, stronger, darker, with more depth and intensity of scent and flavour—in fact, more like the wines of Montilla, a district to the north-east of Jerez, near Cordoba, which is famous for this type of wine. A fine amontillado is, in fact, much better than the wine it is named after, but the name came in to describe the type at the beginning of the last century, and it has remained.

The word amontillado is now used commercially to mean nothing more than a medium sherry. Real amontillado is medium in the sense that its colour and flavour lie between those of a fino and those of an oloroso. In quality it is far from medium: it has an extraordinary individuality which is, in my opinion, the best thing Jerez produces.

Not all finos turn into amontillados as they grow old. Some just become—though it is rare—old finos: they keep their lightness and freshness even as they intensify with age. Many just lose all their qualities and become good for nothing. But others move gradually through an intermediate stage, which is known as fino-amontillado, until they reach the stature of fully fledged amontillados. Then they are dark, dry, pungent, almost tarry; as nutty as a hedgeful of hazels.

Very often wines which are called amontillados, on the other hand, are medium in the sense that they are neither one thing nor the other. They are blended to be middling-sweet, middling-brown. They are supposed to appeal to everybody and end by exciting nobody.

*Full*    The word full comes into such phrases as "old full pale". It must be construed to mean soft and sweet. The paleness mentioned in this phrase is an exception to the general rule that the darker the sherry, the sweeter it is. Bristol Cream is a pale, very sweet wine.

*Milk*    The word milk only occurs in sherry shipped, or which used to be shipped, to Bristol. It implies sweetness and softness, and I suppose to some extent harmlessness, though there is no particular justification for the latter. There is a story that the Ministry of Food tried to object to the word milk being used on something which did not originate in an udder. Bristol used to be so full of its famous milk that horse-drawn sledges, rather than iron-tyred wagons, were used in its cobbled streets to avoid vibrating the precious wine below.

*Cream*    A cream sherry is one which is older, softer and better than a milk. It is usually a fine oloroso, sweetened and tinged with a lighter colour.

*Golden*    The term golden is virtually interchangeable with cream. Where a range of sherries includes both, however, the cream is usually sweeter than the golden.

*Amoroso*    Amoroso also means very much the same. Although the word means amorous in Spanish, a perfectly appropriate adjective for a soft, sweet wine, it is the name of a vineyard—far removed, I imagine, from the famous Inocente vineyard which produces austere finos. Amoroso is really only another word for oloroso now.

*Vino de pasto* literally means table wine. It is used, though rarely now, on light medium sherries of no special quality.

Brown, or East India, sherry has more in common with Malmsey Madeira than with a fino. It is greatly sweetened and darkly coloured, very rich in taste and often stronger in alcohol than most sherries. To me it is most welcome after a sharp walk in a deep frost.

## Serving sherry

Clearly a range of wines so wide can produce something for whenever a shortish, strongish drink is wanted. Since longer and not so strong drinks are found to be better with meals, sherry tends to be everywhere but at table. Natural dry sherries are supremely appetizing before, sweetened sherries are popular both before and after meals.

If there is any time when a drink is called for with no meal in the offing, sherry—dry, sweet or medium—is the ideal choice. There used to be a custom of having a glass with a piece of cake where now we take tea or coffee at mid-morning—but office-workers and wives in centrally heated houses find that it makes them drowsy.

But there is a place for sherry at table too. A number of the richer kinds of hors d'oeuvre, notably smoked salmon and smoked eel, have a tendency to overpower the light table wines with their oiliness, producing a taste in the mouth which is not pleasant. A dry sherry is excellent with smoked salmon, or with any of the strongly flavoured hors d'oeuvre dishes. At the beginning of a meal when you are going to have a bottle of red wine and feel like drinking something with the first course, but do not want to order a whole bottle of white, a glass of dry sherry is perfect. It is also perhaps the best wine to drink—if you want wine at all—with most kinds of soup. It is good either with or in consommé and all clear soups.

At the other end of the meal sweet sherry is quite good with cheese, though not with sweet dishes. Nuts go extremely well with sweet and medium-sweet sherries, amontillados and olorosos.

Sherry is perhaps the wine which is most often kept in a decanter—especially by the British. Knowing the British habit its makers incline to strengthen their wines enough to preserve them during their sojourn on the side-board. There is no harm in decanting sweet or medium sherry—indeed the extra elegance of the decanter can add appreciably to the pleasure of serving it. But for light dry sherry, finos or manzanillas, it is a disaster. The sooner they are drunk up after opening the better. If there is some left it should be kept tightly corked, in the fridge. In Jerez bars normally serve only half-bottles, the better to preserve the fleeting freshness of this most delicate of wines.

Any smallish, round or bud-shaped glass is fine for sherry. It should never be more than half-filled, or the scent of the wine is lost. In summer some people like it in a bigger glass with a lump of ice, and even a splash of soda. Dry sherry definitely improves with half an hour in the refrigerator at any time of the year. It is best cold, not icy.

## Montilla

It has never been quite clear to me how the shippers of sherry, powerful though they are, have managed so successfully to keep us in the dark about sherry's one possible Spanish rival: Montilla. Montilla is one of Spain's most popular and highly esteemed wines—in Spain. There is a bottle emptying at least as fast as the sherry bottle on every bar. Yet abroad few people know about it, for it is rarely listed.

*[margin notes: Vino de pasto; Brown; Decanters]*

Montilla lacks an ancient reputation for the simple reason that it was always sold in the past, by sherry shippers, as sherry. Only in the last twenty years has Montilla had an official identity of its own. Still to this day a good part of the wine in the bodegas of Jerez comes from this outpost of excellent vineyards over a hundred miles away, in the hills just south of Cordoba.

Montilla has *albariza*: the same chalky soil as the best parts of the Jerez district. But being farther from the sea it is hotter, and it grows the Pedro Ximenez, the super-sweet grape used for sweetening sherry, instead of the Palomino.

Pedro Ximenez and extra heat between them make wine of such high natural strength that there is no need for additional alcohol. When Montilla has finished its fierce fermentation (in open earthenware amphorae, or *tinajas*) it is already about 16 per cent alcohol—enough to secure it from any further attacks by yeast.

The eventual product is classified in just the same way as sherry: as fino or oloroso, or even amontillado (meaning "montilla-ed"). The typical Montilla, however, is the fino rather than the amontillado. It is a pale dry young wine with all the delicacy of a true fino, differing from a sherry fino only in a rather softer feeling, a muted acidity.

Being unfortified, Montilla comes across with its true fino character more vividly than any except the best of commercial sherry finos. But it must be treated as a white wine, chilled and drunk quickly. Ideally the bottle should be started as an aperitif and finished with a first course of hors d'oeuvre or smoked salmon. No wine leads into a summer lunch better.

## The "sherries" of other countries

The other countries of the world which make wine that they call sherry inevitably challenge Spain to a comparison. If their wine is indistinguishable from its original—for even they will not deny that they are copying Spanish sherry—it is hard to make out a case against their calling it sherry. It seems a pity from their point of view that they must admit that the best they can do is to copy someone else. But that is their business.

### South Africa

There are very few people who can tell the best of South African sherry from an ordinary Spanish one of the same character. It is not entirely surprising, because the vineyards of Andalusia and the Cape have many things in common. Their latitude, on opposite sides of the equator, is almost the same. In their climate and their nearness to the sea they are very similar.

Their soil, however, is completely different. The staring white chalk of Jerez is not found in South Africa. The vineyards there are largely sandstone—which you would not expect to give the wonderful cleanness of flavour which chalk gives, whether in Jerez or Champagne. The South Africans, however, use the Palomino sherry grape, and the Pedro Ximenez, as well as a South African variety, the Steen.

They make the wine in a very similar way to the Spaniards, and see to it that *flor*, whether natural or induced, is in every barrel where it is wanted. Indeed, the South Africans discovered, to their great delight, that the mysterious yeast called *flor* was as native to the Cape as it is to Andalusia. This seemed to sanction their calling their wine sherry.

Finally, the best South African sherries are made by the same solera system as the Spanish. Some of the soleras have now been in operation for over twenty years, not the same matter as the century or more that the oldest and most valuable blending wines of Jerez have been in the bodegas, but still a respectable length of time, and enough to have started giving the best oloroso-type wines some of the depth of flavour they should have.

In Britain South African sherries are slightly cheaper than the Spanish wines with which they are bound to be compared. Where they are comparable, therefore, there is an advantage in buying them. But this is only in the middle, medium-to-sweet range.

There are no very dry and delicate South African sherries, nor very full, old and nutty ones. They can be as sweet as you like—and there is probably less noticeable difference between Spanish and South African in the sweet wines than among the dry—but they are not anything like as good as the best of Spanish sherry, sweet or dry.

I have had an old amontillado-type South African wine which should have worried a *Jerezano* seriously. But it was a special bottle from a special solera, not on the market—the old story. I am not saying what South Africa can or cannot do—let alone what she could do if the South Africans themselves were discriminating and devoted sherry-drinkers. But what she does, commercially, is to produce good-quality ordinary, unexciting wine. The only motives for drinking it in preference to Spanish can be economic, or sentimental.

The Kooperativ Wijnbouwers Vereeniging (K.W.V.), by far the largest South African wine-producer, puts out two full ranges of sherry at slightly different prices and qualities. The more expensive, the Paarlsack range, has the edge for age and smoothness, includes a more fino-like dry wine and very good cream sherry. Both are best, I think, in their medium categories—still quite light but distinctly sweet in the mouth. I find these indistinguishable from comparable Spanish wines.

*Australia*  The greater part of the Australian wine which is called sherry finds a totally different market from that of the Spanish wines. Australia's natural advantage is sun. The historic tendency for all Australian wines, with the exception of a few grown on high ground, is to have a great deal of sugar and a very low natural acidity. Sun makes grape-growing easy (so easy, in fact, that Australia has an enormous surplus of grapes, which are processed in whatever way comes to hand, to make raisins, alcohol or wine) but it makes wine-making difficult. A good part of the wine is strong, sweet and rough—qualities which in a well-balanced wine would develop, as port does, into excellence with age, but which in an unbalanced wine lead nowhere.

Where great care is taken to imitate Spanish sherry, in bottles which cost the same as the best South African, Australia makes a pleasant, medium to dry, good-quality wine. But it still would scarcely be mistaken for the real thing, as South African often is. Where Australian wine strives to achieve a light balance it so often goes too far, and achieves wateriness instead. Where it does not, it remains heavy and heady.

The handful of first-class Australian sherries includes Mildara's George, Yalumba's Chiquita, All Saint's Pale Dry Flor and Buring and Sobels' Granfiesta—all of them made with *flor* yeast.

*Cyprus*  The sherry-type wine of Cyprus is not the most successful of the island's wines. At its best it tastes like a moderate parody of sherry, at its worst the name does not fit it at all.

This is not to say that there are not excellent Cyprus wines. Table wines from Cyprus are often very good. The island's own sweet dessert wine, Commandaria, is like nothing else—and is none the worse for that. But Cyprus sherry, except in the sweetest categories where it is a good, smooth, intensely sweet drink—indeed almost more like a port than sherry—has little except extreme cheapness to recommend it.

*British "sherry"*

One in every four bottles of wine sold in Britain is not wine at all, by any strict definition. These British wines, which the wine-trade knows affectionately, and not inappropriately, as sweets, are made of preserved and concentrated grape-juice. The grapes are pressed and their juice dehydrated in the country where they were grown, which is often Cyprus or North Africa, before fermentation has a chance to begin. The solid concentrate which is shipped to England is non-alcoholic and hence pays less duty. On this fact, and the saving it achieves, hangs the prosperity of the British wine-industry.

British "sherry" at its best, when it is still only about half the price of the cheapest Spanish, manages to conjure up a taste which reminds one of sherry. The greater part of it, however, is designed merely to be a sweet, smooth, strong and consistent drink. It succeeds in being the cheapest form of alcohol, money for degrees, in Britain outside the old last resorts of methylated spirits and rubbing alcohol.

*California*

It is a great pity that sherry is almost a dirty word in the United States. The fault for its low reputation lies with the Californian producers who have made it merely a cheap, strong wine. "Sherry-drinkers" used to be the term for ragged layabouts borrowing rides on freight trains and drinking from the bottle. The wine, needless to say, was not sherry at all. It was cheap southern Californian wine, more or less processed by cooking to give it a kind of burnt taste which was supposed to bear some resemblance to sherry.

California still produces considerably more wine which it calls sherry than the sherry area of Spain (according to Frank Schoonmaker's invaluable *Encyclopaedia of Wine*, over three times as much). I personally do not find that the "sherry" sold in gallon jars in supermarkets in the United States has any of the aperitif qualities, or indeed anything except alcohol in common with sherry.

# Champagne

Champagne has the stimulating qualities of an aperitif, rather than the savoury, mouth-watering ones, in the highest degree. It owes a large part of its reputation, in fact, to its magical effect on the morale.

To say that it is more often drunk for its boosting qualities than for its taste is not to belittle its taste: there is nothing else which has an even comparable stimulating power.

It was by some of the neatest and most painless public relations the world has ever seen that champagne came into power. Somehow, at the end of the last century and the beginning of this, it just seemed to fall into its ready-made slot in the social pattern. What, we now have to ask ourselves, did they drink at weddings, dances, christenings, launchings, comings-out, before they had champagne?

Good champagne has an incomparably fresh and delicate taste of grapes. There is hardly any sugar in it at all, but just enough to balance a slight acidity—the perfect balance of, say, a crisp golden-green apple. It has an extraordinarily pungent smell—you can smell a bottle being opened in the next garden—and yet the scent in the top of your glass is as delicate and fresh as the wine itself. Finally it has a perfect mill-race of pin-point bubbles, slowly settling down to gently racing streamers from the bottom of the glass. The total effect of the wine is one of richness, belying the fact that it is completely dry, and never, at least in my experience, cloys.

No other wine has these qualities all together—or indeed any of them so perfectly. There are innumerable other sparkling wines, a great many of them imitating champagne, but there are still hardly any effective substitutes.

### The name champagne

So successful is champagne that it continually has to defend itself against the danger of becoming a notion rather than a wine. Its name is borrowed by anything that wants to sound gay, luxurious and expensive. The hint of old-fashioned elegance it carries with it has been used to sell almost anything—including other wine.

But Champagne is a place, like Bordeaux, Alsace and the Loire. It is one of the few world-famous wines which does not have an English name. We call Bourgogne burgundy, Jerez sherry, Rhine-wine hock, red Bordeaux claret. All these names, being our inventions, have been borrowed by imitators. But Champagne is an area, a small county of French soil, and its name should only be used for wine which comes from its superlative vineyards.

### The champagne country

The vineyards of Champagne are the nearest vineyards to Britain. To reach them is barely half a day's drive from the Channel ports. Reims, the capital, is familiar to anyone who has driven south from Calais on the way to Switzerland and Italy. It is not a particularly beautiful town, due to the First World War, which razed most of its fine old buildings, but its glorious Gothic cathedral, wonderfully restored after having been completely gutted, is sometimes called, with full justice, the Parthenon of France. Reims is honeycombed with cellars. Some of them are said to have once been Roman stone quarries. In many cases the galleries through the chalk under the city are three or four storeys deep—all full of champagne.

All the vineyards lie to the south of the city, above and around the valley of the Marne. It is neither majestic nor pretty country, but simply peaceful, and in autumn, when the leaves of the vines are red and gold and the smoke of bonfires rises quietly into the cool air, marvellously beautiful.

No wine region throws open its doors more readily to the visitor. The shippers are always ready to welcome people and show them round their colossal establishments. It is not uncommon for a firm to have ten or fifteen miles of dank chalk cellar to show anyone who is that interested. Above ground the buildings are no beauties; most of them were built during the nadir of architecture at the end of the last century and the beginning of this. The Avenue du Champagne, though, in Epernay, the second town of Champagne, is worth seeing. For half a mile the top-heavy mansions of the shippers alternate with the huge courtyards of their *maisons* (as they call the office-cum-cellars-cum-factory where the wine is made). Never did proprietors live so near their work so pleasantly. It was one of the houses in this street, the house of the Pol Roger family, which Sir Winston Churchill once called "the greatest address in Europe".

At no moment of the day is champagne not being drunk somewhere in Epernay—and the visitor is sure to get his share.

## The wine

Champagne, the wine, is the outcome of an ideal site for the growing of vines, being so far north that the coming of cold weather influences its making. The chalk soil is perfect for a clean, dry, white wine. Its arrangement in gentle slopes, sheltered from the north and canted towards the sun, is perfect for ripening grapes, which need all the sun they can get. But being so far north the harvest is late, and the grapes are not over-full of sugar when they are picked. Formerly, before the technical revolution of recent years, they fermented slowly, and were still in the last stages of fermentation when the winter caught up with them. Cold weather temporarily stopped the fermentation. The characteristic of champagne was that when the spring came and the temperature of the wine slowly rose it began to ferment again. This is the so-called secondary fermentation. It was used to make champagne a sparkling, rather than a still, wine.

Sparkling champagne is a wonderful example of how experience has taught the grower to bring out the best in his wine—even at great risk and expense. Champagne without bubbles is perfectly possible, in fact very good. But it has the drawbacks of delicacy. It is fine in Champagne. But bring a bottle to England and it has lost its character. There is obviously no very profitable market for such a wine—and yet there was the potential of making millions of gallons of it. The answer to the riddle is traditionally ascribed to a monk, the legendary Dom Pérignon.

## Dom Pérignon

Pérignon was the cellar-master at the Abbey of Hautvillers, a lovely spot looking southwards over the wide valley of the Marne. Tradition says that he was blind. He conceived the notion of bottling the wine, in which he had discovered the tendency to ferment and become fizzy again in the spring after the vintage, while it was thus troubled. Furthermore, he was the first man to use corks for the job. Previously an ineffectual stopper of rags had been used. Thick bottles were needed, and stout string to keep the corks in, but those that survived, among the many that burst with the pressure of mounting bubbles, became a most marvellous drink. The monks found, in place of the fragility and tartness of the still wine they were used to, a fine, more fragrant, more robust, more spirited wine, better than they had ever been able to make. Best of all, it had lovely bright ribbons of bubbles, rising and waving endlessly in the glass. There was no instantaneous gassiness about it; the bubbles seemed to appear from nowhere at the bottom and form columns processing upwards. The gas, the by-product of fermentation, having no room to go elsewhere, had dissolved in the wine.

Champagne, however, did not just appear fully fledged from the blind master's cellar one fine spring morning. He worked on it constantly for year after year. Naturally he found, as every wine-grower finds, that one year produces fine, full-flavoured wine, another a liquid which is hardly wine at all. He discovered, in addition to this, that the vineyards of the area had qualities which separately left something to be desired, while their finest points could all be brought to the fore in a blend.

*Blending*      Thus the wine of the Marne valley slopes of what is called by courtesy the Mountain of Reims was as round and full-bodied as any in the area. Those of the gentle slopes to the south, on the other hand, from Avize and Cramant, had more of the qualities of finesse and brightness in the mouth. The cellar-master saw in his mind's eye the notional champagne—a perfectly balanced blend of these desirable characteristics. It could be, he thought, the finest wine on earth.

But there was a serious problem yet to be dealt with. The fermentation which brought the bubbles had other side-effects. As yeast cells multiply in the bustle of fermentation the old ones die. The fermentation itself leaves a deposit of solid particles, all of which are trapped in the bottle. Instead of a clear golden wine you have a thick unhappy-looking one full of "fliers". It may taste good, but it looks most unappetizing. This is the great difficulty in making champagne.

If you ever see an eighteenth-century champagne-glass—and there are not many, for the fashion had not really begun—you will see that it is frosted like a bathroom window. It will be flute-shaped, a long thin V, the classical and still the best shape for sparkling wines, but you will not be able to see the wine in it. That was before the problem had been mastered.

The cellar-masters of Champagne gradually developed ways of removing the débris from the bottle. To filter it was fatal; all the sparkle went too. Somehow it had to be done under pressure or with the pressure released only for a moment. They had, in fact, to take the cork out, remove the sediment and get the cork back in again without letting the wine, or the gas, escape.

*The widow*      The credit for finding the way the whole vast industry does it now
*Clicquot*      goes to another of the legendary figures of Champagne, the widow Clicquot. Her husband was, among other things, the head of a small wine-making business in Reims. As the story is told in a little book published by the widow's firm and written by the Princesse de Caraman Chimay, the wife of a former director, the young couple would drive out in their trap round the vineyards, learning about every stage in the making of wine, from winter pruning to the treading of the grapes at vintage time. Madame Clicquot became fascinated by the many skills, the patience, the naturalness of everything that went on in the farms and the cellars. But the idyll was shattered. A fever took away the young husband and the wife was left a widow.

She carried on. She built up a trade and a reputation for the wine with her husband's name. She found partners and took risks, chartering ships and following up contacts. Russia was her principal market, for the Russian army was quartered in Reims in the final campaigns before Waterloo, and had acquired a thirst for champagne which went back home with them. To Prince Serge Alexandrovitch Wolkonski, their humane and convivial commandant, Reims owes a great debt. The widow Clicquot is supposed to have pondered the problem of the bits in the bottles until she came to the logical solution. The bits must be obliged to collect on the cork, where they can be removed without affecting the rest of the wine. To do this she had a big table pierced with holes, and stuck the bottles in the holes upside-down. In some the deposit, which looks like a line of fine white sand along the lower-most side of the bottle, obediently slid to the cork. In others it stuck.

Then was devised the simple expedient of giving the bottle a gentle shake, lifting it slightly from its hole, giving it a slight clockwise turn, and knocking it against the wood as it was being put back. It had to be done discreetly, or all the accumulated deposit would be shaken back into the wine, and the whole process would have to start again. The trick was called *remuage*, or moving.

### Remuage

Refinements followed. The tables were leant up at a sharp angle so that they took up less room, and the holes ovalled slightly so that the bottle could still be stood almost on end. In this form they were christened *pupitres*—desks. The *remuage* was brought to a fine art, so that an experienced *remueur* could, using both hands, shift three thousand bottles an hour. Instead of just being upside-down from the start they were tilted more and more each day, so that the deposit rolled slowly down the hill to the cork. Even so it took three months in the *pupitres* for a bottle to be ready for the next stage.

### Dégorgement

This was the disgorging (*dégorgement*). The deposit was now resting on the cork, the bottle standing on its head. It remained to get the cork and the deposit out, and another cork in, as quickly as possible. To do this, a man took each bottle in turn, upside-down, cut the string, pulled the cork, let out the first two inches of wine holding the waste matter, topped it up with a little more and handed it to his neighbour, who rammed in another cork. Then more string to hold the new cork in against the pressure, and the job was done.

There was one more modification. The wine, at the end of its second fermentation, is always completely sugarless and dry. The Russians, in particular, liked it sweet. So the topping-up wine became a mixture of sugar, wine and—just to make sure the wine would stand up to its long journey—a drop of stabilizing brandy. And so (except that most firms now leave out the brandy) it is today.

### Dosage

The sweetness of champagne is easy to adjust. It is simply a matter of how much sugar is put in the *dosage*, the topping-up. In theory, *brut*, the driest champagne, has none, but is topped up with wine alone; *sec* has a little, *demi-sec* more and "rich" a good deal. In practice even *brut* has a little.

Since the process—the whole of which is known throughout the world as the champagne method—became established at the beginning of the nineteenth century the principle has not altered. Modern methods have been able to speed up and simplify some things, but *remuage*, for example, still baffles the makers. New ways of doing it by machine are continually being invented, but none of them work as well as the patient men with cold hands down under the chalk.

One deyelopment has helped a great deal. The neck of the bottle, containing the deposit to be removed, is now dipped into a freezing mixture just before the disgorging, so that the wine in it becomes ice.

When the cork is removed it is a plug of frozen wine that shoots out, to be replaced by the *dose*. A lot of wine has been saved this way.

Further developments are taking place all the time. Most of the big firms now use concrete or glass vats for the first fermentation of the wine instead of the traditional barrels. It is notable, though, that two of the firms which all connoisseurs of champagne agree in calling the best at the present day—Krug and Bollinger—still use oak barrels.

Large firms are also changing over to crown corks from the more expensive and laborious real cork for the first fermentation. Again, some firms are resisting it. It is these little differences, they are sure, which add up to the big difference between the best possible champagne and a passable one.

But more important by far than the details of processing is the wine which is processed. The deciding factor in the quality of champagne is the original wine that goes into it. All champagne, you remember, is a blend. A shipper may grow his own wine or he may buy it from farmers. But wherever he gets it, if it is not good in the first place he cannot turn it into good champagne.

*Classifying the vineyards*

The vineyards of Champagne have their own classification. You cannot buy a first- or a second-growth champagne, because it is all blended. The object of the classification is not to help the consumer; it is a scale of prices for the farmer.

Each of the villages of Champagne has been given a percentage figure. Ay, the most famous of the black-grape-growing villages, and Avize, the most famous of the Côte des Blancs, for example, are among those classified as 100 per cent. Some villages are 95, some 90, etc.

At each vintage time a committee of growers, shippers and other interested parties get together and decide the price for the year. They take into account the quality, the quantity, the stocks, the demand and anything else that crops up. Then they announce so many francs a kilo for the grapes. Ay and Avize get 100 per cent (the whole price), Hautvillers 80 per cent and so on. It is equitable, it reflects the value of the land, and everybody is happy.

Therefore a shipper who is buying grapes to make his wine can decide to have more or less of the 100 per cent in his blend, to fill up with cheaper wines or restrict himself to what he can afford of the more expensive ones. It is here, at this stage, that the quality of champagne is really decided.

The vineyards of Champagne are roughly divided in two; those which grow black grapes and those which grow white. Both, needless to say, make white wine. The black-grape country is the valley of the Marne and the Mountain of Reims, the wide, plateau-topped hill which lies to the south of Reims, between the city and the Marne. Its slopes to the north, east, south and south-west are a solid mass of vines. The flat top is wild forest country. No vines grow there.

Over the valley of the Marne, beyond the town of Epernay is the Côte des Blancs, the white-grape country. It stretches out along a line of hills for ten miles south.

*Blanc de blancs*

Classical champagne is a blend of the wines of these two regions. Each has something to offer the other. In the last ten years, however, champagne made of the juice of white grapes alone, called *blanc de blancs*, has been widely sold, under the guise of being lighter than the traditional kind. I have not met anyone who has found the old kind of champagne too heavy, but the power of suggestion is great, and since "lighter" Scotch has been such a success, and the lighter rum and drier gin and vodka—with no taste at all—have all proved extremely popular, it seemed a reasonable assumption that the public would swallow the same thing with champagne.

It is usually sold at a higher price than classical champagne, though in what way it can be worth more it is hard to say; white grapes are no more expensive than black ones. It is, in fact, a fashion, which will eventually stand or fall on its merits. But it is a pity that anyone should be misled into thinking that no champagne is good enough unless it is *blanc de blancs*.

*The vintage*

At vintage time, which varies in Champagne from mid-September in a good year to mid-October in a sunless one, parties of pickers, many of them mining families from the industrial belt up near the Belgian border, descend on the vineyards. Hampers are dropped from trucks along the lanes through the vines, each marked with the name of the shipper who has bought the crop, or who owns the vineyard in question. They might be mistaken for laundry-baskets. They fill quickly, as messengers go back and forth between them and the picking parties with little wooden trug baskets, maintaining an endless chain. Before the trucks come back for their load some of the women of the party have been sorting all the grapes, sitting at trestle tables in the lanes, rejecting any that have mildew or are muddy or in any way undesirable.

The trucks or tractors go on their round again, and the baskets go straight to the pressing station. Sometimes this is close by, at a farmhouse in the fields or in the nearest village; sometimes they are taken straight into the headquarters of the firm in Ay or Epernay.

*The pressing*

Then the grapes are pressed. The presses are enormous: some of the biggest used anywhere: four tons of grapes go into one press at a time. They are wooden, round or square pens with slatted sides. Into the top of the enclosure descends a wooden grill with tremendous force, imperceptibly slowly, pressing all the juice out of the grapes and into the runnels, whence it runs down to a waiting vat or cask below.

The press is used three times on each load of grapes—once for the *cuvée* (the best of the wine); once, harder, for a second batch of wine which could be used for blending or sold to brokers who carry stocks of such wine in case they are needed; once, a third time, after the *marc* (the remains) have been broken up and rearranged with spades, for ordinary wine for the workmen. (In Champagne even the *marc* is used: it is distilled to make eau-de-vie.)

In the casks the wine begins to ferment quickly if the weather has been good and there is plenty of sugar in the must, slowly and reluctantly if a wet summer is being followed by a chilly autumn. It goes on until most of the sugar has been converted into alcohol and the night-frosts have set in. Then in former times the shipper threw his windows open to let the cold air circulate round the casks and vats to stop the fermentation. Today he adjusts his thermostat.

*Blending*

The vital process of blending takes place in the spring. The directors of the firm meet in the tasting-room, sometimes day after day for weeks, to examine all the wines that have emerged from their vintage of six months previously. It is then that they discover whether they have bought well, and got what they need. For their object now is to make up the *cuvée*, the blend, which will eventually bear their name.

Most of the well-established firms follow a fairly standard buying pattern year after year. They know that the particular kind of light or not so light wine for which they are famous demands a certain proportion of grapes from the village of Ay, a certain proportion from the village of Verzenay, and so on.

Needless to say, there are always opportunist firms who buy whatever they can get at a cut rate, and try to disguise its faults as best they can, but the good firms will let nothing seduce them from obtaining and blending the best possible wine, for the vintage, that their experience and ingenuity can manage.

I say "for the vintage": if it is a fine year, with all that a great champagne needs—body, balance, bouquet—the blenders have the opportunity of modelling their very finest and most individual product, a vintage champagne.

*Vintage champagne*

Vintage champagnes are only made in extra-good years. In Champagne this almost always means years with more than the usual amount of sunshine. More sun produces riper grapes, and riper grapes richer wine. A vintage champagne, therefore, though not sweeter, is always a heavier, fuller and rounder wine than the ordinary, non-vintage kind. It has more individuality; it is not made to be as similar as possible to the current wine of the same firm. On the contrary, it is planned to be unmistakable as the wine of this particular year—the year when the grapes were ripe by, say, 10 September, or the year the flowering happened before the children went back to school; the year we never thought the thunderstorms would hold off, or the year of the Anniversary celebrations.

In fact this is not quite true. To a certain extent a good shipper will cheat over a vintage wine if he feels he can make it still better by adding something he has in reserve. This was true of some of the 1959s, which were almost too rich, and lacked the balance of acidity. Several shippers provided what was lacking—and made a better wine—from the stocks of the leaner wine of the year before. The shipper can never use this as a means of stretching his vintage, because he is not allowed to sell more wine of any given year than he has made. In a certain sense, therefore, you can say that a vintage is a shipper's first-quality champagne. The principle remains, however, that a vintage champagne should be true to the date which it shows and thus reflect the character of that year.

*Non-vintage champagne*

Most champagne is non-vintage. It does not carry a date on its label. The making of the *cuvée* is done on a different principle in the spring following an ordinary or mediocre year. The object is to maintain the constant standard of the brand by combining the new wine with stocks of the previous year or years to obtain a result as similar as possible to the wine of the current non-vintage. It is easy to see that this is one of the most skilled processes in the whole tricky field of wine-making. The tasters have to be able to foresee the future, after a further fermentation and three years in bottle, not of one wine but of a complicated combination of perhaps a dozen which they have before them. Only experience, of course, can make this possible. When the decisions have been taken and the *cuvée* made up and thoroughly mixed together, it must be bottled.

The young wine used to be bottled haphazardly, the makers knowing its tendency to ferment again in its bottle, but not knowing exactly how much it would ferment and what the resulting pressure in the bottle would be. Innumerable burst bottles were the result. It was not unknown for half the wine of a vintage to be lost in this way. When one bottle exploded, the sides of its neighbours would be stove-in, and the destruction would spread. The floors of the cellars were running with wine and crunchy with broken glass.

*The second fermentation*

It is now possible, however, to add exactly the right quantity of sugar-syrup to the wine as it is being bottled, so that it will ferment a predictable amount, and the pressure in the bottle will rise to a predictable and tolerable level. Bottle-bursts are very rare now, although the champagne bottle still has to be much thicker and heavier than all other types.

The wine is required by law to be at least one year in its bottle before the long and elaborate preparations for its final appearance begin. In practice the best firms allow it three years. During this time it is lying in a stack in the cold, damp cellar, and the fermentation of the extra dose of sugar is imperceptibly going on. With no more oxygen than the tiny amount in the bottle and what can get through the cork, the life of the yeasts is not so energetic as it is in an oak cask. It will take them at least a year to convert all the sugar to alcohol. Occasionally the cellar-man will come along and rouse them up, giving each bottle a hearty shake to mix all the yeast thoroughly into the wine again and keep the fermentation going.

Only at the end of all this is it put in the *pupitres* to collect the sediment on the cork. To keep this process going all the time the shippers have to have enormous stocks of literally millions of bottles—another addition to the eventual cost of the wine. In this state, undisgorged, champagne will keep in perfect condition almost indefinitely. I have had a wine from the last century that had been kept *sur pointe*, standing on its head, for the last sixty years and only disgorged ten minutes before we drank it. But this pleasant habit can only be indulged by shippers and their friends, and by them only in their own houses above the cellars where the wine is kept.

*Ageing champagne*

Once the champagne is disgorged it is, in theory, ready to drink. In fact it improves immensely if it is kept a little longer for the dose to marry with the wine. There is a surprising amount of disagreement among experts on what should be a very easy thing to decide: whether it goes on improving after this, and whether it is, in fact, a wine which you can lay down with profit (not that there are many people who would or could) or not.

To me there is no question about it. A bottle of champagne is always worth keeping for a year or two before drinking. Vintage champagne can be worth keeping for ten years. In the course of time even non-vintage champagne seems to lose its sharpness, and broadens out in flavour. After several years it begins to lose a little of its sparkle, and become noticeably richer in flavour and colour. Eventually it will probably go almost flat and acquire what some people call a chocolate taste. It is usually avoided in this condition, and for this reason old champagne, if it ever crops up, is often sold for less than new. In fact it can be superb and you should never pass by an opportunity of tasting it if you are offered it.

*Buying
champagne*

There are, broadly speaking, four classes of champagne on the market. The cheapest is that sold by a retailer under his own brand-name, which is known as his "Buyer's Own Brand". It is always recommended for parties, and there is rarely anything wrong with it. On the other hand, it is seldom the wonderful drink that champagne can be. Champagne is so expensive anyway that it seems a pity not to pay the little extra which is necessary to get a really good one.

*B.O.B.*

B.O.B.s can do the champagne industry a great deal of harm by disappointing people who, tasting them, wonder what all the fuss is about. On the other hand, there are some which, in all fairness, are as good as or better than some of the shippers' marques.

*Non-vintage*

The second class is non-vintage champagne with the French shipper's name. The leading dozen-odd names in the industry are household words. The biggest house, Moët & Chandon, has an astonishing turnover. The thirteen commonly thought of as the finest shippers are the following: Bollinger, Charles Heidsieck, Heidsieck Dry Monopole, Krug, Moët & Chandon, Mumm, Perrier Jouet, Piper Heidsieck, Pol Roger, Pommery & Greno, Louis Roederer, Taittinger, Veuve Clicquot.

To these might be added the names of Ayala, Besserat de Bellefon, De Castellane, Delbeck, Deutz & Geldermann, Henriot, Irroy, Lanson, Mercier, Ruinart, Veuve Laurent Perrier.

Some houses raise their standards and some lower them as time goes on. No rating of these houses has any permanent value. It is nonetheless worth mentioning that if an *hors concours* class were to be made at present, the names which are likely to appear in it are among the following: Bollinger, Krug, Pol Roger, Louis Roederer, Veuve Clicquot.

Non-vintage champagnes from this class are good enough for practically anybody and practically any occasion. They are lighter than vintage wines and almost better, therefore, as aperitifs. For a party they are ideal: one could ask for nothing better.

*Vintage*

For vintage champagne the same names apply. Normally nowadays a vintage is not put on the market until the stocks of the preceding one have been sold. This is a pity, because it deprives us, unless we have the forethought to keep some ourselves, of the pleasure of comparing two vintages side by side. Vintage champagnes are the ones to drink with food, if any are. Otherwise they are for keeping for occasions even more special than those that call out the non-vintage.

*Tête de cuvée*

Several houses have put out a brand which is supposed to be even better than their vintage wine. In some cases it is a *blanc de blancs*, which is not necessarily better, though it may be more to your taste—lighter, more delicate, thinner in body. Some of the others, though, are what is known as *tête de cuvée*: wine made only from the first and most gentle pressing of the finest grapes, blended in the usual way but intended to be a superlative—even better than the same firm's vintage wine. Dom Pérignon, Moët's champagne named after the old monk, is the original one of these: it first appeared as long ago as 1921. There is always a suspicion that these wines are made only for people who are anxious to spend as much as possible on a bottle; for whom the best is not good enough. Some *tête de cuvée* champagnes, in short, are the superlatives they are said to be, some are merely good champagne gift-wrapped. To buy one because it is more expensive is to lay yourself wide open to having your leg pulled.

My personal favourites in this "extra special" class (based I'm afraid on less experience than I should like) are Roederer's Cristal, Ruinart's Dom Ruinart, Pommery & Greno's Avize Blanc de Blancs, Laurent-Perrier's Grand Siècle, Taittinger's Comte de Champagne and Heidsieck Monopole's Diamant Bleu. Bollinger's R.D. is another excellent wine. R.D. stands for *récemment dégorgé*—the wine is aged (for ten years or so) in the bottle containing the sediment before it is disgorged. Thereafter it is ready to drink without more ageing. There is an extra depth of flavour given by this method, which is why most champagne houses keep a few bottles undisgorged until the last minute for their own pleasure.

*Rosé*      Pink champagne, made by mixing in some red wine, is very pretty. It used to be a fashion, and could, it seems to me, easily become one again. Nothing is more suggestive of pretty girls and shady lawns. What is more, with age it takes on a pale tawny colour which, lit with bubbles, is a most beautiful sight. In taste it is very similar to ordinary champagne. It is most certainly worth trying.

*Crémant*      *Crémant* means "creaming". Fully sparkling champagne is *mousseux*. *Crémant* has about half as much fizz. It is for some reason rarely seen, but it can be superb. The village of Cramant (in the white-grape area) is famous for it, which causes rather a confusion of names. *Crémant* should certainly be sought out by people who swizzle out the bubbles in normal champagne—a complete waste of all the long and expensive process of putting them there. It tends to be extremely light and delicate, gentle both in bubbles and taste—another drink which could easily become a craze.

*Consumption*      It is surprising to find that by far the greater part of the 125-odd million bottles of champagne which are sold every year stay in France. (In fact, 80½ million of them, according to the 1973 figures.) The French are devoted champagne drinkers. There is hardly a café in the whole of France which cannot produce a bottle of a good make to order—and this despite the fact that it is often more expensive in France than it is abroad.

*Serving champagne*      I have put champagne, you notice, among the aperitif wines. It is often said that champagne is the ideal wine right through any meal. This may help to sell more of it, but I do not think it is true. For almost any part of any given meal I could name a wine which was more exactly appropriate, and would make a better meal. To use champagne as we use *vin rosé*, to avoid making up our minds what other wines to choose, in the spirit of compromise, is to do it a great injustice.

Champagne is wonderfully, uniquely stimulating before a meal or at a party. On the other hand it has lost more potential admirers by being served when something else would have gone better than almost any other wine.

It loses friends by the dozen in cold marquees at tea-time on a rainy wedding-day, when a hot cup of tea would be far more to the point. It loses more friends when it is served with a great mound of roast beef, when the soul yearns for a fat red wine, and loathes the thin white one which is the only thing in sight.

One of the chief reasons why so many people say they do not like champagne is because they have it when they do not really want it—in that dripping marquee—and do not have it, because it is so expensive, when they do want it.

As an appetizer, or a party-maker, champagne is without a rival.

The physiology of it—why champagne has a different effect from every other wine—seems to be something to do with the dissolved carbon dioxide in it. Although you see a good part of it escape in bubbles before you drink it there is still a good deal left dissolved when it goes down. The gas escapes, and carries the fumes to your head. Or alternatively it makes it easier for the stomach lining to absorb the alcohol. Whatever the reason, champagne produces its effect more quickly, keeps you on a pleasant level more steadily, and lets you down more gently than any other wine. It is the easiest of all drinks to serve. One of the effects of its long conditioning in the cellars of Reims or Epernay is that it is as stable as a rock. You never have to worry—as you do with other wines—about whether journeys have shaken it up, or whether a hot summer or a cold winter has spoilt it. It survives all these things.

*Temperature*   The only care you must take is not to shake it about too much in the hour or so before you uncork it, and see that it is reasonably cold. There is a tendency, particularly in the United States, to serve champagne as cold as a freezer can make it. This is quite a good way to serve a money-saving substitute for champagne, but it is a waste of the real thing. Neither the scent nor the taste can come out when it is icy. The temperature of a deep cellar is best: distinctly cool, perfectly refreshing, but not searingly cold in the throat like a can of lager straight out of the ice-box.

*Glasses*   Any big glass is good for champagne. There is no need for special glasses of any kind, though the beautiful flutes and tulips look very pretty. A goblet is good. A silver mug can be splendidly appropriate. André Simon, who so characteristically described the champagne on a picnic in the country as "a bottle of something cold", had the most perfect glasses for it I have ever seen. They were crystal half-pint mugs, each with a constellation of five stars engraved inside the bottom from which five columns of bubbles ascended in a steady stream.

There is one kind of glass which is no good for champagne, or any wine—the kind caterers, who have vast stocks of them they have to use, insist on calling a champagne-glass—a saucer on a stem.

*Quantities*   Each person has his own experience of his friends' drinking powers. Without experience it is difficult to predict how much champagne anyone will drink. Half a bottle per head is a minimum allowance for a party where champagne alone is being served. A man can usually drink a whole bottle in two hours without ill effects: there are only five or six (depending on the size) glasses in a bottle. For this reason it is always worth getting champagne for a party in magnums, which hold two bottles. There are half as many corks to pull, and the sight of a magnum is a generous and cheering one. A magnum would last four people for a whole evening, or eight just for drinks before dinner.

Champagne can be bought in quarter-bottles (one good glass), half-bottles, double magnums and even bigger sizes. Anything bigger than a double magnum, however, is very hard to handle.

## Other Sparkling Wines

*France*   The champagne method is now used all over France. There is hardly a wine-district which does not have a sparkling wine of one kind or another. The trouble, however, with most of them is that the process is used to make poor wine marketable, rather than—as is the case with champagne—to bring out the natural qualities of the best wine that can be made.

*Vouvray*

The best of the other sparkling wines comes from the Loire. If any of the districts can be said not to be following champagne, but making a first-class sparkling wine in its own right, it is Vouvray, in the ancient province of Touraine. Sparkling Vouvray tends to be a little richer and rounder than champagne, a reason why a good many people prefer it, if they would but admit it. There is more flavour of grapes about it, if a little less subtlety. It is never as dry as the driest champagne, but it is none the worse, in many people's opinion, for that.

The Vouvray vineyards cover a hill of chalk in the same way as those of Champagne, and, as in Champagne, the cellars are cut out of the chalk beneath. At Vouvray even the houses of the vintners are often cut straight into the rock. The wine they make is either made sparkling or left still; still white Vouvray can be a very good, rather sweet wine.

*Saumur*

The Saumur area, following the Loire downstream and westwards, also produces a great deal of sparkling wine of very much the same kind as Vouvray, possibly not quite so good. The difference in price between these wines and champagne, once relatively slight, has increased so markedly recently that few people can afford not to try them. Many, if they are honest with themselves, would actually be happier to be given the Vouvray. The slight extra "generosity of flavour", as they say in the trade, can be very "comforting".

The most famous of the sparkling wines of Saumur in Britain is Golden Guinea—a medium-sweet, gently Muscat-flavoured wine, far from being typical of the region. The brand has been popular for over fifty years. Oddly enough, such wines as this, brands which are well known all over the country, never excite comment nor even get a mention in wine textbooks. The wine-conscious overlook them, but the public goes on buying them, which probably says more for their quality than a little passing acclaim.

Three other districts also have a long tradition of making sparkling wines (tradition is a thing worth taking into account, for it means they have not just jumped on the bandwagon to use up stocks). Their wines are St-Péray and Clairette de Die, both from a long way south down the Rhône valley, and Seyssel, from higher up the same valley.

*St-Péray*

St-Péray and Clairette have nothing in common with champagne except the sparkle. St-Péray is strong, golden and dry, a much heavier wine than any champagne, and to that extent better with food, if you like sparkling wine with food at all. Clairette de Die (Die is in the hills to the east of the Rhône valley, almost in Provence) is a slightly muscat-flavoured, slightly sweet and generally very well-made *méthode champenoise* wine without much delicacy. Seyssel, on the other hand, could be confused with champagne if anything could. It is not often seen, but when it is, it should be tasted. Dry, delicate and pale, it has the aperitif qualities to a high degree.

*Clairette de Die*

*Seyssel*

*Sparkling burgundy*

Sparkling burgundy is as often red as it is white. Sometimes it is made by the champagne method, sometimes not. The thing to bear in mind is that no-one would waste good burgundy by making it sparkle. To me there is something absurd and ungainly about sparkling red wine. It is like a fat old man dressed up as a fairy. Perhaps the best of the sparkling burgundies is neither the red nor the white but the pink, which glories in the name of Oeil de Perdrix—Partridge Eye. I do not remember ever having waited until I saw the pinks of a partridge's eyes, but it is expressive as a name, and the wine is good. There is excellent sparkling white burgundy to be had, too, but its recommendation is rather a negative one: it does not taste like white burgundy at all. It seems a pity for a wine to give up its native character, for it can never adopt another successfully. But good, if rather neutral, sparkling white burgundies there are, made by the champagne method. Kriter is far and away the best-known brand made in Burgundy, though it does not claim to *be* burgundy.

*Blanquette de Limoux*

Of the other French wine areas, those without a long tradition of making sparkling wine, the most remarkable at present is Limoux, in the hills west of the Languedoc just south of Carcassonne—one of the last places you would look for the delicacy and acidity that sparkling wine needs.

The Limoux growers' cooperative, one of the largest in France, has taken the plunge and bought extremely sophisticated wine-making weaponry. Their press-room, with two banks of eight of the biggest horizontal presses, controlled from an electronic bridge, is a traditional wine-lover's nightmare. Yet they use the laborious *méthode champenoise* for the ageing and sparkle-making of their wines, and the results are a real surprise. They lack champagne's flavour and finesse, but lightness, delicacy and the true racing bubble they do have—at about a third of champagne's price. Their *Appellation Controlée* is Blanquette de Limoux.

*Cuve close*

There are two common short-cuts in the making of sparkling wines. That of simply pumping them full of gas is only used for the very cheapest. It can never make bubbles which stay in the wine after it has been poured out. The wine froths for a moment and then is flat. The other method, perfectly respectable but still nothing like as effective as the long laborious business of the second fermentation in bottle, is known as the *cuve close*. By this method the wine is made to have a second fermentation, but in a pressurized vat rather than a bottle. The carbon dioxide is not allowed to escape, so it stays in the wine. The difficulty with the sediment is overcome completely: it is simply filtered out as the wine is bottled. Wine made like this foams well, and keeps a sparkle for a while—though not as long as the *méthode champenoise* wine. It is the sensible way to make cheap sparkling wine; the labour involved in doing it the long way would be out of all proportion to the value of the wine being treated.

*Sparkling Bordeaux*

*Cuve close* is used in Bordeaux to make very pleasant sparkling white wine. If a bottle of sparkling wine says nothing on the label about the champagne method being used you are pretty safe in assuming that this is what has been done.

## Italy

The most popular sparkling wine of Italy is Asti Spumante (*spumante* being Italian for sparkling). The characteristic taste of Asti is muscat. It is an unmistakable scent wherever the grape is used in a wine, even in small quantities, for no grape has such a strong smell. Even its skin is perfumed.

*Asti Spumante*

Asti Spumante is always more or less sweet—sometimes ravishingly so, the most honeyed mouthful imaginable. What makes it so drinkable is that the bubbles prevent the sweetness cloying. It is even refreshing, despite its sweetness. If there is any wine for a picnic by a stream, in long scented grass, with the sun winking in the ripples, it is Asti Spumante.

The town of Asti is in the hills south of Turin, not far from France and the Mediterranean, the country which grows several of Italy's best wines. It is a small country market-town, modest in its attractions and accommodation, but the scene of a major wine-converting industry. The local muscat wine is made there into either Spumante or vermouth. The firms of Martini, Gancia, Cinzano all make both.

It is a good idea to serve Asti Spumante very cold—much colder than champagne. When it is at all warm the taste seems to get out of hand, but when icy it is nicely balanced and slips down easily. It has a surprisingly low alcoholic strength—less than normal table wines—making it all the more suitable for drinking in warm weather.

*Other spumante*  There is hardly a corner of Italy which does not make sparkling wine of some sort—but it is limited to local consumption and rarely worth seeking out. One or two have a name and reputation, and others deserve one.

Signor Ferrari of Trento, in the Italian Tyrol where German is almost as commonly heard in the streets as Italian, is typical in the scale of his operations, if not (unfortunately) in the quality of his wine. His premises are no bigger than the cellars of an old bishop's palace. (Trento was full of bishops for the twenty-odd years it took the Council of Trent to deliberate its counter-Reformation policy.) When I went there the labelling of the bottles was being done by two small boys: the smaller one licked the labels and put them on, the larger one put them straight. The wine which was bottled under these conditions was much the best Italian sparkling wine I have had; very clean in taste, as dry as all but the driest of champagne. But it is not, I fear, typical.

## Germany

In Germany a vast industry, as big as the champagne industry itself, has grown round the process of converting ordinary wine into sparkling wine. The product is known as Sekt—by tradition because an actor who was famous for his Falstaff was always calling for sack when he wanted what used to be called *Schaumwein*, foaming wine.

Sekt varies from the rather nasty, cheap, chemical-tasting varieties to wines which are almost as expensive as champagne, and are therefore bound to be compared with it. I have never known one which did not suffer by the comparison, though one or two are excellent drinks of a rather different kind.

*Sparkling Moselle*  The chief fault they have in common, to my taste, is rather too strong a flavour. The best I know is a sparkling Moselle, with many of the qualities of the still wine—but this is the best that can be said of it. The sparkle seemed to me to add nothing: perhaps it was hiding something. Wines from individual and famous estates are also, oddly enough, sometimes processed into sparkling wine. Presumably they are the wines of poor vintages. It would be a terrible waste of their successful wines.

The greater part of Sekt, however, is made from wine imported in tankers to Germany from wherever it is cheapest—Italy, France, Africa or Spain. The processing of this wine is analogous to the making of vermouth rather than the making of champagne. The first object must be to remove whatever character of its own the wine has so that it can be made to taste "German" by the addition of flavouring.

Such wine is immensely popular in Germany. There alone the annual sales are greater than those of champagne in the whole world. On top of this Germany is no mean market for French and other sparkling wines. One of the best things to do with Sekt is to mix it with fresh orange-juice; to make, in fact, the drink which, made with champagne, is called Buck's Fizz. Sekt, in any case, should be served very cold. It is usually made dry but a sweet type is also available.

*Spain*  Catalonia, in the north-east, is the sparkling wine area of Spain. It was Perelada, one of the wines from this district, which lost a London High Court case brought by the champagne industry to prevent it being sold in England as Spanish champagne. *Xampan*, the Spanish phonetic equivalent (as *coñac* is of cognac) is still seen on labels in Spain.

Many of the Spanish sparkling wines are very good. In general they are made by the *méthode champenoise* rather than by any of the short-cut methods. Some sparkling white Rioja is made in the district near San Sebastian which is responsible for all the best Spanish table wines, but it is from Catalonia that the best *Espumoso* comes. It is never very dry, and rarely very sweet, but maintains a very pleasant drinkable middle path. The names Codorniu and Frexenet I can vouch for personally.

*California*  Californian sparkling wine is sold as champagne. It deeply vexes the French originators of the idea and the method, but there seems to be little they can do about it. The *champenois* can take some crumb of comfort from the thought that at least the wine which is sold under their name is one of the best made by their method in the world. Some of the *brut*, the driest, Californian sparkling wines are very fine— among California's best produce. A simplified version of the champagne method is now being used by some producers. They avoid the laborious process of *remuage* and *dégorgement* by decanting the wine, after it has re-fermented in its bottle, into a tank, and thence filtering it into another bottle. Almaden and Paul Masson are among the pioneers of this method. It results in rather shorter-lived bubbles than the original *méthode champenoise*. Adherents to the old way (Korbel and Schramsberg are good examples) are now labelling their product "fermented in *this* bottle", to emphasize the difference.

None of these wines taste like champagne exactly, but they are superb aperitifs; light, delicate, as dry as can be. In Britain they are only of academic interest, because American production costs combined with high freight charges make them as expensive as champagne. In the United States, however, they are of the greatest possible *New York State*  interest. New York State "champagne" is often called the best of the New York State wines. Very few of the wines of this state, however, are made of real wine grapes.

*Moussec*  Moussec is British sparkling "wine", made by the *cuve close* method of second fermentation from concentrated grape juice brought from the borders of the Champagne area. The factory in Rickmansworth near London produces two kinds, sweet and dry, the sweet having, to my mind, a shade more character. Most of the firm's business is done in little one-glass bottles in bars. Only one champagne-shipper, they say, comes near the volume of their sales in England.

# Madeira

Sherry is first and foremost the drink for before a meal. Port is first and last the drink for after one. Madeira is not so simple, and not so fortunate. It seems almost to have lost its way. There was a time when

Madeira was the first wine at every dinner: later it appeared as the last. The island still makes wines to fill both bills, but none of them succeed in the way port and sherry do.

Madeira's trouble was two terrible outbreaks of vine plague in the second half of the last century. Oidium was the first, phylloxera the second. It has never quite recovered from the blow. Nevertheless the wine made today is extremely good value and—unless you remember the wine they used to make—nothing to complain about. The main thing is that it has Madeira's unforgettable special burnt taste.

*The island*

Madeira was the first of Portugal's finds when she began sending out her explorers in the fifteenth century. The island lies five hundred miles out in the Atlantic, west of Casablanca. Prince Henry the Navigator, the sponsor and inspiration of the voyages of discovery which brought to light, among other things, both the Cape of Good Hope and Cape Horn, took Madeira under his wing. When it was found the island was naturally enough uninhabited, but covered from shore to shore with trees. Prince Henry had these burnt, in a forest fire that lasted for years and covered the island with ash. On the bare and ashen remains he ordered the planting of vines.

Thus was consciously founded what later became, at one point, the greatest vineyard in the world. The wood-ash made the volcanic soil fertile, and Mediterranean sweet-wine vines were planted. The vines, ash and lava established the special sweet, sharp, smoky character of Madeira wine.

*Ageing treatment*

Experience showed that long exposure of the wine in its cask, after it was made, to the sun and air improved it enormously. Madeira is constitutionally strong: stronger than any other wine. Treatment which would finish off a lighter-built wine completely only brings out its finer points. Long sea voyages, which were in any case inevitable in delivering the wine to the Portuguese colonists round the Cape in the Eastern trading stations, were best of all for it. A combination of a year or two of cooking in the sun, and four or five months of rolling and pitching in the bilges of a galley or a carrack, smoothed and rounded it in an amazing way. The return voyage to the Indies, involving nearly a year of tropical heat and ship's movement, brought it to perfection. And yet the wine was still as tough as ever. It has never been known to have travelled too far or grown too old. As far as anyone knows it is immortal.

It is still possible to buy Madeira a hundred years old. A few merchants in Britain and the United States list vintages from 1845 or so until about 1900, to this day. For wines of this age they are ridiculously cheap. Furthermore, unlike any other wine as old as this they are a completely safe buy: they have never been known to go off, or even fade, except in colour.

*Today's wines*

But the Madeiras we are considering as aperitifs are a slightly different matter. Modern Madeira is classified under four headings, corresponding to four different types of vine which are grown on the island. Two are dryish; the kind of thing you would drink before a meal. The other two you would be more inclined to drink after.

Only a few of the very finest of the dessert wines, the Malmseys, are aged today in their casks under the sun. The rest are artificially heated in big sheds called *estufas* (stoves).

*Sercial and*     The two drier types which are made in this way are called Sercial
*Verdelho*     and Verdelho. What proportion of the wine actually comes from these
two classical vines depends on the quality of wine you buy, but the
idea is to follow their characters.

Sercial is the drier. It is a full, brown wine, with a superb perfume,
but markedly sharp, which helps to make it appetizing. Verdelho is
almost equally dry, but with a little fatness—a beginning of the
peculiar buttery scent and soft flavour which distinguishes the dessert
—and the best—Madeira wines.

*Rainwater*     A third kind, made, in theory, by blending the two above, is sold
under the name of Rainwater. This unflattering, if rather pretty,
name comes from the United States, which has traditionally been the
island's best customer. A Mr. Habisham of Savannah, Georgia, used to
sell a particularly light and pleasant Madeira which was given this
name, perhaps because he had the curious habit of leaving his casks
outside, like rainwater-butts.

## Fortification

Madeira is a fortified wine, like port. The principle of its making is
that a part of the sugar of the grapes—large for dessert wine, smaller
for aperitif—is prevented from fermenting by the addition of
alcohol, traditionally in the form of cane-sugar spirit, a first cousin of
rum. Thereafter it is stored in an *estufa* at a high temperature for at
least a year. This treatment gives it its slightly burnt, caramel flavour.
In California, curiously enough, a similar technique is used to make
so-called sherry.

*Shippers*     There used to be a good score of Madeira shippers, as there is of
port shippers today. But lack of interest in Madeira, and the shortage
of first-class wine, has led to massive amalgamation, so that, for all
intents and purposes, Madeira today comes from one large enterprise,
still using, however, the old companies' names, among which are
Blandy, Cossart Gordon, Leacock, Henriques & Henriques, and
Rutherford, Miles.

In most cases these names appear on two ranges of wines, under the
grape-names Sercial, Verdelho, Bual and Malmsey, making eight
wines in all—a complete scale from dry to sweet in two price-ranges.

*Serving*     Sercial, Verdelho and Rainwater are all equally suitable for drinking before a meal, in place of sherry. Like dry sherry, they are much
better for being chilled for half an hour before they are drunk. As the
rich and powerful scent is half the joy, it is important to use large
glasses, in which it gets a chance to expand.

## White port

A full account of port comes later, in the After-Dinner Wines
section. It occurs here, however, in its white version, which has
recently been launched in England as an aperitif. Personal taste is
bound to obtrude into a book about wine, and I might as well come
clean. White port is not my drink.

There is no difficulty about making port with white grapes instead
of red, or about making it dry instead of sweet. The difficulty comes,
it seems to me, in making it taste as though it was a good idea.

It is not a new idea. Port has been made white as well as red for
centuries. But the reason it has not been popular in all these years is the
reason it is not particularly exciting now: it is heavy, ungraceful. It
cannot stand comparison with even an indifferent sherry.

*Tawny*     In fact tawny port (see the After-Dinner Wines section, page 230)
makes an excellent aperitif—much better than white port. Both need

chilling if you are going to drink them as appetizers; either by being left in the refrigerator for half an hour or with a lump of ice in the glass—one lump, not the full "on the rocks" treatment.

*Other aperitif wines*

There is no sharp dividing-line between aperitifs and table wines. Most people find that high-strength and sparkling wines are better on their own before a meal, but there are a great many wines which are neither high-strength nor sparkling which go as well as ever before a meal. One or two, in fact, have the aperitif qualities in such a degree that there seems to be no better time to drink them.

*Château-Chalon*

Château-Chalon is the most peculiar of these. It is most like very light sherry: yet it is not sherry. It is never fortified, yet it lives to a great age and builds up to a good strength.

It belongs to the family of *vins jaunes*—yellow wines—from the Jura mountains in eastern France. The town of Arbois nearby is famous for a number of wines; white, grey (the local name for rosé), red and yellow. Arbois yellow is unusual, and good with the dish of chicken which is cooked in it, but Château-Chalon is a different wine altogether.

Its oddity is due to the fact that, through some vinish freak, it is the only French wine to grow the *flor* which is found on the best sherry. Southern Spain has it, South Africa has it and this one village in France has it.

*Flor* gives Château-Chalon the ability to age for seven or eight years in cask, far longer than would be good for a normal white wine. It also gives it the strange, yeasty, soft freshness which is found in a good fino. In fact it is lower in strength than sherry, less dry and more acid. It is remarkable, perhaps, more because of its peculiarity than because of its ultimate quality. Yet—and also despite its formidable price—it is well worth trying. It is a good reminder that there are worthy things in the world of wine outside the usual circle of sherry, hock, claret and port.

The Château-Chalon bottle is unmistakable. It is short and dumpy —locally called the *clavelin*. It is worth using large glasses to enjoy the special scent. Overchilling kills it.

*Chinese dry white*

Into the category of unusual wines which are really best drunk before a meal comes perhaps the greatest curiosity of all, a Chinese white wine—a red Chinese white wine, in fact. It comes from Shantung, or so I gather from its modest label. It is extremely palatable, very dry, with a reasonable scent and a distant cousinship of flavour to a light sherry. It is only available in half-litre bottles, and is by no means cheap, but its sheer curiosity value and, to some extent, its quality make it well worth trying.

*Lagoa*

There is a less exotic wine, similar to sherry, from the Lagoa vine-yards in southern Portugal, called Afonso III. There is an excellent

*Vernaccia*

high-strength dry white wine called Vernaccia in Sardinia—there are, in fact, wines of this type from more places than I shall ever know about. But they are almost never shipped to be sold abroad. The wine trade has to specialize to some extent. Nobody would argue that in choosing sherry among all these strong wines to specialize in it has neglected anything which is even comparable in quality and range.

*Muted wine*

In the Frenchman's ceaseless quest for new things, and particularly new, sweet things, to drink—he is the mortal enemy of his liver—he has produced countless curiosities. Fortified wine is not—may I be forgiven—France's forte. But she has a product called muted wine, which has never been allowed to ferment at all. In this case, brandy is added to fresh grape-juice before fermentation has started. The yeast is doped by the alcohol and never gets to work. The resulting drink is as sweet as the grape-juice and as strong as the brandy, without having the characteristic winy taste of anything which has ever fermented. The two most famous of these concoctions are the specialities of the Cognac and Champagne areas. They are called, respectively, Pineau des Charentes (the two Charentes are the two *départements* of France in which cognac is made) and Ratafia. When they are old they can be good, though I think it is fair to say that they are a taste that has to be acquired. Ratafia is sometimes flavoured with almonds. It was a favourite cordial of Victorian England, but rarely seen today.

*Pineau des Charentes Ratafia*

## Vermouths and Patent Aperitifs

*Quoique ce soit*—"whatever this may be"—was the name of a French patent aperitif in the last century. It might be the motto of all patent aperitifs to this day.

A vermouth, or a patent aperitif—and in this class go all the tribe of Byrrh, Dubonnet, Campari, Lillet, Pernod—is a conspiracy of silence. It is offered as a drink with one particular, unchanging taste. You can take it or leave it. You will never know what is in it.

*Vermouths*

Vermouths are flavoured and fortified wine. Wine is their base and gives them their character. Its strength is brought up to about the strength of sherry, or a little above, with pure alcohol. It is sweetened with sugar, and flavoured with any number of herbs and spices. Among the classical, and probably universal, flavouring agents is wormwood, whose German name, *vermuth*, gives the drink its name.

Vermouth has its origin in the medieval, and even older, practice of improving wine which had gone sour, or which was otherwise not worth drinking. Honey and herbs were the original additives. It has developed into a major industry, particularly in Italy.

The vermouth country is the foothills of the Alps on both sides of the French and Italian border. Turin is the capital city of vermouth. Broadly speaking there are two kinds, which still tend to be known as French and Italian, although both are made in Italy now more than in France. French is the drier, and Italian the sweeter of the two. Italian comes in two colours, *bianco* and *rosso*. Each of the major Italian manufacturers therefore has at least three main products: dry white, sweet white and sweet red.

The dry white vermouth is the flavouring in the gin of a dry martini, the most famous of all cocktails. It is highly perfumed, with an elusive herb-and-spice scent which makes it a very good drink on its own, iced, on the rocks or with soda. Noilly Prat is perhaps the most famous of the French manufacturers of this style of vermouth. The vermouth of Chambéry, a small town near the Italian border, is less known, but is generally considered to be France's best. It is particularly dry, rather lighter in flavour than most, and mixes well. The firm of Dolin in Chambéry have a particularly delicious speciality of making their vermouth with the juice of wild strawberries. The pink, slightly sweeter than usual Chambéryzette, as it is called, is a wonderful spring and summer aperitif. I sometimes make a cup by mixing it with *vin rosé* which, if you are susceptible to pretty colours, is agreeable.

*Noilly Prat*

*Chambéry*

*Chambéryzette*

*Cinzano bianco*

The sweeter version of white vermouth is typified by Cinzano bianco. It seems usually to have a rather more richly coloured label than the pale green of the dry one. (Vermouth labels all follow a pattern of curious circus-poster Baroque which suits the drink so well that it could never be changed.) Bianco is perhaps less good for mixing, and better on its own, than dry vermouth. It needs icing; without ice it is rather syrupy. With an edge of lemon and a touch of soda it is excellent.

*Rosso*

Red vermouth is the essential ingredient in any number of well-known cocktails. Americanos and Manhattans depend on it. I prefer it half and half with the dry white to straight, but as a straight drink it is treated in the same way as the bianco.

Whether and how much better these, the classic and original vermouths, are than their many modern imitators I have never been at great pains to find out. God preserve me from a vermouth tasting. But since vermouth is essentially a matter of cookery the question of geography cannot enter into it as much as it does into the making of natural wines.

## Quinine aperitifs

On the fringe of vermouth and almost overlapping into the next section, patent aperitifs, there are one or two Italian dark and sweet ones with the addition of quinine. Quinine provides a bitter element which is strangely appetizing. The finest example of this type is Carpano's famous Punt e Mes. The name means "point and a half", and has its origin among the stockbrokers of Milan who used to order it, for some reason, with this cryptic phrase. It is at the same time extremely sweet and extremely bitter, a contradictory but compelling combination. It needs icing.

*Punt e Mes*

In places this craze for quinine has got quite out of hand. In Spain you will meet with Sherry Kina, sherry with quinine added, which has a certain saloon-bar public. In Italy there is a Chinato made from Barolo, the best of Piedmontese red table wines. Cynar, another curious aperitif with quinine flavour, is made from artichokes, and has a faint, rather pleasant artichoke flavour. The most popular application of quinine in England, of course, is in tonic-water.

*Sherry Kina*
*Barolo Chinato*
*Cynar*

*Do-it-yourself*

So well-trained are we by advertising to buy famous brands these days that the idea of actually making something oneself seems quaint, even faintly dotty.

For just this reason I must make the point that it doesn't take a chemist with a computer to concoct anything worth drinking. To prove it let me pass on a recipe for a *vin de noyer* which was given to me in the Dordogne by a housewife of the old school, Mme Cassin of Castillon-la-Bataille, in whose house everything is home-made: one feels reborn in tasting the freshness of every mouthful. It makes an aperitif a hundred times better, to my mind, than some of the most widely advertised brands—and at half the price.

You must have fresh walnut leaves, gathered in the second or third week in June, while they are tender. (If you crush any walnut leaf and smell the oils within you will get an idea of the flavour.) You need fifty grammes of walnut leaves, one litre of eau-de-vie (good brandy, but not necessarily cognac), one kilo of caster sugar and four litres of sound young red wine.

Steep the walnut leaves in the eau-de-vie in a covered jar for two weeks. Then strain off the eau-de-vie and discard the leaves. Dissolve the sugar in the red wine. The best way is to pour two hundred grammes (I prefer it rather less sweet, with only one hundred and fifty grammes) of sugar into litre bottles containing four-fifths of a litre of wine, and to shake them until the sugar is dissolved. Then add one-fifth of a litre of the eau-de-vie to fill up each bottle. Shake, cork and leave the bottles for a week or two. You can then start drinking them as a marvellously reviving winter aperitif with nuts and biscuits, or as a summer drink with ice cubes. I know of no better (to use the old word) cordial.

## Patent aperitifs

Patent aperitifs are so nearly related to vermouths at one end of the scale that it is hard to distinguish them. At the other, however, they get nearer to gin. They can, in fact, be either based on wine or on spirits. The dividing-line is easy to spot by the price, if nothing else. The spirits are twice as expensive. I include them here for clarity's sake, although they have nothing to do with wine.

The enormous family of drinks which the French use before meals, or at any other time, are evidence of the nation's sweet tooth. All French aperitifs are sweet. They drink port as an aperitif; they have never heard of sherry. It is a curious contradiction that, as far as aperitifs go, the French are children: as far as everything else concerning the stomach goes, they are gods.

*Dubonnet*
*St-Raphaël*
*Lillet, Byrrh*
*Cap Corse*

I cannot hope to repeat all the names of all the potions stocked by French bars. They greet you, often in truncated form, among the peeling posters at the entrance to every grey French village: Dubonnet, both red and white (which is also made under licence in California); St-Raphaël, red and white; Lillet, white (drier than most); Byrrh, red; Cap Corse from Corsica. In bars in France they are often served at bar temperature. They all taste much better iced.

The other names you see in France, Italy and increasingly at home are those of spirit-based aperitifs, which cover an even wider range. It is perhaps useful to divide these into bitters and sweets.

*Campari*
*Amer Picon*
*Fernet Branca*
*Underberg*

*Suze*

Bitters are either always diluted to some extent for straightforward drinking, or are dripped into other drinks to point up the flavour. The chief drinking-bitters are Campari (the brilliant red, extremely bitter Italian champion, which is also sold in little bottles already mixed with soda), Amer Picon, Fernet Branca and Underberg. The last two are medicinal, and are claimed to be good for hangovers. Amer Picon is black and bitter; it needs the addition of orange-juice or grenadine to sweeten it. There is also a strange French drink called Suze, which is bright yellow and tastes of gentian. It is good on the rocks; too pungent for mixing.

*Angostura*

The bitters you drip need not keep us long. Angostura—the Worcestershire Sauce of the drink world—is the best known. The best use I know for it is in making what its advertisements call Pink Ice—adding it to the water in the ice-cube tray. It can easily be overdone.

*Pernod, Ricard,*
*Pastis, Ouzo*

The sweet section is the monopoly of the *anis* drinks: Pernod, Ricard, Pastis from France and Ouzo in Greece. When neat, they are clear and slightly yellow. Diluted with water, which is how they must be drunk, they go cloudy like milk. There is no absinthe in them, as there once was, but they nonetheless need watching. They taste insidiously harmless and soft, although they are stronger than brandy.

# White Table Wines

Any wine which is not distinctly red or pink is described as white, whether it is really the palest possible gold or almost brown. There is far greater variety among white wines than red. Among the reds there are no differences as great as that between a tart, prickling Moselle and a deep gold, syrupy Sauternes. As the companion of food white wine ranges much wider, too. There are many dishes which would taste distinctly odd with a red wine, but hardly one which has not a perfect match somewhere in the endless list of the world's infinitely varying white wines.

With a few exceptions—which include some of the most wonderful wines of all—the essence of white wine is freshness. It must always have a suggestion of acidity about it—just as even the ripest of peaches does. We drink white wines cold so that the temperature adds to the sensation of freshness in the mouth, playing down the flavour. Most white wines also have a little sweetness in them—enough to balance the sharpness of fruit. Those with a great deal of sugar—so much, sometimes, that the liquid moves like oil in the glass—are kept for drinking after the meal as dessert wines.

*Extracting the juice*

The real difference between white and red wines lies not in the colour but in the way that they are made. Briefly, white wine is pressed, while red wine is crushed.

Each wine-making area has its own methods, which vary in detail so much that sometimes they are hardly recognizable. Yet the underlying rule is universal: to make white wine you get the juice out of the grapes as quickly as possible, separate juice from skins and let the juice ferment and become wine on its own. For red wine you merely break the grapes open to get a pulpy mass of juice, pips and skin. Fermentation starts with the complete crushed grape. Each component contributes something to the eventual wine.

Since white wines are made without the grape-skins it does not matter what colour they are. Some white wine is made from white grapes, some from black, some from both. What matters is that the juice is white. One class of grapes has not only black skins, but red juice as well. They are known as *teinturiers*—dyers—and are the only ones which cannot be used for making white wine.

Unlike red wines, white wines start life ready to drink. Their make-up is simpler. The extra flavours which red wine gets out of the skins during fermentation take time to settle down. While they are very young they are (there are exceptions to this rule, of course) hard to the taste—positively unpleasant to hold in your mouth. Most ordinary white wines, on the other hand, are drinkable the day they stop fermenting. The better wines still have a great deal to gain by staying in barrel for a while, and some, mainly the best ones, from being kept for several years in bottle, but there is nothing inherently undrinkable about them new: they are merely not at their best and not giving you their full potential.

**Dryness and sweetness**

The natural process of fermentation makes grape-juice into wine by converting sugar into alcohol. The amount of sugar in a normal ripe grape can all be turned to alcohol without any trouble. If the fermentation is allowed to go on until it finishes of its own accord there will —unless the grape is abnormally ripe, as it is in making Sauternes—be no sugar left. The wine will be completely dry, or very nearly so: the natural state of light white wine.

Something has to be done if the wine-maker wants to produce medium wine, as he often does. He has to stop the fermentation before all the sugar has gone. What is more difficult, he has to prevent it starting to ferment again, as it normally would, at some later stage. He does this by getting rid of the yeast, without which the fermentation cannot take place.

To stop his wine from fermenting out, and drying out, completely, the vintner either doses it at the appropriate stage, when there is little sugar left, with sulphur dioxide, which puts the yeast to sleep, or he refrigerates it, or he seals the tank where it is and puts the liquid under high pressure. In any of these circumstances fermentation will stop.

He then has to get rid of the yeast, which he can do in various ways, of which fine filtering is one. He must then keep the wine under completely sterile conditions and finally put it, with another dose of sulphur dioxide, in sterilized bottles.

All this is extra trouble and expense to him. Wine processed in this way is therefore certain to cost more than the natural wine. It obviously has a wide appeal, or he would not trouble to do it, but it is never as good, in any real analysis, as wine which has gone its own natural way and ended up dry, with scents and savours of its own.

You can be pretty sure that this denaturing process has been applied to any fairly cheap, sweet or medium-sweet, light and low-strength table wine—unless, like most modern German wines, the sweetness has been added artificially afterwards, in which case the same precautions are needed to stop the sweetened wine fermenting. Very sweet wines are a different matter (see the After-Dinner Wines section).

# The White Wines of Burgundy

If it mattered whether or not the wines in this book were put in order of importance, there would be two major rivalries: between Bordeaux and Burgundy for the first place among red table wines, and between Burgundy and Germany for the first place among white table wines.

Having rated white burgundy as the finest white wine in the world I must immediately qualify this claim. I am not comparing it with champagne or sherry, and both Germany and Bordeaux produce equally glorious white wines of a completely different kind. But the principal glory of Sauternes and the German vineyards is wine so sweet that it leaves the ranks of table wine. Nobody would want to drink it during the course of a meal. It is for sipping with dessert, with a peach or some grapes or on its own, and belongs to the After-Dinner Wines section. So white burgundy is left as the greatest still, dry white wine grown anywhere in the world.

Its qualities are essentially savoury ones. The least among white burgundies is fresh and fair, refreshing and enticing; the greatest is rich and sappy, dry without exception, but fat with flavour. Its perfume can have a haunting fruitiness, a really peach- or apricot-like quality, without being sweet. It can be either soft and succulent or hard and strong.

*The Burgundy district*

Burgundy is not one neat continuous wine-district, growing white wine here, red there, but an old and extensive duchy in which several separate wine districts happen to lie. In French it is *Bourgogne*. It is odd to think that the splendid name of Burgundy, with its undertones of thunder, should not be its own, but a mere anglicized version of the real name, for it is tremendously evocative of the ancient glories of France. I can never say it without seeing in my mind's eye the grand gaunt figure of the Duke of Burgundy in *Henry V*, pleading for peace:

> Her vine, the merry cheerer of the heart,
> Unpruned dies; her hedges even-pleached . . .
> Put forth disordered twigs; her fallow leas
> The darnel, hemlock and rank fumitory
> Doth root upon, while that the coulter rusts . . .

His velvet cap and gown, regally red, his voice, a reverberating bass, stand for a land of country riches, of fat pastures and rich upland, of farmyards full of poultry and fields full of cattle—above all, for the long broad-backed hill of vines called the Côte d'Or.

The Côte d'Or (Hill of Gold) is Burgundy's backbone from north to south. Its eastern flank supports half of the most famous names in the whole wine-drinking world: Chambertin, Clos de Vougeot, Romanée, Nuits-St-Georges, Corton, Beaune, Pommard and Volnay for red wines; Montrachet, Meursault and Corton-Charlemagne for white.

And yet Burgundy has more. To the north, as though hurrying to get to Paris, lies Chablis; to the south, heading for Lyons, lie Mâcon, with the white wines of Pouilly-Fuissé, and the Beaujolais, the lovely high hills round Beaujeu, a cornucopia of light, sweet, succulent red wine. If you go west, over the mountains of the Morvan or the Charollais, famous for France's best beef, you come, within eighty miles, to the upper valley of the Loire, where the spice-scented white wines of Sancerre and Pouilly-Fumé grow. If you go east, across the wide plain of the river Sâone, you come to the Jura, where the wine is a rainbow of red, white, pink and yellow.

*The heart of France*

Burgundy, in short, lies in the heart of France. On one side of her the beef is, say the French, the world's best; on the other side, in Bresse, it is the chickens. It is simple farming country. Burgundy has none of the orderliness, daintiness even, the feeling that vineyards are a form of parkland or that each grey château is the manor of its particular plot, which is the characteristic of Bordeaux. There is a noticeable lack of seigneurial houses dominating the Côtes. In fact there are very few large estates.

In Burgundy most of the land belongs to small farmers. They live in the villages, make their wine in the villages, and go out to work with their own, and their families', hands among their own vines. Where, at the harvest, many of the proprietors of Bordeaux can fill two or three hundred barrels with their new wine, most Burgundian farmers are lucky if they can fill thirty or forty. The total production of fine wine in Bordeaux is often ten times that of Burgundy.

Burgundy, therefore, is a picture of small units in a small frame. The finest burgundies come from a pitifully small slope of hill. The world demand for them is insatiable. In view of how very little wine there is and how many people want it, it is quite extraordinarily cheap.

*Names and the trade in Burgundy*

Much as everyone would like everything about Burgundy to be as straightforward as the rows of vines and the cherry-trees in the peaceful landscape, the situation, unfortunately, has become more and more confused over the years. Stories of faking and cooking come to be attached to Burgundy more than any other wine-district. Before looking at the wines it is worth seeing how they get their names.

*Climats*

Like any European countryside, Burgundy consists of parishes and, within the parishes, fields. Where in England there might be a hillside divided into fields called Acre Piece, Colman's Bank, Half-mile Bottom and Tinkerpot Shaw, in Burgundy you have Cailleret-Dessus, En Champans, Carelle-sous-la-Chapelle, En l'Ormeau, Les Mitans, Brouillards. The Burgundian name for these fields, where they are planted with vines, is *climats*.

As time goes on it becomes apparent that some of these *climats*, despite changes of ownership, always tend to make better wine than their neighbours. As these names become known the wine from the lucky plots goes to market with its own name while the rest simply goes under the name of its village. In some cases, where the village was not on a road and the local market was in another, more accessible, village, the wine might even not bother with its own village's name, but be sold, and asked for again, under the name of the market where it was bought.

Thus, for example, the red wines of the villages of Chassagne and Santenay used to go to market at the village of Pommard. Their wine was known as the wine bought at Pommard (which in any case is a good simple name to remember). In fact, it was often considerably better than the wine grown at Pommard itself.

*Control and confusion*

This loose, informal trading system was adequate for simpler times. At the beginning of this century, though, it was being so much abused that action had to be taken. A law was passed, a well-meaning but misinformed attempt to regulate the use of names. Pommard, it said, must be grown in Pommard: Santenay must be sold as Santenay.

The situation now was not good, either for Pommard or for Santenay; least of all for the customer. Any wine, however poor, grown in Pommard now had the sole and exclusive use of all the reputation and goodwill built up by Pommard in conjunction with its neighbours. Santenay, on the other hand, had no market at all. No-one had heard of it.

Certain towns and villages which had always been centres of commerce and handled the wine of the whole region—Beaune, Meursault, Pommard, Volnay—were sitting pretty. Many of the others, to identify themselves, adopted the names of their best-known wines, a habit which had been growing for many years. Thus Chassagne took the name of the famous Montrachet *climat*, which lies half in the parish, and became Chassagne-Montrachet. Gevrey took the name of Chambertin. Puligny, which has the other half of Montrachet, also attached its famous name and became Puligny-Montrachet. Nuits became Nuits-St-Georges. Chambolle claimed the splendid name of Musigny. Vosne, where the Romanée vineyards lie, called itself Vosne-Romanée. Gilly, the hamlet dwarfed by the great Clos de Vougeot, was known as Gilly-les-Vougeot for a while. But now the Gilly has almost been forgotten—it is referred to simply as Vougeot.

Naturally this move had the desired effect. Chassagne had been unknown, and unsaleable. Chassagne-Montrachet was unmistakable. Of course, it had something to do with that wonderful Montrachet. There is always the possibility that someone may think it is better, in the way that Fotheringay-Jones is better than plain Jones.

The fact that the only connection between a Chassagne-Montrachet and a Montrachet is that they have the same parish priest and the same postman is not immediately obvious. The important thing, that they have different soil on a different slope, and that Montrachet comes from one specific, superlative vineyard, and Chassagne-Montrachet from any old patch of vines within the village boundaries, can easily be forgotten.

*The vineyards are subdivided*

The complications of Burgundy do not end here. Even within the illustrious *climats* whose names have been borrowed all is not as simple as it seems.

Hardly any of the vineyards belong to one man. The wine which any two men make, even of the same grapes from the same soil in the same season, will not be identical. One leaves it to ferment longer, one not so long; one has older vines than another, or vines from a superior "clone"; one picks out the unripe or overripe grapes, another leaves them in; one starts picking two or three days before the other—one, in fact, will always be better than another. When you have narrowed it down to one vineyard and one vintage, therefore, in Burgundy you will still be offered, perfectly honestly, several different wines.

And in some cases the fault is partly that of the vineyard itself. The soil of a hillside is never exactly the same from top to bottom and from side to side. Yet several vineyards spread from the valley right up the hill, from flat land to a steep tilt, through a variety of soils. The wine, therefore, although all bearing the vineyard's name, will vary enormously according to which part of the vineyard it comes from. The most notorious example of this is the famous Clos de Vougeot, whose one hundred and twenty acres include everything from Burgundy's best soil to the most ordinary flat valley-land, all entitled to the same great name.

These are the internal difficulties of the trade in Burgundy. The result of it all is that the dealers in wine have to resort to blending. It is impossible to trade with goods which have so little consistency, unless they are worth the very high price which this kind of specialized business is bound to charge. In Germany until recently there were cases where the wines of different casks, even of the same picking and pressing, were kept apart, unblended, and were eventually labelled with their cask numbers. But such wines cannot possibly cost less than £8 or £9 a bottle; as collector's items they cannot be the basis of a consumer trade.

Burgundy has kept both kinds of business as far as it can. On the upper level it maintains a business in individual wines from individual growers in named vineyards—a business which can only be done with wines which are intrinsically worth the extra trouble and extra costs involved. For the rest it buys in bulk from anyone who has wine to sell, and makes up what it hopes are typical and representative wines in the blending vats.

The first and most important thing, then, about Burgundy is to distinguish an individual estate wine from a merchant's blend. Unfortunately, one sometimes has to do this with less than the full co-operation of the designers of labels. But the first thing is to know which is the name of a village and which the name of a vineyard.

*Classification*    The official, definitive classification of the vineyards by quality has never been done in Burgundy as it has in Bordeaux, or at any rate part of Bordeaux. The Burgundian system, which is generally accepted, though not official, takes a local view of comparative excellence. The best vineyard of each *finage*, or parish, is the *tête de cuvée*, or *grand cru*. Where more than one are superb there are several *grands crus*; where none reach the right standard there need not be any. A *grand cru* has its own appellation: not that of its parish.

Vineyards of the second rank are known, confusingly enough, as *premiers crus* (first-growths); third-rank vineyards are called second-growths.

Not too much weight is placed on these rankings. Unevenness of quality from *finage* to *finage* means that the *grand cru* of one may be less good than the *premier cru* of another. In practice, the *grand cru* wines very rarely mention their rank on labels, nor do any wines below *premier cru*. The thing to remember, in fact, is that when you see *premier cru* on a label, with or without the name of the vineyard (if it is without it will probably be a blend of several), it does not mean first-growth in the Bordeaux sense. It really just means one of the good growths.

*Domaine-bottling*  The usual Burgundy word for an estate is domaine. Domaine-bottled is the equivalent of the Bordeaux château-bottled. Domaine-bottling in Burgundy is slightly less prevalent than château-bottling in Bordeaux, though in both it is very much on the increase. Comparatively few estates in Burgundy have the facilities for bottling. Some wine-merchants have even overcome the problem for the growers by having a truck fitted up with all the necessary equipment and backing it into their courtyards, bottling the wine there and then and carrying it away with them, domaine-bottled.

Although domaine-bottling is usually only carried out with good wines it is no real evidence of their quality. It could be done by anybody. Many people say that some British wine-merchants are better at the cellar-work of bottling than many Burgundians.

In the United States, though, it is almost assumed that a wine has been tampered with unless it was bottled at the domaine or château. Domaine-bottled wines are, therefore, the rule there rather than the exception they still are in Britain.

## Chablis

Less than a quarter of the wine made in Burgundy is white. All white burgundy is dry. It ranges in price from almost the cheapest French white wine to over the price of a bottle of vintage champagne. But at that you have one of the very finest wines that money can buy.

Chablis and Sauternes are probably the best-known, and most imitated, white wines in the world. Chablis is taken to be the archetypal dry young white, very fresh, rather hard, a trifle green. The description fits the ordinary cheap wines of Chablis well enough, and they are the kind which are best known, but it comes nowhere near the extraordinarily scented and powerful great growths. It is a common mistake to think that Chablis is just Chablis and that's that. From the tiny town, in fact, comes as wide a range of quality and price as from the whole of Burgundy.

Chablis is only fifteen minutes' drive down Sussex-like lanes from the autoroute from Paris to the south. The little town lies in a valley, straddling the dreamy little river Serein, all ducks and reeds. It is grey, a good part of it is very old, and by eight in the evening it is dead. Round the bridge, as in so many towns of central France, the old buildings have been destroyed and ugly new concrete ones have taken their place. It was a tank battle that ruined the centre of Chablis.

But it is not the town, but the hills to the south and north-east which are important. Immediately above the town to the north they are at

*Grands crus*  their steepest, and here, for a stretch of a mile and a half, the *grand crus*, the superlative wines, grow. The names of the Chablis *grand cru* vineyards are Bougros, Les Preuses, Vaudésir, Grenouilles, Valmur, Les Clos and Les Blanchots. In the area round them are several other bigger vineyards which are perhaps better known, since their wine has a wider circulation. They include La Fourchaume, Monts de Milieu, Vaulorent and Montée de Tonnerre. There are about a dozen

*Premier crus*  of these, which are entitled to call themselves Chablis *premier cru*. Below this level the wine can only be called plain Chablis, without a

*Petit Chablis*  vineyard name. There is an appellation below that of Chablis; Petit Chablis, used for light wines from the outlying parts of the district

"Fermentation comes naturally to grapes. Wine did not have to
wait to be invented. Everything needed to make wine is there
already when the grape has ripened on the vine."
**Above:** the red flood of must begins its tumultuous fermentation
in an open vat, as Bordeaux has been made for centuries.

The basic wine-making process is the same whether in a château or a more modern winery like the growers' co-operative (**above**) at Parnac, near Cahors. The more fastidious old-fashioned Bordeaux growers first de-stalk the bunches by rubbing them through a wooden grille, as at the Château Margaux (**below**). Ways of crushing the grapes range from the traditional bare feet of the high Douro (**right**) to hydraulic presses (**top right**).

The cooper (**above**) who makes and mends barrels is still an essential craftsman in a winemaking community. Bordeaux, burgundy and similar red wines spend about two years in barrel, gaining smoothness and subtlety. The cellar-master (**right**) re-examines each barrel constantly to check its healthy development.

**Above:** the typical modern cellar of gleaming stainless steel and glass, whether in California or a co-operative in the Midi, is about as picturesque and atmospheric as an operating theatre. By way of contrast (**right and below**) in Burgundy below ground, in Portugal above, wine is stored in the traditional material, oak, and kept as cool as a vault or a high roof can make it.

which have less alcohol than Chablis proper. In poor, sunless years it is common for even good growths to fail to contain the necessary amount of alcohol: in this case, so long as they achieve 9.5 per cent alcohol, they can call themselves Petit Chablis.

In general, then, the identifying mark of the best Chablis is one of the seven names of vineyards above, plus the term *grand cru*. No-one is obliged to name the vineyard if he does not want to. It could just be Chablis *grand cru*, but it is unlikely. Chablis *premier cru*, on the other hand, since not all the vineyards entitled to call themselves this are well known, is much more often found without the name of the individual *climat*.

The taste of one of these great Chablis is bone-dry, but by no means thin. They have a remarkably powerful scent, and a flavour which I can only describe as slightly mineral, rather than fruity. In alcoholic degrees they can be formidable. I have heard of one wine which in 1959—admittedly a very hot year—reached an unprecedented 17 per cent alcohol. The Chablis qualities which are found all the way down the line to the Petit Chablis are the same, only less marked. It is never remotely sweet, always slightly stony in flavour. What you are paying for in one of the superior growths is greater strength—of everything, not just alcohol: strength of character, of scent, of taste, and length of rich lingering after-taste.

In poor years, which are common, none of these things are found. The best wines are cut down to size and the worst wines are not worth drinking. Most of the common wines of Chablis, in any case, are drunk in the restaurants of the neighbourhood and Paris.

Chablis grows something like a tenth of the wine which is sold as Chablis. It is one of the world's most imitated wines. There is very little hope, in fact, that a carafe white wine in fish restaurants which is called Chablis really is. On the other hand it is usually agreeable, and answers its purpose of washing down oysters and sole well enough.

*St–Bris–le–Vineux*

There are a number of white wines from the same area which might be described as sub-Chablis. The village of St-Bris-le-Vineux has evidently been noted for its contribution for some time. It makes a very light dry wine from the Sauvignon, the white grape of Bordeaux and the Loire rather than of Burgundy. The effect, here, however, is to make something a little like the familiar Muscadet of Brittany. It is not a wine which is often shipped, but it is a good example of the kind of thing to look for among the local wines when you are travelling in France. Drink St-Bris in the restaurant of the Hotel de la Ville d'Auxerre at Toucy, between Auxerre and Briare, before eating the *Escalope de veau á la tante Nini*. Aunt Nini's sauce is made with sorrel, lemon-juice and cream.

*The Côte de Nuits*

Having started in the north of Burgundy with Chablis we will take the other white-wine vineyards in order as we go south. The first we meet are in the line of hills between Dijon and Nuits-St-Georges, the part of the Côte d'Or which is known as the Côte de Nuits.

The Côte De Nuits is in fact almost pure red. Only four of its villages make any white wine at all, and that in quantities so small that it is almost never seen. It is, however, supremely good, as good as any other white wine in France except that from just down the road. It is one of the curiosities which make wine all the more fascinating to find the name of a familiar red wine on a bottle of white. It can happen with Musigny, a superb, full, dry wine, with Morey-St-Denis, Clos de Vougeot, and with Nuits-St-Georges. The peculiarity of these wines is their similarity to their red brothers. It is perfectly possible to shut your eyes, drink an old Clos Blanc de Vougeot, and imagine that you are drinking the red wine. You can always spot the difference, but it is the similarity which is more striking.

*The Côte de Beaune*

The southern half of the Côte d'Or, after the town of Nuits-St-Georges, and a break in the hills where the Comblanchien free-stone quarries have turned old vineyards into an ugly scar of industry, is the white-wine half. Beaune, the beautiful old walled town which gives this part of the Côtes its name, lies near its northern end.

*Beaune*

Of the wine of Beaune itself only a very small part, from the vineyard called Clos des Mouches, is white. It is very good, but Beaune means, almost exclusively, red wine.

*Savigny-les-Beaune*

The same is true of Savigny-les-Beaune, the little village with one of Burgundy's few châteaux which borders Beaune on the north-west, up under the hillside. Most of its wine is red; a little is white. They are not Burgundy's very best, but they are almost always worth buying, and are comparatively cheap.

There are three key white-wine names in the Côte de Beaune: Corton-Charlemagne, Meursault and Montrachet. Together with Chablis and Pouilly-Fuissé they make up the total of the great white burgundies—or rather the white burgundies which can be great, for the names of Montrachet and Meursault, in certain combinations, are as applicable to run-of-the-mill wine as they are to fine or great wine.

*Corton-Charlemagne*

Corton-Charlemagne is exceptional. There is only one Corton-Charlemagne. It is the vineyard on the upper half of the western end of a curious round hill which juts out from the Côte north of Beaune. The eastern end, above the village of Aloxe, is a red-wine vineyard, Corton. No visible line divides the two parts, but in mid-hillside the exposure changes from south-east to south-west and the grey stain of limestone in the brown marl fades, making all the difference between a wine for the fish and a wine for the beef.

I cannot describe the taste of Corton-Charlemagne, but I can differentiate it to some extent from the other great whites of the Côte de Beaune, Meursault and Montrachet. Of the two, it is more like Meursault, but it is not so soft. It is what is known as a bigger wine, with a mouth-filling savour which has a noticeable tendency to linger in your mouth after you have swallowed it. In hot, ripe vintages it can become so charged with flavour as to seem almost ponderous. It has been called monotone in flavour; the first impression is very like the last (some wines, on the other hand, "develop" in the mouth, surprising you by starting succulent and ending astringent, or vice versa). Corton-Charlemagne is very elusive: Burgundians like to say that it smells of cinnamon, and yet suggests flint and steel to the taste. This is the kind of thing that one is up against when trying to describe the taste of a wine.

*Corton*

There is a slightly less exalted white wine made in a small part of the Corton vineyard, next to Corton-Charlemagne. In this case what is usually true of Burgundy, that the wine with the shorter, un-qualified name (Corton as against Corton-Charlemagne) is the better, is reversed. Corton for red wine is the supreme name; for white it is second best.

*Meursault*

Meursault is the biggest village of the Côte de Beaune. It is pretty, but grey and far from animated. In fact it always seems asleep. The wine of Meursault is remarkable for being very dry and at the same time soft and mellow. It is described by some people as mealy, reminding them of oatmeal, by others as being like hazelnuts. In its colour, which is very pale gold, there is a suggestion of green.

It is remarkably consistent. It is never the cheapest white burgundy, and never the most expensive. There is no single Meursault vineyard as superb and world-famous as the neighbouring Montrachet. But the best vineyards of Meursault, to the south of the village, which are called Les Perrières, Les Charmes, Les Genevrières, and some slightly less exalted ones (the best of which are Le Poruzot and La Goutte d'Or nearer the village, and Blagny, higher up the hill in a south-facing fold of stony ground) produce the most appealing of all white burgundies: a soft, smooth and scented wine.

A friend of mine is a typical grower of Meursault; burly, perhaps fifty, given to wearing open-necked khaki shirts. He might almost be a tea-planter. He has small parts of the Goutte d'Or, Poruzot and Charmes vineyards. He cycles from one to the other (they are quite widely spaced on the gentle slopes of this part of the Côte) on his Mobilette, working all day among the vines on his own.

His cellar, though not large, is stately and vaulted. The casks are in single file on the floor round the walls. In one corner a bin of slats holds treasured old bottles. I once asked him about the keeping qualities of Meursault. Before I could stop him he had found a bottle of his wine of 1929, unthinkably old from any commercial point of view, and started to open it. Time had done nothing but round off its formidable qualities into a beautifully polished prism of scent and taste. It had not even taken on, as white wines usually do, a darker colour, but had remained as light and vital as the day it was bottled.

Plain, unqualified Meursault could vary as much as any burgundy from merchant to merchant. Nevertheless in my experience it is one of the most reliable names. Production is comparatively large, and no superlative name has given the whole area a false glamour.

*Auxey-Duresses*

Above Meursault the steady slope of the hill falters and lets a road through. In this gap stands a pretty little village, primitive and flowery, the gateway to a lovely pastoral valley of rocks, meadows, birches and a stream, the way to the fortress of La Rochepot and the main Paris road. Auxey-Duresses is not one of the famous names of Burgundy, but its white wines, neighbours and cousins of the Meursaults, are excellent and very similar to the more famous growths. In a good year they are touched with sweetness; lively, fresh and slightly green. Their biggest advantage of all is that they are not a fashion: they fetch no fancy prices. An Auxey-Duresses on a wine-list is almost certainly a sign of careful and imaginative buying.

*Montrachet*

Montrachet has a habit of being the one name people remember when they think of white burgundy. In the United States, where "greatness" is at a premium, it is linked with Romanée-Conti, representing the best red burgundy, Château Lafite as the best claret and Château d'Yquem as the best white Bordeaux. Then comes Krug as the best champagne, Steinberger Kabinet or Schloss Vollrads as the best hock, Bernkasteler Doktor as the best Moselle. It is a simple and trouble-free approach to wine, and hideously expensive. For these wines, whatever their actual or relative quality from year to year, have been enthroned as the best. Sad to say, they are probably drunk more by people who drink what they are told is good and less by people who appreciate their extraordinary qualities than any lesser growths. Their price, moreover, often bears little relation to their value. At its worst, Romanée-Conti comes down to something like twice the price of any other red burgundy. Nobody seriously claims that it is worth it, but it will fetch it.

*A tasting*

What is it that makes Montrachet stand out from the wines of the surrounding countryside, not as a giant among pigmies, but as a colossus among giants? It is simply the power and beauty of its taste. I will never forget a long tasting of new wines in the cellars of M Remoissenet in Beaune, standing among the casks in the half-light with Ronald Avery of Bristol, who is his agent in England. The wines were the new 1964s. We started by tasting four Meursaults—the peculiar mealy Meursault taste ran through them all. Some brought it to more fruit, more freshness, more vitality than others. Les Perrières seemed to have most to offer.

Then came Corton-Charlemagne, which tasted strong and forceful after the Meursaults. "Suave but broad-shouldered", I put down in my notes. (They demonstrate very clearly the difficulty of finding words for tastes; every expression you use has to be borrowed from some other sense, except the four words sweet, sour, salt and bitter. Words follow lumberingly after the clear, precise and yet indefinable impressions of the tongue.) The Corton-Charlemagne, I noticed, had less scent than the last Meursaults, and yet came and went with a marvellous evenness of power, lingering at the back of the tongue and in the throat, perfuming the breath.

Then followed the Montrachets; a clear ascent from a Puligny-Montrachet, a village wine (though a beauty, flowery and fresh), through Bâtard-Montrachet ("capped it completely; what could be more perfect? The same flowers on a sunnier day; somehow much more clean-cut; authoritative is the word"), to Le Montrachet. "Still fermenting a little in its second fermentation," I have down. "Nevertheless a tremendous heady scent of peaches and apricots and an intense sweetness of character, though fully dry, in the mouth. It declares itself immediately to be something *very* special."

That was Le Montrachet before it was even fully made, let alone bottled and ready to drink. The notes I have made on older bottles of it—the 1953, for example—would make me blush to repeat them. What one can say is this: the character of Montrachet is that of the complete balanced white wine. It is sweet in its nature, yet there is no spare sugar; it is not syrupy, but dry and lively. It is soft to drink, but firm and clear-cut. It suggests, without imitating, all the ripest and most perfect of fruit.

*The Montrachet vineyard*

The Montrachet vineyard which is responsible for such ecstasies lies in both the villages of Puligny and Chassagne, both of which have availed themselves of its name, at the southern end of the Côte de Beaune. The hill is solid with the clear green of the vineyard, but it is divided, by tracks and crumbling stone walls, into three parts across the slope. The centre part of the hill is Le Montrachet, the lower part Bâtard-Montrachet and the upper part, from Montrachet itself up to the crest, Chevalier-Montrachet. When one says that Bâtard and Chevalier are lesser vineyards it is not to belittle them. Many find them more drinkable than Le Montrachet.

Montrachet has five owners of any consequence: the Marquis de Laguiche, Baron Thénard, the Domaine de la Romanée-Conti, Calvet and the firm of Bouchard Père et Fils. The rest of its area is divided in lots so small that the wine cannot be made on its own, for it will not fill a cask for its fermentation. It must be mixed with the same owners' grapes in other plots in Bâtard or Chevalier which also belong to them. It loses its identity, and also its right to the great name.

It is worth going off the high road to see the Montrachet vineyard, if only to see how Burgundians concentrate on essentials. Its dry stone wall is worse kept, if anything, than its neighbours. Its simple, wide open gate is tottering. But still at half-past eight on a summer evening the sun is flooding down the alleys of vines, painting them bright apple green and giving the brown earth a touch of auburn. Despite the fact that the hill seems to face the morning sun, the sun is still on it after the workmen have had their summer-evening supper. It is such tricks of topography as this which give a vineyard a slight advantage over its neighbours.

*Bâtard-Montrachet* And what of its neighbours? Bâtard-Montrachet and Chevalier-
*Chevalier-Montrachet* Montrachet are still pure nectar, if they are not Jove's own selection. Bâtard is, perhaps, the more tasty and solid of the two; Chevalier the more ethereal and delicate—but we are splitting hairs. Both these wines are the glories of the village of Puligny-Montrachet, which is lucky enough to have them within its boundaries.

Bâtard-Montrachet overspills, like Montrachet itself, into the next village going south: Chassagne. Along the southern wall of Bâtard is another vineyard in the same class: Criots-Bâtard-Montrachet. Its opposite number in Puligny is called Les Bienvenues-Bâtard-Montrachet.

*Puligny-Montrachet* These are all superlative wines. Hardly less good are the other
*Chassagne-Montrachet* named vineyards of Puligny and Chassagne, with the usual kind of Burgundian names: Combettes, Les Pucelles, Cailleret. Even below named-vineyard level the plain village wines, the ones most often found on wine-lists in Britain, are as fine as any in France. Ordinary Chassagne-Montrachet is thought to have just the edge on plain Puligny-Montrachet for delicacy. Either, in any case, from a good merchant, should be a really fine wine.

*Montrachet* It is difficult to know what to eat with a wine which has as much
*and food* personality as Montrachet. I am of the school of thought which would drink it alone, if not, as Alexandre Dumas claimed was the correct procedure, kneeling, with head bared. I do not know the food that would not be completely overpowered by it.

I have enjoyed Le Montrachet immensely with a cold salmon-trout early in the summer, but that was not a wine of one of the great, powerful vintages, when ripeness makes it really full-blown in scent. I think I would fall back on a chicken, plainly roasted or grilled or even boiled. There is no better accompaniment to any great wine, white or red.

With Le Montrachet we are discussing the food that goes with the wine; with its Montrachet cousins, for the most part, we are back in the realms where wine goes with food. Where do they fit in?

At dinners which aim to show the best of French (or indeed of any) wine against a formal menu, where fish comes before meat, white burgundy is almost always represented by a hyphenated Montrachet. The perfect menu, I have heard many good eaters say, has white burgundy for the first wine, claret for the second. White Bordeaux is never that wonderful. Red burgundy after white fails to use the amazing potential of France. Between them, white burgundy and claret represent the best of everything. In these circumstances there is no fish or shellfish which would not be a good match for a Meursault or a Puligny- or Chassagne-Montrachet. The same would be true of a meal in which fish was the main or the only dish. It is the quality of the fish, in fact, which is on trial in the presence of wines as delicious as these.

But nothing limits them to fish. Chicken, veal, ham—anything without red blood and strong savour—match them well. Whether it is habit or prejudice, I do not like them with lamb, beef or game.

## Côte Chalonnaise

### Cheilly, Dézize and Sampigny-les-Maranges

The town of Chagny (a little wine bears its name) brings the Côte de Beaune to an end in the south. The villages immediately south-east of Chagny make good white wine. Their lovely names of Cheilly, Dézize and Sampigny-les-Maranges might be seen on the list of an enterprising merchant who found better value for money among their unknown wines than in the villages down the road whose names ring round the world. But their yield is so small that it is not worth anyone's while building up their reputations.

After Chagny the hills have nothing like the old consistent sweep. The Côte, such as it is, is broken up into puny mounds, which nevertheless bear the name of the Côte Chalonnaise, from the town of Chalon-sur-Saône in the valley to the east. Rully, Mercurey, Givry and Montagny, the villages of the Côte Chalonnaise, all make white wine. Of these, Rully and Montagny make mainly white wine, the others only a little. But all can be good, and Montagny in the hands of Louis Latour has moved up into near-Meursault realms of prestige and price.

### Rully, Mercurey and Montagny

None of these wines has the power or apparent strength of the great white burgundies, none the way of expanding in the mouth, lingering in the throat or scenting the air. They are pale, light, clean-tasting and capable of becoming more interesting with age—a test no second-rate white wine will pass. All, on the other hand, if you can find them, are almost certainly good value.

## The Mâcon area

South again, between Chalon and Mâcon, the next big town as we follow the river Saône, the hills return again, and the countryside changes character. Still the Côte faces east across the river, but behind it the ground is broken up into a much more confused formation. These are young mountains, as hard to follow in their convolutions as waves in a choppy sea.

### Mâcon Blanc

The white wine of the Mâcon area, simply Mâcon Blanc, is the white-burgundy equivalent of the Beaujolais, unqualified by any village or vineyard name, which is to be found everywhere in France, Switzerland or England. Some, indeed, is sold as Beaujolais Blanc.

### Mâcon Supérieur

Mâcon Blanc is usually the cheapest of the white burgundies on any list. The second cheapest may well be Mâcon Supérieur. They are not to be despised for this; the production is large, over a considerable area, and there is every chance for a shrewd wine-merchant to find something exceptional at a very reasonable price. The village of Viré in particular has made its name over the years for wine of more than common power and character. Two Viré estates, indeed, the Clos du Chapitre and the Château de Viré, regularly reach Côte de Beaune standards. Ordinary Mâcon Blanc is not as dry as Chablis, nor as soft as Meursault. It is a little more yellow in colour than either, firm and strongish in taste; rarely acid. In fact it is as good as any general-purpose carafe white wine, for fish or fowl or drinking in hot weather to quench your thirst.

The Mâcon area has one wine, however, which steps straight into a different class; whose equivalent can only be found among the better, if not the best, wines of Chablis or the Côte de Beaune. It is Pouilly-Fuissé—a name well enough known to be a victim, at times, of its own popularity.

*Pouilly-Fuissé*    Five villages sell their wine under the name of Pouilly-Fuissé: Fuissé, Pouilly, Solutré, Vergisson and Chaintré. They stand in tumbling, tender-green countryside with farmhouses which are beginning to get a look of the south about them. The light is very bright and strong violet shadows cut the stone-walled roads in half down the middle. A field here and there, fallow or pasture, stands out from the hillside vines as a flat rectangle among endless stripes of green, tilted every way.

The Château de Fuissé, the fifteenth-century manor of this tiny village, is a property bigger than most, producing some of the finest wines of the area. Its proprietor, Marcel Vincent, is the fourth generation of his family to make wine there. His son is being trained to follow him. In Vincent's cellar, going from cask to cask among the new wine, I first understood what makes Pouilly-Fuissé, which I had always thought of as a moderate, often dull wine, a great one. They are qualities of tenderness, gentleness, freshness and clarity.

In the courtyard of the Château de Fuissé under the apple trees is a little mossy tank of trout, looking marvellously cool in the bright dusty afternoon. The trout and the apples seem to symbolize Pouilly-Fuissé; not powerful or stimulating, but gentle and reviving.

Vincent, not Marcel but another, is the patron saint of wine. Just outside the cellar door, which is insulated with wool and brown paper to keep it cool inside, Marcel Vincent keeps a little shrine to the saint: a wooden statue, a little table, a bowl of marigolds. He is a big proprietor for these parts, with about seventy acres of the best vineyards of the commune, from which he makes several distinct wines every year. The wine which goes out under his own label as Château de Fuissé is his best. Only in good years does he give it a vintage. The wine of indifferent years he puts out as a non-vintage under the title of *cuvée privée* (private selection)—"Like M Krug of Champagne."

The comparison with a champagne-shipper is apt in a way. Vincent is not typical of the peasant proprietors of Fuissé, though with his working-clothes and thick pebble glasses, until you hear him talk, you might take him for one. He is educated. He sells his own wine. He has capital and bargaining power.

*Solutré*    A typical peasant, like Emile Renault of Solutré, the next village, is in a different boat. He has two acres of vines, from which he is perfectly capable of making good wine, but he has nowhere to keep it, and no contacts except unsolicited visits from dealers. His eight or ten *pièces* of wine, in fact, are kept in the back of the garage with the cows and the oil for the tractor, protected only, like the rest of the tumble-down farm, by the nightly closing of the old gate on to the village street. Ask to taste his wine and he will produce, as all Burgundians will, his silver or silver-plated *tastevin* from his pocket, where he keeps it wrapped in a handkerchief. The *tastevin* is used everywhere in Burgundy for tasting wine from the cask. It is like a small ashtray with a handle and a hill in the middle. The light reflected off the middle through the wine shows its colour well in a dark cellar, where a glass would hold too much wine for the poor light to give an accurate idea of its shade.

*Pouilly-Loché*
*Pouilly-Vinzelles*

Two villages beside the five I have mentioned make wine of the same kind as Pouilly-Fuissé, and have the right to attach Pouilly to their names. They are Loché and Vinzelles. Pouilly-Vinzelles can be found in London at about half the price of Pouilly-Fuissé, offering nine-tenths of the quality.

Since 1971 there has been another appellation in the district for seven or eight villages on the Pouilly outskirts whose wine is deemed to deserve a better name than Mâcon Blanc. The name to watch for is St Véran. One of the villages is called St Vérand (sic). Another, St Amour-Bellevue, is better known for its red wine—one of the best *crus* of Beaujolais.

Pouilly-Fuissé closes the list of fine white burgundies. It has all the character, and—almost as important—it has the quantity, to support a world-wide reputation. For meals of sea-food, for the opening of formal dinners it can be one of the best white wines of France.

*White Beaujolais*

Farther south, where Burgundy ends with the beautiful Beaujolais mountains, it is almost exclusively red-wine country. A little white Beaujolais is made, and sold as such, but there is no real reason to make white wine in country which is so justly famous for its red, and whose red, for that matter, is in chronically short supply. White Beaujolais is an adequate, dry and middling-strong wine, full of the taste of the grape and attractive, but it has none of the character and style of either Pouilly-Fuissé among white wines, or red Beaujolais among red.

*Bourgogne*
*Aligoté*

The controls on the naming of the wines of Burgundy are very specific about which variety of grape will be cultivated. All the great and classical red wines of Burgundy are made from the Pinot grape, all the whites from the Chardonnay. One other white grape which is grown a great deal (for local consumption as much as anything) from end to end of Burgundy is called the Aligoté. Wine made from the Aligoté is only allowed to call itself Bourgogne Aligoté, without mentioning a place-name. If you are in Chablis you will, if you ask for Aligoté, be given Chablis Aligoté, if you are in Meursault it will be Meursault Aligoté, but if you are in England or America there is usually no evidence of where it comes from. It is never, in any case, anything very special. In the hands of a good wine-maker, on the other hand, it can be surprisingly delicate, like the shadow of his Chardonnay wine from the same district. A good wine-merchant can find a good one and list it at a very reasonable price as his burgundy *ordinaire*.

# The White Wines of Bordeaux

Bordeaux stands apart from every other wine-growing area. It is not only supreme for quality; it produces gigantic quantities. The vineyards cover a large part of the land for about fifty miles in one direction by about seventy in the other. They have been known to produce over a hundred and thirty million gallons of wine in a good year, while the top figure for Burgundy (including Beaujolais) is about fifty million.

The best wines of Bordeaux come into other parts of this book. Best of all are the great red wines, known to forty generations of Englishmen as claret. Almost equal to them in a completely different way are the supremely luscious sweet wines of Sauternes. (There is a full description of the Bordeaux area in the Red Wines section, page 167.) However, under the heading of white wines for the table, for drinking with food, we are restricted to the dry or medium-dry or medium-sweet wines which we think of under the broad heading of Graves, but which are grown in almost all districts of Bordeaux.

*Graves*     Graves is a district name. The Graves country, in which the city of Bordeaux itself lies, and which stretches away to the south among old buried sand dunes and straggling pine woods, makes better red wine than white. It makes some of the finest of all clarets. Yet, curiously enough, the name of Graves is only used on labels to indicate the district's less important white wine.

The red wines bear the names of their distinct parishes within Graves—Pessac, Léognan, Gradignan. There is no red wine called just plain Graves. But the white wine of the area can call itself Graves if it contains 10 per cent of alcohol, or Graves Supérieures if it contains 12 per cent.

*Graves Supérieures*     Graves (and Graves Supérieures) is one of the most popular basic white wines in Britain. At its best it is dry and full-flavoured and mellow, somehow not quite clean-cut, having something rather like a hint of vanilla at the end of its taste, the result of ageing in oak casks. Cheap versions are just plain medium-sweet and insipid.

As it grows older both taste and colour grow stronger. Old Graves of a good year is more like Sauternes without the sweetness. Young Graves is just the average, medium, useful white wine.

Graves is the only part of Bordeaux where the red and white vineyards share the honours of the land. Several of the best estates grow both. Their red wine is almost always better than their white, but tradition seems to dictate that certain parts of the countryside are planted with the white-grape varieties, and indeed new white Graves vineyards are tending to spring up now, since it is easier to sell white Graves than red.

*Château Haut-Brion*     Even the great Château Haut-Brion, the brightest star of Graves, and the only wine of the area to be included in the famous claret classification of 1855 as a first-growth, or at all, has a small plot of white wines, and makes a wine which few have tasted but all agree in praising. The honours for the best white Graves in the traditional full-blooded style would probably go either to Haut-Brion, to Château Laville Haut-Brion (the white-wine vineyard of the superb La Mission Haut-Brion next door) or to the remote Domaine de Chevalier, which rarely fails to make some of Graves' best wine in both colours.

A list of other good white Graves châteaux should be headed by Châteaux Olivier and Carbonnieux, both more famous for white wine than red, and should certainly include Château Bouscaut, Couhins (which also makes a good rosé) Malartic-Lagravière, Latour-Martillac and Baret. Château Smith-Haut-Lafitte has also recently started making a very good crisply dry pale white wine—which seems to be the direction for Graves in the future. Graves, in fact, is at a turning-point. The old style of golden white has had its triumphs, but most of it is dull wine, with a miasma of sulphur as its most memorable characteristic. Business has stagnated compared with the growth of other wine regions. Graves' growers could hardly fail to look enviously at the success of Loire white wines, becoming more and more fashionable, largely at their expense. Especially galling is the fact that Sancerre and Pouilly-Fumé, the new rage, are made with the Sauvignon, *their* grape—or one of them.

Graves is traditionally made of Semillon grapes, which make a soft wine, blended with a proportion of Sauvignon, which add aroma and "backbone". But there on the Loire is Sauvignon alone, selling like cigarettes. The message is clear enough.

*A changing market*

Forward-looking proprietors in the Graves today are increasing their plantings of Sauvignon, and aiming through temperature-control to make lighter, Loire-weight wines. Perhaps most important they are reconsidering the use of oak barrels (which are moreover becoming alarmingly expensive). Without the vanilla-taste of oak Graves changes character radically. Now, even in the Graves communes nearest to Sauternes, whose wines traditionally inclined towards the soft and gold, go-ahead growers can be found who are making it almost fiercely fresh and green.

This is not to say that Graves has changed overnight, or will. Most of it, sold as a négociant's blend, will no doubt remain as dull as ever. Nor is Haut-Brion or the Domaine de Chevalier suddenly going to abandon the old heroic style.

Of the thirty-odd communes which are included in the Graves area the most distinguished by far are the northern group near Bordeaux. All the châteaux named above lie in this part.

*Château de la Brède*

The showplace of Graves stands in the middle of the region. Every visitor to this rather sad, sandy country must see the Château de la Brède. It was the home of the philosopher Montesquieu and still stands as he left it two hundred years ago, inhabited by his descendants. But its history goes back long before its most illustrious owner. It is a medieval moated castle, sitting in a meadow with the trees standing back from it, for all the world like something out of an illuminated Book of Hours. The Comtesse de Chabannes, its present owner, drinks a glass of her white wine before lunch out on a little lawn by the old narrow defensive bridge, waiting to greet visitors, who have to pass under the old portcullis. It is a short walk through the meadow to where the *chai* (the Bordeaux word for where the wine is made and kept) stands by the wood, like a little farm. It is pitch dark inside; slowly you can make out the forms of barrels resting in rows on the earth floor, with chickens scratching around among them. A glass of the cool yellow wine, smooth, dry and satisfying, is drawn out with a glass "thief"—a pipette—from one of the casks. You go outside in the sun to sip it and look back at the castle. Such a homely jumble of cottages and fortress it looks that it seems impossible that it has been standing like this for five hundred years, silently reflected in its moat.

## The Médoc

Almost every part of Bordeaux makes a little white wine, and some parts a great deal. Graves has the best of the dry wines, but the Médoc (treated at length under Red Wines) makes a little very good dry white. Even the great first-growth Château Margaux makes some, which it calls Pavillon Blanc du Château Margaux. It is like a good dry Graves. Château Loudenne in the Médoc makes a very popular dry white, and Château La Dame Blanche, just north of Bordeaux, makes another.

*Entre-Deux-Mers*　　Across the river Garonne the enormous district of Entre-Deux-Mers, between the Garonne and the Dordogne which comes to meet it from the east, is known chiefly for its medium, neither dry nor sweet, white wine. The growers of the area evidently feel that the wind is blowing in the direction of drier wine, for their produce is getting drier. They are selling it with the idea of it going with the oysters which everyone eats in Bordeaux—excellent fat ones from the Bay of Arcachon just over on the Atlantic, forty miles away. Their motto, *Entre Deux Huîtres, Entre Deux Mers*, Between Two Oysters, Between Two Seas (the two rivers which enclose the region), though laboured in the telling, has had deserved success.

A complex pattern of different appellations for scarcely different wines makes this part of Bordeaux, the wrong side of the river, a puzzle which few wine-merchants have thought it worth while to solve. It is a land of half-, or often quarter-hearted viticulture, where ranks of high-growing vines, Austrian-style, alternate with fruit trees and humbler crops. Broadly speaking, the proportion of white wine to red increases as you go south from Bordeaux, on this side of the Garonne as on the other. And by the same token the white wine tends more to sweetness as you go south until the communes opposite Sauternes, Loupiac and Ste-Croix-du-Mont, give, at their best, wine you could easily mistake for one of Sauternes' juicier growths.

The recent track-record of this area has not been very good, but one must always keep an open mind. The important firm of Sichel has started making lighter wines, both white and red, here in a very modern installation under the name of Domaine de Belair.

Similar useful wines, with their regional character not so much in evidence as their simple grape origin, are beginning to come from modern-minded producers in an area spreading wider and wider from Bordeaux, mounting the Dordogne to Bergerac and beyond.

# The White Wines of the Loire

The wines we call Loire wines come in so many guises that the portmanteau term is more misleading than helpful. We call them Loire because they are strung out along the length of that river and its tributaries. But the Loire is six hundred miles long, and a lot can happen to the geology and climate in six hundred miles. Both are vital factors in determining the character of a wine.

Thus at the source end of the river, only eighty miles from the famous Côtes of Burgundy, the white wines of Pouilly-Fumé and Sancerre have a near-burgundian character. A hundred and fifty miles farther west the sweet white wines of the Côteaux de la Loire and the Côteaux du Layon are more like white Bordeaux. And the westernmost wines of the Loire from the vineyards clustered round the port of Nantes are a completely different matter again; forceful dry wines, more like, if anything, the wines of Chablis than either of their namesakes.

The Loire wines have grown in popularity in the last decade faster than almost any others. Everybody agrees to call them "charming", which is a pity because it sounds so patronizing. Very few people call them great wines, and then only a very small quantity of the sweet wines from curious idiosyncratic vineyards, and then only at a considerable age.

*Muscadet*

The seaside wines of the Loire are called Muscadet. Muscadet is not a place, but the name of the grape from which they are made. They are the *vin du pays* of Brittany. Fortunately, in view of their situation so near some of the busiest fishing ports of France, they go perfectly with almost anything that comes out of the sea. The Brittany fleets fish the Grand Banks off Newfoundland, the waters of Iceland and the Channel as well as the Bay of Biscay. Their haul includes cod, whiting, sole, skate, turbot and squid. For shellfish they have mussels, scallops, lobsters, langoustines, shrimps and excellent oysters. With all these things Muscadet is in its element.

Being a light, yeastily fresh wine, tending to softness rather than acidity, Muscadet has nothing to gain from being kept. It is often treated as the white equivalent to Beaujolais in Paris cafés and sold as soon after the vintage as they can get it as the *vin de l'année*. Muscadet bottled in the March after the vintage is called, and often labelled, *sur lie*—on its lees. A certain amount of deposit is normal in it—though it is very hard to convince any but the initiated that this does not mean there is something wrong with it.

The vineyards of the Muscadet area, around the city of Nantes, are desultory in appearance. The vines, low on the ground in single, pale-leaved bushes, are scarcely distinguishable from the cabbages with which they share the fields.

Nobody claims greatness for Muscadet, and yet it is one of the most useful of the lesser wines of France. From a mere *vin de pays* it has established itself in the last decade as something which no self-respecting restaurant can do without. Its price, correspondingly, has gone up recently to equal that of a minor white burgundy. It has to be a very good specimen to be worth that much, but domaine-bottlings are coming in to help you to be selective. A number have already built up reputations for wine of more-than-usual strength and cleanness, the attributes of upper-class Muscadet. Château de la Galissonnière, Château la Noë, Château de la Cassemichère and Domaine du Cléray are four of the best I know. Half (on the whole the better half) of the Muscadet vineyards are in the *département* of Sèvre-et-Maine. Sèvre-et-Maine is therefore a good indicator on an unknown label.

*Gros Plant*

The same district also has a secondary grape variety, the Gros Plant, whose wine is sold, like Muscadet, under the varietal name. Gros Plant remains cheap, but is not to be despised as a stand-in for Muscadet. It is similar in character, only a little coarser.

*Sancerre and Pouilly-Fumé*

Odd though it seems to jump from the Atlantic coast to the centre of France to talk about the almost-burgundian wines of the upper Loire, they are, in a sense, next in order. They serve the same purpose as Muscadet at table. They are drunk young, often in their first year; are very dry and light in alcohol. Their colour, like that of Muscadet, is very pale and their whole character leans towards summer drinking and plates of oysters or shrimps.

Sancerre, Pouilly, Quincy and Reuilly are the four wine-villages of the district. The first two are the better known. Pouilly on the Loire, the one in question, is often confused with the Pouilly near Mâcon, which produces a superior wine, Pouilly-Fuissé. That one wine should be called Fuissé and the other Fumé seems to be designed to confuse. There are only eighty-odd miles between them.

Pouilly-Fumé is an appellation reserved for wine grown at Pouilly-sur-Loire from the grape called here the Blanc Fumé; elsewhere the

Sauvignon Blanc. If the wine is made from any other grape it can call itself Pouilly-sur-Loire, but not Fumé. This grape's special contribution, in combination with the chalky soil, is to give the wine a strong scent of what is technically known as gun-flint—like the puff of smoke given off by striking two flints together.

In Pouilly-Fumé the scent is aromatic, obvious and unmistakable—often too much so for my taste. In sunny years it is overwhelming, attractive for the first few sips, but growing rather dull after a while.

In poor years, on the other hand, the wine can be searchingly acid, the scent almost rank.

The Sancerre district lies across the Loire on the west bank, on similar chalky clay but with more sheltered south- and east-facing slopes scattered among its five main villages. As a general rule its wine benefits from the difference: the grapes are riper and the whole effect more fruity and harmonious. But with the hillier countryside the quality is less even. In Sancerre, more than in Pouilly, vineyard names are specified. The sites of Les Mont Damnés in Chavignol and Le Chêne Marchand in Bué, both excellently sheltered slopes, command a premium.

Rather unexpectedly sharing the slopes of Sancerre with the Sauvignon vines there are remnants of a once-important acreage of red burgundy grapes—Pinot Noir—which once made a valued red wine in good years, and in bad years white wine which was sold to the Champagne houses of Reims.

Neither Quincy nor Reuilly has found the same sort of place in the modern world as Pouilly and Sancerre. Off the Loire, and off the main roads, their vineyards have dwindled. In small quantities, though, they still grow the Sauvignon and the new Sauvignon cult is obviously having its effect.

Sancerre and Pouilly-Fumé are now firmly entrenched on wine-lists as alternatives to the medium-priced growths of white burgundy. Compared to these they may seem rather thin and unsubstantial at first, particularly in winter—their turn comes with summer food, very cold, in large glasses beaded and dewy with the chill. Sancerre gains little by being kept more than a year—indeed has much to lose. Pouilly-Fumé is said to improve a little in bottle. But it is certainly not a wine to lay down. Pouilly's biggest estate, the Château du Nozet, unquestionably produces its most famous (and most expensive) wine.

## Touraine

If you follow the Loire downstream, north-west at first and then almost due west, from the old dukedom of Berry where the Pouilly is Fumé, Orléans is the first of the large towns. Orléans wine used to be well known, possibly because it is so near Paris, but now it is famous only for the vinegar it makes. After Orléans comes Blois, and after Blois, now in the middle of the château (real château, not wine-château) country, Vouvray. Vouvray is famous for its white wine.

### Vouvray

It is the curious character of these wines of the middle Loire that they are neither dry nor sweet in the sense we can usually give these useful—though overworked—words. Vouvray can manage to be both dry and sweet at the same time or, if you like, neither at all, in a way of its own. In poor years it is thin and meagre, more acid than anything else, struggling to keep a hint of grape-sugar in it. In exceptional years it becomes really syrupy—and yet still not entirely sweet; there is always a sharp touch about it. It is often strong, and has the capacity, astonishing in such an apparently light wine, to live to a great age—at a great age, indeed, it can improve; I have had a thirty-year-old Vouvray which was like glorious flower-honey. Most often, however, it is marketed as a medium wine, to appeal to everybody, and this is how it is generally known. If nature gives a light and acid wine the Vouvray merchants are not above helping it along with a drop of grape-juice which has been muted (prevented from fermenting by adding brandy or sulphur) and thus kept sweet. A great bottle of Vouvray is so rare that it virtually never makes an appearance outside the grower's own home. It may well, if you ever find it, come *Jasnières* from the diminutive vineyard of Jasnières which is in reality outside the Vouvray area, but which is said to surpass true Vouvray in good *Montlouis* vintages. Mountlouis, on the other hand, which faces Vouvray across the Loire, and thus faces north, always produces lesser wines.

Elsewhere in Touraine the Sauvignon is gaining ground on the traditional vine, the Chenin Blanc. Touraine Sauvignon, indeed, with its own reputation still to make, can be a real bargain.

## *Anjou*

The border country of Touraine and Anjou, the next region travelling westwards down the Loire, is given, in the main, to red and rosé wines. The next white wines are from vineyards lining the north bank of the great river, and of three of its tributaries, the Loir (masculine, not to be confused with la Loire) to the north, and the Aubance *Coteaux de la Loire* and Layon to the south. Those of the Coteaux de la Loire, as the north *Savennières* bank of the Loire is called, are best known. Savennières is the most famous name, and at Savennières two vineyards command higher prices than any others in the whole of the Loire valley in all its six *La-Roche-aux-Moines* hundred miles. They are called La-Roche-aux-Moines and Coulée de Serrant. These are essentially dessert wines—big, full of alcohol and sugar, and yet they are not at all sweet. They have a fine scent, a kind of balance of qualities which reminds you rather of the great German wines, but to someone who is used to the great growths of Sauternes they lack richness.

They are virtually impossible to match with food; a peach would probably be the best thing, or, better still, nothing at all. But their place is not necessarily after a meal. I believe they are really more enjoyable quite divorced from any meal at all, when you are simply sitting at a table by the river with legs outstretched and time to think.

*Quarts de Chaume* Quarts de Chaume from the north bank of the Layon to the south is similar to these, but markedly sweeter. It is a little less highly regarded, perhaps not so delicately scented, but the third great name *Bonnezeaux* among dessert Loire wines. Bonnezeaux, its neighbour, is similar. *Coteaux du Layon* For the rest, the wine of Anjou tends to be firmer and more positive in character; better, in short, than the wine of Touraine. You can expect a plain Coteaux du Layon to be a light, rather sweet wine, almost apple-like in a way, easy to drink at almost any time, excellent with pork or ham.

# The White Wines of Alsace

If it were not for Germany, France could claim to have a royal flush of all the best table wines in the world. But Germany has mastered a style of wine to which France has no real rival; soft and gay, sweet and sour, thirst-quenching and light, wine which asks to be drunk as a long drink and yet is so aromatic that the drinker pauses, and sniffs again, and is carried back in imagination to harvest-time; low sun and leaves turning to red and gold.

The wines of Alsace are France's answer to Germany. Indeed, from the Franco-Prussian War to the end of the First World War Alsace was part of Germany. In those days nobody heard of its wine. It was sold anonymously as *vin ordinaire*. Alsace has had to make its reputation for good wine since the Second World War, when the vineyards and villages were fought over again. It has succeeded, and now stands high as one of the most consistent producers of good reasonably priced wine in the world.

The wines of Alsace are dry and full-flavoured. They do not flirt with sweetness as German wines do, but tend to be stronger, in taste and alcohol, less delicate and less interesting in your mouth.

*Wine for rich food*

They are, above all, table wines, wonderful with food, especially rich and creamy food. The special taste of Alsace is spicy and aromatic. With pig and goose, the fat creatures which are often found in Alsatian, and indeed German, cooking, they get along very well. If they were any sweeter the arrangement would be sickly, but, as they are, they act as excellent seasoning. *Foie gras* is Alsace's most famous dish. It can profit enormously from a piquant cold Traminer. There are some who like Sauternes with *foie gras*; honey, as it were, with cream. I would rather have the touch of seasoning, the mustard on the beef, which an Alsace wine provides.

*The slopes of the Vosges*

The Alsace vineyard, like the bulk of the German Rhine vineyards farther north, faces east across the Rhine, but on hills (in this case the foothills of the Vosges) set back from the river by several miles. Through these hills, never particularly steep or spectacular but always shifting and rolling in perspective, narrow stone-walled lanes twist overshadowed with vines. Here the vines are strung on poles as tall as hop-poles, emphasizing the green leafiness of the plants. Tendrils reach out for you as you pass.

Such old villages as the war spared are almost absurdly picturesque, with the painted eaves and gables, the cobbles, the wellhead, the baskets of geraniums, the archways, the clocks and bells, the leaded

*Riquewihr*

panes of an opera-set. Riquewihr is the one perfect survival. It looks as though it has just been built. In fact it has not changed seriously since the town-hall was built in the early eighteenth century, and under its streets long vaults are stocked, as they always have been,

*Colmar*

with the new wine of the neighbouring fields. Colmar, less involved in the making of wine itself, since it is down in the flat valley-bottom, but the scene of a great annual wine-fair, has an old area, and a big one at that, which no amount of tourist-literature can prepare you for. It is beautiful, busy, natural; the Middle Ages still seem to be in full swing.

*Varietal names*

The wines of Alsace are not known, as all German wines and most French wines are, by the names of vineyards or villages. They are identified by the grape-variety from which they are made, the name of the maker (as in Champagne) and sometimes by a qualifying phrase such as *réserve exceptionelle*, which leads you to expect a higher price, and indeed a better wine.

*Riesling*

The grape-varieties are all-important. The best, beyond a doubt, is the great German grape of the Rhine and the Moselle, otherwise not grown in France, the Riesling. Riesling wine has a quickly recognizable kind of floweriness, not obvious but always true to type, and greater delicacy than almost any other. Normally it tends to sweetness, at least when the grapes have had a chance to get fully ripe, which is later in the year than most. In Alsace the wine it makes is not sweet, but it has more power than usual. Power and delicacy, floweriness and balance—this is not really describing it. Nothing can: it is a wine you must taste.

*Gewürztraminer*  The next grape of Alsace is the Gewürztraminer—the really spicy one. A grape called the Traminer used to be used, and the name is used still to denote a less than full-powered Gewürztraminer, but the Gewürz (or spicy) is now the one in use almost everywhere in Alsace.

This is the most characteristic wine of Alsace. Its aroma is strong, its taste is strong; it does not just slip down, but seasons (as I have said) every morsel of food that goes with it. It is almost always fully dry, though sweeter ones from late-picked and very ripe grapes are sometimes made.

*Muscat*  The Muscat is also grown in Alsace. Normally it is associated with very sweet, very grape-like wine, but here even this is used to make a dry, and surprisingly delicate, one. The firm of Dopff & Irion, whose headquarters is in the old Château de Riquewihr, owns a vineyard called the Clos des Amandiers (there are almond-trees in it), which is planted with Muscat grapes and which produces one of the few Alsace wines sold under a vineyard name. It is light, pretty, only gently Muscat-flavoured and possibly even a little bit almond-like. A good aperitif and excellent with trout.

*Sylvaner*  Two lesser wines are made from other grape-varieties, the Sylvaner
*Pinot Gris*  and the Pinot Gris (or Tokay d'Alsace). Sylvaner is the local tap wine (superior taps often have Riesling). The Tokay is increasingly and rightly fashionable. Pinot Noir is also used to make a rosé, which is extremely good. If an Alsace wine does not state the grape it comes from you may assume that it comes from obscurer varieties and is probably a blend (*Zwicker*) of several. The words *grand vin* can only be used on a wine coming from the superior grape-varieties (if blended, *Edelzwicker*), and containing 11 per cent alcohol, which is the same as most white burgundies.

*Shippers*  Alsace wines are always bottled in long thin Moselle-type bottles, either green or brown; often slightly larger and longer than the German ones. The best-known shippers are Hugel (who makes some superb special, more expensive late-gathered wines under the description *réserve exceptionelle*, as well as a normal range and a very popular, cheaper blend called Flambeau d'Alsace), Dopff & Irion, Dopff (a separate firm, just as there are three Heidsiecks in Champagne), Faller, Beyer, Josmeyer, Mure, Schlumberger (whose wines tend, I think, to be a shade softer and sweeter than some), Trimbach, and Preiss Zimmer (lovely delicate wines). Several growers' co-operatives also make excellent wine—that of Kaysersberg-Kientzheim in particular.

I said that Alsace wines are not known by their vineyard names in, say, the German fashion. But vineyard names do sometimes appear on the labels of (usually) the better wines. In such cases they may be genuinely topographical (Schlumberger's Kitterlé and Trimbach's Clos Ste-Hune are examples). Or they may be more emblematic—a sort of trade-mark.

# The Rhône Valley

Wine is made in the valley of the river Rhône all the way down from its glacial beginnings in Switzerland to its turbid dispersement into the Mediterranean. When we say Rhône wines, however, we mean those of the hundred-and-forty-mile north-south stretch from Lyons to Avignon. Châteauneuf-du-Pape, the wine of Avignon, is sometimes called a Rhône wine, sometimes a wine of Provence. Geographically it is both. In character it belongs more to the Rhône.

The white wines of the Rhône are rich and strong, full yellow-gold in colour and nine-tenths dry. The best of them has a superb scent and lingering lusciousness—is, in fact, one of France's very best white wines—the least is still strong and fine-flavoured. As value for money, all Rhône wines are above average. Their production is low and reputation limited, they are by no means listed everywhere, but a bad one is seldom found and they can cost barely more than half as much as an equivalent burgundy.

They are strong, both in alcohol and flavour; not the wine for delicate food or lunchtime on a busy day. But their richness, sharpened to a flinty edge, is a wonderful accompaniment to dishes which are themselves rich. I have had a white Hermitage with a steak of grilled salmon which seemed at the time one of the most perfect of wine-and-food combinations.

**Château Grillet**

The best and most famous of white Rhône wines is called Château Grillet. It comes from a tiny vineyard on the western bank of the river, producing so little wine—a mere thousand bottles or so in many years—that it can never be more than a curious rarity. It is hopeless trying to describe it, beside saying that it is fairly deep-coloured, very scented, full and suggestive of spice in your mouth, and has a long unfading soft and dry aftertaste which still remains a full minute after you have swallowed it. Many people, Germans particularly, compare it with the great German wines—usually to their advantage. It is bottled in long thin Moselle-type bottles. It is necessarily extremely expensive from sheer rarity. Sooner or later every wine-collector has to try it. Vienne, the town twenty miles south of Lyons where the Rhône vineyards start in earnest, is the place to go to have your sample. The Pyramide restaurant there has from time to time been called the best in France.

**Condrieu**

Beside the ultimate rarity of Château Grillet, the village of Condrieu produces similar and less-serenaded wine from the same rare local grape, the Viognier. There is not much of this either, and it is almost never exported, but those who try it locally will find it excellent, elusively flower-scented, sometimes slightly sweet. Such a wine would be good with a chicken cooked in cream—the kind of rich food for which the Rhône valley is famous.

**Hermitage**

There is a gap of thirty miles after Condrieu before the next white-wine vineyards—here in country which is more famous for its red wine—at Hermitage. The hill of Hermitage on the east bank of the Rhône at Tain, opposite Tournon, is alone allowed to call its wines Hermitage, but those from several villages round about are able to label themselves Crozes-Hermitage (Crozes is a village just to the north of the sudden bleak Hermitage hill).

**Crozes-Hermitage**

White Hermitage is fat with a richness which fills your mouth, but also with a flinty edge. It is one of those white wines which you could, with your eyes shut, almost mistake for a red. Its colour, in fact, is singularly golden. Again, there is little of it, but it is exported, stores and travels perfectly, improves with age (even, I believe, with great age) and costs less than some lesser wines from better-known areas.

The Crozes-Hermitage area, too, produces similar and excellent white wines. Of the white Hermitages the best known is Chante-Alouette (Lark-song). There is also another called Chantemerle (Blackbird-song).

Hermitage used to be reckoned about as far south as a white grape could grow without losing face. True, there was a tiny production of white Châteauneuf-du-Pape, but it was strong and dry with some of the dryness of a hot wind off the desert. Its main characteristic was what the wine-trade so happily calls "stuffing".

Happily, though, new techniques (above all refrigeration) are beginning to give us white wine of Hermitage (or at least Crozes-Hermitage) standard from a hundred miles farther south. The fifteen villages which make up the newly prosperous appellation Côtes-du-Rhône-Villages have great potential in white wine as well as their main production, red.

## The south of France

It is best to take the south of France in two bites: to the east and west of Provence and the Rhône delta. The eastern bite has much less, but on the whole better wine; the western has the vast bulk of *vin ordinaire*, but one or two notably superior growths.

### Haute-Savoie

The mountains of Haute-Savoie, south of Switzerland, have several white wines whose names are more familiar than their tastes even to devoted bottle-collectors. Crépy, Seyssel, Abymes and Apremont are some of the most familiar names. All are dry and none of them are very strong. There is a tendency to sparkle which is encouraged in some places, discouraged in others. They are essentially wines to study on the spot, where both the food and the scenery, whose fame far outdoes that of the wine, can be taken into account.

### Côtes de Provence

### Cassis

The Côtes de Provence, which is the name allowed for all the wine from the eastern coastal belt which satisfies the authorities as to its strength and quality, are better known. Cassis, from the very doorstep of Marseilles, is perhaps the best known of all. It is offered almost as a matter of course with the inevitable *bouillabaisse* in Marseilles. Indeed, it is ideal to quench the thirst which follows this peppery dish.

Great confusion is caused by the name Cassis. It is both a wine and a blackcurrant liqueur made in Burgundy. A *vin blanc cassis* is an aperitif made by pouring a glassful of white wine on to a spoonful of the liqueur, whereas a *vin blanc de Cassis* is a white wine from the Cassis district, on its own. The mixed aperitif does not need a wine as good as the fresh and tasty Cassis. It can be made well enough with any dry white wine.

### Bandol

Bandol, only a step eastwards along the coast, is better known for red wine, but produces good white not unlike Cassis. Farther east in the Var *département*, round St Tropez and Hyères, it is red and rosé wine rather than white which has a reputation. The best of the white is often described as *blanc de blancs*.

In the hills north of Marseilles, on the other hand, near Aix-en-Provence and in the valley of the Durance, good white wine is made. Château Simone has a virtual monopoly of the name of Palette and hence of the local wine section on lists at Aix-en-Provence. Its white is not quite as good as its red, which tastes of the pines and herbs of the countryside.

The Massif of the Lubéron which rises to the north of the valley of the Durance has surprisingly delicate white wines, at least one of which—that of Lourmarin—makes a good, and remarkably cheap, *Côtes du Lubéron* sparkling version. The name Côtes du Lubéron is the thing to look for.

## West of the Rhône

There is no need to dwell on the *départements* of Gard and Hérault west of the Rhône delta. They are red-wine country, and not very good red wine at that. There are two or three local white specialities, but local is the operative word; the grapes they grow, notably the *Clairette* Clairette which gives its name to some of the wines, only emphasize the softness and flatness, the lack of essential acidity, which is the bane of white wine in the south.

Only one spot on the long coast round the Golfe de Lyon to the Spanish border makes white wine of real note: the geological freak known as La Clape, a limestone massif for all the world like a Greek island blown ashore on the sand-flats at the mouth of the Aude. The vines scattered among pine-woods on this quasi-island give white wine of power and personality—in tiny supply, but worth trying.

The vast influx of tourists to the new resorts of this coast (an architect's dream: miles of uninhibited apartment blocks where ten years ago there were only marsh and mosquitoes) is nonetheless having its effect. Listel with its Vins de Sables or sand-wines, long (and justifiably) neglected, is suddenly on a main road. It is beginning to dawn on the dogged wine-growers of the south, usually with the wrong grapes in the wrong places, that science is going to be their fairy godmother. The Camargues of all places suddenly has one of France's most advanced experimental wineries. The perfectly acceptable wine it has started making, even from vines planted for their high yields alone, may well lead to better vines being planted, and ultimately to a new source of good wine for the world.

*Limoux* Meanwhile only Limoux, in the extreme west of this wide area in the hills south of Carcassonne, has good fresh white wine in ample supply. Sparkling wine is the Limoux speciality, but the tart still *blanc de blancs* they also make is very agreeable.

*Gaillac* To the north of this region, the mountains round the lovely gorge of the river Tarn, the Gaillac white wines are made. This used to be a district of sweet white wines, but modern trade has encouraged the growing of a complete range of wines—dry white, rosé and red. The white is perhaps the best of them; not a wine of great character, but cheap and honest.

*Béarn* Farther west yet, in the Pyrenean foothills of Béarn, whose capital is Pau, a more than adequate *blanc de blancs*, not unlike that of Limoux, *Jurançon* is made. But the most famous wine of this area is called Jurançon. It should be, and traditionally is, supremely sweet, and said to smell of carnations and taste of cloves. Tall tales are told of the high-strung vines and heavenly mouthfuls of Jurançon. Sad to say, the only one of its wines which is exported, as far as I can discover, is a dry one of no amazing distinction.

## The Jura

The most characteristic and best white wines of the Jura are the *vins jaunes*, strange, strong and dark, more of an aperitif than a table wine (see under Aperitifs, page 46) or the raisin-like *vin de paille* (see the After-Dinner Wines section, page 230).

The Jura also makes white table wines, but they are not as good as the pink and yellow ones. Under the broad description of Côtes du Jura good *ordinaires* are found, in one case well described as a *vin de campagne*—a country wine. Rather better ones are made within the controlled area of Arbois. An Arbois *blanc* can remind you of a Pouilly-Fumé; a good dry white wine, perhaps a little strong and obvious in scent and taste, but good for country food.

*Arbois*

Both the ordinary Jura and more special Arbois wines have a smell of their own which I have not met elsewhere—a rather fat, nutty scent which might lead you to think that they are going to be better than they really are. One firm also makes a *Blanc de Blancs du Jura* from white Burgundy grapes—a lighter-weight wine with much the same character.

# German White Wines

France, Spain, Italy, Portugal, Austria and Switzerland are real wine-countries. They have wine as their national drink—it is as much a part of their diet as bread. Only as a hobby of a few and the preoccupation of vineyard proprietors does connoisseurship come into it. You might say that wine works upward from a broad base in these countries. It is assumed that everyone will drink it; it so happens that a few take a special interest in what they are drinking.

*Wine for wine's sake*

Germany, though, is more like England in her attitude to wine. Wine, for all the two thousand years it has grown on the vertiginous hillsides of the Rhine and the Moselle, does not come naturally to her. Her total production is barely a tenth of that of France. In perhaps three years out of five the grapes in German vineyards never ripen properly at all but remain green and acid, giving (unless they have the help of added sugar) a thin sour wine. Making fine wine under these conditions is not just farming, it is craftsmanship, and of a particularly laborious and dogged kind. The results, when they are good, are expensive, but they are unique: they are wine for wine's sake. In a good vintage a good German vineyard-owner is not making something just to quench thirst, or even to make a perfect drink with a fine meal. He is trying to give his wine all the individual flavour of his own land in its highest possible intensity. He considers his wine to be better or worse according to the clarity and strength of the taste by which it expresses its difference from all other wines. He will make as many different wines as necessary—even keeping the contents of each cask separate from all the others and thus adding immensely to his problem of selling it—to make sure that the best he has to offer is the best his land can possibly produce. Compared with this dedication to the wine itself the most perfectionist of French growers is commercial and carefree. Even an estate as famous as Romanée-Conti or Château Lafite makes all its wine of a year together, giving the poorer parts of the crop the benefit of mixture with the ripest and the best. But this does not happen in Germany. A German grower thinks it is a sin to level down his masterpiece, even to improve his other wine. Hence the multiplicity, and in a sense obscurity, of German wine-names.

*New controls*   Their obscurity, in fact, has often been exaggerated. What they suffer from is excess of clarity: they are not dark but blindingly light. They tell you, albeit in German, often in archaic gothic type and in astonishingly long words, exactly what is in the bottle in your hand. Or rather, they did, very satisfactorily, until the advent of a complete new set of rules in 1971. Up to 1971 it took only a clear head and a steady hand to interpret any reputable German wine label. Unfortunately the new laws have introduced ambiguities which only the most dogged use of reference books can elucidate. Whether there was a publisher on the committee that framed them I don't know. But there can't have been a consumer.

When we describe these wines labelled in such elaborate detail we are speaking of the traditional, and by far the best, German product; not about the bulk of that which is made now. A vast number of small quantities of different goods is hardly a sound basis for trade. Besides, in most years most of the wine of Germany is a long way from being worth the trouble of individual bottling and labelling, let alone marketing. Logically enough, then, the wines of poorer years and more ordinary vineyards are blended together to give a good average product which can be made consistently to order, and so is susceptible to modern marketing and advertising. This is the story of most German wine today.

*The taste of German wine*   The immediate and most noticeable difference between German and French wines is that German wine tastes weaker. It is a matter of body, or of what wine-merchants call vinosity—the mouth-filling sensation of alcoholic strength peculiar to wine. French white wines, as a rule, have plenty of it—most German wines have much less. Their taste is somehow clear and tenuous, not reinforced by an impression of warmth and strength. This does not mean that they are sour, but rather that their fermentation does not go so far and produce so much alcohol. Their light body is the perfect vehicle for their delicate taste, in which sweetness is balanced against acidity.

The balance which good German wines achieve between sugar and acid is a lull in a perpetual struggle between the two elements. The acidity wins more often than the sweetness, in poor, cold and wet years, resulting in sour wine. On the other hand, when the sweetness predominates, the wine is hardly any better: it is dull, flat, unrefreshing. A balance of the two is essential.

The ideal, reached naturally only by fine wines in fine vintages, is a great measure of both: enough sugar to make the wine like syrup coupled with enough acidity to make it fresh and uncloying. The ideal is expressed in terms of the laboratory as 10 degrees Oechsle (the specific gravity of the unfermented grape juice; the factor which determines strength and/or sweetness) to one gramme per thousand of acidity. In terms of the nose and mouth, it is a wine which is a sheer pleasure to smell and drink, giving you the feeling that you could go on for ever and never grow tired of it.

*The scent*    Despite their delicate flavour, German wines have a more powerful perfume than any others. None, perhaps, in the world can compete with a fine young Moselle for sheer volume of scent. As soon as the cork is out it can be smelt all over the room. It is a blossom-like, spring-flower scent with a hint—sometimes a very noticeable one—of pear-drops. If the other German wines are not quite so pungent as Moselle they are still highly, and delightfully, scented—as much so as any wine from France, except possibly champagne.

*German wine and food*    Wine like this—delicate in body, fresh and balanced in taste and scented like a garden of flowers—is a different matter from the savoury and appetizing white wine of, say, Burgundy which goes so well with food. Good German wine is not really table wine in the French sense at all. It is not so good with a meal as on its own. There are many exceptions to this—the wine of the Palatinate being the most important—but the rule holds for the best wines of Moselle and Rheingau, which are Germany's best. No matter what the meal, what the dish, they are wasted on it; their appeal is a matter of subtleties, and food simply gets in the way.

A German, then, drinks his best wine on its own, in morning, afternoon or evening—it is not very strong, so it does not matter. At mealtimes (if he drinks wine at all) he drinks something simple and straightforward—often the local "open" wine sold by the glass. He might drink one of the advertised national brands or, if he wants a particular type of wine—say, a light Moselle to drink with trout, or a heavy spicy Palatinate to drink with some game—he would have the less expensive wine of the appropriate region, without all the trappings and extra expense of estate-bottling.

*The Rhine*    The wine-country of Germany is the basin of the river Rhine and its tributaries. The Rhine cuts Germany in two from south to north on its way from the Alps to the North Sea. Wine of some kind is grown along most of its route, but by far the best of the wines of the Rhine are those grown in the fifty miles or so above and the twenty-five miles below a great bend in the river where the Main flows in from the east. The Rhine wines from this area have been known for the last century or more in England as hock. Hock is supposed to be a contraction of hockamore, which in turn is an anglicization of Hochheimer, the wine of a fine vineyard-town right on the river bend, by repute the favourite of Queen Victoria.

Rhine wine used to be called Rhenish in England. It is Rhenish, not hock, which is referred to (as a superior kind of wine, fit for courts and feasts) in Shakespeare's plays. But the Rhenish of those days seems to have been a red wine, whereas now all hock, and indeed all the German wine which is considered good enough for export, is white.

*The Moselle*    The other German wine which equals Rhine wine in its reputation, and nowadays more and more often surpasses it in price, is Moselle. The river Moselle, coming out of France beside Luxembourg, carves its way north-east through a range of pine-covered mountains to join the Rhine at Koblenz. In its central section it has had a nightmarish time getting through the mountains; every mile to the north-east has meant a detour of six or seven miles to west, east or south. As a result, its banks may face any point of the compass. Where they face south, regardless of how inaccessible or steep they may be, they are planted with vines.

Two tributaries of the Moselle, and two more of the Rhine, also have fine vineyards on their banks. The little rivers which join the Moselle at the top of its German course are the Saar and the Ruwer. Both have some wines which are among the world's very finest. Of the Rhine's other tributaries, the Nahe, which lies between the Moselle and the great hock bend, makes wine which is always treated as Rhine wine. The Main, whose vineyards lie far to the east, round Würzburg in Franconia, has a different character, a different bottle, and a reputation of its own.

All the wines which come into the Moselle complex are shipped in slim, sloping-shouldered, green bottles; those which belong to the Rhine appear in brown ones. The Franconian bottle is like a gourd.

## South Germany

These are not Germany's only wines, nor even the greater part of them. The south is more prolific than the north, and the consumption of wine is a far more everyday affair in districts whose wines have scarcely been heard of abroad. The shores of Lake Constance, the slopes of the Baden hills which face Alsace across the Rhine, and, above all, the banks of the river Neckar in Württemberg, far above where it joins the Rhine at Heidelberg, are the home of *Konsumwein*—ordinary daily wine—red, white or a mixture of the two. Good growths and even great vineyards are not unknown in these regions. The Kaiserstuhl, a hill like an island in the broad valley of the Rhine north of Freiburg, has several famous growths—Ihringer, Ach-karrenner, Oberrotweiler—which are offered with pride in, for example, the Casino at Baden-Baden. They are strong-flavoured, fruity wines in a good year. When young they are fine, and they are no doubt used for blending with hock when supplies are short. Their fault is usually that they are made from a haphazard variety of grapes and not a single, classical stock like the Riesling, which gives the lovely cleanness of the great German wines.

### Württemberg

### The Kaiserstuhl

## "Commercial" wines

The wine-trade often uses the word commercial to describe the wines it can buy and sell in large quantities at a reasonable profit to earn its living, as opposed to the finer wines whose minute quantities and vast variety make them a barely economic proposition. Obviously, there is nothing pejorative in the term, unless it is applied to a wine which has pretensions to being in a higher category.

Commercial wines have a more important rôle in Germany than anywhere else, partly for the reason I have mentioned (that there is such a tangle of nomenclature that few drinkers can be bothered to sort it out) but also, more pressingly, because of the weather.

It is common for three-quarters of the wine in Germany in a bad year to need sugar adding to it to make it drinkable. In the worst years even the best vineyards simply have to sell their wine to be turned into Sekt. But in almost any year there is a great deal of wine which needs improvement either by sugaring or blending, and often both. The world relies on these circumstances to keep it supplied with its regular meal-time German wine—among others, its Liebfraumilch.

*Liebfraumilch*
The name Liebfraumilch on its own means quite simply Rhine wine. It is not wine from a particular place or of a particular kind. In combination with one of the famous brand-names applied to it by the great shippers (of which Sichel's Blue Nun, Deinhard's Hanns Christoff Wein, Langenbach's Crown of Crowns and Hallgarten's Blackfriars are the most famous), it is a complete guarantee of a good-quality blend of medium-price, soft-flavoured, faintly sweet and eminently harmless hock. Without a good shipper's name attached it might be anything.

A Liebfraumilch offered at half the price of a good brand will not be a bargain; it will be half as good—if that.

In the city of Worms in Rheinhessen (the district which produces most of the Liebfraumilch-type wine), there is a church called the Liebfrauenkirche, surrounded by a small vineyard. This is where the original Liebfraumilch is supposed to have come from, although its wine today is known as Liebfrauenstiftswein.

*Moselblümchen*
An approximately equivalent wine to Liebfraumilch from the Moselle is sometimes called Moselblümchen, which means Little Moselle Flower, but the name has never achieved the popularity of Liebfraumilch. The most popular Moselle wines, on the other hand, are almost the same kind of thing—a broadly regional blend. Deinhard's Green Label is a good example; in this case of wine from the area (*Bereich*) of Bernkastel.

Compared with Liebfraumilch, such commercial Moselles as these typify the difference between Rhine and Moselle wines. It is a difference which is well symbolized by the colours of their respective bottles; the Rhine a warm reddish-brown, suggesting a soft, sweet, full-flavoured drink; the Moselle a cool green, the colour of sharp, refreshing fruit. To put it another way, if a hock were a peach, a Moselle would be an apple.

## Wine and the chemist

I spoke above of the ideal balance in German wine, and implied that —in this most northerly of the world's wine-regions—it is rare for it to happen naturally. In most vintages it needs to be helped along.

In former times there was only one way the wine could be helped, if the natural Oechsle level was too low (to make say 8 or 9 degrees of alcohol and still leave a touch of sugar in the wine for balance). You had to add sugar and water (the water helped to reduce the wine's acidity) and then stop the fermentation from finishing up every scrap of the sugar with a dollop of wine's age-old antiseptic and general panacea, sulphur. A century ago the weaker kind of German wine used to be stuffed with sulphur like an exhibition whale with formaldehyde. The miracle was that, in the hands of skilful wine-merchants, the sulphur disengaged itself from the wine and the drinker was unaware of it. If he was less skilful it stank like a gasworks.

*The quiet revolution*
The passing of sulphur in the last generation or so has been one of wine's silent revolutions. German scientists have been at the heart of it. In place of such heavy-handed methods of keeping the yeast quiet they have devised filters of such perfect fineness and sterility that the yeast can simply be eliminated from the wine when the fermentation has gone far enough. Without yeast, and protected from the air, the wine is perfectly stable.

But in Germany there has been a further development which has made still more difference to the character of German wine. In the past only the expensive late-gathered wines were positively sweet.

The rest just had a few grammes of residual sugar, as I have said, for balance. But the current technique is to ferment the wine to the full, using up all its natural sugar plus any extra sugar it may have needed; and then to add sweetening to the resulting dry wine to match what is thought to be the popular taste.

*Added sweetness*

The sweetening agent is grape juice which has never been allowed to ferment at all—again by means of sterile filtration. Up to about a quarter of the total volume today can be this *süss-reserve*. If anyone has wondered why German wines seem to have got much sweeter recently this is the reason. I personally think it is often terribly over-done: the whole character of a fine and delicate wine can be overlaid by the blanket of sweetness. Given time, I am told, it will marry very well with the wine, enriching the flavour and losing its excessive sugariness. But unfortunately all the trends in German wine-drinking are towards younger and younger wine; each vintage supersedes the last like a fashion in hats. So it is a poor outlook for the man who wants natural dry or nearly dry wine with all its character on show. Again, he can only find it by discovering which estates have the lightest hand with the *süss-reserve*, and buying their wines.

## German wine-labels

To understand the basis of the German wine-laws, and the philosophy behind German labelling, you must accept the German grower's fascination with the weather. It is natural enough, in the most northerly vineyard. Ripeness is all.

The German theory of wine quality works entirely on the basis of the natural sweetness of the wine. Theoretically in Germany any vineyard can make wine as good as any other vineyard. There is no classification of land as there is in France—no official recognition of the built-in superiority of, let us say, the middle Moselle to the lower Moselle. Oechsle is king, and there is no way of avoiding some sort of familiarity with his majesty.

In former times a German wine-label was quite straightforward, however long-winded. First came the name of the village, then the name of the individual vineyard, then (usually) the grape variety, then the quality category, corresponding to the degree of ripeness of the grapes.

*The new controls*

The new laws have made such a generalization impossible. Under certain circumstances the same rules apply. But now there are so many alternative possibilities that, however reluctantly, you have to read the fine print.

In the first place the new laws have reformed the geography of German wine; making new divisions and sub-divisions, enormously reducing the number of individual vineyard names from the former figure of thirty thousand (which was admittedly quite unmanageable) to a mere two thousand seven hundred, and introducing a new concept, the *Grosslage*, or big vineyard. It is the last which the innocent drinker must watch like a hawk.

The broadest of the new divisions is perfectly simple: the *Weinbaugebiet* is just the part of the German wine-country in question: Baden, Rheingau, Rheinhessen, Mosel-Saar-Ruwer . . . they are all familiar names to drinkers of German wine.

*Bereich*

The first of the new divisions is the *Bereich*: a word which first appeared on wine labels in 1971. *Bereich* means district, more narrowly delineated than the *Gebiet*—though not much more: and not in every case. The whole of the Rheingau, for example, is in the Bereich

Johannisberg. Here comes the first confusion of the new law; for Johannisberg was formerly and is still the name of one of the best villages of its region. The village name has now been applied to the whole *Bereich*. It would be a comparable case if, say, the name Meursault were suddenly to be allowed for any white wine from the Côte d'Or. The only proviso is that it must be accompanied on the label by the word *Bereich*. British wine-merchants would like to be allowed to translate *Bereich* into "district", but so far the law says no.

*Einzellage*        The final true geographical division recognized by the new law is the *Einzellage*—or single vineyard. It is in this category that the most drastic pruning has been done. Thousands of traditional names; Red Mountains, Church Paths, Knight's Ways, Spice Gardens, Hare-leaps, have been suppressed. In each village the names of a handful of the best-known *Lagen* or vineyards have been bestowed on their neighbours: a very reasonable act of consolidation. In places there has been a remarkable sense of the integrity of a particular plot, even one as small as three or four acres, which from its unique location, or in some cases its ownership by one grower, has an identity which would be lost if it were touched.

All the finest German wines will bear an *Einzellage* name, as they have always done. This in itself would make them easy to identify, if the law had not also brought in the new concept of *Grosslage*.

*Grosslage*        A *Grosslage* is not a piece of land, like an *Einzellage* only bigger, but the name which a grower may use for his wine if it is a blend of two or more *Einzellage* wines, or if for some reason he thinks it would help to sell the wine (e.g. if he judges that the *Grosslage* name is more famous than his particular *Einzellage*).

The catch is that *Grosslage* names sound exactly like *Einzellage* names—most of them in fact were *Einzellage* names before 1971—and that the label does not tell you which level of demarcation you are dealing with. More surprisingly, it is not allowed to tell you. The law is very specific on this point: anything which is not required by law to be put on the label is positively banned.

*Caveat emptor*        An example will clear the air. Bernkasteler Graben is the name of a vineyard in Bernkastel—an *Einzellage*. So, until 1971, was Bern-kasteler Badstube. But by the law of 1971 the name Badstube has been stopped as an individual vineyard name and made available to all growers in the vineyards of Graben, Bratenhöfchen, Matheis-bildchen and Lay.

The label, however, will only say Bernkasteler Badstube as it always did, leading you to think that Badstube has the same standing as, let us say, Graben which remains a very special hillside site.

Meanwhile growers in the six other *Einzellagen* of Bernkastel have the possibility of using the *Grosslage* name Bernkasteler Kurfürstlay. But so also do the growers in Wintrich, Brauneberg and six other villages upstream. So even the village name (Bernkastel) no longer necessarily means what it says.

In theory, say the officials, everyone will get to know which are the *Grosslage* names in time. But there are three hundred of them. I shall not even attempt to name and describe more than a handful of the most important in this book. You will, in other words, need a reference book specifically on German wine constantly at your side. Unless, and this is the crux of this tirade, the law is changed and *Einzellage* wines are allowed to identify themselves on their labels.

Unofficially, of course, there is still the most certain way of all of getting first-rate German wine, which is by knowing the name of the grower. I need hardly say that what a good man puts in the bottle is still the best he can make. But even if the grower is right it is nice to know exactly what the label means.

*The Oeschle scale*

Good king Oechsle and his part of the laws are interwoven with the geographical side to make the whole grand bureaucratic daydream. It works like this:

There are three levels of wine quality corresponding in spirit, but by no means in the letter, with the Italian *denominaziones* and the French *A.C.*, *V.D.Q.S.* and the rest. The humblest level is *Tafelwein* or table wine. Regulations are minimal. It can be sugared, blended, concentrated, even helped along with imported wine up to 25 per cent of its volume. The idea is a good cheap drink. It can claim to come from a given district (not vineyard or *Grosslage*) but it doesn't have to.

*Q.b.A.*

The second level is *Qualitätswein bestimmter Anbaugebiete*, or *Q.b.A.*, or quality wine from a named area. This is the class for all wines which have some pretensions to quality but which have had to be sugared to achieve a certain minimum strength. In this class the regulations are stricter, the wine must pass a test and wear on its label its test number, and correspondingly it can make definite assertions about where it comes from—even down to the actual vineyard. It can state that it is estate-bottled (*Erzeugerabfüllung*)—which, incidentally, "improved" (or sugared) wine could not under the old laws. It must all come from one area of Germany.

*Q.m.P.*

The top division rejoices in the untranslatable name of *Qualitätswein mit Prädikat*, or *Q.m.P.* "Quality Wine with Special Attributes" is the official version. *Prädikatswein* is perhaps the simplest way of referring to it with any chance of being understood.

This is the bracket for all natural wines made without sugar. But the sugar content decides where in the *Prädikatswein* league table the wine will come: whether it will be simple *Kabinett* (73 degrees Oechsle), the basic level for any natural wine, or *Spätlese*, which demands another 12 degrees Oechsle—enough to give the wine noticeably more strength and richness, or *Auslese*, which means very ripe grapes and 10 degrees more sugar than *Spätlese*, or *Beerenauslese* or *Trockenbeerenauslese* which call for really spectacular Oechsle-readings: respectively 125 and 150 degrees . . . readings which are often exceeded, and have even, in record-breaking cases, been doubled.

Here we are back among distinctions familiar to old hands with the old wine laws. There is no change in the basic meaning of these terms —only a more categorical interpretation of them. And of course the new law bans the old home-made distinctions made by proud and devoted cellarmen; such phrases as "best cask", "finest *Auslese*" and actual cask-numbers which used to appear on labels—sometimes, admittedly, to add a spurious glamour, but more often because the wine-maker could not bear to see his handiwork muddled or mistaken for anything else. All this has gone, and Oechsle reigns in its stead.

*Quality prizes*

In place of the old home-made distinctions has been erected a formal system for giving a wine credit for being better than the minimal standards to get into its class. When each wine is tested for its proof-number it is marked out of twenty, with marks for colour, clarity, scent and flavour. Oechsle degrees apart, it has to get eleven points to be a *Qualitätswein*, thirteen to be a *Prädikat Kabinett*, fourteen to be a *Spätlese*, fifteen to be an *Auslese*, sixteen to be a *Beerenauslese* and seventeen to be a *Trockenbeerenauslese*. If it does better—if a *Spätlese*, say, gets eighteen points—it qualifies for a variety of prizes. The whole rigmarole is far too involved to set out in detail, but in order of importance the prizes are *Deutsches Export Weinsiegel* (German export wine-seal; amusingly enough the lowest prize); *Deutsches Weinsiegel*; *Bundesweinprämierung* or national wine prize at three different levels—bronze, silver and gold; and *Gebietsweinprämierung* or regional wine prize, which has a slightly different qualifying system, for some reason a shade less demanding for wines up to *Ausleses* but from *Auslese* and up calling for an outright twenty out of twenty for its gold medal, as against the *Bundesweinprämierung*'s 19.5/20.

Obviously no one is expected to carry all this in his head, but it is just as well to know what the little prize stickers which are appearing as neck-labels on so many German wine-bottles are all about. If you remember that a bronze label is good, a silver better, and a gold best you are on the right lines.

*Diabetic wine*

Finally there is a special category for dry wine, which is a help for those who find the degree of *süss-reserve* in most German wines too sweet for their liking. If they have less than four grammes of sugar per litre, which is very little indeed, they can wear a *Diabetiker-Wiensiegel* or diabetic wine-seal label. It doesn't sound very appetizing, but if you like your wine tart and enjoy its herby and grassy flavours unmasked by softer notes diabetic wine is well worth looking for.

*The grower's prestige*

The last part of a German label is, in a sense, the most important part of all. It tells you the name of the grower and where the wine was bottled. With all the finest wines it is the commonest thing for the wine to be bottled on the estate where it was made, and thus to qualify for the phrase *Erzeugerabfüllung* or *aus eigenem Lesegut*. Which of the proprietors of the vineyard (for the great majority of famous vineyards in Germany have several owners) it comes from is vital. Growers' names mean even more in Germany than they do in Burgundy. A few (on the Moselle several of them religious foundations, in the Rheingau most of them old noble families, and throughout Germany very prominently the Federal State) have such high reputations that any wine from them can be assumed to be reliable.

## The Moselle

The Moselle comes into Germany out of France and Luxembourg already dressed with vines. Luxembourgeois Moselle is a caricature of the kind of wine the valley will produce later in its path. It is very light, sharp, often bubbly in its bottle from the effects of unfinished fermentation, almost colourless and wonderfully refreshing to drink. It is rather like miraculously light and scented cider, or the *vinho verde* of Portugal.

*The vineyards*

For most of its way through Germany the river is accompanied by the tilting green lines of vineyards on little terraces and precipitous slopes far above the valley floor. Sometimes, where a bend gives the whole bank for a mile or more a directly southern exposure, the hill of vines is continuous from the river's edge to the crest six or seven hundred feet above. The Moselle vineyards are some of the world's most beautiful, and must certainly be the world's steepest. In places, ladders laid on the ground are the only way of getting up the hill. A glance below your feet shows the river as a mere stream. A stranger on these slopes can hardly make his way about at all, but the men and women who work all year on the vines have adapted themselves to their cliff-hanging life. At harvest-time they run up and down all day with hods of grapes, weighing a good hundredweight, on their backs.

The soil of the Moselle is grey slate. It is thin, and looks poor, but the hardy Riesling vine, which is grown there to the exclusion of all lesser types, thrives on it. The light slaty soil has one great advantage: rain falls straight through it. Where in the sandstone vineyards of the Rhine the surface traps the water, turns to runny mud and pours down the hill, the slate of the Moselle stays in its precarious place. If it were not for this fact, a heavy rainstorm would leave the roots of the vines bare, and the vineyard would slide to the bottom of the hill.

Only a small part of the Moselle, however, grows fine wine. It is a series of curves in the central part, known as the Middle Moselle, which contains all the best vineyards of the river itself. These, and a few villages in the tributary valleys of the Saar and Ruwer farther up-stream, comprising at most only a quarter of the whole river's wine-production, are the wines which are exported, and are known by name all over the world.

*The Saar*

The Saar valley is the southernmost of these districts. There are seven great wine-villages on the Saar, with barely fifteen hundred acres of vineyard between them. Their names are Wiltingen, Ayl, Oberemmel, Saarburg, Serrig, Ockfen and Wawern. In very good vintages they produce what some consider the best of all Moselle wines; in a bad year, on the other hand, their wine is hardly drinkable at all without sugaring.

In 1968, for example, even the best estates in the valley had to sell all their wine to the Sekt producers, so sour and—as they say—*stahlig*, steely, was it. Yet in 1971 the best Saar wines were among the finest in Germany. Their greatest appeal to wine-lovers, in fact, is in the hint of hardness—again, this steeliness—which they keep even in warm and ripe years. Rather as a Chablis, however rich in flavour, always has a stony, austere finish, the Saar wines keep their firm, ungentle individuality.

The greatest name of the Saar is the splendid straight hillside known as Wiltinger Scharzhofberg, and the best-known single estate that of the Egon-Müller family.

Unfortunately, however, the *Grosslage* name chosen for the whole of the Saar and all its wines (a four-thousand-acre area covering much more than the classic heart of the region) is Wiltinger Scharzberg. Did it occur to anyone that the three letters of "hof" might possibly not be missed?

At least half a dozen vineyards here have names worth committing to memory. The Ayl vineyards of Kupp and Herrenberger; the Ockfen vineyard of Bockstein; Wiltinger Braunfels, Klosterberg and Rosenberg; Schloss Saarfelser and Vogelsang at Serrig, and Warwerner Ritterpfad all produce great wine in great years (and bad wine in bad ones).

At Serrig and Ockfen the State Domain has excellent vineyards. The black eagle on the label makes it easy to recognize State Domain wines. Other very important holdings belong to the various religious foundations of the city of Trier, which lies on the Moselle only a short way downstream from the mouth of the Saar.

*Trier*

At Trier, more than any other town in the wine-growing world, the endowment of charities with vineyards is a flourishing concern.

The secular foundation of the famous hospital at Beaune, which operates on the proceeds of the sale of its wines, has several counterparts in Trier—some religious, some not. The Catholic cathedral itself is an important vineyard owner (it adds the word *Dom*, meaning cathedral, to the names of the wines it sells from its vineyards). The Bischöfliches Konvikt (a boarding-school), the Bischöfliches Priesterseminar (a training-college for priests), the Friedrich Wilhelm Gymnasium (the school where Karl Marx was educated) and the Vereinigte Hospitien (an almshouse) are all endowed with excellent vineyards, and belong to an association, known as the Great Ring, which sells part of its wine by annual auction, setting a very high standard and allowing none but natural wines under its rules. The labels of these foundations are some of the best known and most reliable on the Moselle, for their estates are dotted over all the finer stretches of the river. There is no finer German wine.

Trier is the business centre of the wine-growing Moselle. It is the oldest city in Germany. A completely preserved Roman gateway still dominates it, although most of the city was destroyed in the Second World War and there are few old houses left. Until the new wine laws few wines actually bore the name of Trier. Only one vineyard, the Tiergarten (which means "zoo") was famous. But now the name Trier applies to a much wider area, including a detached but important little hill of vines belonging to the Cathedral and the *Avelsbach* State Domain in the hills just outside the city of Avelsbach. The wines formerly famous as Avelsbacher Hammerstein and Rotlay are now Trierer Hammerstein and the rest.

Trier, in fact, has linked up with the little vineyard region on the banks of the Moselle's next tributary, the Ruwer. Eitelsbach on the Ruwer shares Avelsbach's fate: its name disappears from labels—except those of one of Germany's most illustrious vineyards of all, the Karthäuserhofberg. Lovers of the most delicate and haunting, lightest and tenderest of all German wines may even now still call it Eitelsbacher Karthäuserhofberg.

## The Ruwer

The wines of the Ruwer have even less alcohol than those of the rest of the Moselle. Like the Saar wines they need a hot summer to ripen properly, and can be worthless in bad vintages. But in a fine year (1971 was an example) there are people who argue that they are Moselle's, Germany's, even the world's best white wines. The villages of Mertesdorf, Waldrach and Kasel are the only three of any consequence, with only about five thousand acres between them. Apart from the Karthäuserhofberg, the greatest estate of the valley is called Maximin Grünhaus, the property of the von Schubert family. The beautiful leafy label of this estate has brought more pleasure into my house than almost any other on earth.

The *Grosslage* name for this whole region is Trierer Römerlay. Altogether it covers some eighteen hundred acres of vineyards.

## The Middle Moselle

From the mouth of the Ruwer downwards the Moselle is accompanied by vineyards, but the hills stand back and the essential combination of steep slopes and the twisting river, which seems to be a prerequisite for the best wines here, is lacking. The *Grosslage* names that cover this area are Longuicher Probstberg (about seventeen hundred acres) and Klusserather St Michael with five thousand five hundred acres. As soon as the river plunges back into the hills, however, the vineyards come clustering round, and the names of Trittenheim, Neumagen and Dhron, though not on the top level, are familiar from good wine-lists.

*Piesport*

Piesport is the first village in the Middle Moselle which grows wine in the highest category. It stands on the outside of a broad bend in the river at the foot of an amphitheatre, two miles long and five hundred feet high, of solid vines. The name of one Piesport *Einzellage*, Goldtröpfchen, had rather got out of control under the old regime: wine from miles around was selling as "little gold drop". The new law, however, restricts Goldtröpfchen to two hundred and fifty acres of the big hill and installs Piesporter Michelsberg as the *Grosslage* name for a long stretch of the river up- and down-stream (which was what Goldtröpfchen had virtually become by default). The *Grosslage* has three thousand four hundred acres. Treppchen, Falkenberg and Gunterslay are the other important Piesport vineyards now.

*Brauneberg*

The wines from Piesport, and from the next stretch of the river down to Brauneberg, are some of the least characteristically sharp of the Moselle. The north bank of the river here is a continuous wall of vineyard above the villages of Wintrich and Kesten, and opposite the little town of Brauneberg. Kesten is known for the fine wine of one vineyard, Paulinshofberg, which is very like Brauneberg wine. Brauneberg has more spiciness and richness than any other Moselle. It is the most hock-like wine of the river and, perhaps for this reason, used to be considered easily the best in the last century. Brauneberger Juffer is the best-known site.

Brauneberg is one of several villages on the Moselle which are across the river from their vineyards, leaving the south-facing slopes entirely free for vines. Before the bridge was built it meant that the growers had to go to work by boat, and bring their grapes to the press-house by boat at vintage-time, but they believed that it was better than giving up good vineyards to mere houses.

*Bernkastel*

From Wintrich downstream the *Grosslage* Bernkasteler Kurfürstlay (with about four thousand five hundred acres) takes over from Piesporter Michelsberg. The town of Bernkastel-Kues straddles the river round the next bend. The river at Bernkastel makes such a sharp turn that the vineyards cross over and face south from the right bank. From the bridge between Bernkastel and Kues there is one of the finest views on the whole river, looking north-west downstream at an unbroken cliff of vines six or seven miles long, with the vineyards of Bernkastel merging into the vineyards of Graach, and those of Graach into those of Wehlen. This, by common consent, is the greatest stretch of the Moselle from the point of view of wine.

Bernkastel is one of the prettiest of all wine-towns. Along its front runs the river, high above hang the vineyards and the ruined castle of Landshut, and in the centre is preserved a perfect medieval town square of brown and white timbered houses, inclining in gossiping attitudes over narrow alleys. Right over the town, gazing down its chimney-pots from a slaty slope as steep as a gable, is one of the most famous vineyards in Germany, Bernkasteler Doktor. With the site which flanks it, Graben, it makes what many consider the best Moselle. The Doktor is only a small vineyard but it has three owners: Dr Thanisch, Deinhard & Co and the Lauerburg estate. If these are considered the supreme Moselle wines, many others from the neighbouring Bernkastel vineyards of Bratenhöfchen, Mattheisbildchen and Lay, and particularly the wine from the scattered properties of the Parish

Church (called Pfarrgut St Michael), are also magnificent.

The typical Bernkasteler is one of the drier of the Moselles, with something of the stony, mineral taste that occasionally reminds me of Chablis, yet no less of the fragrance of Riesling grapes than any other. Now, however, the wave of fashion which made the Doktor the best-known wine of the river has passed downstream, and higher prices are paid for the wines of Wehlen.

*Graach*  Bernkastel's vines merge with those of Graach. Graacher Himmelreich and Dompprobst, and the von Kesselstatt's estate of Josephshof, are the best-known growths. They are very fine, but they tend to be overshadowed by the reputations of their neighbours. Exactly where *Wehlen* on that mighty hill Graach ends and Wehlen begins I am not sure, for there is no break in the vineyards, but at Wehlen we come to the Moselle's most highly prized site, Wehlener Sonnenuhr. *Sonnenuhr* means sun-dial, and there is a massive one shaped out of an outcropping cliff halfway up the vineyard. The best Wehlen wines (all from Sonnenuhr; Nonnenberg opposite is not in the same class) are rich and full-flavoured for the Moselle, but manage never to overbalance into heaviness. There is always an underlying delicacy about them which distinguishes them clearly from, for example, a great hock of the Rheingau. They fill your mouth and linger on your palate not out of strength, but simply out of lovely freshness, with always a suggestion of the taste of honey.

There is one great name in Wehlen: the Prüm family and its connections. Various branches of the family make all the finest Wehlen wines. They live in solid big houses down by the river's edge, gazing up at the sun-dial—for Wehlen is another of the villages which is across the river from its best vineyards. You might easily pay twice as much for a bottle of their best wine as for any claret or burgundy in the world.

*Zeltingen*  Wehlen does not end the great hill. Its vineyards merge in turn with those of Zeltingen-Rachtig. Zeltinger has long been one of the Moselle names most often seen on good-value bottles of middlequality wine. It has indeed a hundred acres of the superlative Sonnenuhr within the parish, but the huge Himmelreich is less even and Schlossberg across the river is largely in the same case as Wehlener Nonnenberg: on the shady side of the hill. The *Grosslage* name here (for all Zeltingen-Rachtig, Wehlen and Graach) is Graacher Munzlay.

*Ürzig*  After Zeltingen the river bends again, and the best vineyards cross over back to the left bank, which is once again the northern one. On *Erden* the bend lies the town of Ürzig, whose vineyards join those of Erden immediately downstream, on an even steeper slope and in even more difficult and rocky conditions than those we have just passed. Production here is small, but in good vintages the wine is excellent and full of the spicy, fragrant character suggested by the name of Ürzig's best *Einzellage*: Würzgarten or spice-garden. Erden and Ürzig can be considered the last of the parishes in the classic heart of the Moselle. In their wines the slightly mineral quality we met in Bernkastel takes a different turn. If Bernkastel suggests flint, Ürzig suggests (suggests not resembles) salt. There is a blunt, earthy quality underlying the fragrance and delicacy here. All their vineyards have similar conditions, making them good names to look out for—only bearing in mind that Ürziger Schwarzlay is a *Grosslage* of three thousand acres covering a number of parishes with none of these special qualities.

*The Lower Moselle*

The great stretch of the Middle Moselle ends here. Farther downstream the vineyards are vitally important as the suppliers of bulk Moselle, and there are three or four names of real value, but nothing of the supreme quality we have just passed.

The best-known names of this stretch are those of Kröv, the next but one parish to Erden, with its Nacktarsch (bare bottom) vineyard—now a *Grosslage* including twelve hundred acres—and Zell, whose Schwarzer Katz (Black Cat) is now a sixteen-hundred-acre *Grosslage*.

Less-known parishes to look out for are Kinheim, Traben-Trarbach and Enkirch—particularly the latter, whose site is almost an echo of Bernkastel's site upstream. I have also come across wines of considerable quality from Reil and Neef—but these are names you will rarely meet outside Germany.

*The Rheingau*

The Taunus mountains are really no more than hills, forested with pine and beech to their crests, but they cause the Rhine to change direction and, instead of flowing north, to skirt them to the west, running along their south side for twenty-five miles between Mainz and Rüdesheim. The combination of shelter from the hills to the north and the moisture and warmth of the wide river to the south is supposed to be the secret of the best of all Rhine wines, for the foothills of the Taunus coming down to the river are called the Rheingau.

The Rheingau is to the Rhine what the great cliff between Bernkastel and Zeltingen is to the Moselle: the best of many good things. The little towns along its busy riverfront from west to east are Rüdesheim, Geisenheim, Winkel, Mittelheim, Oestrich, Hattenheim, Erbach, Eltville and Walluf. In the hills behind these are Johannisberg, Hallgarten, Kiedrich and Rauenthal. All come into the single *Bereich* of Johannisberg. All, except possibly Mittelheim, are or can be the names of great wines.

Rheingau wines come in great variety. It is harder to generalize about them than it is to generalize about, say, the Médoc. But of all hocks they are the best balanced, most firm (as opposed to soft) in your mouth, with most scent and the cleanest, most positive characters. They owe some of these qualities to the fact that the Riesling is grown on most of the sites, exclusively on all the best ones, of the Rheingau, whereas along the rest of the Rhine the more prolific Sylvaner and lately the Müller-Thurgau is dominant.

At the western end of the Rheingau where the river turns north the hills are cut clean through by the stream. The two high banks crowd together over a little castled island, and the water runs in rapids as though it is still only just breaking through. This is the Bingen Hole. It is as far up the river as ships from the sea used to get before the days of steam-tugs. To it the town of Bacharach downstream owed its reputation for wine—it was once thought to be the source of all good Rhine wine—although its vineyards are insignificant.

*Rudesheim*

On the Rheingau side this flurry of rock and water is overlooked by the castle of Ehrenfels on the Rüdesheimer Berg. The Berg is the high hill behind and downstream of the town of Rüdesheim. All the best Rüdesheimer vineyards are on it, and three use it as an additional name, so that, for example, the wine from above Schloss Ehrenfels is known as Rüdesheimer Berg Schlossberg. Rüdesheimer wines are called variously the softest wines of the Rheingau (by those who do not like them) and the most delicate (by those who do). It is agreed, though, that they have the curious habit of being better in fairly wet years than in very hot summers. The drainage of the steep hill is so effective that without rain the vines fail to grow and ripen properly, so that the lesser wines of Rüdesheim are the ones to choose in a great vintage. For the last few years the Berg has been the scene of a rationalization scheme for consolidating properties, to simplify the endless subdivision of vineyards. It has been done by the direct method: with a bulldozer. Machines levelled the tiers of old terraces into great smooth slopes on which, though they are steep, some kinds of mechanical aids can work. One grower calculated that when the changes were finished the work which used to be done by twenty-five men could be done by ten.

Rüdesheim is a resort—and in summer a place to avoid. It sums up the life of the Rhine-front, with its crowds, its ferries, the throbbing barges and the clattering trains which pass just under all the towns' windows along the river.

Rüdesheimer Burgweg is the *Grosslage* of Rüdesheim—and also of Geisenheim upstream and Lorch downstream; a parish which cannot be said to be in the same quality-class. Immediately downstream from Rüdesheim and round the corner of the Berg is the one parish of the Rheingau which makes red wine: Assmanshausen. Assmanshausen is famous and much appreciated in Germany—largely owing to the big holding of the State Domain which is in a good position to sell its wines well. But to a non-German there is little to be said for these pallid reds, either of Assmanshausen or of the Ahr, the little district farther downstream still, towards Bonn, which is Germany's only uniquely red-wine area.

*Geisenheim*

The wines of Geisenheim, the next little town going upstream along the Rhine-front, are some of the Rheingau's least well known, but are no less excellent for that. On the far side of Geisenheim rises the most unmistakable, and perhaps the most famous, vineyard in Germany, the hill of Schloss Johannisberg with the castle on top, its

*Johannisberg*

vineyards falling away round it like skirts. Schloss Johannisberg really belongs to the wines of the river-front rather than the hills behind, although the village of Johannisberg and most of the other vineyards with its name lie farther back in the hills. It is the property of Prince Metternich. Schloss Johannisberger wines are distinguished from each other in quality by a series of coloured capsules on the bottles, in which it is hard to discern any logic. You would be fairly safe in assuming, though, that of any two of the wines of any given year the more expensive of them would be the sweeter. Of all the great wines of the Rheingau they are perhaps the mildest and most delicate in flavour, for among the others there are some powerful and spicy mouthfuls.

Johannisberger Erntebringer, formerly a highly esteemed vineyard of the parish, is now a *Grosslage* including all Johannisberg and a little of Geisenheim, Winkel and Mittelheim. Bereich Johannisberg, as I have mentioned, is now a name available to any wine from the whole Rheingau.

*Winkel*

At the foot of the Schloss Johannisberg hill to the east the vineyards of Winkel stretch down to the river and up into the hills behind. Their most famous site is known without the village name, simply as Schloss Vollrads, but sandwiched between the two schlosses lie a number of really excellent sites, the best known of which is Winkeler Hasen-

*Schloss Vollrads*

sprung, or Hare-Leap. Schloss Vollrads lies well back from the river in a fold in the hills, with an air of great dignity and reserve, beneath its mighty square tower. It is the estate of Count Matuschka-Greiffenclau, whose family have lived there since the fourteenth century. Here again, quality is designated by a system of coloured capsules and different label markings which very few people alive can know by heart. Many argue, however, that the best of Vollrads, with its extreme elegance and lovely bouquet, is the best of the Rheingau, and therefore of the Rhine.

*Mittelheim and Oestrich*

Mittelheim and Oestrich continue the vineyards along the river. Oestricher Doosberg and Lenchen are the best of half a dozen good vineyards, producing wine with a certain attractive earthiness and a marvellous long flavour. The Oestrich *Grosslage* is Gottesthal. The next town of Hattenheim has it both ways; three very fine vineyards down by the river and one supreme one up in the hills a mile behind. The riverside sites are called Nüssbrunnen, Heiligenberg and Mannberg. The hill site, famous enough not to use the name Hattenheimer, is Steinberg.

*Hattenheim*

*Hallgarten*

Steinberg stands on a steep slope to the south-west nearer to the village of Hallgarten than to Hattenheim. Hallgarten is a dull little place, the highest in the hills of the Rheingau villages, with three very fine vineyards, Würzgarten, Jungfer and Schönhell, which give good, strong and long-lasting wine. Steinberg, however, has the advantage not only of a magnificent situation, surrounded by a wall (a cousin of the famous wall at Clos de Vougeot in Burgundy, built by the Cistercians seven hundred years ago), but of having one owner, the Federal State Domain. Not all its sixty acres are of the same quality, but it must be considered among the greatest German vineyards.

*Steinberg*

*Kloster Eberbach*

The monastery which created the Steinberg, Kloster Eberbach, still exists in perfect preservation in a little green valley behind it. It was secularized by Napoleon, and now belongs to the State, which uses it for official receptions and wine-auctions, as well as for the cellaring of Steinberger wine. It is hard to say which is the most fascinating part of this lovely place; the great empty church with its magical echoes, the cloisters, the vast dormitories or the old press-house, where the giant wine-presses of the Middle Ages still stand.

Beside the State Domain the most important proprietor in Hattenheim is Count von Schönborn. Its *Grosslage* name is Deutelsberg.

*Kiedrich*

*Erbach*

The next of the hill-towns, Kiedrich, is not particularly famous, though it has three vineyards in a class not far from the top—Wasseros, Gräfenberg and Sandgrub. Erbach, down on the Rhine, has a much higher reputation, no doubt because of its one supreme site—Markobrunn (or Marcobrunn, for different owners spell it in different ways). The river-front at Erbach is dominated by Schloss Reinhartshausen, the mansion of the late Prince Friedrich of Prussia, which he made into an hotel.

Markobrunn is perhaps the most surprising-looking of all great vineyards, for it is on almost flat land, a mere slope, down by the railway near the river. The soil and drainage must, however, be perfect, for its name is certainly among the top six, possibly among the top four, of the Rheingau. Erbach wines can be sold under the Hattenheim *Grosslage* name: Deutelsberg.

*Eltville*

Eltville, which virtually joins Erbach on the east, might almost be called the Zeltingen of the Rheingau; it touches the greatest but itself produces large quantities of fine and reliable, reasonably priced wine. In Eltville live two of the great growers of the Rheingau, Baron Langwerth von Simmern and Count Eltz, beside the headquarters of the State Domain, the biggest proprietor of all.

*Rauenthal*     Behind Eltville in the hills lies the final jewel—the most highly valued land in Germany, the vineyards of Rauenthal. The name of Rauenthaler Baiken is not as familiar as, for example, Schloss Johannisberg, but its wine regularly fetches a higher price, the highest price of any Rhine wine. The other great vineyards are Gehrn, Nonnenberg, Rothenberg, Wulfen and Langenstück. Rauenthalers are big and strong, spicy and smooth, marvellously flower-scented and astonishingly delicate in the complexity of their flavours. The Rauenthal *Grosslage* name, Steinmacher, applies also to the wines of Eltville and those of the more obscure parishes of Martinsthal and Ober- and Nieder-walluf which bring the Rheingau to an end at the outskirts of the big city of Wiesbaden, the capital of the state of Hesse.

*Hochheim*     There remains only Hochheim, the origin of the word hock, which officially lies in the Rheingau, though in fact it is some way off to the east on low hills overlooking the confluence of the Rhine and the Main. A few growers at Hochheim maintain exceedingly high standards which keep its name among the better Rheingau wines. Werner, Pabstmann and Aschrott are the growers, and the most famous vineyards Domdechaney, Kirchenstück and Königin Viktoria Berg, named after Queen Victoria by an enthusiastic proprietor on hearing how fond she was of "hock".

## Rheinhessen

Rheinhessen is the opposite bank of the Rhine to the Rheingau, and its huge hinterland. Its best vineyards lie a little upstream, above the river bend at Mainz, on a long slope set back from the river.

Most of Rheinhessen is devoted to quantity production of second-rate wine, using the Sylvaner and Müller-Thurgau grapes. Except under certain rare conditions, the Sylvaner gives wine with nothing like the balance and clarity of flavour, the scent or the refreshing acidity of the Riesling. Sylvaner wine, the typical Rheinhessen wine the bulk of which is sold as Liebfraumilch, has, as its fault or virtue according to your taste, a softness of character which makes it pleasant, unobtrusive and not particularly memorable. Less than 10 per cent of the Rheinhessen vineyards are planted with Riesling, but these 10 per cent grow virtually all the best wine.

There are only half a dozen parishes in the district which make outstandingly fine wine. One of them is probably the best known of all the wine-towns of Germany abroad; not only, however, because of the quality of its best wine but because its name has long been what is known as generic—in other words free to be used by any who fancy that their wine is similar enough for them to get away with it.

*Nierstein*     The famous name is Nierstein. It stands right on the Rhine, about ten miles above Mainz, with its great sand-red slope of hill behind it. Along the hill are ranged the sites whose famous individual names are still intact—Hipping, Rosenberg and Pettenthal. Pettenthal at the

*Nackenheim*     north end runs on into the parish of Nackenheim, where it is called Rothenberg. These wines, both Niersteiners and Nackenheimers, are the finest of Rheinhessen, as scented as Rheingau wines, as solid, full-flavoured and individual. The name Rehbach used to be of similar renown: today it is reduced to the ranks as a *Grosslage* name.

Niersteiner Gutes Domtal, the new version of the old "Niersteiner Domtal" (a name which used to be taken in vain more often than any other in Germany) is now the *Grosslage* name for thirty-one vineyards in fifteen parishes in the district.

*Oppenheim*     The next town upstream from Nierstein is Oppenheim, hardly less famous and only slightly less fine. Sackträger is considered the best vineyard, along with Kreuz, Herrenberg and Daubhaus.

This little group of villages represents all the great wine of Rheinhessen. To the north the neighbours, Daubenheim and Bodenheim, and to the south Dienheim, Guntersblum, Alsheim and Mettenheim, produce some similar wines but more of the common kind. Otherwise the only wine of Rheinhessen which deserves to be called fine comes from the far corner of the district, across on the Rhine facing Rüdesheim at Bingen, where the tributary Nahe breaks the hills of the left bank to pour its contribution into the main stream.

*Bingen*  The hill above Bingen on the east, seen from down by the Nahe, seems to ape the Rüdesheimer Berg, across the Rhine, giving its vines a perfect exposure to the south and south-west. It may be the sandstone which gives the hill its name—Scharlachberg, the scarlet hill. It is said about Bingen wine that it has a slightly smoky taste from the smoke of the trains which pass the vineyards. The same thing has been said of the Bernkasteler Doktor—that it tastes of the smoke of the chimneys below it. Of the many tall stories about wine this is perhaps the tallest. Whether the change to diesel engines and central heating has given the wines a taste of oil I have not heard.

## The Nahe

The Nahe is not a dramatic stream where it joins the Rhine. It has been flowing straight through flat country for fifteen miles. But in its upper reaches, where it winds through the lower hills of the Hunsrück —the mountains which put the loops into the course of the Moselle— it has the kind of pretty scenery which seems unfailingly productive of good wine.

Nahe wine is described as halfway between Rhine and Moselle, which is exactly true geographically, but less so gastronomically. The Nahes are like very fine and rather delicate Rheingau wines. Some Rheingau wines have a faint taste of earth under their floweriness, as though you were drinking the whole garden. This seems to me to be the taste of the Nahe: others have described it as blackcurrants or honeysuckle, but in so subjective a matter language is more likely to give the wrong impression than the right. Perhaps it is better to play safe and say that Nahe wines are (with one or two notable exceptions) comparatively light and mature quickly, but nonetheless have excellent scent and a flavour which puts them among Germany's very best.

*Schlossböckelheim*  The Nahe is divided into two *Bereichs*: the upper river under the name of Schlossböckelheim, and the lower under the name Kreuznach. The two names have for long been the most famous on the river: Schlossböckelheim (in reality a tiny village) for its two superlative vineyards, Kupfergrübe and Felsenberg, the source of a very limited supply of wine of the highest possible quality, and Kreuznach as the name of the main town of the district, a famous spa (Bad *Bad Kreuznach*  Kreuznach is its full name) and with its big vineyards a notable source of good upper-middle-class wine.

Massive Nahe vineyards scattered over an upland area twenty miles by thirty, which can only be rated with the bulk of Rheinhessen wine as fair-to-middling, come under these *Bereich* names. It is worth committing to memory six or seven of the parish names of the Nahe, even if they are little known compared with those of, say, the Moselle. Bad Kreuznach is already well known; particularly its vineyards of Kahlenberg, Schoss Kauzenberg and Brücken (bridges) which

*Niederhausen*

occupy the best slope south-eastwards over the river. Schlossböckelheim will always be in demand. But Niederhausen is surprisingly little known for the headquarters of perhaps the most distinguished of all the State Domain estates: its vineyards of Hermannshöhle, Hermannsberg and Steinberg are unsurpassed. And at the village of Traisen lies a vineyard with a unique aspect and conditions, whose wine can at its best be equal to any in Germany: the tiny six-acre Bastei which is no more than the crumbled detritus at the foot of the six-hundred-foot cliff of red sandstone which drops to the river, facing due south, before the Kreuznach bend.

Below Bad Kreuznach (which is almost as famous for its Seitz factory, where the original and best wine-filters are made, as for its wine) the outstanding vineyards are fewer and more scattered. Winzenheim, Langenlonsheim, Laubenheim and Münster-Sarmsheim are probably the best parishes. The last, whose wine is labelled Munsterer so-and-so, contains State Domain vineyards, including the redoubtable Dautenpflänzer whose name I find hard to forget.

Beside the State Domain the firms of von Plettenberg, Herf and Anheuser make some of the best wine of the Nahe. But it is a region of high standards, with excellent co-operatives as well as many good growers. The words *Winzerverein* and *Winzergenossenschaft*, which both mean co-operative, are not to be despised in any part of Germany.

## The Palatinate

The Palatinate (in German Pfalz) is not far south of Rheinhessen— Worms is indeed almost in both regions—but it seems to enjoy a completely different climate. It is more like Alsace, which is said to be the sunniest part of France. The orchards of the Palatinate, which cover the valley-floor on the left bank of the Rhine up to the base of the Haardt mountains (the range which at its French southern end is called the Vosges) are full of southern fruit—figs, peaches and almonds. The foothills of the Haardt are covered with Germany's most extensive vineyards, growing wine in easier conditions than anywhere else in the country.

Only a small part of this region, as in the case of Rheinhessen, concerns itself with fine wines. A great deal of Palatinate wine is intended for immediate drinking, and the extremely *gemütlich* little cafés, heavily timbered in the German forest manner, supply excellent open wine which is much stronger than that of the Moselle, and is best, I think, when it is rather sweet and very fresh. When it is dry it is heavy and rough. All Palatinate wines, however, have more flavour and fuller body than other German wines—and usually rather less scent. For this reason they are the ones to drink with food. With the game of the forests, which is always the best thing to eat in this part— and most parts—of Germany, they are perfect. Venison and wild boar are commonplace, I should add, and by no means the exotic luxuries they sound.

The Palatinate divides naturally into two parts of roughly equal length with the town of Neustadt in the middle. It has two *Bereich* names corresponding with this division. The northern part, known as the Mittelhaardt, is the one known for all the finest wines of the region. But the southern part, Südliche Weinstrasse (or southern wine-road), deserves more notice than it usually gets (from myself, among others).

*The Südliche
Weinstrasse*

The Südliche Weinstrasse has commonly been dismissed in the past as the bulk-wine region, with no pretensions to quality. But conversations and tastings at the Wine School in Neustadt, one of the most highly regarded in Germany, have convinced me that we can look for better and better wine from a whole hillside of parishes as yet virtually unknown. Starting in the north of the region, just south of Neustadt, the villages of Hambach, Maikammer, St Martin, Edenkoben, Rhodt, Birkweiler, Leinsweiler, Ilbesheim, Eschbach, Billigheim (whose best vineyard rejoices in the name of Venusbuckel) and Bergzabern are all known to me for better than ordinary wine. You are not, for the moment at least, likely to see many *Einzellage* wines from this sort of area. Much use is made of the *Grosslage* names. Rhodter Ordensgut, Eschbacher Herrlich, Berzaberner Kloster Liebfrauenberg, and the southernmost, right on the French border, Schweigener Guttenberg are prominent. But things are made no easier by the fact that any of the parish names from within the *Grosslage* might turn up in combination with the *Grosslage* name. For example, instead of Berzaberner Kloster Liebfrauenberg, you might see Göcklinger K.L.—which would of course mean that the wine comes from Göcklingen but is taking advantage of the theoretically better-known name of Kloster Liebfrauenberg, as it now legally can.

*Grapes: old and new*

If the place-names all seem a bit daunting down here, so do some of the grapes. This is not Riesling country. Sylvaner and Müller-Thurgau are the most popular vines to grow, but there are quantities of kinds only seen on an experimental basis in most of Germany. Scheurebe (an old cross between Riesling and Sylvaner) can make excellent wine in a heavy, perfumed style. Murio-muscat carries the same style to extremes: it is much too aromatic for my liking. Gewürztraminer is grown, but with nothing like the success it meets in Alsace down the road. Weissburgunder or Pinot Blanc is very happy (particularly on chalky soil) and ripens well in nine years out of ten, making good clean full-bodied wine, often among the best of the district. Ruländer is the same as the Tokay of Alsace.

Then there are plantations of really new grapes whose performance is still being closely watched. Kerner is one of the most popular, though I am not entirely convinced by the wine I have tasted. Ehrenfelser is said to come nearest to Riesling. The air is bracing with experiment, and every restaurant provides an opportunity to form opinions: you can get most of the dozens of wines they list by the glass. In some they have special numbered holders for eight glasses at a time, each filled with a different wine. Lunch can take quite a while.

*The Mittelhaardt*

North of Neustadt in the Mittelhaardt the atmosphere is rather different. Long-founded prosperity is written all over the villages. So grand are the growers' and merchants' houses that their high walls and towering entrances give the narrow village streets an almost Andalusian air. The middle of the Mittelhaardt must be compared with the Moselle below Bernkastel, or the Rhine below Oppenheim, for its concentration of valuable and prestigious land. Kallstadt, Ungstein, Bad Dürkheim, Wachenheim, Forst, Deidesheim and Ruppertsberg are the parishes in question. Of these, Wachenheim, Forst and Deidesheim are the *crème de la crème*.

Much of the best land in these three parishes belongs to three all-powerful growers whose names all begin with B: Bassermann-Jordan, Bürklin-Wolf, and von Bühl. Undoubtedly they had some influence on the law-givers, for a clutch of their best *Einzellagen* remains virtually intact: notably Wachenheimer Goldbächel, Rechbächel and Gerumpel, Forster Jesuitengarten, Kirchenstück and

Freundstück, and Deidesheimer Hohenmorgen, Kalkofen, Grain-hubel and Leinhöhle. These top names have a *Grosslage* name virtually all to themselves: Forster Mariengarten. But there are a lot of *Grosslage* names to learn here: Kallstadter Kobnert in the north, Dürkheimer Feuerberg, Wachenheimer Schenkenböhl, Forster Schnepfenflüg, Deidesheimer Hofstück, and then, going south to Neustadt, Gimmel-dinger Meerspinne.

Deidesheim and Forst have more Riesling vines than anywhere else in the Palatinate. The Traminer, Scheurebe, and Muscat are grown to add spiciness to the flavour of the wine. In these near-perfect grape-growing conditions there is a considerable emphasis on late-gathered wines, *Auslesen* and really sweet *Beerenauslesen* and *Trocken-beerenauslesen*. Often, here, they are magnificently rich in flavour, deep gold-orange in colour and almost tropical in scent.

## Franconia

Franconian wine is the only German wine which is bottled in anything but the familiar long thin flask. The Franconian bottle is the *Bocksbeutel*, a flagon shaped like the kind of wineskin which would swing from the girdle of a well-fed monk. It is a jealously guarded right to put wine in this kind of bottle, which establishes the individuality of Franconia's wine—usually called, generically, *Steinwein*— perhaps better than the wine, bottled normally, would do.

### Steinwein

Steinwein, from the banks of the Main in and around Würzburg, is the most similar to French wines of the wines of Germany. You can often honestly use the word dry about it, which you cannot do with most German wines. Instead of balancing between sweet and sour, Steinwein has strength and stoniness, slight earthiness perhaps, not unlike Chablis. Both the Riesling and the Sylvaner are grown: many say that here is the only place where the Sylvaner makes really fine wine. Not all Steinwein is made dry, however. *Beerenauslesen* as sweet as any in Germany are made in hot years.

The best Steinwein parishes are, above all, Würzburg itself, the capital of Franconia, Randersacker, Iphofen and Escherndorf (whose best vineyard is called Lump, which means idiot). The finest grower is the Juliusspital, a hospital in Würzburg. The normal, not late-gathered, Steinwein of any of these villages in a normal vintage is the most suitable German wine of all for drinking with a meal, and makes a very fine match with fish. Here its comparatively non-aromatic and more substantial nature stands it in good stead.

These are Germany's great wine regions, but not its only ones. We shall have more and more motive to explore farther in the future; certainly south up the Rhine to the vineyards of Baden, (where Germany's biggest co-operative is making a spectacular mark both on the landscape and the market for soft and strong white wines). For the moment there is plenty to study in these traditional areas. One of the most remarkable things about them is that their wine has stayed, in comparison with, for example, Bordeaux, quite reasonable in price. At present there is no French wine of the quality of a fine Moselle or Rheingau, estate-bottled and of a great vintage, at anything like its price.

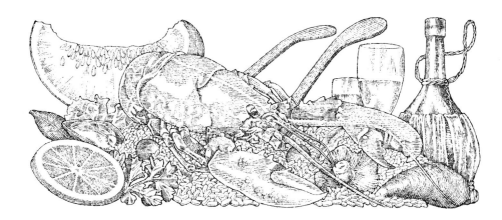

# Italian White Wines

Nobody knows all the wines of Italy. It is the biggest wine-producer in the world, and the most disorganized. There are trends and tendencies in this region or that which can be recorded without too much trouble, but there is always the individual to be considered. In Italy he still rules the roost.

So when I say that the best of the wine in such a village is white, you are not unlikely to go there and taste a red wine which is just as good as the white wine, or perhaps better. When I say that it is still, it is very likely to be sparkling; when it is supposed to be dry it will turn out sweet. It will certainly be a mistake on my part. It may even be a mistake on the part of the grower. But Italy is like that. Its most sedate bottles are liable to explode into fountains of delicious froth; its most publicized wines to lack anything worth talking about and its unknown ones to be like nectar. Next after a corkscrew, what you need to enjoy Italian wine to the full is a sense of humour.

In the last decade the Italian government has made valiant efforts to change all this. In 1963 they passed a new set of wine laws, intended to do for Italy what the laws of *Appellation Contrôlée* have done for France. It is more than laws can do to change the Italian character, but what laws can do they are doing. Certainly one's expectations from a bottle of Italian wine can be higher today than ten years ago.

*Red versus white*

The white wines of Italy never quite achieve the distinction of some of the reds. The best that I know have good clean characters, sometimes the right balance and the right shade of acidity, sometimes a refreshing scent, sometimes a lovely greeny-gold colour. Soave, for example, can have all of these. But they tend to be dull. It has often been said that no wine can achieve dullness under certain characteristically Italian conditions—under an arbour of vines, on a terrace high above the sea, in the square facing a cathedral—but this is not a comment on the wine.

Taken out of their context, with their props, so to speak, removed, they are very often a disappointment. There is a mediumness about their characters which I long to force one way or the other. Those that do commit themselves to something definite (some Sardinian wines, for example), carry it off beautifully. But whether it is a matter of over-careful or over-careless making, or whatever it may be, the majority are not inspired.

## The wine-making industry

The truth is that in many parts of Italy there is still no middle stage between the totally primitive state of affairs where the farmer's son treads the grapes in a wash-tub, hanging on to the side of an open-ended barrel—the family fermenting-vat—for support, and the new, hygienic *cantina sociale* (or co-operative), with every device for avoiding the old weaknesses of inconsistency and cloudiness and fermentation in the bottle, including sterilizing and pasteurizing plants. They are justifiably proud of producing a stable wine, as bright as a new pin. They have achieved a good deal. But they have thrown out the baby with the bath-water.

This makes you realize the tremendous achievement of the French wine-industry. Somehow in France exactly the right degree of orderliness, of regularity and cleanliness to make fine, secure, characteristic wine has been reached by peasants of no more apparent intelligence than their Italian counterparts. Yet both have been making wine for an equal length of time. It is simply that in Italy a tradition of craftsmanship has never grown up. There has never, until just now, been the large middle-class market to urge on the grower. Where he is making wine only for his village his standards do not matter. But in producing wine for the cities he is completely out of his depth, and the *cantina sociale* has to come and do his wine-making for him.

You can never expect to find in Italian wine, then, the quality which we call greatness in a French or German one. It can be very fine indeed, but (so far) that is where it stops.

## Italian wine-names

In Italy vineyards are almost never named on labels as they are in France and Germany. The name of an Italian wine is either that of the grape-variety involved or of the district where it was made, or, in a few cases, a simple name such as Lachryma Christi or Est Est Est, implying that it comes from the particular place which is famous for this wine, but not explicitly saying so.

Which are the grapes and which the villages is not always obvious. In Piedmont, for example, Barolo is a place, but Barbera a grape. In Alto Adige, Termeno is a village and Teroldego a grape. Certain grape-names—Nebbiolo, Trebbiano, Malvasia, Moscato, Aleatico, Sangiovese—occur again and again. Eventually one learns them, but there is no golden rule. Italian wine-labels are a law unto themselves. I have seen a modest ordinary red wine in Italy labelled Château-bottled Vintage Claret, whether out of sheer exuberance or in the hope of finding some exceptionally gullible customer it is hard to say.

Under the new laws Italian wines, like German, are divided into three levels of quality. The lowest, more or less equivalent to the German *Tafelwein*, is known as *denominazione semplice*. All the producer or merchant is allowed to state is the broad region of production. No special standards have to be met.

The second level can be broadly equated with the French *Appellations Contrôlées*. The term *denominazione di originè controllata* (or *D.O.C.*) applies only to wines of set standards from recognized and defined areas. At present most of Italy's best wines wear a *D.O.C.* label. The system can honestly be said to have raised the general standard of Italian exports immeasurably since it was introduced—as soaring export figures have shown. What it has done, above all, is to give the scrupulous merchant an advantage over the unscrupulous.

A third level is allowed for in the 1963 laws. Wines from certain top producers which pass rigorous tests are allowed to use the term *denominazione controllata e garantita.* They must be shipped in the bottle with a seal over the cork. For the moment, however, the development of the hierarchy is still in its early stages. Lack of *e garantita* on a label is no indication that the wine is less than first-class.

Come to that, even the process of defining the D.O.C. areas, the first geographical delineation of Italy's better wine areas and an enormous task, is still not quite complete. Such zones as Chianti Classico, long ago defined by their own *consorzi*, were the starting point. But *consorzi* only existed in the more sophisticated regions: elsewhere the local infighting has sometimes dragged on for years.

## Piedmont

Piedmont, on the French border in the north-west, is the country of Italy's best red wines. White wine, apart from the vastly popular Muscat, most of which is made into Asti Spumante, is almost ignored.

### Cortese

Cortese is the best-known white. It is a dry, light, savoury kind of wine with a peculiar scent and enough taste to linger in your mouth, without being very appealing. Some of the best Cortese is sold under the name of the village of Gavi, as Gavi Bianco.

### Liguria

From Genoa and the coast of Liguria come a number of white wines: Coronata, Portofino, Vermentino, which are all middle-weight, more or less dry, and subject to the Scenic Fallacy. Look out for them there, in other words, but not here. Liguria's most famous wine is Cinqueterre, famous perhaps more for the spectacular tilt of the vineyards into the sea and the fact that in places the grapes have to be fetched off by boat than for any special qualities.

### Cinqueterre

## The Veneto

Crossing the north of Italy to the more important vineyards of the north-east you encounter little white wine with a name of its own. Brescia and Pavia have their own. Vino Pavese I have not tasted, but the Pusterla of Brescia is good, a little aromatic, dry, clean and light.

### Pavia

In the Veneto, which stretches all the way from Venice to Lake Garda, down to Ferrara in the south and north to, at one point, the Austrian border, wine is everywhere. Soave, to start with, which is grown at and around the pretty old village of Soave, north-east of Verona, is often called Italy's best white wine. To me it has never really been better than satisfactory: dullness is its fault; freshness, balance, even delicacy its virtues. It is a pale, dry, "fish" wine, as they say in Italy, bottled in narrow green bottles, like Moselle. The first secret with Soave is to catch it young. The second is to pay a little extra if you can for the Soave Classico. In Soave, as in a number of other D.O.C.s (the neighbouring Valpolicella is an example), the Classico zone is an area-within-the-area where higher standards and slightly greater strength (of character and alcohol) are expected. An enormous *cantina sociale* accounts for the majority of Soave, and does so very well. The Soave of the house of Bolla is perhaps better known.

### Soave

### Bianco de Colli Euganei

South-east of Verona in the lush volcanic Euganean hills sweet, light-weight and very drinkable white muscat wine is made. Wine which is simply called Bianco dei Colli Euganei, on the other hand, is not sweet *moscato* but a mixture of grapes, giving a yellow wine which may be sweet or dry, good or not so good.

### Prosecco

Farther east, north of Venice, Conegliano is well known for rather sweet white wine called by the name of the Prosecco grape. The Prosecco of Treviso, on the other hand, is more delicate and dry.

The same area, and the easternmost province of northern Italy, Friuli, use a minor burgundian grape, the Pinot Gris, which they call the Tocai (it is the same as the Tokay d'Alsace, not the famous Hungarian kind). It gives an aromatic, yellow-lit dry wine which makes a good aperitif. The name Verdiso is another grape-variety, making a dry wine without much strength or character.

*Friuli*  Friuli, to make matters worse, has another grape called the Verduzzo which gives a wine more like the Tocai, often a little sweeter—but once you start going into detail about the different varieties there is no end to it. It is hard enough to know which is the place-name and which the name of the grape in Italy. One is tempted to fall back on the familiar—which is provided in these parts by considerable new plantings of Bordeaux's Sauvignon Blanc, Alsace's Sylvaner, Pinot Grigio and the Italian Riesling. How good their wine will eventually be I cannot say, but so far it is not spectacular.

*Trentino-Alto Adige*  Things are made rather more simple in the province north of Veneto, tucked away between the Dolomites and the Alps to the north of Lake Garda. Many of the people at Bolzano, the more northerly of the two big towns of the region, are German-speaking, and correspondingly more organized about their wine. The Trentino-Alto Adige area makes some of Italy's most attractive and reliable light wine. This region is probably the area of all Italy where most has been done to standardize names and types, to raise standards and to increase sales. It accounts for nearly half of all Italy's wine exports—Austria and Germany take most of them. Names of grapes which are familiar north of the Alps—Sylvaner, Traminer, Riesling, Pinot Blanc and Pinot Grigio—are common. Traminer, indeed (so the locals claim), is a native of these parts. Certainly the German name of the village of Termeno near Bolzano is Tramin.

These are the same vines as the Alsatians grow. The wines rarely reach Alsatian standards, but their characters are easy to guess from a knowledge of Alsace wines. Traminer is spicy and aromatic; Sylvaner lighter and fruity, a little green in taste; Riesling well balanced.

There seem to be good grounds for singling out the neighbourhood of Terlano, between Bolzano and Merano, as the best site for white wine in the upper valley of the Adige. On the steep slopes facing south-west across the river the grapes, mostly Pinot Blanc and Sauvignon, ripen to real sweetness and the wine is strong. Very young *Terlaner*  Terlaner I have tasted in the cellar has been heady, stiff, lively—almost like the best new Austrian wine. The Pinot Blanc was lighter and appley, the Sauvignon recognizably gun-flinty but full-bodied and almost nutty. A touch of bitterness underlies the flavour of most Alto Adige wines as a very agreeable *gout de terroir*.

*Emilia-Romagna*  The little river Trebbia joins forces with the Po at Piacenza, in the west of the long province of Emilia-Romagna, which almost cuts Italy in two south of Milan and north of Florence. The Trebbia has its *Trebbiano*  own grape, the Trebbiano, which makes the sweetish local wine of Piacenza. Presumably this was its first home, but now it is found throughout Italy.

*Scandiano*  As you go south-east across the province, Parma comes next, then the industrial town of Reggio, whose white wine is called Scandiano.

After Reggio comes Modena, famous for motor-cars and the fizzy red wine of Lambrusco, and after Modena, in this flat and tedious *Albana*  landscape, Bologna. Bologna's white wine is Albana. It is middling in every way except in its strength, which can be formidable.

## Tuscany

Tuscany is overwhelmingly the country of one red wine—Chianti. There is such a thing as white Chianti, but it is in no real way the counterpart of the characteristic red. Any white wine grown in the country between Florence and Siena (or, I suspect, anywhere else) can be sold as white Chianti. You can expect it to be quite strong, pleasantly hard, rather earthy and dry.

### Chianti Classico

But in the territory of Chianti Classico, nearer Siena than Florence, a number of once-feudal estates make small quantities of wine in the patient, painstaking way of the French or the Germans, experimenting all the time and perfecting styles of their own. A small part of this wine is white.

### Brolio Bianco

The Barone Ricasoli at Brolio (of whose family I shall say more) makes a Brolio Bianco of a surprising mixture of grape-varieties: classical burgundian Pinot Noir and German Riesling. Neither grape is usually grown in Tuscany at all. The results, with the first-class technique of expert wine-makers (a different matter from the traditional methods of most of Tuscany), are extremely good. Brolio Bianco is one of Italy's best white wines. It has a very marked scent and great delicacy and freshness. You would drink it happily with trout.

### Bianco Val d'Arbia

The more traditional white wine which Ricasoli also makes, and which is made by others, too, in his immediate area, is named after the little river Arbia. Bianco Val d'Arbia, or just Arbia Bianco, is more the wine for salmon than for trout.

The house of Antinori also makes an excellent white under the name Santa Christina. In fact of all Italian white wines I have tasted recently I think this is my favourite: the southern touch of ripeness is there but with a cleanness and polish which is something quite new.

## Elba

The island of Elba between Tuscany and Corsica produces both red and white wines. The white, though rather strong, is dry and refreshing; exactly the thing for open-air suppers of fish and shellfish. Whether it is possible for wines to take on a tang of the sea or not—it may easily just be imagination—Elba to me has something distinctly maritime about it.

## Central Italy

Chianti apart, central Italy is essentially white wine country. It has three names which are familiar to wine-drinkers everywhere. Verdicchio (dei Castelli dei Jesi, to give it its full name) is the dry wine, the fish wine, of the Adriatic coast. Orvieto is the golden dessert wine of Umbria. And Frascati is the eternally memorable, impossible to classify, wine of Rome.

### Frascati

Of the three Frascati is certainly my favourite. Romans complain you can never find a genuine one. All the Frascati in restaurants, they say (except in *their* little place) is made of carrots or old engine oil or no matter what. I seem to have been luckier. The villages south of Rome in the Alban hills, of which Frascati is one, have miles of perfectly good vineyards, and not a few diligent and honest wine-makers. Give me a bottle of San Matteo or Orfevi and I will show you a real Frascati. The word dry gives the wrong idea about this savoury, pale-golden wine. It is not, or should not be, sweet—but rather full of the lush flavour of white grapeskins (Italian white wine is often fermented on the skins), with a certain note of firmness and strength.

The great Frascati experience is to drink it served in a pitcher at a trestle table under the planes outside the cellar. Street-corners in Frascati have stalls selling hot roast pork in chunky salty sandwiches with crumbling bread. The sandwich goes in your right hand; in your left, a tumbler. It is one of Nature's perfect matches. Frascati is as sweet a wine as pork is a sweet meat.

Below ground in Frascati stretch cold, cavernous, musty *grottas* which no modern vintage has been able to fill; the wine-stores of every age of Rome's history.

The villages of Marino, Grottaferrata and Monteporzio Catone all make wine which is sold as Frascati. Other places in the area make similar wine but give it their own name: Albano, from Lake Albano, a volcanic crater-lake hidden in the hills, full of huge tough trout; Castel Gandolfo, where the Pope has his splendiferous summer villa; Velletri; and Colonna.

*Falernum*  Of the favourite wine of ancient Rome, Falernum, a pale shadow (one must presume it used to be better) now remains. It is now a rather heavy dry yellow wine from the coast half way between Rome and Naples.

I should add that like many Italian wines Frascati is also made in a sweet—*amabile*—version. Have nothing to do with it. The *secco* is the real thing.

## Umbria

If you are driving south from Florence to Rome down the Autostrada del Sole you will see the town of Orvieto occupying the top of a table mountain a mile or two away to the right. Orvieto produces one of Italy's most famous white wines: its *abboccato*.

*Orvieto*  All Orvieto is white. It is never very dry (though there exists a so-called *secco*), but always a little soft and velvety. At its best it is comparable with a good minor Sauternes. It is comparatively light in alcohol, or seems so after the Frascati of Rome, which is described by its growers as "food as well as drink".

In places like Orvieto, with its world-famous name, the wine-trade has reached a pitch of sophistication which is not entirely typical of Italy. The firms whose names appear on the bottles are often not growers but shippers, like the makers of sherry. Many buy the produce of small farmers who make their own wine in the countryside, where vines have taken over completely; orchards, cabbage-patches, everything is a mass of vines.

Orvieto is the *locus classicus* of "promiscuous cultivation", as the old style of viticulture is so accurately called in these parts. It seems Virgil's *Georgics* are still used for ready reference on some of these farms: such festoons and swags of vines ramp from tree to tree. In the midst of it all the flat-topped hill stands up, bearing the walled town with its glittering-fronted cathedral, its frescoes, its pottery market and its deeply delved cellars. Wine-making is a patient, undynamic business here. The wine is left to ferment on the farm for the winter following the vintage, and only brought to Orvieto in the spring. The best of the wine is then allowed to go on fermenting very slowly, turning more and more of its rich store of residual sugar into alcohol, for two or even three years, in casks under the earth.

After such a long time in wood it is natural for a wine to be completely dry; all the sugar will have fermented away. The *abboccato* for which Orvieto is famous has to be made by adding a little intensely sweet and scented wine made from dried grapes to the normal, nearly dry, type. There is a modern short-cut—that of stopping the fermentation with sulphur before all the sugar has gone—but the best firms resist it.

It is interesting that even the firms which are most proud of their wine—Barberani and Cortoni is one, Petrurbani another—sterilize and pasteurize before they sell it, so that it cannot change at all once it is in bottle. I suspect this is because nothing they can do, besides leaving it in cask for years so that all the sugar disappears and it is bone-dry, will prevent the fermentation from tending to restart after bottling. Nonetheless there is a real depth of flavour in good Orvieto. It is not so sweet as to go with ice-cream. I would suggest plain cake or a pear as a good accompaniment.

## The Marches and Abruzzi

### Verdicchio

The Adriatic coast opposite Umbria is the province of Marche. Inland from the port of Ancona in the Apennine foothills a small district called the Castelli dei Jesi, a group of five or six villages, makes wine from the Verdicchio grape. It is a fresh and appetizing wine, without much scent or particular character, but pleasantly dry and even a little bitter in your mouth. It has, in fact, more delicacy than most white wines from so far south. It is more like Soave, for example, than Frascati. To this it owes its wide fame. It is sold, either as Verdicchio dei Castelli dei Jesi or just plain Verdicchio, in amphora-shaped bottles all over Italy and is often one of the few Italian wines appearing on wine-lists abroad. You might call it Italy's Muscadet: the standard wine for feasts of fish.

South of the Marches the Trebbiano grape crops up again. Its yellow, rather strong wine is what you are most likely to find in the high empty spaces and lost little towns of the Abruzzi.

## Lazio

### Est Est Est

In the north of the province of Rome the town of Montefiascone has a reputation for a wine called Est Est Est. The story of how it got its name is the only memorable thing about it—and this only because it is impossible to repeat such an absurd name without being asked its meaning.

A bishop called Fugger was on his way to Rome. His servant went ahead of him to report on the facilities (which meant, as all beds were hard and all food tough and poor, the wine). The servant's method was to chalk on inn-doors a cryptic *Est* if the inn passed muster, *Non Est* if not. Arriving saddle-sore and thirsty in Montefiascone, and downhearted by the dismal appearance of the town, he alighted and ordered wine. By some miracle they gave him a good one, because he was moved to give the first three-star accolade in history by scrawling *Est! Est! Est!* on the inn-door. The curious thing is that Fugger went no farther, but ended his days drinking Montefiascone, and no doubt boring his boon-companions to death with the story of the name of Est Est Est.

According to all history and tradition Est Est Est is a white wine. If you ask for it at Montefiascone they will, however, offer you red as well. I think the red (which is sweet and fresh) has a slight edge on the white. Neither is particularly well made, and thick bottles are necessary to avoid bursts from unfinished fermentation. Commercially Est Est Est is normally a semi-sweet or sweet white wine.

South of Rome there is a pause in the wine-country. You still see vines taking their ease over every cottage and up most trees, but there is nothing you would call an industry as such. Oddly enough it is here that most of the favourite vines of ancient Rome were grown. I have never heard a satisfactory explanation of why there was good wine then in places which have none now.

**Campania**

The pace quickens when you come to Campania. Inland from Naples and south down the coast wine is a flourishing business. Not many of these wines are what you would call export quality, but there are some that are very good indeed, and there are some that are exported anyway.

At Naples we have virtually reached the southern limit of white wine making. The ordinary wine here which would come under the heading of white—since it is not red—is brown. It has the flat, oxidized taste of overheated fermentation and overripe grapes. If you do not treat it as white wine (above all do not ice it), it is drinkable. A splash of water often improves it.

**Lachryma Christi**

Most famous of the Campania wines must be Lachryma Christi del Vesuvio. Old crumbled lava clothes the slopes of Mount Vesuvius. Lava soil is ideal for certain varieties of vine. Real Lachryma Christi is the wine of three different white grapes grown on the volcano's flanks. In fact much wine is labelled Lachryma Christi which is grown far from the mountain, and is even red.

The best I have had has come from the firm of Giuseppe Scala in Portici. Mastroberardino is another good producer. Both make pale gold wine of genuine character and delicate sweetness that make delicious drinking.

Individual firms and their products are the things to look for in southern (or indeed in any part of) Italy. The Caruso family, who own the grand old Belvedere Hotel at Ravello, sharing an unbelievable view of the Sorrentine peninsula with the remains of an old Papal

**Ravello**

palace, make some admirable wine. Their Ravello comes in three colours: red, rosé and white. The white is heady but pale and tart enough to be refreshing—qualities it owes to the altitude of the vineyards, the sea-mists which gather in the mountains, and the fact that most of the vines are grown pergola-fashion, even in arbours forming tunnels over the twisting road.

I have no doubt that dedicated research will be rewarded with very agreeable wine in many other places, too. I for one would like to try the strange-sounding Asprinio from Potenza, which Cyril Ray recommends as being pale, light-weight and *frizzante*: the last thing you would expect from such a source.

**Capri**
**Ischia**

Very little of the wine called Capri comes from Capri and I have never had any which was any good. Ischia, on the other hand, has some excellent white wine which, whether it comes from the island or not, is worth looking out for. Two Ischian wines in particular which I have had, Forastera and Biancolella, were good.

**Sicily**

Sicily, funnily enough, has been quicker than the rest of southern Italy to change with the times. A number of Sicilian brands are already quite widely known. Corvo from the estate of the Duca di Salaparuta near Palermo is well made and sound: the red perhaps better than the white. Val di Lupo and Regaleali are other good and similar brands; both, again, from the lands of the nobility. The wines of Etna's slopes are locally well regarded—particularly the Ciclopi, named after the Cyclops whom Odysseus blinded at a spot on the coast just north of Catania (where the rocks the giant threw can still be seen). I'm not sure that Sicily's heart is in white wine making, though. At best they are dull wines. Where Sicily excels is in the making of treacly sweet wines—but these belong in the After-Dinner Wines section.

# Portuguese White Wines

To be in Portugal at vintage-time in September is to see that the whole country north of the river Tagus—about two-thirds of the total—is kept busy by wine. On every road the ox-carts are lumbering and groaning their way to and from the vineyards. In every village street the heady smell of wine-making fills the air. Donkeys jog by with laden panniers. The fields are dotted here and there with working-parties. As you drive through the country details change: ox-harness or the shape of tumbrils for the gathered grapes or the baskets on women's heads or donkeys' backs alter in inexhaustible variety even from village to village. It is not surprising that the wine does too. Most of these country wines are good, but not many of them even have names.

I remember at a little inn at Alcobaça (under the shade of the most superb of monasteries, a palace whose kitchen was designed for titanic feasts—a trout-stream bubbles in at one end, and the chimney is like a blast-furnace) the white wine with a savoury dish of minute clams had a distinct and delicious scent of wild strawberries. It was the local ordinary wine. It would have been welcome anywhere, but it did not even have a name. This is always happening in Portugal. To go through a list of the Portuguese wines which are at all generally available is not necessarily to name the best ones. The list, in any case, is absurdly short, because no-one has studied them properly, or exploited any except the easiest to buy and mature.

*A great producer*

In some ways Portugal comes second only to France among the wine-countries of Europe. She not only produces a great variety of excellent wines, but seems to do it without effort. Some of the things which are true of Italy—that naming is careless, wine-making sometimes amateurish (and sometimes overcommercial), that vineyards' names are never used and vintage dates are used with gay abandon—are true of Portugal too. Organizations and supplies are unpredictable. And yet the wine always seems to reach the standard required. Furthermore it is the cheapest good wine anywhere.

It is literally impossible to pay as much for a bottle of the best Portuguese table wine in the best hotel in Portugal as a carafe of ordinary wine would cost you in England or America. Nor have I ever been given in Portugal any standard open wine which was not as good, or better, than such a wine would be in France.

All the conditions for wine-growing seem to be perfect. It is all too easy to despise the wine merely because it is cheap. If any wine-merchant would seek good growths, make sure that they are well bottled and offer them in England or America, he would be doing a public service.

*Unknown wines*

As things are, the only wines which are offered for sale abroad are the easily handled brands which can be made in sufficient quantity to be worth advertising. They are often far from being Portugal's best. In some cases I was amazed to find when I went to Portugal that what I had taken to be the name of a village was, in fact, just a brand-name (this is the case, for example, with the very good brand of Serradayres).

The government is starting to legislate to rationalize things by approving appellations of origin not unlike those of France. But so far this is not notably successful or fair. All *vinhos verdes*, for example, are approved just because they are *vinhos verdes*, regardless of quality.

But some of the best of all Portuguese white wines, being brands, are unapproved.

These problems are not our concern. I mention them because they underline, and to some extent explain, the foreign wine trade's concentration on wines which are not necessarily the best the country can offer.

Of the appellations which are approved by far the biggest (about three-quarters of the total) and most exploited name is *vinho verde*.

## Vinho verde

Portugal's real speciality among white wines bears the strange name of green wine. It is green in the sense of being young and unstable. Sometimes it seems barely alcoholic: sometimes it is just like new cider. It can even be red, and still be called green.

*Vinho verde* comes from Portugal's northernmost province, the Minho, named after the river which washes the Spanish border to the north. The southern limit of the province is the river Douro in its lower reaches, below the mountains where port-grapes grow. Oporto, in fact, is the city both of port and of *vinho verde*, possibly the two most dissimilar wines in the world.

No countryside compares with the Minho for garden-like beauty. It is astonishing at first that what you are seeing is farmland, and not some vast pleasure-ground. It is small-scale country, where streams and hillocks rather than rivers and mountains divide up the land into a series of little amphitheatres. The eucalyptus tree with its narrow leaves and peeling trunk is the biggest object in sight. Medieval farms, sometimes a little chapel with its cloister converted into a farmyard and full of barrels, two-house hamlets and buried leafy lanes are the landmarks. But the prettiest thing of all is the fields.

*The vines*

Around every field, held high on pergolas to form a maze of green arbours, vines make a border. In the centre, as irregular in shape as pieces of a jigsaw puzzle—octagons, hexagons, wedges, parallelograms—are patches of maize. There are no vineyards, no serried ranks of trimmed and sulphured bushes. The vine grows as it grew in Eden.

The object of holding the vine high and surrounding it with green and growing things is to stop the grapes overripening in the blazing summer sun. White wines as far south as this are usually strong, not refreshing. But by preventing the heat from reflecting off the ground on to the grapes, as it does when they are trained low, and also stopping the residual warmth in the earth at night from continuing the sun's daytime work, the growers of the Minho have contrived to make just the wine they need. It is often only about 9 per cent alcohol, and carries a refreshing trace of acidity. Even the peaches and pears of the Minho, they say, are sharp. The wine needs no maturing, but is drunk while there are still traces of fermentation; tiny bubbles cling to the side of your glass. Above all, you can drink a lot of it. A bottle each is a reasonable lunchtime ration on a Portuguese summer's day.

White *vinho verde* is a marvellous drink on its own. It is often drunk with Portugal's superb fish and shellfish; a good idea when the weather is hot, though a good rich dish makes it taste very thin and watery. If it is simply a matter of quenching thirst, in fact, it is ideal.

*Reputable brands*

Despite the fact that it is a quickly made, quickly drunk wine there is considerable variety in the kinds that are made. The cheaper ones are sometimes no better than water with a squeeze of lemon-juice. Widely known brands such as Casal Garcia, Aveleda and Casal Mendes are the safest. There are a few even better ones: Vinhos de

Moncão's Alvarinho (the name of the grape) Cepa Velha, which bears a vintage year and is bottled in a long green Moselle-type bottle, is perhaps the best—but it is almost leaving the simple, ordinary field of *vinho verde*. It lasts well and even improves in bottle, developing a fine and delicate, almost freesia-like scent, staying fresh but turning into a full-scale table wine. This is not normally the idea. Most *vinho verde* should be drunk as young as possible.

It is so obviously the kind of wine which will appeal even to people who find most wine too strong-tasting, too dry or too heavy—some even, searching for a word, call all wine "bitter"—that the exporting of it has become big business. There never was a wine with less chance of travelling well. Everything made it likely that it would lose all its qualities en route. But careful research has made it possible to ship a slightly sweetened, not quite so fresh version—the Casal Garcia, Casal Mendes and the rest which are gaining ground in Britain and the United States. It is odd that the Portuguese wine which should have most success abroad is the one which is least suited to foreign travel—and far better at home.

## Vinho maduro

Wine which is not green, but which has had a year or two in barrel to settle down and finish fermentation, is described as mature wine—*vinho maduro*. In this category come all the best wines of Portugal.

Five regions producing white *maduro* wines are "approved" by the law. They are Colares, near Lisbon, whose crop is nearly all red; Carcavelos, a little nearer the capital, whose diminutive produce is elaborated as a sort of Madeira; Bucelas, north of Lisbon; Dão, in the north of Portugal but south of the Douro; and the river Douro.

### Carcavelos

Carcavelos I've been very lucky to taste at all, since almost all of what used to be its vineyards are now the suburbs of the resort of Estoril. Since it is in all the reference books, however, I should report my findings. The produce of the Quinta do Barão, the only Carcavelos still sold (as far as I know) is very good wine indeed. I would have guessed it to be a very gentle and exquisite madeira verdelho, with less than madeira's characteristic acidity. Which means that it is sweet, and presumably fortified.

It was the Duke of Wellington's troops who started a craze for the wines of the Lisbon area which lasted for two generations after the Peninsula war. One might surmise that it was they who encouraged the growers to fortify Carcavelos, to make them a local madeira. There is no obvious reason why they should have done so otherwise.

### Bucelas

Bucelas, the other Lisbon vineyard (just north of the city, as Carcavelos is just west) makes its white wine straight, and makes it on the whole very well.

Bucelas, indeed, seems to be something of a cult in Lisbon. The firm of J. C. Alves is the big producer, and his wines are relatively dear and hard to find. There are so many good bottles of white wine to be had in Portugal that I did not find them exceptional; merely dry, fairly fragrant, clean and well made.

### Dão

Dão is the white *maduro* that has most prospects for the future. It is Portugal's white burgundy. It is dry, savoury and clean. It could do with a little more of the richness (as in cream) which makes white burgundy so lovely. But that is a lot to ask. In every case where a very dry white wine is needed—and a soft, not a sharp one—Dão is a great standby. It does not age well, as red Dão does, but grows very flat with time. I have found that it pays to open a bottle an hour before drinking it if possible. There is often a smell of sulphur about it at first, but it quickly dissipates in the air.

*Douro*

The Douro is amazing. It grows good wine of every kind. It is not commonly known that the famous Mateus Rosé has a white twin (and also a red one). The red comes from the Dão, but both the pink and white are Douro wines. Vila Real, the town where Mateus is made, is in the northern part of the Douro district, near the border of the Minho, the *vinho verde* country. It is curious to think that Britain has now gone crazy about a sort of pink sparkling port.

Little white wine is sold using the Douro appellation. I believe Ermida, one of the best dry white brand-named wines, does come from the Douro, but it does not say so. Douro white wine is generally dry and has the quality of hardness and freshness which Dão sometimes lacks. It ages well. By far the greater part of it is country wine, never bottled but freely drunk with the various dishes of salt cod, the famous (or notorious) *bacalhau*, which they never stop eating in Portugal. In any part of Portugal it is not only safe but wise to ask for the wine of the house when eating in a restaurant.

*Names to look for*

Brand-named wines come from every part of Portugal. Some of the best known are Almada, Arealva, Justina, Estoril, Serradayres, Allegro, Campo Grande, Solar, Serrador, Realeza or just plain Branco Seco (dry white). They are not meant to be anything more exciting than cheap blends, but they are usually good value.

*Reserva and garrafeira*

For the finer wines there is nothing for it but to visit Portugal. The words to look for which indicate that the wine is a special selection are *reserva* and *garrafeira*. Both are usually followed by a date, which is (more or less) that of the vintage year. The idea of a vintage year is not nearly so strictly adhered to as it is in France or Germany, where it makes all the difference between good wine and bad. The climate of Portugal is more equable, and variations are rarely great. Where a label says *Garrafeira* 1957 it means that the wine was specially made in 1957 from the best of that year's wine—and perhaps a little good wine of the previous year or so if it helped the blend. In any case the *reservas* and *garrafeiras* are the best the firm in question can do (or, rather, *reserva* is better and *garrafeira* is best).

White *reservas* you may find in Portugal include that of the illustrious house of José-Maria Fonseca, their Branco Seco Especial; the Ermida I have mentioned; Gaeiras; Lagoa (a rather strong dry wine from southern Portugal, in its humbler forms the ordinary wine of the Algarve); Lezirão; Planalto; Quinta d'Aguieira; Sanguinhal and Tres Cunhas. The makers of Serradayres have a wine called Caviar. There is quite a good sweet one called Grandjo.

*The food*

As it is one long sea-coast, Portugal has a great deal of sea-food. Apart from the universal *bacalhau*, there are magnificent lobsters and wonderful little clams which come in many guises, either on their own or in a very good dish with pork. The dry white wines, therefore, are on every table, and constitute perhaps the most typical of Portugal's wines. It is a mistake to think that *vinho verde* is the only or even the best of them. Richer dishes call for *reservas*. Fish restaurants in Britain and America could do worse than to find some good ones.

It would take longer than I have been able to spend in Portugal to discover where all the wines come from, or even to taste them all. I have not met anyone who has really made a study of them. But there are some really excellent wines among them. The field is wide open.

# Spanish White Wines

Spain produces very little table wine which can compete in the international market by any virtue except extreme cheapness. The one important exception to this is the Rioja district in the north—and even in Rioja the red wine is better than the white.

The Spanish climate is not at all conducive to white wine. Common wines (of which vast quantities are made all over the country, except near the Atlantic coast or on very high ground) have some of the characteristics of sherry—high alcohol, strong colour, abundant flavour. But they lack the vital quality of acidity—the balancing, refreshing factor in every good white wine—and the result is flatness. Sherry is a lonely miracle. And yet sherry is not as different from other Spanish white wines as we tend to think. In fact, to the Spanish, it is simply the best of them, not separated in their minds from all table wines in the way it is in countries where it pays a different duty and fulfils a completely different function.

Given the overabundance of sun in Spain it is clear that the best wines (always excepting sherry) will be in the north. The province of Catalonia, the northern part of the Spanish Mediterranean coast, has some of them. Rioja, far away beyond Aragon and Navarre, where the Ebro breaks out from the Cantabrian Sierra to begin its long search for the Mediterranean, has most. The uplands of the north, towards the Portuguese border, have a few. And Galicia and Asturias, the Atlantic provinces, between Portugal and Biscay, have their wild, cider-like country wine.

*Alella*  The districts of Alella and Panades lie on either side of Barcelona. Alella is to the north, on the coast and the coastal hills, between Barcelona and Mataró. Panades, a much bigger district, centres round the town of Vilafranca de Panades between Barcelona and Tarragona. The seaside resort of Sitges lies on its coast. Alella wine is some of Spain's best *vino corriente*, open carafe wine for cafés and restaurants. Some of the best of Barcelona's excellent fish restaurants sell it—or rather give it with bread as part of the cover. Superior white Alella is sometimes put into long green Moselle-type bottles. Modern techniques have gone a long way towards ironing out the faults of the old *vino corriente*—heaviness, strength and flatness. Unfortunately, they have also made a new-style Alella sweet. It is the old story of the baby and the bath-water. Special Alella costs three or four times as much and has about half the character.

*Panades*  Panades gives the greater part of its best white wine over to the manufacture of Xampan—sparkling wine. The town of San Sadurni de Noya in the north of the district is one of the most important centres—is said, indeed, to have the biggest sparkling wine cellar in the world. Otherwise white Panades is made either dry or sweet, is always fairly strong, and at its best is rather like Alella. Torres is the best-known brand. Their white Viña Sol is unexceptionable—and very dry.

*Rioja*  The Cantabrian Sierra cuts off the north coast of Spain from the rest of the country. South of it the old kingdom of Castile stretches in wild open country and range upon range of bare hills. Almost on the borders of Navarre in the north-east the river Ebro comes south through the Sierra, still only a stone's throw wide. Its green valley, just below the entry of its tributary Rio Oja, which gives its name to the country, is Spain's best table-wine vineyard.

A good deal of the white wine of Rioja has been sold, over-modestly, as Rioja Chablis and Rioja Sauternes, the names corresponding to the sweeter and drier types, though neither is particularly like the French wine whose name it has borrowed. Some of the Spanish wines which sell themselves as Spanish Chablis and Spanish Sauternes would be unsaleable without the borrowed names—they are young and horrible. But the Rioja wines would do much better to keep their own names and sell on their own considerable merit.

The wines do fall into two broad kinds, sweet and dry. There is none of the peculiar "noble rot", which gives Sauternes its intense creamy sweetness. Rioja is never normally more than weakly sweet. The dry white, though, is excellent. It is a strongly built, not a light-weight, wine, aged for two or three years in barrel, having a good gold colour, a faint but clean scent and a flavour rather like a white Rhône wine; round but a little hard. The best of these dry whites age extraordinarily well; even for as much as a decade in barrel without being exhausted. A fifteen-year-old Viña Tondonia from the bodega of Lopez Heredia had developed a very striking flavour: full, balanced and lingering, with the appetizing vanilla smack of oak dominant.

For that matter I have had a very old Brillante, one of the brand-names signifying sweet wine, a 1910 from Bodegas Bilbainas, which genuinely had some of the deep honeyed sweetness of great Sauternes.

Probably the best known of all white Riojas is the Monopole of the important firm of C.V.N.E. (Companhia Vinicola del Norte España). But in most ways it is untypical: lighter, paler and more in the modern style than, for example, the very good Banda Dorada of Federico Paternina. With white Rioja you have a choice: to catch them young and stony or to leave them to mellow, which they do singularly well. The vintage year on the bottle (white *reservas* usually carry one) is very likely accurate, even if it seems improbably antique compared with current vintages of, say, white burgundy.

The names of some of the best Rioja bodegas (or wine-houses) will be found under Rioja on page 216.

## Other areas

The white wines of the rest of Spain are of local interest only. There is white Valdepeñas from La Mancha. I have had it served in crystal by a white-gloved butler without managing to enjoy it. Tarragona, Valencia and Alicante all produce white wine. I never understood why until I went to stay with a friend near Alicante. His cook, clearing up after a meal, poured any left-over red wine down the sink. But white wine and water she religiously put in their carafes in the fridge.

Then there is the white wine of the north and north-western provinces: the very opposite to the heavy Mediterranean brew. Galicia has its exact equivalent of Portuguese *vinho verde*—which we may well see exported one day. As at Moncão, the banks of the Minho give estimable wine from the Alvariño grape.

## Chacolí

Finally, there is the wine the Basques would not wish me to call Spanish at all: the Chacolí which redoubtable diners at Basque restaurants in Madrid challenge each other to drink without a grimace. Chacolí is the inevitable product of one of the rainiest corners of Europe: a wine of steel. Yet curiously this thin, scarcely alcoholic, squeeze-of-lemon wine can be the very thing with heavy Basque country cooking.

# Swiss and Austrian White Wines

Switzerland and Austria are both real wine-countries. That is, they not only grow wine; it is their habitual drink. Germany is far more famous for her wine—and produces much better wine than either—but to a German it remains a drink for special occasions. Only in the heart of the wine-making Rhine country is it on every table.

Switzerland is the biggest wine-importer in the world. More burgundy, for example, goes to Switzerland than anywhere else. Austria is one of Italy's best customers for wine. No two capitals are more in the heart of wine-country than Vienna and Geneva. Grapes grow right in the suburbs of both cities. All their best wine, in both cases, is invariably white.

*Switzerland*

In Switzerland the main vineyards follow the course of the river Rhône from its headwaters in the Bernese Oberland, down the long, cliff-sided, flat-bottomed Valais and along the north shore of the Lake of Geneva. If you drive over the Simplon Pass from Italy and follow the road to Lausanne you pass almost all the best vineyards of Switzerland. Indeed at vintage-time you can hardly get along the road in some places for the carts and lorries parked on the verge, loading hideous red and yellow plastic boxes of grapes.

*Visperterminen*

Up near the head of the valley, where a southern side-valley leads from the ski-resort of Zermatt down to Visp in the Valais, the highest vineyards in Europe, the near-vertical Côtes of Visperterminen, face a glorious prospect of Alps and birches and snow. Lower down the Valais the rocky citadel of Sion stands out in the widening alluvial plain, providing more slopes, and more exposure to the sun, for the mellow Fendant grapes which make the Sion wine.

In the Canton of Vaud, where Lausanne follows Vevey and Vevey succeeds Montreux with hardly a break for countryside, the vines and villas, road and railway have become inextricably entangled. It is hard to see how they cultivate the little wedges of vines trapped between railway and lake.

Elsewhere in Switzerland, on the north shore of Lake Neuchâtel, round Zurich, Geneva and in Italian Switzerland, Ticino, wine is grown. Of these areas only Neuchâtel makes export-quality wine.

*Fendant de Sion*

The wines of the Valais are usually known by the name of the grape-stock and often by a brand-name as well. Only occasionally is the name of the place used. Wine made from the Fendant grape at Sion makes mention of the fact, but not all Fendant de Sion necessarily comes from Sion. In addition, there are two wines named after the wines of other countries—Johannisberg and Hermitage—made respectively from the German Sylvaner and the French Rhône Marsanne grapes.

The Fendant (light, soft, good café wine), Arvine, Amigne and Humagne are all white wines, more or less dry but tending to lack balancing acidity. Malvoisie is a sweet wine used as an aperitif and after dinner. The *vin du glacier* used to be a peculiar speciality. It was taken when it was young from the valley vineyards to the cellars of high, cool villages to finish its fermentation very slowly, and developed a hard, almost bitter taste and more than usual strength. Of all these wines only Fendant and Johannisberg are commonly exported. Both could be described as light wines in the German, or perhaps rather the Alsatian, manner.

*The Vaud*

The Canton of Vaud, in which lies the north shore of Lake Geneva, includes all Switzerland's most reputed growths. Three districts lying on both sides of the city of Lausanne produce them. Of these the

*Lavaux*

best is called, confusingly, Lavaux. It is on the steep lake-shore to the east of the city.

The best growths of Lavaux are Dézaley and St-Saphorin. Their wines are dry, not too strong and often thought to be the best in Switzerland, although they are rarely exported. The Clos des Abbayes at Dézaley, the property of the city of Lausanne, is sometimes called Switzerland's best vineyard.

*La Côte*

To the west of Lausanne the La Côte district is bigger but less distinguished. East of the lake altogether, where the Rhône widens out into a delta-shaped plain and the mountains fall back, the third district,

*Chablais*

Chablais, occupies the spectacular near-cliffs of the north side. Aigle and Yvorne are the best names here, making richer wine than Lavaux. They cannot be much more than ten miles, as the crow flies, from the border of France. All the good Vaud wines are made from the Fendant grape, though in the Vaud it is known as the Dorin. All in all, it is Switzerland's best.

The white of Neuchâtel is almost comparable with the Portuguese *vinho verde*; a wine of minimum alcoholic content, a good streak of tartness and a perceptible bubble, which is often encouraged to the point of sparkle.

## Austria

Austria has traditionally been a land of vineyards fragmented among thousands of small growers, none big enough to enter the market with consistently good wine—though many capable, on occasion, of producing first-class wine on a domestic scale.

To this extent the traditional picture of Austrian wine as a tavern drink is accurate. Still, most of the best vineyards supply light, fruity, hurriedly made wine of almost miraculous characteristics straight from the barrel, but once in bottle (if anyone were so rash) a dreadful disappointment.

*Vienna*

Even Viennese wine is like this. For the wine of such a sophisticated city it seems distinctly rough and ready. Yet in its context, from a cask in a *Heurige*, it has a captivating heady freshness. There is no real translation for the word *Heurige*. It means both the new wine and the grower's cellar or terrace where he offers it for sale from the barrel.

Vineyards still occupy what must be some of the most valuable land in Vienna: as central as, for example, Montmartre in Paris or Hampstead Heath in London. They infiltrate the beginnings of the Vienna woods to the north, commanding a superb view of the city and the Danube. And scattered among them, in residential districts and out in country lanes, the *Heurigen* attract the Viennese of all classes. In most you can eat, in some dance under the trees, in all drink new wine until your joints ache—which won't be all that long if acidity takes you that way.

Grinzing is probably the most famous of these wine-districts. But between Grinzing and Nüssdorf and Kahlenberg and Sievering, and their respective Grüner Veltliner (the most Austrian of grapes and my personal favourite), Traminer, Sylvaner and Riesling, there are a thousand debates, and no doubt duels fought, every night.

Viennese wine, however, is a perfect example of what is meant by wine "not travelling". To take it out of context by exporting it would be to ruin it.

In all Austria there are only two districts with a real tradition of exporting wine, and even they have rarely exported their best. The Wachau is the more distinguished of the two—yet there is something about the name of Gumpoldskirchen, the other, which makes it hard to forget.

*The Wachau*

The Wachau vineyards occupy one of those sites which God clearly intended for vines. At a point fifty miles above Vienna where the river Danube flows in broad curves eastwards, the north bank rises in broken hills to a thousand feet above the water. The pivot of this region is the little town of Dürnstein. Dürnstein has Austria's biggest and best Winzergenossenschaft, or co-operative winery—a union of nearly all the growers on these difficult and fragmented slopes. Their bottlings are some of Austria's finer and more reliable wine.

The bulk of Wachau wine is made of the common Sylvaner for rapid consumption. Under the name Schluck this wine has made a reputation for being adequately fresh and fruity at a very low price. But the *pièces de resistance* of the Wachau are the Grüner Veltliner and the Rhine Riesling—the latter making a more complex and distinguished wine, the former the characteristically full and forthright kind with panache. Fritz Salomon and Petermichl both bottle good ones. The place-names to look for are Weissenkirchen—sold by the co-operative as Achleiten—Dürnstein, Stein and Krems.

Just downstream of the town of Krems the hills move away from the river and wander off north-eastwards. The small town of Röhrendorf, just round the corner, has a particularly important place in viticulture. It is the headquarters of the firm of Lenz Moser, one of the most original and skilful wine-growers in Europe.

*Lenz Moser*

Lenz Moser has given his name to a revolutionary way of growing vines, widely spaced and relatively high above the ground, producing more and better wine from fewer plants with less work and less chance of disease. He has also demonstrated that it is not only the traditional vineyards of Austria which can make the best wine. At a tasting in his cellars I met wines from districts I had never heard of which were among the best Austrian wines I have had.

One was a Grüner Veltliner from Mailberg in the north, in the district known as the Weinviertel—which, although the name means wine-quarter, has always been better known for quantity than quality. Another was a Riesling from a strange and rather depressing district down near the Hungarian border—the sandy shores of the shallow, reed-fringed Neusiedler See. The west shore of this distinctly odd lake, which is said to be wadable right to the middle, boasts one historic wine-town—the town of Rust. Ruster Ausbruch—Ausbruch is the Austrian for syrup, what the Hungarians call Aszu—was once famous as a near-Tokay. But this wine came from the east side of the lake, from the little-known village of Apetlon.

I look on my Apetloner Rheinriesling Auslese, now that I have some at home, as the perfect wine for startling and baffling friends who think they know German wine backwards. It has the quality of a very fine German wine—but it also has that Austro-Hungarian attack, that stirrup-cup-before-battle feeling you get from the best wines of this old Imperial corner of Europe.

*Gumpoldskirchen*

I have been less lucky with my Gumpoldskircheners. Even the bottled wines have varied widely in quality and style. Sweetness was the only thing they had in common. Some had the acidity and fruit to back it up; others did not.

Gumpoldskirchen lies on the Südbahn, the railway south from Vienna which has given its name to the vineyards which stretch due south from the city. These slopes are the last gasp of the Alps in the face of the central European plain. Their name of Thermalpen comes from the hot springs which break the surface at Baden and Bad Vöslau, and furnish the wooded slopes with hundreds of little stucco villas suitable for convalescent water-drinkers. Alsace, the Mittelhaardt, the Côte d'Or are all famous wine-districts with almost identical sites: foothills facing east across a plain.

Gumpoldskirchen is the white wine centre of the Südbahn: Baden and Bad Vöslau specialize in red wine. Neither is specially noteworthy —probably owing to the local grape-varieties.

Trying to see Austrian wine whole is hard at the moment. Export strategy is still developing. Estate-bottled wines are making an appearance, but none so far (except for Lenz Moser's) are as exciting as their labels. For the moment the most important Austrian wine in our lives is the good, plain, blended Hirondelle. But how much of that started life as an Austrian grape is never certain; Austria is a considerable entrepôt for the wines of eastern Europe, Romania and Bulgaria, which despite their quality find it hard to make headway under their own names.

# Eastern European White Wines

The operations of a socialist regime have their effect on wine, as they do on every aspect of life. They level standards. The best may come down, but at least (in the case of wine, anyway) the worst improves. The fascination of individual growths and the exercise of the critical and comparative faculties disappear. But we are offered very sound, safe, miraculously consistent and very reasonably cheap wine in compensation. Indeed, we do nothing but gain from the agricultural revolution in the countries of eastern Europe, however the farmers feel about it. It has given us a greater choice of better cheap wine than we have ever had before.

All the Communist countries concentrate on a range of standard lines, varying as little as possible even from vintage to vintage. Vintages are sometimes given, but never with the element of choice; one vintage is used up before another is offered. If a date is put on the bottle it can be used as an indication of age, but there is no question of whether or not it was a good year. The wine, they will tell you, is always good. The date is there for prestige.

Yugoslavia and Hungary are the two best wine-countries of eastern Europe. Their wine can be taken seriously, not as a cheap substitute for French or German, but as something excellent, and of great character, in its own right. Both make better white wine than red, but their red wine is not by any means to be rejected. Both also make among Europe's best rosés.

*Hungary*
*Tokay*

Hungary undoubtedly makes the finest wine of the Communist world, Tokay. Tokay is in the same class (see After-Dinner Wines) as Château d'Yquem or the *Trockenbeerenauslesen*, which are the apotheoses of German wine-making. It is honey-sweet, relatively old and necessarily expensive.

The other white wines of Hungary have nothing like the same

reputation in the English-speaking world. Our sights tend to be rather narrowed to France and Germany, Italy at a pinch, and Spain and Portugal for their specialities and their cheap wines. The Poles and the Scandinavians know better. They are great drinkers of the outlandish-sounding Badacsonyi Szurkebarat and Debroi Harslevelu.

Most Hungarian wine is on the heavy side and inclined to be sweet. The word the Hungarians often use for it, fiery, has all the wrong implications for us. It reminds us of rough hooch, bath-tub whisky or emery-paper Algerian wine. What I think they mean by it is that it is encouraging, warming, generous stuff. Their thin light wines they drink with soda as thirst-quenchers (*froccs*): by serious wine-drinking they mean beakers of something rich and strong.

I find Hungarian wine delicious. Running through it all there is a thread of a special flavour, the same flavour as Tokay has *in excelsis*, something I can only describe as being rather like overripe butterscotch. There is a Hungarian scent, too; a sort of floweriness which is somehow more autumnal and less spring-like than the German bouquet. In the way of lusciousness—drinkable, acceptable, not cloying lusciousness—they follow close on the heels of all but the best of German wines.

The names are admittedly a problem. I once learnt how to pronounce them impeccably, but I promptly forgot again. If I did not think that a wine's identity was its most precious possession, and that to lose its name is to become, as Cassio said, poor indeed, I would say that they should go in for simple and memorable brand-names like the German Liebfraumilch. Happily, there are not many to remember though, for as in all Communist countries the state is the sole exporter and no names of individual estates or merchants appear. In Britain, apart from the deservedly popular ordinary Hungarian Riesling, which is very much in the same class as the Yugoslav Riesling, there are only about half a dozen white table-wines available.

*Lake Balaton*   Lake Balaton is the biggest and most important wine-district, leaving aside Tokay. Its shores yield district wines, in the broad sense of being no more specific than by saying, for example, Bordeaux red, of very high quality. The Riesling, as familiar as any grape to the English, takes on a new richness here, making round, golden wine with a hint of the familiar Hungarian overripeness. The other grape they use widely, the Furmint, which does not seem to appear anywhere except in Hungary but in Hungary is supreme, has the Tokay taste (it is the Tokay grape) to a marked extent—although, of course, nothing like its sweetness.

Both Balatoni Riesling and Balatoni Furmint are table wines in the sense that they would do no dish any disservice; both, on the other hand, have the strength and style to be good drinks on their own, either as aperitifs or, for example, at a party or when you are sitting reading late at night. Their touch of sweetness makes them as adaptable as this.

*Badacsonyi*   The best wine of Lake Balaton comes from a hill on the north shore —the hill of Badacsonyi. Here are grown the Riesling again, a grape called the Keknyelu and another called the Szurkebarat (which means Grey Friar). (I mention the grape-names not out of sadism but because they appear on the labels as they do with Alsace wines.) Badacsonyi wine is sweeter than plain Lake Balaton wine, stronger and more aromatic: in fact, to the Hungarian way of thinking, better. The best vintages made from the ripest grapes are purely dessert wines; the rest—including those which are exported—are for people who like these qualities in a table wine.

My Hungarian topography and much else I owe to a little book on Hungarian wine by Zoltan Halasz, published in Budapest. I cannot resist quoting him on the delights of Badacsonyi:

> One could hardly wish for a better way to relax than by taking a rest on the terrace-dotted slope of the hill, settling down on a small cask on a sawn log as a seat in front of the wine cellar. Laid out on a trestle table, an assortment of cold meat—sausages, greaves, smoke-cured bacon—soft bread and pickles lure the rover, who feels a gnawing hunger from the bracing air of the lake.

The wine he is offered with most pride by the cellarer, who goes on to invite him into his stone-and-thatch press-house, is the Keknyelu, a "stiff, manly, fragrant wine".

*Somlo* Somlo and Debro are the other great white wine-districts of Hungary. Somloi (the name has a final "i" in the same way as a German place name gets an "er" when it refers to a product) does not seem to be shipped to England. It is strong and fragrant, typical of Hungary. Its reputation is that it causes the begetting of male children.

*Debro* Debro in northern Hungary grows the Harslevelu, which gives a strong-flavoured but not quite so luscious wine as those from Balaton. It would be more suitable with fish. Eger also, better known for its red Bull's Blood, makes excellent white from the Leanyka grape.

*Mor* Finally there is Mor, from which comes Mori Ezerjo, possibly the most familiar and certainly the shortest of Hungarian wine-names. Mor lies to the north of a line from Balaton, which is in the south-west of Hungary, to Budapest. Its wine is considerably less luscious than the rest (although again, in good years, it is said to produce very sweet wine). For the ordinary table uses of white wine, and particularly with oysters or other shellfish, Mori would probably be Hungary's most suitable produce. It is a wine for the drinkers of white burgundies rather than hocks.

I find that these rather sweet and very prettily scented wines lose a great deal by being served too cold. Like all white wines, they are best decidedly cool, but anything approaching iciness kills the floweriness and lusciousness which are the whole point. They are worth big, beautiful glasses and time to ponder and discuss what the smell reminds you of.

## Yugoslavia

*Slovenia* The Riesling, the vine of hock and Moselle, is responsible for most of the Yugoslav wine exported. It is at its best at Lutomer in Slovenia, the north-west corner of the country near the Austrian and Hungarian border. Here there are even estate, rather than regional, wines. The Kapela estate near the town of Lutomer is famous for its Renski (Rhine) Riesling.

*Serbia* Much of the wine which is shipped as simply Yugoslav Riesling, without the superior name of Lutomer attached, comes from Serbia, the area in the north-east where Belgrade lies, and where the Danube turns to wash the border of Romania. To the north-west of Belgrade the Fruska Gora mountains face the wide, monotonous plain of the Sava. These are the biggest vineyards in Yugoslavia.

The Riesling in this case is not the Rhine version, but an inferior vine known sometimes as Italian, sometimes as Welsh(!) Riesling, common all over middle Europe. The northern vineyards also grow

*Macedonia*

other grapes familiar in Germany and Alsace, the Sylvaner and the Traminer. Serbian Traminer is splendidly rich and luscious.

Farther south in Macedonia, the familiar names of Riesling and Sylvaner disappear. Native grapes take over, and the names become Balkan and bizarre. This should not be a deterrent from buying the wines—we do not hesitate about buying Chianti because it is not made of Pinot Noir. The Zilavka of Macedonia is one of the most bewitchingly different grapes. It gives a wine with a sweetness of savour and scent, and a dryness of final taste, which are astonishing in something so cheap and unknown. It would take the place of white burgundy at dinner perfectly well—not perhaps every day, but every now and then. Each of the islands of the Dalmatian coast has a wine of its own. Most are dry, many are good—but all tend to be overstrong. Grk, from Korcula, is notorious.

All these wines so far have been in the dry or semi-dry class; as sweet as Liebfraumilch at the sweetest. There is also a Lutomer late-picked wine, Tigermilk, or Ranina Radgona Spätlese, which is very much sweeter and more like a Hungarian wine, though not as good.

# The Black Sea

The vineyards of Russia and the Balkans are grouped about the Black Sea. Going eastwards round its shores, there are vineyards in Bulgaria, in Romania, in Moldavia, the Crimea, the Russian Republic, Georgia and the Caucasus (Armenia). All the wine they export is made from large co-operative vineyards working to a standardized pattern, and is pasteurized when it is bottled, so that it can neither improve nor deteriorate—nor ever be more than an ordinary, rather dull brand. For variety they look to different grapes, each being made to give a stylized consistent wine. It is rather as though we asked all our best painters to paint exactly the same picture over and over again. There is interest, for a while, in comparing artist with artist, but it is not long before we long for them to paint something else.

The red wine of the Black Sea area tends to be better than the white. Romania and Bulgaria make better wine than the Soviet Union. Romania has, if anything, the better name of the two for white wine.

*Romania*

Within this century Romania has been the third most prolific wine-country in Europe, and there are signs that wine has a high priority in her economy. She has, however, lost Bessarabia, her chief wine-making region, to the Soviet Union (it was liberated, as they say in those parts, and re-christened Moldavia in 1940). Cotnari is her best—a rarity today. Most of her white wine is rather sweet and not particularly good. Murfatlar and Muscat Ottonel are both in about the range of sweetness of Orvieto—too sweet, to my mind, to enjoy with most food but not quite sweet enough for after dinner. The Riesling of Tirnave is Romania's best-known white wine abroad. The Riesling of Perla is a sweeter version. Both are comparable with Yugoslav or Hungarian Riesling. The Chardonnay of white burgundy is also grown in Romania, I believe, although I have not tasted a Romanian one. In Bulgaria it makes an excellent clean and dry white wine—one of the nearest approaches to a white burgundy which I have tasted outside France.

*Bulgaria*

The Black Sea coast is the chief white-wine region of Bulgaria. Some of its vineyards are beautiful, sloping right down to the yellow sandy beaches between groves of oak trees like the setting for a Greek tragedy. The Dimiat and the Grozden (both apparently relations of the Riesling) and the Misket, a kind of Sylvaner, are grown on the coast and all make adequate white wine. I must confess that on my one visit to Bulgaria I was not always sure what I was drinking. The custom is to start every meal with the delicious white plum spirit, slivova, which has a numbing effect on the palate. Despite this, the Bulgarians are wine-drinking people. There is always wine on the tables in the cafés. The vaults of the opera house of Sofia, where the youth and beauty of the capital gather late in the evening to talk, has the atmosphere of a Rhineland *Weinstube*, with the addition—universal in Communist countries—of an energetic little orchestra.

*The Soviet Union*      I have frequently had leaflets from what is euphemistically called the Russian Information Service about enormous new tracts of the Soviet Union being turned over to vines. The production of Champanski, in particular, seems to double every year or so. Few white wines, however, appear in the West. In Britain we see Tsinandali and Gurdjani, which are both Georgian wines—the former light and harmless, the latter more courageously exotic. Both are dry. I prefer the Gurdjani because it has more taste. There is one other white wine —the one product of the Russian Republic itself which is exported— Anapa Riesling, which fails to reach the standard set by Romania in this field.

## Californian White Wines

The United States is second in size of the vineyards of the New World (Argentina is first), but in prosperity and overall quality she has no rival in the New World and very few in the old. The growth of California's vineyards, and the market for their wine, has taken on gold-rush proportions in the last three or four years. A by-product of California's success has been the birth—in some cases the re-birth—of wine-industries in other States of the Union. Leaving aside the long tradition of wine-making in upper New York State, which has a character of its own outside the mainstream of the world's wine, a good dozen States now have the beginnings of wine-industries. If California looks with apprehension at any of them (which she has no reason to do) it will be at Oregon and Washington, whose temperate west-coast climate has already produced a few wines of considerable quality.

In the New World outside the USA California has only Australia to fear. In terms of average quality California is safely in the lead. In terms of ultimate quality the question is more open. Australia did not suffer the self-destructive aberration of Prohibition as America did from 1919 to 1933. In many senses her wine industry (though much smaller) is more mature, and in a few cases her wines show it.

*The reasons for success*      One of the main contributing factors to California's brilliant success as a wine-maker, climate and soil apart, is the rich, cultivated and demanding audience her wines have had in San Francisco and Los Angeles. South Africa has comparable natural conditions. But who is there in South Africa to patronize, criticize, encourage and support the efforts of experiment and investment needed to improve the wine year after year? In California's social climate there is room for the world's biggest winery, but also for dozens of tiny individual enterprises dedicated to making wine as well as they can, regardless of cost. Without both kinds (and the ones in the middle) California could never have gone so far so fast. Nor could the whole team have found its form without its remarkable coach, the Department of Viticulture and Enology of the University of California at Davis near Sacramento.

*Classification problems*

The newcomer to Californian wine has a hard time of it these days. However complicated and confusing the picture of European wine there is a pattern and a discipline there for the student to grasp. In California there is no such thing: just a happy American free-for-all of brands fighting with the weapons of advertising and marketing. No quality classification has ever been attempted or even suggested. Vineyard-names are almost non-existent; wineries use grapes from distant districts; ripeness comes too easily to be (as it is in Germany) a deciding factor; labelling laws are distinctly good-neighbourly. To catch up with the hundreds of brands at one moment in time is a considerable challenge: to keep up with them from there on, with every winery having a brain-wave (or a take-over, or both) every season, is a life's work.

*Jug wine*

The first and most exciting lesson California teaches a visitor is that she is sitting on an artesian well of sensationally good *vin ordinaire*. Its producers hate the word ordinary—understandably, since the quality of much of it is not. The term "jug wine" is a useful let-out—though even this gives the wrong idea. None of it ever gets in to jugs. Every drop is bottled at the winery. Broadly speaking, "jug wine" is the harvest of the great interior valley, the San Joaquin, with Fresno as its capital; a land of intensely hot, utterly dry summers.

Until recently, more grapes were grown here for raisins than for wine, and those which were made into wine were made into "sherry". But the last few years have seen a revolution. A new generation of wine-drinkers found table wines more to their liking than the old heavy dessert wines. At the same time a new understanding of grape growing and wine-making made light wines possible even in such a hot area. The technological innovations were basically refrigeration and rigidly keeping oxygen away from the wine in the making, which meant, among other things, using steel tanks in place of wood. But equally important has been the study of what vines to grow where.

*Grape varieties*

California has concentrated more than any other wine producer on the question of varieties of vine. The University Department of Viticulture made a famous survey of the State, dividing it into five temperature zones. For each zone they recommended the grape varieties that should do best—based largely on their performance in comparable zones in Europe. Zone 1, the coldest, which includes parts of Napa, Sonoma, and Mendocino counties, can be compared with parts of Germany. Zone 5, the hottest, which is the greater part of the San Joaquin valley, has conditions not unlike the south of Spain.

For the central valley the University was able to recommend grapes which maintain a balance of acidity even in extreme ripeness (among them grapes the French use for making brandy, whose high natural acidity is unusable in Europe except in this way). The classical vines of Germany, Bordeaux and Burgundy found their exact niches in the coastal counties, above all in the counties surrounding San Francisco Bay. Here the influence of the Pacific and its great land-bound extension, the Bay itself, moderates the climate. The nights are cool.

Often heavy sea-mist rolls in over the Coast Range at night to provide moisture for the vines. South from Monterey Bay a sea-breeze sweeps up the Salinas valley in the afternoon. Hot as it may be here in the sun there are cooling movements in the air. Instead of the grape roasting it gently ripens.

It is sometimes hard to believe, as you see the strange juxtaposition of vineyards and cattle-ranches, of bare grass hills—the West of horse-opera—with Pinot Noir and Chardonnay, the delicate grapes of Champagne, that anything but a fancy drink for cowboys can come of it. Yet of all the places that have set out to imitate the great wines of Burgundy and Champagne and Bordeaux, California has come as near as any to succeeding. I am not using the word "great" loosely. There are a handful of wine-makers in the Napa, Sonoma and Salinas valleys who have demonstrated that what they can make is comparable with a Montrachet or a Château Latour; not just a vague white burgundy or claret. If such wine-makers are very much in the minority, it is worth remembering that so they are in France, too.

## "Generic" wines

At jug-wine level the brand-name is the only sign-post. Most wines still have "generic" names—i.e. the borrowed names of European wines. Chablis, Sauterne (usually, in California, without the final "s"), Rhine and Burgundy are taken to be wine-types, and interpreted as the wine-maker sees fit. The unchallenged leader in this field is the firm of E. & J. Gallo of Modesto, which is said to account for over a third of the whole American wine industry. Gallo Chablis Blanc and Hearty Burgundy are their key "straight" white and red wines (they make fruit-flavoured wines too). Chablis Blanc is in fact rather more like German wine than Chablis, with just a kiss of sweetness. What is beyond question is its consistent quality. Tens of millions of bottles of it come off a production line which starts in a glass factory. There is no enterprise like it in the whole world of wine—unfortunately for us Europeans, who can only gaze on it with envy from afar.

There are, of course, other huge mass-production wineries in the same business. Italian Swiss Colony, Guild, and Franzia are the giants. Nearly all have, as it were, Italian blood, whose influence can be detected in some of their products. Before the present wine-boom it was the Italian Americans who were the mainstay of the wine industry, and their taste is still well catered for.

## "Varietal" wines

At the next price level, among what begin to be called "premium" wines, the old generic names have been abandoned. California's pre-occupation with grape varieties has led to an enormous increase in "varietal" wines; wines, that is, named for and in theory made out of (or at least deriving their character from) one single variety of grape. The names of Semillon, Sauvignon, Chardonnay and Cabernet have already become part of the Californian language, strange as it may seem. Frenchmen who have been drinking the juice of these grapes all their lives may well have hardly heard of them, but you will hear sun-burnt, slow-walking ranch-hands drawl them out like the names of their home town.

## Vintages

These grape-names, with the name of the winery, usually constitute the whole nomenclature of fine Californian wines. Some, but they are a minority, carry the vintage year; whether they do so or not is largely a matter of commercial convenience. It is not always convenient that wine is made in annual harvests, with inevitable (though

# The Work of the Wine-Trade

"Being importers, seeing wine as a luxury, England and America
have developed a highly specialized and immensely skilful wine-
trade. With no commitment to or against any country or district
we have learnt how to bring home the best from everywhere."
**Above:** wines are chosen from unlabelled samples in the
clinical atmosphere of the tasting room.

After grape-juice has been extracted, fermented and aged, it still has a long way to go before it reaches the table. There is the work of the professional taster (**above and left**), who sniffs the wine, examines its colour, rolls it round his mouth and spits it out, and that of the auctioneer (**right**). The price of a burgundy vintage, for example, is largely determined at the famous November auction of the Hospices de Beaune. The wine must be bottled, too, whether in a modern bottling line (**below**) or by old-fashioned methods. Ordinary Spanish wine is still sold in wicker-jacketed *bombonas* (**below left**), while in Chablis (**below right**) used bottles are carefully washed by hand, before re-use.

There are still small private cellars, as here in Beaujolais, where
everything, even sticking on the labels, is a hand operation,
meticulously done by someone who lives by and for wine.

in California slight) variations, and not in a steady consistent stream. To the consumer the main interest in a vintage date on a California wine is to tell him how old it is.

Appellations of origin, in the European sense, do exist in California, but their usefulness as a guide to quality is strictly limited. If you see "Coast Counties" on a label it will mean what it says. If you see a county name such as Napa or Sonoma used, you will know that the wine comes from this prestigious district rather than from all over the State. There are even one or two narrowly geographical appellations coming into being. Alexander Valley in Sonoma is an example. But the apparent converse of these appellations, that wine without them is inferior, does not stand up to examination. Wine-making in California is still an open-ended and experimental business. If a wine-maker thinks he can improve his wine with grapes from near or far he will use them. If he sacrifices his exact appellation in the process, he will think it a small price to pay.

The human factor, in other words, is more important than the geographical—at least within the broad contexts of coastal or inland wineries.

## Labelling

The exact nature of the human factor—that is who grew the grapes, who made the wine, who cellared it and who bottled it—is less easy to discern in the small print at the bottom of the label. There are enough variant wordings here to make the subtleties of Burgundy's *mise du* or *mise au domaine* and the rest mere child's-play. Only the phrase "grown, produced and bottled by . . ." tells you the whole story. But since few wineries do all their own growing, or even "producing" (meaning fermenting) it is unusual. "Produced and bottled by . . ." is the usual phrase for first-class wines. But there are also eminent wineries who buy a good proportion of their wine already fermented. They are limited to some such phrase as "cellared and bottled by . . ." or "perfected and bottled by . . ." or simply "made and bottled by . . ." The consumer should not lose sleep over these ambiguities. They can only indicate; they cannot guarantee. By far the most important words on the label are the name of the firm that takes responsibility for the contents. And after them, the grape variety.

## Popular varieties

The list of Californian white wines is longer than the list of reds. The white grapes of Bordeaux, Burgundy, Alsace and Germany, the Loire and the north of Italy—though not, strangely enough, of southern Italy or Spain—are all grown with considerable success. One grape above all, though, gives wine as good as any but the greatest of its native land—and even that qualification is in doubt. The grape

### Pinot Chardonnay

is the Pinot Chardonnay, or just plain Chardonnay, the white grape of Burgundy. It is almost always the most expensive Californian white wine, for the yield of grapes per acre is small, and farmers in the past were reluctant to plant the variety.

In richness and freshness of scent, in savouriness and complexity of taste, and in balanced and appetizing dryness, however, the Chardonnay is so outstanding that vast new plantings have been made to increase the supply. It is grown in the beautiful and fertile Napa and Sonoma valleys north of the Bay, the Livermore valley east of the Bay, and Santa Clara, Monterey and San Benito counties to the south—all the best areas of the State. It is commonly thought to reach its very best in Napa and Sonoma, in the hands of such small-scale wineries as Hanzell, Heitz, Freemark Abbey and Stony Hill. Recently Chalone vineyards in Monterey county, however, have brought it to astonishing perfection. But wines like these are rare and expensive. They are seriously to be compared, in value and price, with fine Meursaults and even Montrachets. The wines made on a more commercial scale by the best of the larger wineries—Beaulieu, Wente, Charles Krug and Louis Martini are perhaps the best examples—are far more widely available, and less distinguished only in the proportion that a good plain Meursault comes below, let us say, a Meursault Perrières. On a mass-market level Almaden and Paul Masson also present the true Chardonnay—scaled down, to keep the analogy going, to something on the Mâcon Blanc level. In other words, by no means to be sneezed at.

*The taste of oak*
With Chardonnay, more than any other grape, California vintners have found that they can not only compete with, but they can really mimic, French wine. The secret of the flavour of white burgundy, they have discovered, lies not only in the grapes but in the barrels. Few Europeans, even Burgundians, realize just how much of the characteristic rich, dry white burgundy flavour is really the taste of Limousin or Nevers oak. But Californians found out, by going to Europe and buying the same barrels for themselves. Not all Californian vintners approve: some are too proud of the wine flavour to mask it with tannin and vanillin, the barrels' contribution. Their wines are considerably less burgundian in style—though not necessarily less good, by any means. As one cellar-master said to me, in California all the wine-makers watch each other's experiments with scepticism, have a good laugh, and then try the same thing themselves.

*White Riesling*
Next in prestige to Chardonnay comes the white Riesling, or Johannisberg Riesling—the Riesling of the Rhine and Moselle. There is no danger here of confusing the Californian with the European wine. In this climate the Riesling ripens uniformly and fully, giving a rounder, softer and above all more alcoholic and "winy" wine than in Germany—unless, perhaps, one compares it with the few Rieslings of Baden. At its best it achieves very considerable delicacy and complexity, but of a different kind. Despite this apparent lack of acidity (relative, that is, to German wine) the good California Rieslings can do with a little time in bottle to develop character. If they are good young, they are noble after two or three years, gaining the deep, almost sour smell only old Riesling achieves. Again, the Napa valley is the classic Riesling area, but again, it is being challenged today by new plantings to both north and south.

*Sauvignon Blanc*
The other white grape which is, or can be, on equal footing with France in California is the Sauvignon Blanc. Bordeaux has one (or two) ideas about the Sauvignon. Basically it likes its wine strong, broad and either dry or very very sweet. The Loire, on the other hand, emphasizes its potential for flinty, sometimes piercingly flinty, freshness. Both styles have their adherents in California, and both do exceedingly well. It is only those that are half-heartedly sweet that fail.

To my mind the classic California Sauvignon Blanc was that of Wente Bros, made in the peculiar conditions of the gravelly but fertile Livermore valley just east and inland of the Bay. I say "was" because my last impression of it was less happy. In its heyday it was California's best easily obtainable white wine: golden and smooth but austere, of a quality rarely achieved in Graves—for it was a white Graves it most resembled.

The other dry Sauvignon style, that of Pouilly-Fumé and Sancerre, was brought to California by Robert Mondavi who left Charles Krug to start his own ultra-modern Napa winery. He called his version Fumé Blanc. Not being the greatest lover of the Loire "fumés", which can be pretty mean and piercing, Mondavi's wine struck me in its first vintage as a great Californian contribution: the flinty flavour in a softer (though not a sweet) wine.

*Gewürztraminer*

Being a variety so open to interpretation Sauvignon is the least reliable to recommend, however great its potential. Perhaps the safest of the whites, because it wanders so little from its peculiar path, is the Gewürztraminer—the grape that is almost synonymous with Alsace. Its pungent spiciness, a cousin of the Muscat flavour, is recognizable anywhere. In Alsace it is firm, dry, highly seasoned; an almost aggressive wine. California tames it down to a smoother and softer character. The least Californian of the Californian Gewürztraminers, in this sense, are Louis Martini's, for long the leader of the field, and the recently introduced Mirassou wine. To my mind these are far and away the best.

*Chenin Blanc*

The Chenin Blanc is one of the latest white grapes to have come into fashion. Its name is little known in Europe. Touraine and Anjou are its headquarters, and its products those mid-Loire whites, Vouvray, Saumur and the Layon wines, which hesitate between sweet, very sweet and sweet-sour. Sourness (which comes from underripe grapes) is never a problem in California. Without it, however, the Chenin Blanc can make rather wishy-washy wine. The best California versions, therefore, take steps to keep something like a European balance, creating a general effect rather like a German wine. The Christian Brothers make one like this, lightly sweet and very pleasant. Paul Masson makes another. Charles Krug's version (called, for some reason, White Pinot) is rather drier. The new Chappellet winery in the hills above the Napa valley has made one with an intensity and depth of flavour which would have done credit to a Vouvray. But these are examples almost at random from a wide and growing field. Chenin Blanc is clearly going to be a Californian standard.

*Semillon*

Semillon is probably slowly fading from the scene. Its best wines are sweet—it is, after all, the nobly rotting grape of Sauternes. But Europe makes no wine from Semillon on its own, unblended with other grapes. Sauternes is a mixture of Sauvignon and Semillon, with or without a little Muscatel as well. California, having adopted the varietal idea, seems reluctant to make the blends which give so much complexity and subtlety to Europe's wine. It is the same story with Cabernet Sauvignon, as we shall see when we come to California's reds. Semillon waits for an inspired compromise. Straight, it sticks.

There are other old-guard white varieties on California labels. There is Pinot Blanc from Burgundy, Grey Riesling whose ancestry reputedly lies in the Jura, Sylvaner from Germany. It is hard to get excited about the wine of any of these grapes. They may well, indeed, be allowed in due course to die out. The zones to watch are the new-

*Emerald Riesling*

guard grapes which are peculiar to California, of which Emerald Riesling is the best so far, and one or two minor European grapes whose Californian potential is only just emerging: notably the French Colombard and Folle Blanche.

What these varieties have in common is plenty of acidity. Any grape that can ripen in the Central valley and still make a fresh white wine has a future in California.

*The eastern States*

The wines of California are all made of European vines—or at least from varieties of the European vine species, *Vitis vinifera*. But America has its native vines, too. The wild vines whose exuberance made the first Norse discoverers of the continent christen it Vinland have been selected and bred for wine-making since Colonial times. There is a basic difference in flavour between their wine and that of *Vitis vinifera*: it finds few admirers among those who are accustomed to European-style wine. But native vines have the advantage of thriving in the fiercely extreme climate of the eastern States, where *Vitis vinifera* has never (at least until recently) flourished. The important New York State wine industry round the Finger Lakes in the far north-west corner of the State was based on American vines— originally, overwhelmingly, the dark-juiced Concord. Today it still uses them and their hybrids for nearly all its wine, which makes it hard for me, with my prejudiced palate, to say anything constructive about it.

*"Champagne"*

The most acceptable of the traditional New York wines to a European-wine drinker are the "champagnes". In the context of a sparkling wine the odd scented flavour of American grapes (technically known as "foxiness") is less striking. The Pleasant Valley Wine Company's Great Western and Charles Fournier's Blanc de Blancs are good examples.

*Dr Frank*

The most interesting development in the area (again, to a European-wine drinker) is the work of Dr Konstantin Frank, the founder of the Vinifera Wine Cellars at Hammondsport on Lake Keuka. Dr Frank comes from Russia, where winters even colder than those in New York fail to kill *vinifera* wines. He was employed in the early 1950s by Charles Fournier (himself a native of Champagne; former wine-maker of Veuve Clicquot), to try to vindicate *vinifera* vines in New York. He planted Riesling, Chardonnay, Gewürztraminer and others with complete success—even discovering that the Finger Lakes climate is conducive to "noble rot": he has made a Riesling *Trockenbeerenauslese*. The industry, however, to his chagrin, has been unwilling to follow him. Instead, it has temporized and either planted hybrid vines, crosses between the European and American species, or stuck to its old ones. Knowing that fine wine can never come from either, Dr Frank believes that New York State is throwing away its chance of ever becoming a great vineyard. The truth seems to be that America has two co-existing markets for wine, and that the wineries who supply the strictly "American" one would be rash to give it up and compete in the other. Widmer's, another big Finger Lakes wine-company, who recently planted five hundred acres of vineyard in Sonoma county, California, clearly believe that it is possible to have the best of both worlds.

# Australian White Wines

Australia is no beginner in the wine business. It is an exceptional wine company in Australia which is not a hundred years old: several have been in existence for one hundred and fifty years. The industry is mature, and was, until 1966 or so, settled in its ways. Nobody asked anything much of it except strong, sweet dessert wines and "tonic burgundies". Britain was the main market for them, and Britain used them arrogantly and contemptuously. One of the Seppelt family told me how, after his twelve-thousand-mile sales journey, he was kept waiting half a day in the outer office of a big London customer. When he was finally admitted, it was to a brief session of bargaining, in which his profit was eroded to practically nothing. As he left he offered the samples he had brought. "Samples be damned," said the customer. "If the wine's no good I'll send it back."

*Unknown wines*

Meanwhile Australia's considerable production of her own sort of table wines went on, ignored by the outside world. Virtually nobody outside Australia had any notion that old vineyards and long experience were making wine—red wine especially—of excellent, and sometimes superlative, quality. Inevitably it was heavy-weight wine. But this was no disadvantage to the reds, which only needed long ageing in bottle in the old-fashioned way. And the great soft and strapping whites found their own circle of admirers.

## The wine revolution

In 1966 what might be called the modern wine movement hit Australia. The movement, here as in California, consisted of two complementary forces working together: a new demand for light table wines coupled with the technical ability to make them. Australia's vintners were enthusiastic, ingenious and splendidly uninhibited about embracing every conceivable modern wine-making dodge. So now there co-exists in Australia a fair-sized segment of the old order side by side with a bustling, booming, often brilliant party of the new.

*The old tradition*

The old tradition is best embodied in such wines as the much-loved "Honey Hunters"—broad, soft and golden white wines from the Hunter valley in New South Wales. Sydney's cognoscenti dote on them. Or in reds in the quite extraordinary South Australian Grange Hermitage of Penfold's, Australia's most luxurious wine. Or more humbly in some of the dark, strong, but ultimately (after due bottle-ageing) remarkably fine and complex reds of such roasting inland areas as Rutherglen in northern Victoria right on the New South Wales border.

*The new idea*

The new idea is summed up in the almost-fizzy water-white "pearl" wines of Gramp's in the Barossa valley, or the feather-weight grape-juicy Lexia made by McWilliams in the Murrumbidgee irrigation area of New South Wales—as unlikely a spot for good wine-growing as any classical vigneron could imagine. At McWilliams' winery at Griffith in the irrigation area (a former desert to which water is brought by canal a hundred miles from the Murrumbidgee river), I have tasted a Traminer which was beautifully fragrant and ready to drink at three weeks old. The physical mastery of wine-making is complete. Australians can have all the fresh, clean, uncomplicated white wines they want.

The very best white wine Australia can make, however, is emerging as something between the old style and the new. After a few glasses—let alone a few wineries—full of relentlessly clean modern wine, one longs for some of the fullness and complexity of the old. I called at Angove's at Renmark in South Australia one evening after a day of Riesling that tasted more of grapes than wine. I was given a glass of Bookmark, the Angove Riesling still made in a semi-traditional style. Never was the pale golden colour, the faint flavour of oxidation more welcome. Seeing my appreciation John Angove opened a twenty-four-year-old bottle of Queltaler Hock. It tasted indescribably deep and delicious after so much brisk refreshment.

*Riesling*   It is the Riesling grape which is making Australia's best white wines today—but the Riesling in special situations: above all in cooler areas. The little district of Coonawarra in the south of South Australia, two hundred miles south of the Barossa valley, is making excellent Riesling—as well as the red wines for which it is already famous. Round the Barossa valley it is vineyards at twelve hundred feet or more such as Yalumba's Pewsey Vale, Penfold's Eden Valley or above all Gramp's Steingarten which make the best-balanced, most satisfying wines. Gramp's have gone to greater lengths than anyone to give their Riesling quasi-German conditions. Their Steingarten is literally a field of stones; the schistous summit of the tawny sheepwalks high above Rowland Flat. The Kaiser Stuhl winery, the Barossa valley growers' co-operative, sometimes makes a *Spätlese* or "late picking" Riesling from an individual grower's vineyard on the high ground. Some of these wines have richness and acidity in such perfect proportions that one instantly thinks of German wine.

There is a bad Australian habit, however, of which one must beware. The word Riesling is used with abandon. Without qualification it often means, for some reason, Semillon. Any real Rhine Riesling will say so—either as part of its name or on the back-label.

*Other varieties*   Riesling apart the white-grape repertoire is not impressive. The Chardonnay which makes California's best white wines is hardly grown in Australia at all ... so far. There is some Verdelho (the Madeira grape), Chasselas from Switzerland, Blanquette from the south of France, Palomino from Jerez, Marsanne from the Rhône, the Traminer I have mentioned and a little Sauvignon Blanc. None of these, however, makes a particularly distinguished "varietal" wine on its own. One has to learn one's way among the unhelpful generic labels, the Chablis and white burgundies, to find some of Australia's other good white wines.

*Labelling*   Australian labels, unfortunately, do little to help. Each company has its own labelling philosophy. Some tell you just what the wine is and where it comes from in simple terms. But more use intricate systems of brand names and bin numbers—impossible to remember—to distinguish their different products. Most confusing of all, most of the big wineries are established in two or more of the vineyard areas and blend their wines without hesitation. It is common for one bottle to contain wine from two, or even three, different States. So even rudimentary ideas about the characteristics of regions are of limited value.

There is some guidance in the medals with which many of the best Australian wines are adorned. The old idea of the agricultural show is not precisely in fashion in Europe. Château Lafite would not send its wine to the Bordeaux or the Zurich fair to establish whether it was better than Château Latour. In Australia, however, the circuit of shows—Adelaide, Sydney, Brisbane and the rest—is watched by wine-lovers with bated breath. The judges are some of the key figures in the wine-world. A gold medal can mean a great deal in reputation, sales and prices.

What is perhaps hardest for the British to appreciate is that Australia is immensely wine-conscious. Barry McKenzie is no sort of indication. Australians can be very serious about wine and pick their way among brands with a skill we cannot hope to emulate. The best wineries are catering for so much amateur technical knowledge by printing more and more details on labels: some of them look more like laboratory reports than tags of identification. But there is no substitute for a formal and universally accepted labelling system such as France provides.

# South African White Wines

The climate of South Africa has more in common with Spain and Portugal, the countries of strong aperitif and dessert wines, than it does with France and Germany, the countries of fine white table wines. But Portugal, with its exposure to the west and the influence of the Atlantic, has good white wine to its credit. The western province of the Cape is in a comparable position. The vine, in fact, could hardly find more perfect natural conditions.

In the last century its famous Muscat, Constantia (which must have been similar to Portugal's Setubal), was one of the world's most expensive wines. What South Africa has lacked in the development of her modern wine-industry has been a body of discriminating drinkers. South Africans have always preferred drinking brandy to wine.

*The K.W.V.* The enormous national co-operative, the K.W.V., which was founded in 1917 to regulate an industry in chaos, was based on the control of wine for distilling as a way of disposing of a huge surplus. But its effect, providing as it did a secure market for poor wine, was to increase quantity and lower quality, encouraging the planting of high-yield grapes in hot areas where irrigation made them yield even more, and worse.

Only since 1960 has there been any emphasis on table wine in South Africa. But progress has been rapid: given modern cold fermentation, conditions in the western Cape are good. Luckily one of the white grapes already massively planted turned out to be excellent for nearly-dry light wine. Almost without effort, it seems, South Africa has turned herself into a source of table wine as good as most of Europe, or better. New (1974) legislation along the lines of *Appellations Contrôlées* concerns her determination to compete internationally with her wines.

*Steen* The good white grape is the Steen, which has no exact equivalent elsewhere but which may be a relation of the Sauvignon Blanc of Bordeaux. Steen wine has no very marked character, besides a very agreeable freshness, but it has the liveliness to taste good with a trace of sugar left in it. There is dry Steen, and *Spätlese* or late-picked Steen which is medium-sweet, and both are good. The K.W.V. ships both, and so does the excellent old private estate of Twee Yongegezellen, or Two Bachelors. A South African law decrees that no wine (with very rare exceptions almost calling for a special Act of Parliament) can contain more than two per cent sugar, which inevitably prevents anyone from attempting the manufacture of the old Constantia.

*Riesling* Steen is South Africa's national white grape. Its only challenger is the Riesling of the Rhine—a rarity a few years ago, but now being planted in some of the best vineyards of the Cape, round Paarl and Stellenbosch, thirty miles east of Cape Town, and at Tulbagh, fifty miles north of Paarl. There are relatively few estate wines: grape farming on the old co-operative basis is still the general rule. But a few estates do offer Rieslings. The best known is Nederburg near Paarl. Bellingham near Franschhoek in the same valley sells a Riesling under the name of Johannisberg. At Tulbagh Twee Yongegezellen is again the best-known name.

# White Wines of the Eastern Mediterranean

Although the eastern Mediterranean made wine long before France did, the hand of the Prophet was laid on it in the early years of Christendom. The Koran forbade (though not always successfully) the drinking of wine, and it died out in its own home-country, giving place to the wines of the upstart Europe.

There is no long tradition of wine-growing, therefore, in most of the eastern Mediterranean countries which are now growing wine again. Their wine comes into the category of the New World's wine —a direct transference of the grapes and the styles of wine from its most famous homes. The new Israeli wine, for example, sometimes compares itself with Alicante—unambitiously enough, for it has chosen about the worst example of any traditional wine that it could find. Even Cyprus, whose wine-growing tradition was never really stopped by the Turks, uses terms such as burgundy for its very un-burgundian produce.

*Greece* Greek wine, it is true, lies right outside the mainstream of wine tradition in a backwater of its own. The Greek taste for putting resin in the new wine makes it a struggle for anyone who is not used to it. Retsina, with its taste of turpentine, becomes a memory of Greece which it is difficult, once you have drunk it there, to forget. No country expresses itself so uncompromisingly in its wine—but wine is hardly the word for it. I first discovered its merits in a little inn in Thrace where the beans in oil, the potatoes in oil and the hard grey bread desperately needed something to take the taste away. The taste of turpentine was distinctly better than the musty oil and the soggy hopelessness of the food. Subsequent indifferent meals at expensive restaurants have convinced me that this is Retsina's ordained role.

There are, however, a number of unresinated wines in Greece, of which the white, on the whole, are more pleasant than the red. The *Samos* sweet muscat of Samos has the greatest reputation of these, though I have never had a very wonderful bottle. Of the others, the brands Domestica and Pendeli are widespread and adequate, and a number of *Rhodes* the islands make better than average whites. That of Rhodes (superior Rhodes wine goes under the name of Lindos) is better than most in my experience, but I would recommend conversation with one who has really drunk his way round the Aegean rather than reliance on my limited experience.

*Cyprus* All the eastern Mediterranean wines suffer from the excess of sunshine so far south. They are all scaled up in strength, so to speak, so that, for example, Cyprus rosé has the sort of flavour you associate with a very stout southern French red, while Cyprus red has more the impact of port. Ordinary white wine has most of the power of sherry. They are a race of superwines. But to those who are used to French wines they tend to be too much of a good thing; rather than quenching thirst they set your head spinning. The kind of new techniques which Australia is using, however, are coming into play. Refrigeration is making a great difference. No doubt there will one day be excellent Cyprus white wine (at the moment the red is better).

*Israel* Israel is already making some very light dry whites with a good deal of character of their own. Some have a slight background taste of raisins, reminding one of how hot it must have been in the vineyard at vintage time, but there is no reason why the original lands of wine should not come back to their inheritance and, with modern methods, add yet more good wines to the vast variety we have to choose from. At the moment, I should add, most of the Israeli wines are rather sickly sweet.

## Rosé Wines

The word "rosé" has moved into the English language. Pink was too undignified a word for wine. Rosé is simply French for rose-coloured. Its similarity to *arrosé*, which means watered, is quite coincidental.

It is useful to have a wine which you can fall back on at any time, which is good as a drink on its own, or good for a glass with lunch, good for sipping as you cook or good for supper in the garden. No wine has a monopoly of these qualities; many fine German wines, for example, would be good for any of these things, or with practically any dish. But German wine is expensive, and not so very simple. Rosé is cheap, has no long pedigree, needs no special serving—is in fact, the all-purpose wine for thirsty people.

Rosé has, besides, the prettiest range of colours of any wine. Colour is not everything, by a long way, but a really glowing coral glass, a cherry-coloured one or one with a touch of tangerine about it fairly beckons you in. The wine-makers themselves have toyed with the poetic in their words for the pinkness of their wares—*oeil de perdrix*, partridge-eye, is one the lipstick people might try. *Pelure d'oignon*, onion-skin, would probably go less well.

There is no great range of tastes and scents among rosé wines. It is the connoisseur's—many, unjustly, would say snob's—argument against them. The grower making a rosé is not following, as more serious wine-makers do, the specific practice of his region to bring out the regional character and make a wine which could be recognized anywhere. Character is considered expendable for pink wine. What the maker is after is the simple taste of wine; the lowest common denominator (or, if you like, the highest common factor) of all wine. He will make it sweeter or drier, still or a little sparkling, to suit your fancy, but his art touches that of the confectioner rather than the ancient skills of making wine. The colour comes, as does the colour of red wine, from the skins of black grapes. For rosé fewer skins are left in the fermenting wine for less long—the length of time depending on the colour and richness of flavour the maker wants. No doubt there are those who make it by mixing red and white wine, or even putting cochineal in white, but they work by night if they do.

Whereas in buying most other kinds of wine I would counsel you to buy the best you can afford, with rosé I would say buy the cheapest you can find, for there is not very much to choose between them. Rosés from northern parts, it is true, tend to be weaker in flavour and alcohol than some from farther south. Italian rosés, which are in the main more like light reds, have more character than some French ones. Portuguese rosés are usually shocking pink with titillating little bubbles. But basically the same, essential, appealing wine is there behind the frills and frou-frou. It is the wine for lunches, picnics, kitchen-parties—but not for fine food at a good dinner.

*France*
*Tavel*

One of France's rosés takes itself, and is taken, more seriously than the others. It is Tavel, the pink cousin of Châteauneuf-du-Pape, from just across the Rhône in the same hot and stony countryside. Like its cousin it is a strong wine, leaning towards the onion-skin (imagine the colour Cézanne would have painted an onion) in colour, high-flavoured, not remarkably scented but pungent and assertive, happy with the strong-flavoured food of Provence. It goes equally well with the herb-smoky grills and the astonishingly thirst-provoking *aioli*, or with that strange Provençal concoction, the oily, creamy cod porridge known as *brandade de morue*.

But even Tavel, leader of the *vins rosés*, is not regarded as a wine of vintages or a *vin de garde*—a wine to keep. It is drunk, like all pink wines, regardless of its vintage but on the understanding that it is not more than two or three years old.

*Côtes de Provence*

Provence produces a great many *vins rosés* besides its most famous one. They are among the most plentiful and best wines of the Côtes de Provence region which stretches east from Marseilles behind all the resorts of that crowded coast. They all tend to be dry and strong rather than soft and sweet. This tendency is sometimes reversed in the cause of commerce; some of those which are shipped abroad in rather more fanciful bottles than good wine usually needs are medium-sweet, without much of the clean refreshing taste which makes them such good drinking in Provence. The Vacation Syndrome, or whatever you like to call it, works powerfully against the rosés of Provence in a foreign land; we ask them to take us back to our summertime Garden of Eden, we expect a sip to transport us, like the N.7., to Nice. There are wines which can give satisfaction when so much is asked of them, but Provençal rosés are not often among them.

*The Loire*

At the other extreme of wine-growing France, in the Loire valley, the rosé is blessed by nature with all the qualities its tender pinkness promises. It is light, soft and slightly sweet. It should be the perfect thing for a kind of party I shall never be invited to—a gathering of ladies for lunch. Suppose they are going to eat a chicken salad, or some veal or even just starch-reduced rusks and cream cheese, I propose the rosé of Anjou as the wine. There are two kinds of Anjou rosé in circulation, the cheaper known as plain Anjou Rosé and the (slightly) more expensive as Anjou Rosé de Cabernet, made of the Cabernet, the black grape of Bordeaux. The Cabernet wine is usually less sweet than the other, but more scented.

Burgundy does not waste much time with rosés. A small part of

*Beaujolais*    the produce of Beaujolais is made into rosé instead of red—and suffers loss of character accordingly. At the northern end of the Côte de Nuits,

*Marsannay*    near Gevrey-Chambertin, the village of Marsannay specializes in rosé, and makes a very fine, very pale one which is popular in the United States but rarely seen in Britain.

*Alsace*    A small part of the crop in Alsace is also made into rosé, and is excellent, but is not widely circulated in the wine-trade as the white Alsace wines are.

*Bordeaux*    Bordeaux also produces good rosé with very little fuss, cheaper than most and just as good. It is comparatively dry, and light and clean to the taste. It could even be the wine which made the English call all red Bordeaux claret, which was certainly pale red—though perhaps not quite so pale as the modern rosé.

*The Jura*    Last of the big rosé-producers of France—every area produces a little—is the Jura, whose lovely unvisited hills are like a ramp up to Switzerland from what feels like the heart of France. The Jura owes its fame to some small quantities of unusual white, brown and red wines, but not less to large quantities of rosé of very high quality. The Jura word for a rosé, just to round off the spectrum, is *gris*—grey.

Jura pink wines are, in taste, light red ones. They are made from the same two local grapes, the Poulsard and the Trousseau, as the velvety local red wines. Their quality varies more or less in proportion to the amount of Poulsard and the amount of Trousseau each wine has in it. The Poulsard is the better, although each contributes something to help the other. There is always some Trousseau, even when the finest quality is the object.

*Arbois*    The best part of the Jura area for red wine is the neighbourhood of its chief town, Arbois. The same is true for rosés. Rosé d'Arbois is therefore a superior appellation to Rosé du Jura. Beyond this it is hard to specify, because most of the wines have brand-names. Their quality is deliberately related to their price.

A good Arbois rosé has more scent than most pink wines, the characteristic kernel-like scent of the Poulsard. It is round, satisfying and faintly sweet—simply, as I have said, a pale red. Compared with it a Jura rosé seems a little thin but has, on the other hand, a kind of individuality, a rather stony quality, which is very attractive. There is one called Cendré de Novembre whose name alone goes a long way to persuade me. It is not difficult to imagine that you see the glow of embers in its colour, as its name suggests. November, on the other hand, is not the month I would choose to drink it. It is a carafe wine for summer, a picnic wine, a really refreshing mouthful for a hot day.

## Italy

The best of Italy's pink wines, too, is a pale red rather than a true rosé. It is Chiaretto, the wine of the calm lakeside of Garda. At the south end of the enormous lake which divides Lombardy from the Veneto the steep, misty, olive-clad hills which surround its north, east and west subside. In these faltering hills the wine is bright cherry-red. Under typical Italian holiday circumstances, in hot weather, with

*Chiaretto del Garda*    pasta or salads and on picnics, Chiaretto del Garda is perfect. The best Chiaretto of many good ones I know is made at a little place called Moniga on the south-western corner of the lake, by the firm of Nino Negri. Moniga is a tiny walled town, no bigger than a big farm, surrounded by vineyards. Its wine is sold as Moniga del Garda, with Chiaretto added as though as an afterthought.

To the north of Garda in the Italian Tyrol a paler, delicately bitter

*Lagrein Rosato* — and very attractive pink wine with the name of its grape, Lagrein Rosato, is made. It is curious that these wines are hardly shipped to Britain at all. They are certainly among the world's best rosés, and there is every sign that the market for rosés is expanding. The greater part of the produce of the Tyrol at the moment goes to Austria and Germany.

*Ravello* — Italy's two other famous and noteworthy *rosatos* come from the other extreme, the farthest south. Of these Ravello is the better known. Of the three shades of Ravello wine which are well known, particularly in the United States, pink is the most popular, though I personally think least good. It is a bit too strong for my taste, at any rate at home. It is remarkable how the rapid evaporation from the body in hot weather makes degrees of alcohol less noticeable. The wine which seems more or less normally strong when you are by the Mediterranean can be far headier at home in cold weather simply because the pores are shut and it has no way out.

*Rivera* — The much less frequented Adriatic coast of Italy at Bari makes an extremely good *rosato* called Rivera. I have not yet seen it exported anywhere, but no doubt it will be, and will be as good abroad as it is at Bari—or, come to that, in Rome, where I first met it.

## Switzerland and Germany

In Switzerland the vineyards round Lake Neuchâtel produce good rosé. In Germany a small amount of rosé is made, but it is never particularly distinguished and is rarely exported. On the other hand the very pale—it seems almost accidentally pink—Schillerwein which is made in the southern Rhine vineyards of Baden-Württemberg is a local speciality you will be pressed to try if you go there.

## Eastern Europe

Two of the best and cheapest rosés you can buy in Britain come from eastern Europe. They are the equivalents of the Riesling which has had such success. Perhaps they are even more outstanding.

*Hungary*
*Yugoslavia* — Hungary's rosé is a very pale tangerine colour, Yugoslavia's a deep plummy pink like a light red wine. They have as much character as rosé can—the Hungarian light and refreshing, the Yugoslav warm and fruity. The Yugoslav is always known as Ruzica, but the Hungarian might appear under any brand-name. Magyar is one current name in England.

## Portugal

The Portuguese have had the most astonishing success with their pink wine, considering that it costs nearly twice as much as the Hungarian and Yugoslav ones. Part of the high cost is caused by its import in bottle—and very fancy bottle too. Part is due to the various processes by which the wine is made pink, slightly sweet and slightly sparkling.

In the United States, Lancers, which is described as crackling, and in Britain Mateus are the biggest selling wines of all. They are, in a sense, wines for people who do not really like wine. They form an intermediate stage between childish fizzy drinks and the adult taste for wine. As such, they do an invaluable service, for anything which leads more people to drink wine as part of their daily diet helps them towards health and happiness.

## The New World

As you would expect, rosé wine has transplanted to the New World's vineyards better than most. There is no great difference in character between Californian and European rosés, partly because neither has a very strong character to assert. When the grape of France's most famous rosé, Tavel, is used, which is increasingly often, results can be on a level with the French wine. The Grenache is the grape, and its name is seen on the best rosés of both California and Australia. The Beaujolais grape, the Gamay, is also used to make a good rosé.

*California*

Most—possibly all—of the great California wine-firms make good rosé, happy to be compared with French wines, and losing nothing by the comparison. In Maryland the Boordy vineyard makes a rosé with a high reputation, and Widmers make a Finger Lakes rosé in upper New York State which is said to be among the better New York State wines.

*Maryland*

*New York State*

*Australia*

In Australia Lindeman's Grenache rosé wins most prizes. Kaiser Stuhl in the Barossa valley also makes a light Grenache one, a touch sweeter than Lindeman's. Seppelt's Spritzig, on the other hand, obviously draws its inspiration from Portugal, even to the bottle and label. It is, after all, the Portuguese who have done most to make pink wine attractive.

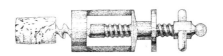

# Red Table Wines

Whereas white wine is made from the juice of grapes alone, red wine is made from the skins as well; and whereas white wine can be made from black or white grapes, red wine can only be made from black grapes. The colouring pigment in the skin makes it red, and various other constituents of the skins alter its taste. In fact, it is white wine plus. But so great a difference do the skins make that it seems like a completely different drink.

Red wines are rarely sweet. While white ones vary from tart to luscious, red stays somewhere in the middle. Some clarets are extremely dry. Some wines from the far south are very rich. Occasionally red wines are bitter. Others have a mouth-coating property. Principally, though, they have the appetizing taste which makes them the ideal companions for savoury food.

Red wines tend to come from hotter places than white, although most of the world's vineyards grow both to some extent. In Germany, the northernmost vineyard, what little red is made is not very good. In the south of Italy, on the other hand, red is far more widespread than white and tends to be better. This phenomenon is not always convenient; we more often feel like a cool white wine in a hot country and a rich red one where it is cold. But white wine needs some acidity, which it loses when the grapes get very ripe under a hot sun. In red wines the balancing factor which keeps them from being flat and dull to drink is tannin.

*Tannin*   Tannin is the substance which is used for tanning leather. It is found in the bark of trees, particularly the oak, in tea and in the skins, stalks and pips of grapes. Its taste is hard and harsh, but this gives it its vital rôle. Without it the wine would be characterless and insipid.

The strength of a red table wine varies from about 8 to about 18 per cent alcohol. The usual figure is 10 or 11 per cent. It can be either more or less strong than a white one, but usually it is a degree or so less. White grapes tend to contain that much more sugar.

The world's finest wines are both red and white; it is not possible to say that either is finer than the other. Most *vin ordinaire*, though, is red. The word "wine", alone, conjures up a glass of something red rather than white. Certainly the first wine was red: separating the juice from the rest of the grape came as a later refinement.

In fact, if it had to be a one-wine world, the majority of wine-drinkers would probably settle for red. There is something satisfyingly complete about it. And there are not many things that it does not go well with.

## French red wines

If there was some doubt about whether France leads the world for white wines, there is none about red. There is no challenger to her position as the producer of the best, and very nearly the most, red wine in the world.

She has such a strong position that there are few red wines made in other parts of the world which can say that they owe nothing to France. A good many owe even the names under which they are sold: claret and burgundy are both English names for French wines which have been used by the whole world to designate two kinds of red wine. Those that do not owe their names very often owe their grapes to the vineyards of France.

### Bordeaux and Burgundy

Bordeaux and Burgundy are indisputably the world's greatest red-wine areas. Even in France there is nothing else to touch them. The Rhône valley comes next, giving wine which at its best is probably as good as any other in the world. Besides these three there are four or five excellent smaller areas and a vast sprawl of ordinary and very ordinary ones.

You have only to look at the proportion of the space taken up on any wine-list by the wines of Burgundy and Bordeaux to see that all the rest of the world's wine together cannot compare in variety and in the care with which individual vineyards are kept apart and given labels and distinctions of their own. Elsewhere—with Germany only excepted—it is enough to say which village, which county or even which country the wine comes from; in Bordeaux and Burgundy, on the other hand, we are told which vineyard, even which part of the vineyard, who made the wine, bottled it, and when and such distinctions are enough to justify enormous differences of price.

You have, then, the prospect of perhaps two thousand different names in Bordeaux, five-hundred-odd in Burgundy and another five hundred in the rest of the country. It is safe to say that nobody knows them all. There are perhaps three or four hundred of these which a regular wine-drinker gets to know in time—which, in fact, regularly appear on wine-lists overseas. It is at least as many names of wines as he will need to know from the whole of the rest of the world put together.

I shall concentrate, in the following pages, on the wines which are best known and most shipped overseas. They include all the best ones. The specialists in the British and American wine-trades often know more about the districts of Bordeaux and Burgundy than the people who live there.

# The Red Wines of Bordeaux

Bordeaux is the largest fine-wine-producing area in the world. Its red wines, which make up a shade under a half of its total production, are known in Britain as claret. Historically, they are the table wine of the ordinary Englishman. There was a long period when this was no longer true—the greater part, in fact, of the seventeenth, eighteenth and nineteenth centuries—but the British have always had a weakness for claret, even when war or taxation have prevented them getting it. Today it is once again the most commonly drunk, as well as the most highly prized, of the red wines which are described as "table" because they are incomparably at their best with food.

*The taste of claret*   Red Bordeaux is among the light and dry red wines. So large an area obviously has wide divergences of style—from year to year as well as from place to place—but the overriding hallmark of claret is to be slightly mouth-drying and at the same time to taste of fresh soft fruit. It is not what is known as "fruity". Very fine old clarets eventually reveal that there is still some sugar in their systems; they seem to allow themselves to smile after decades of keeping a stiff upper lip. But sweetness (except of character) is not the thing to look for in a claret. Spiciness—the kind of scent found in a cigar-box—there sometimes is, and quite frequently a slight hardness and taste of the stalks. In poor years red Bordeaux can seem thin, poor stuff—acid and watery—but it rarely loses its typical, refreshing, individual taste.

*The country*   Bordeaux lies in country which owes its nature to rivers and the sea. The Dordogne, flowing from the east, and the Garonne, running north from the foothills of the Pyrenees, meet some fifty miles before they flow together into the Bay of Biscay. The country round the confluence of those rivers is the Bordeaux country.

*The city of Bordeaux*   The city of Bordeaux lies just above it on the wide grey Garonne. It is a grey city itself, but to anyone who admires the taste of the eighteenth century it is one of the finest in France. Its quarter of a million inhabitants live and work in streets of the period of Louis XVI. Just before the French Revolution, at a time when French taste was at its most perfect, the city was the centre of the trade with the Indies, both East and West. Its merchants and bankers set out to make it one of the finest cities in the world.

As it is today, it is a pleasure to walk along any of its serene, elegant streets. It reminds me a little of Dublin or Edinburgh. The black iron balconies against grey façades, graceful and monochrome, suggest an exquisite charcoal drawing.

The approach to the city on the Paris road, over its busy bridge, is magnificent. It is worth walking out along it (for it is impossible to linger on it in a car). The quay, almost six miles long, stretches as far as you can see in both directions. Spires and towers rise above a lovely even line of buildings which form a low grey cliff down to the river.

*The port*
The quay, not surprisingly, is a mass of barrels. Huge grey and white ships with derricks like the dipping oars of a quinquereme load where centuries of merchantmen have loaded before them with claret for Bristol, Leith, Boston, Bremen, The Hook, New Orleans. Under the splendid terrace opposite the ships the shippers' cellars stretch for miles. There should be sails, furled and spread, and the dark wedges of rigging there to balance the beauty of the old city on the water.

## The vineyards

The vineyards of Bordeaux are all around. Upstream, downstream, almost in the city to the south, across the Garonne in Entre-Deux-Mers, the beak of land that separates the two rivers as they flow to meet each other, and again across the far river, on the hills that over-look Bordeaux from the east. They fill the whole of the *département* of the Gironde, which is the name the two rivers take when they have become one. And they are all legally Bordeaux.

Upstream, to the south, is the country of the white wine. Graves, whose best wine is red but which is most famous for medium-dry white, and Sauternes, where virtually no red wine is made at all, lie in the valley of the Garonne above the city. Across the river the district known as the Premières Côtes de Bordeaux produces good red wine too, but not the best. It is to the north, twenty or thirty miles outside the city, and an equal distance to the east, that the finest wines are made. These are the districts of Médoc and St-Emilion.

They are very different places. The Médoc has a character which you immediately associate with the seaside. Not only is it flat, or nearly so, but the air has that feeling and the light that special lumin-osity. St-Emilion is a hill-town and nothing suggests that it is any nearer the sea than Burgundy. In both—indeed in all the areas of Bor-deaux—the wine-growing unit is called a Château.

## A château

However you translate the word château, referring to the châteaux of Bordeaux, the equivalent is not castle. Farm might almost be a better word, though there are many that are much too elegant, or pretentious, for that. It means any building that is the residence and headquarters of a wine-growing estate, and the estate itself.

A typical château consists of a six- or eight-bedroomed house, rarely lived in all the year round but the scene of splendid lunch- and dinner-parties at vintage-time, and another building, at least as big as the house again.

*The chai*
The other building is the *chai*. The word *chai* is Bordelais for both winery and cellar, that is, both where the wine is made and stored. It is under the control of the *maître de chai*, who takes responsibility for the wine from the moment it is made to the moment it is sold. He is foreman of the château, sometimes responsible to a *gérant*, or agent, sometimes to the owner himself.

Many of the *maîtres de chais* of Bordeaux are famous and formidable figures in their own right. They tend to act the role of host to any casual visitors to the château; they will show their new wine, cold and hard from its cask, to any who come and ask, with a mixture of pride and suspicion.

*The vintage*

At harvest-time the *chai* is a scene of ordered industry. From the vineyard the grapes are arriving in tipping-wagons like coal-scuttles, or in chest-high drum-shaped tubs of wood. A hoist of chains swings out from the building, lifts off the tub and tips the grapes into a chute. The tub goes back to the vineyard to be refilled. The grapes are drawn down into the *égrappoir*, which tears off their stalks and splits them open, and are then pumped up into tall wooden drums or vats (or cold-looking concrete ones more often nowadays) to ferment. As soon as fermentation begins the sides of the vat grow warm, and the air is full of a heady, slightly sickly smell. In hot weather hoses are standing by in case they are needed to cool the vats down to prevent the fermentation running away.

So the must, which soon becomes wine, stays for up to two weeks, fermenting violently at first, then calming down. The mass of skins and pips which rose to the top and formed a cap on the vat sinks as the yeast's work draws to an end. The next job is to draw the wine off the *marc*, as the solid remnants are called. The *marc* is pressed, for it is still full of wine. This *vin de presse* can come in useful, for it is rich in tannin, and if the *vin de goutte*, the unpressed wine, is at all flabby in taste, a little can be added. But it is more likely to be used for the workmen's ordinary ration.

So the young wine is in barrels. The room where the barrels are stored is a long, low barn, its floor a little below ground-level. The barrels stretch in rows like vines from end to end; two, three or four hundred of them, the year's produce. In the bung-hole of each is a glass weight to keep out the air. Once a week this must be taken out and the barrel topped-up with the same wine, a process known as *ouillage*. It prevents evaporation, and the absorption of wine by the new wood, from leaving a gap in the top of the barrel where air could lie and harm the wine. The word has come across into English as ullage. "On ullage" to the English wine-trade means not topped-up, slightly less than full, as very old bottles sometimes are.

*The trade*

So the wine stays for about two years. Courtiers or brokers, *négociants* and possible customers from England and America will come, taste the wine and try and judge what its future is going to be. Some come as early as December or January after the vintage, hoping to get the pick of the crop, while it is still so cold in the *chai* that they can barely taste the wine at all. Muffled up to the ears and wearing three pairs of socks they try to peer ahead into the future of the ungrateful, almost black liquid in their hands. Other more traditional and less frenzied merchants wait until the summer, when the wine has settled down a little, before they make up their minds about it.

Unfortunately, though, not all buying is done with the all-important object, the wine itself, as evidence. More and more it is a matter of speculation. Merchants are prepared to buy even before the grapes are ripe to make sure of their supplies. This buying *sur souche*, as it is called, which means on the vine, does not leave the merchant the alternative of not taking the wine if he cannot honestly recommend it to his customers. He can, of course, try to sell it all to another merchant if he does not like what he has bought. But so lucrative is the trade in good claret that speculation is an obvious way to enter the trade, and more and more people are doing it.

The structure of the trade in Bordeaux is extremely complicated and formalized, and need not detain us here. Many an outsider has stubbed his toe against it, and I do not propose to add my name to the list. However the wine changes hands, therefore, it is eventually sold for shipping, and there are three alternative ways in which it can be shipped. The first, which is universally used by the great classed growths for at least some of their wine, is in bottle, bottled at the château. The second, which is done less and less, is in bottle, bottled by a *négociant* in Bordeaux. The third is in barrel, to be bottled in London, Amsterdam or wherever it may be.

The argument for the first is that it guarantees absolute authenticity, and against it, that it is more expensive, an argument which has no force in the United States. The second must be defended by the supposition that the French wine-merchant is more trustworthy than his foreign counterparts; it is also more expensive, but sometimes merchants who are on the spot are in a better position to find bargains. The value of the third depends on who your wine-merchant is—and nothing else.

The classification<br>of 1855

All France's wine-districts have been divided officially into better and less good parts at one time or other, but Bordeaux is the only one where a list of the best wines, in order of quality, has ever been made. It was done in 1855, on the occasion of the Great International Exhibition in Paris. How well it was done is shown by the fact that it is broadly correct to this day.

The merchants of Bordeaux agreed to accept an aggregate of the prices each wine had fetched over the previous hundred years or so as the measure of its quality. The sixty-five most expensive they divided into five classes; again, natural difference of price indicated where the divisions came. The five classes are the five "growths".

There are several qualifications about the classification, apart from the fact that it is, of course, more than a century old.

The first is that it only includes great wines, whereas the list of good (and occasionally great) wines could have extended it considerably. There are, in fact, several hundred *bourgeois* growths (the name the merchants gave to wine which fell behind the great classic wines) and considerably more *artisan* growths, the category for small vineyards of only moderate quality.

The second objection is that it is territorially incomplete. It takes into account the Médoc area and Sauternes (in a separate sub-classification). It admits its incompleteness in making an exception for Château Haut-Brion in Graves, which lies outside its area, and including it among the first-growths, though it does not mention any other Graves wines. St-Emilion and Pomerol, equally red Bordeaux wines but from the other side of the river, it ignores completely.

The first problem was overcome to some extent in 1932, when the *bourgeois* growths were graded as *crus exceptionnels, crus bourgeois supérieures* and *crus bourgeois*. There were seven of the first, about seventy of the second and hundreds of the third. Below them came the *crus artisans* and below them, though rarely referred to, the *crus paysans*. The sense of hierarchy is evidently strong in Bordeaux.

Classifications of<br>Graves, St-Emilion<br>and Pomerol

More recently Graves, St-Emilion and Pomerol have been given separate local classifications of their own. Unfortunately, each proceeds on a completely different basis. The wines of Graves are merely listed without comment on their relative quality; the ten reds can simply put *cru classé* (classed growth) on their labels. The wines of St-Emilion were divided into *premiers grands crus classés*, *grands crus classés* and *grands crus*. Those of Pomerol are *premiers grands crus*, *premiers crus*, *deuxièmes premiers crus* and *deuxièmes crus*.

So it can be seen that the words "first-growth" are fairly casually flung about. In the Médoc there are only four first-growths: Lafite, Latour, Mouton-Rothschild and Margaux, whereas in Pomerol about twenty-five châteaux lay claim to the title, and a further twenty call themselves "secondary first-growths". As a general rule, in fact, it is a good idea to take the phrase "first-growth" with a pinch of salt.

A new classification of the wines of Bordeaux is always being suggested. The first move was made in 1973, when Mouton-Rothschild, a second-growth long regarded (unofficially) as a first-growth, was officially promoted to the top rung. But though any new classification would be interesting, and no doubt fairer than the present historic document and its successors, it is hard to see what purpose it would serve. It would be far better to drop the classification altogether. A wine, after all, ought to fetch its price on account of its quality, not of its reputation.

## Appellations Contrôlées

In Bordeaux the laws of *Appellation Contrôlée* are not quite as involved as they are in Burgundy. They only really affect anyone buying a bottle of the cheaper kinds of wine. In Burgundy the great vineyards have an elaborate fabric of appellation laws of their own, but in Bordeaux there is no *Appellation Contrôlée* more restrictive than a village name. Château Lafite and the co-operative wine cellars at Pauillac, its commune, are equally *Appellation Pauillac Contrôlée*.

You can safely assume that a Bordeaux wine will always be sold under the highest (or in other words most restrictive and specific) appellation to which it is entitled. Any wine sold as plain Bordeaux, then, will be less than 10.5 per cent alcohol, for more would entitle it to the appellation Bordeaux Supérieur. If it is sold as Bordeaux Supérieur it will not come from any of the better parts of the area with restricted appellations of their own; it will come from one of the undistinguished fringes of the Bordeaux vineyards.

If a wine has any of the wide-ranging district names—Médoc, St-Emilion or Côtes de Fronsac, for example—it may come from any vineyard in that area, be a blend of the wines of that area, or be the wine of a local co-operative. If it has anything to gain by naming its origin more specifically, or by stating which vineyard in the neighbourhood it came from, presumably it would do so.

The level of appellations above districts, that of communes, is as far as they go. The commune names which are protected are Listrac, Moulis, Margaux, St-Julien, Pauillac and St-Estèphe, all within the Haut-Médoc district. The villages around St-Emilion which do not quite merit the appellation St-Émilion also have their own appellations; their own names hyphenated to the name St-Emilion.

So the levels of quality, as far as they can be read from labels, are as follows: Bordeaux, Bordeaux Supérieur, then a district name, then a commune or village name. Some districts are better than others; some communes are better than others. Haut-Médoc, for example, is better than just plain Médoc; Pauillac is better, in general, than Listrac. But it is beyond the scope of *Appellations Contrôlées* that the real interest of different growths in Bordeaux begins. There are nearly two thousand different estates which sell their wine with the intention that it shall reach the eventual drinker bearing its own name. In these wines the appellation, whatever it may be, is only in small type; the important thing is the château's name. There can hardly be anyone alive who knows them all, but it is among these that the wine-merchants pick their way, looking for value. More and more they are finding the kind of wine they want at a sensible price among the *bourgeois* growths. The name has such Marxist-Leninist undertones that it is rather unfortunate, but it should not discourage anyone. It is among them, rather than the great classified growths, that the future of the non-millionaire claret-drinker lies.

## The Médoc

The Médoc is the eastern, or river, side of a long, flat promontory caught between the Gironde and the sea. Its western half is pine forest, sand dunes and long empty beaches. Huntsmen and woodsmen are the only people who go there. Larks and pigeons have the country to themselves.

Even the line of villages along the Gironde, whose names everyone knows—Margaux, St-Julien, Pauillac, St-Estèphe—are lost and sleepy for eleven-twelfths of the year. Their stony vine-covered slopes slip down to the river in a mood of quietness that changes only with the seasons, never with the years. Where they reach the flat land at the river's edge the vines stop, and for a space nothing but coarse grass and blackberries grow. Here fishermen leave their long rods day-long, bobbing over the brown flow of the river, and plovers dip and wheel in still air.

In the Médoc more great red wine is made than anywhere else on earth.

All the finest part of the wine-growing Médoc is included in the area known to the laws of appellations as Haut-Médoc. The word Médoc is used to refer to what was once, less confusingly, called the Bas-Médoc; the north end of the promontory, where less brilliant, though still excellent, wine is made.

## Bas-Médoc

Not many of the wines of the Bas-Médoc are known by name outside their immediate locality. The names of Châteaux Loudenne, Laujac, La Tour-de-By, Patache d'Aux and du Castera are quite often seen on English wine-lists, Loudenne particularly since it has belonged to the English firm of Gilbeys for nearly a century. They bought it as a result of Gladstone's benevolent budget of 1865 in which he lowered duties on table wines, believing that they were far more beneficial than the fortified wines which everybody was then drinking. Up to that time, Gilbeys had been concentrating on selling South African wines, which enjoyed an Imperial preference. This was the only way they could offer reasonable wines that ordinary people could afford. As soon as the Chancellor made it possible they became the first English firm to secure their own supply of good cheap claret.

This is the chief usefulness of the Bas-Médoc. In the finest years some of its wines will rise to the quality of the lesser growths of the Haut-Médoc in normal years. Its prices, however, always stay very reasonable. If you see a Bas-Médoc growth on a wine-list (it will say after its name simply *Appellation Médoc Contrôlée*), you can be fairly confident that the merchant has selected it for solid worth. It is almost always comparatively light, even for claret, which gives it the advantage of needing no more than three or four years of ageing before it is ready to drink.

*Haut-Médoc*

Haut-Médoc begins in the north at the village of St-Seurin-de-Cadourne. From there down to Blanquefort, almost in the northern suburbs of Bordeaux, is a distance of thirty or so miles as the crow flies, as extraordinary as the thirty miles of Burgundy's wonderful Côtes, a long file of good, fine and great vineyards.

There is no chance of mentioning even half of the châteaux of the Haut-Médoc by name. *Bordeaux et Ses Vins*—"The Bordeaux Bible" —by Cocks and Feret, which is reissued every few years, has over two hundred pages on this area alone. Specialized books have given it the detailed coverage it needs. Here I can mention only the greatest of the wines and some of the others which are often seen in Britain and the United States.

*St-Seurin-de-Cadourne*

At St-Seurin-de-Cadourne, Châteaux Coufran, Verdignan and Bel-Orme-Tronquoy-de-Lalande are all well-known *crus bourgeois*. There are no *crus classés*.

*St-Estèphe*

The next village is St-Estèphe. Here, suddenly, we are in the middle of the famous Haut-Médoc, with superlative growths and names known all over the world on every hand. Five of the classic classified growths are in St-Estèphe. Of all the wines of the Médoc they are the strongest in flavour, perhaps the least delicate but some of the most splendid, warm and grand in character. Châteaux Montrose and Cos d'Estournel are second-growths, only one removed from the top flight of all. Each has its character—it is one of the distinguishing marks of the wines that deserve to be called great that they impress you with a personality; they become like acquaintances with characters which can inspire endless discussion.

*Château Cos d'Estournel*

Cos d'Estournel is a curious looking place. The "château" (there is no dwelling house; only the *chais*) was given a façade with Chinese pagodas all over it some time in the last century. The d'Estournelle family fortune was in some way tied up with Chinese trade, leaving this odd and rather ungainly mark on the Médoc. With the familiarity of old customers, English wine-merchants usually refer to Cos d'Estournel (the first "s" is silent) as Coss, like a lettuce. Its wine has more power than most Médocs, and correspondingly is one to keep for a longer, rather than shorter, time to mature. It can be rather hard and fierce in its early years, but in later life it becomes one of the finest of all clarets. This is not surprising. Its neighbour to the south, just over the stream which forms the parish boundary, is Château Lafite.

*Château Montrose*

For Montrose I have a special weakness. The château belongs to Madame Charmolüe, but it is her son and his wife who are always there, and the wine today is his responsibility. The château is a small Victorian house, very mildly assuming the airs of a great proprietor. From its windows you can see the vines sloping away in the distance down to the broad brown Gironde.

Montrose always seems to me to have a touch of lovely sweetness, a trace of some very generous and kindly quality, only partly concealed by the considerable power of a great and classic wine. No doubt memories have coloured it in my mind, for it was here that, on my first visit, M Charmolüe quietly put half a dozen bottles of his wine in the back of my car before I drove away. The next weekend I was on my own up in the lovely remote country of the Dordogne, staying and eating my evening meal at a *routiers* café. I drank one of the bottles of Montrose with my dinner, and was so happy with it that I went out to the car to get the other five and gave them (it makes me sound mad) to the lorry-drivers who were in the café eating their stew. They evidently thought I was mad, too; they had probably never drunk a château-bottled second-growth claret before. In any case, they raised their glasses politely, and were about to empty them, when they stopped in mid-swallow. A look of immense pleasure, the expression of a true connoisseur face to face with a masterpiece, came over their faces. It was the scent of the wine, the clean, sweet, exquisite breath of autumn ripeness, which held them rapt. I do not think I exaggerate. It was a wonderful sight to see those great *onze-degrés* men, those pushers of gigantic trucks and trailers, breathing in the bouquet of a wine which spoke straight to them.

Châteaux Calon-Ségur, Lafon-Rochet and Cos-Labory are third-, fourth- and fifth-growths respectively. The first is a very fine wine; one of the best known of the Médoc as a safe bet from year to year if not one of the most thrilling. The second increases in stature yearly: a new owner has brought it into the limelight in the last decade or so. The third, though thoroughly sound, is less well known than a number of the many excellent *crus bourgeois* of the commune. Châteaux Tronquoy-Lalande, Meyney, Phélan-Ségur, de Pez, Pomys, Marbuzet, Beausite, Beausite-Haut-Vignoble, Capbern, Houissant, La Haye, Fontpetite, Le Boscq are ranked next after the classified growths. Close behind them come Châteaux Les Ormes de Pez, Beauséjour, Ladouys, MacCarthy-Moula, Canteloup, Morin, Andron-Blanquet and Le Roc. Besides all these, any of which you might see on a wine-list, the co-operative at St-Estèphe makes one of the best of the co-operative wines of the Médoc.

*Pauillac*

St-Estèphe borders on Pauillac, the finest and most famous of all the communes of Bordeaux, on the south. Both communes lie beside the river. Pauillac, indeed, has a long quay, for it is more than a village, and has recently become an important oil-refinery centre, which brings in ships from all parts of the world.

In the hinterland behind Pauillac and St-Estèphe good wine is grown, although its name means little beside the superlatives of the riverside. The inland villages are Vertheuil, Cissac and St-Sauveur.

*Vertheuil, Cissac and St-Sauveur*

Châteaux Cissac, du Breuil, Lamothe and Larrivaux at Cissac and Fonpiqueyre, Ramage-la-Batisse, Peyrabon and Liversan at St-Sauveur are the most important.

Pauillac is the only town anywhere which has three of the world's greatest red wines within its boundaries. They are Châteaux Lafite, Latour and Mouton-Rothschild. Lafite and Latour were listed first and third of all the wines of Bordeaux in the classification of 1855. Mouton was placed fifth.

If I had to try to characterize the three wines—for they are very different—I should say that Lafite is (or can be) the most beautiful of the three, Latour the most stylish and Mouton-Rothschild the most tremendous. Yet all are very much Pauillacs. Pauillacs are the most typical of all clarets; strong and clean, dry and scented, incomparably subtle and delicate and yet solid and substantial in your mouth. There is often a touch of the cigar-box scent about them.

*Château Lafite*

Lafite stands well back from the road on a little hill at the northern end of Pauillac. It is not a very striking house, although it is nearer to a castle than most in the Médoc. Inside it is decorated in the grand late-nineteenth-century manner of the Rothschilds, for it is one of the two great vineyards of the Rothschild family—both, they note with satisfaction, among the best in the world. The drawing-room is red and white, the little library dark, meditative green, lit with oil-lamps and, at vintage-time, a bowl of marigolds. Through the french windows on the terrace is a constantly sprinkled lawn, one of the few pieces of grass in Bordeaux which deserve the name.

Lafite's vineyards are large; they cover two hundred of the three-hundred-odd acres of the estate. Formerly only the best of their wine in any year was sold as Château Lafite. The rest was sold as Les Carruades de Château Lafite, or (a third class not often used and only for sale in France) Moulin des Carruades. Little has been seen of Carruades recently, however.

Lafite asks and gets the highest price of any Médoc château for its wine—unfortunately with less regard for the quality of the vintage than in the proud old days when sub-standard wine was summarily disposed of. If it holds its place in the classification today it is because of the real beauty of its most successful vintages: 1945, 1949, 1953, 1959, 1961. As Professor Roger says in *The Wines of Bordeaux*: "The man who has never tasted a great bottle of Lafite cannot know the perfections of which claret is capable." Nonetheless great vintages seem to happen less often at Lafite than elsewhere, and some perfectly adequate years (1967 is an example) have produced a disappointing product from such a sublime estate.

*Château Latour*

Château Latour is the complete contrast: probably the most con-sistent estate in Bordeaux, almost always making a firm, masculine, long-lasting wine. In great years it is superb; in poor years, when many fine châteaux fail to live up to their reputations, it is still superb. Even in such disaster years as 1965 and 1968 Latour, though a mere wraith of a wine, remains recognizably a classic claret.

The tower which gives it its name is no more than an embattled dovecot among the vines. The château itself is a simple, four-square house in a grove of trees. The interest of Latour lies in its *chais*, which lie apart from the house in the vineyard, forming a courtyard shaded by pollarded plane-trees. They were the first of the first-growths' wine-making equipment to be modernized, and to have the old oak fermenting-vats replaced with stainless steel. The fermenting-room is a very different place now from those of most of its rivals, but the quiet lines of barrels holding the wine of the last three vintages are the same as ever. The scene when I first went to Latour thirteen years ago, when old M. Brugière, the manager who must have been over eighty, ran it for the de Beaumont family, when the old house was like a country rectory blinking through its shutters at the sun on the vines and the river, and the sunlight fell in shafts on cobwebs in the dim *chai*, is so very different from the bustle today, with all the shutters thrown back and directors in dark suits everywhere, that it is hard to believe that the wine will be the same. If anything, however, it has been better than ever in the last decade. The new regime has added land to the estate on the landward side towards Batailley and created a new vineyard whose wine has sold (since the 1966 vintage) as Les Forts de Latour. Though it has, of course, no classification Les Forts is a worthy stable-mate of the great château: the newest of the great growths of the Médoc but by no means the least.

*Château Mouton-Rothschild*

Mouton-Rothschild, the third of the great three of Pauillac, makes, as I have said, the most tremendous wine. It is strong, very long-lasting, hard for its first decade at least, pungent and high-flavoured: unmistakably something very special. Such bottles as the 1945 and

1949 are among the deepest, most complex wines I have ever drunk. Mouton today is the work of one of the most remarkable men in Bordeaux, Baron Phillippe de Rothschild. He inherited the little farm with its famous vineyards when he was a young man fifty years ago. The wine has progressed from strength to strength under him, but at the same time he has done wonderful work in forwarding the cause of the whole of the Médoc. Besides Mouton he owns Château Mouton-Baron-Phillippe, a fifth-growth which he has characteristically made, in the words of Cocks and Feret's "Bordeaux Bible"— "*trés supérieur à son classement*". Recently he has also bought another small fifth-growth: Clerc-Milon-Mondon. No doubt it will enjoy the same fate.

At Mouton he has built up a museum of works of art connected with wine, ranging from ancient drinking-vessels to medieval tapestries of the vintage and some of the loveliest glass anywhere. He is also a poet, and the translator of Christopher Fry's plays into French for the stage. He has transformed Mouton from the little farm into a lovely house, and brought to it all the elegance which progress is chasing out of other parts of this quiet country. Yet there is nothing backward-looking about Mouton: its elegance is of today.

*The crus classés*  There are two second-growths in Pauillac, one fourth- and twelve fifth-growths. In reality this classification bears so little relation to the modern standing of the châteaux involved that it is better to consider them all simply as *crus classés*. The two seconds, Châteaux Pichon Longueville-Baron and Pichon Longueville-Lalande, flank the road with their turrets like fairy castles as you drive into Pauillac from the south. Of the two, Lalande is generally thought the better today, but both are worthy of their position.

The fourth-growth, Duhart-Milon, now belongs to Château Lafite and takes the suffix –Rothschild. No doubt it will increase in dignity and esteem. For the moment the two most celebrated Pauillac estates, after the first-growths, are Châteaux Pontet-Canet and Lynch-Bages, among the most popular of all clarets respectively in France and England. Lynch-Bages belongs to M. Cazes, the mayor of Pauillac. The wine is full and fruity, almost sweet at times. He has a mysterious way of maintaining his quality even in poor years. Pontet-Canet is the property of the Cruse family, one of the great merchant houses of Bordeaux. Its vineyards (the biggest of any *cru classé*) border on those of Mouton-Rothschild. They have been known to make a wine as superb as that of their neighbour: the 1929, in particular, is one of the finest clarets I have ever drunk. Recent vintages, however, have been disappointing for such a thoroughbred property.

The other Pauillac classed growths, very roughly in order of size and importance, are Châteaux Batailley, Croizet-Bages, Grand-Puy-Lacoste (very good and increasingly popular), Haut-Batailley (ditto; under the same ownership as Château Ducru-Beaucaillou in St-Julien), Haut-Bages-Libéral (Cruse property, like Pontet-Canet), Pedesclaux, Grand-Puy-Ducasse and Lynch-Moussas.

The names of some of the *crus bourgeois* of Pauillac are also often seen listed. The most prominent are Châteaux Haut-Bages-Averous and Haut-Bages-Monpelou, La Tour-Milon, La Tour-Pibran, Anseillan, Bellegrave, Fonbadet, Pibran and La Couronne. In this class

*Mouton Cadet*  also comes Mouton Cadet, the younger cousin of Mouton-Rothschild, though no blood relation. It is said to be the world's biggest-selling claret. It is a blended wine; not as good value as some of the unadvertised *bourgeois* growths, but more consistent from vintage to vintage. Besides all these the wine of the Pauillac co-operative, La Rose Pauillac, is well worth looking out for.

## St-Julien

St-Julien is the next of the great riverside communes. Pauillac has more superlative wines, which take longer to mature and eventually reach greater heights, but St-Julien has perhaps the highest average standard of any commune. It has no first-growths but it has five seconds, two thirds and five fourths. Two of its fourth-growths are among the best wines of Bordeaux in many years.

The St-Julien characteristic is often described as tenderness. Its wines nonetheless improve over a very long period, and might be called the safest wines of the Médoc. The demand for them is correspondingly high.

*The Léovilles*

The best wines of the commune are those nearest to Pauillac, the three châteaux which share the name of Léoville: Léoville-Las-Cases, Léoville-Poyferré and Léoville-Barton. The first of the three is biggest and perhaps best known, although in England Léoville-Barton is more often seen. Léoville-Barton, with the third-growth Langoa-Barton next door, belongs to the English Barton family, who have been merchants and growers in Bordeaux since the beginning of the last century. Ronald Barton is the present owner. Château Langoa, where he lives, is a typical eighteenth-century Bordeaux country-house. It is elegant, quite small, one long storey perched over its ground-level cellars, and by its shape—all the main rooms in a row so that each room has two main outside walls—subject to all the draughts of a long winter by the sea. In a corner of the Barton *chai* is one of the enormous old kitchens which are only brought into play at vintage-time, where the soup for the vintagers is stirred in cauldrons over a wood fire.

*Château Langoa*

Château Ducru-Beaucaillou, a palatial establishment on the riverside of the village, makes a superb wine which seems to get better with each vintage. Château Gruaud-Larose, the other second-growth, is also one of those which rarely produces anything but lovely, round, easy-to-drink claret. Gruaud-Larose and Château Talbot, one of the St-Julien fourth-growths, both belong to the big Bordeaux shipping house of Cordier. In Bordeaux the Cordiers have a beautiful eighteenth-century town-house called La Bottière. All three are among the showplaces of the countryside; their upkeep, furniture and elegance are as studied as the silky wine of their cellars.

*Château Beychevelle*

The rest of the fourth-growths, the united St-Pierre-Bontemps and St-Pierre-Sevaistre, Branaire-Ducru and Beychevelle, are led by Beychevelle. This is one of the most magnificent of the châteaux and most distinguished of the wines of the Médoc. It is reputed to have got its name from the salute of a dipped sail which passing sailors gave to the Lord High Admiral of France, the Duc d'Epernon, who lived there. The order "*baisse les voiles*" was corrupted to Beychevelle. Now the house is the home of the Achille Fould family. Beychevelle can be a rather thin and sharp wine in poor years, but in hot summers it sometimes overtakes every St-Julien in all the classical qualities of balance and finesse. The 1959 Beychevelle was such a wine.

*Château Lagrange*

Compared with these eminent fourth-growths the third-growth Château Lagrange has sunk into obscurity. It lies in the backcountry of St-Julien, its vineyard reduced from one of the biggest of the Médoc, its park in disorder, its lake silted up.

*Château Gloria*  The leader of the *crus bourgeois* of St-Julien would undoubtedly be among the classified growths if a new list were ever made. Château Gloria, while probably the least impressive château, has one of the best vineyards in the district. It is due to Henri Martin, the owner, who is also prominent in all the organizations for promotion and teamwork among the Médoc growers. His creation of a great new vineyard from scratch is remarkable—although perhaps the phrase from scratch gives the wrong idea. His land used to be part of the vineyards of Gruaud-Larose and the other classified growths. His neighbour to the north, Château Glana, now makes almost equally distinguished wine. Châteaux Grand-St-Julien, Médoc, Moulin-de-la-Rose, des Ormes and Bontemps-Dubarry are also well-known *crus bourgeois*. The

*St-Laurent*  hinterland of St-Julien is the commune of St-Laurent, which, although its only appellation is Haut-Médoc, has a good fourth-growth, Château La Tour Carnet, and a well-known fifth-growth, Château Belgrave, as well as several lesser-known *bourgeois* growths.

For a while south of St-Julien the best vineyards leave the river-banks and keep to the gravel ridges which here go inland. The next

*Moulis and Listrac*  two villages to have their own appellations, Moulis and Listrac, are well west of the road which leads straight up from Bordeaux along the Gironde. Neither has any classified growths, although Châteaux Chasse-Spleen and Dutruch-Grand-Poujeaux in Moulis and Châteaux Fourcas-Dupré and Fourcas-Hosten in Listrac would probably make it next time. Châteaux Villegeorge and Citran in the neighbouring

*Avensan*  commune of Avensan are also well known. These wines are all similar in a way, rather hard and solid, perhaps more like St-Estèphes than the wine of Margaux or St-Julien, their two great neighbours. Châteaux Pierre-Bibian, Clarke, Duplessis, Dutruch-Grand-Poujeaux, Maucaillou, Moulis, Gressier-Grand-Poujeaux, La Closerie-Grand-Poujeaux, Pomeys and Semeillan are all in this area. All are *crus bourgeois*, which are likely to be bought by British wine-merchants particularly and appear, as the classified growths all used to year after year until they became so expensive, on British wine-lists.

The villages of the river road below St-Julien (below on the map, above in terms of the stream of the river) are of less importance until we get to Margaux and Cantenac.

*Cussac*  Cussac, Lamarque, Arcins and Soussans all have the appellation Haut-Médoc, but none of their own. At Cussac (not to be confused with Cissac near St-Estèphe) Château Lanessan is the best-known wine.

*Lamarque*  At Lamarque, the sleepy old village whence the ferry plies over the river to Blaye, making a short-cut of about fifty miles—instead of going into Bordeaux—to the road north, the war-like old Château de Lamarque makes a good wine, and Château Malescasse has recently

*Arcins*  been bought, its *chais* rebuilt and its vines replanted. At Arcins the best of the wine has traditionally been used up in various more or less underhand ways by the growers of rich Margaux, down the road.

It is strange that a place like Arcins, so near Margaux, one of the richest townships in Bordeaux, and with not dissimilar soil and growing conditions, can be almost a depressed area, as it is. The root of the trouble is partly the archaic laws of inheritance, by which at every death, unless there is a well-paid family lawyer to do something about it, the land is divided among all the relations until there is hardly a grape for each of them in a small vineyard.

A young Englishman called Nicolas Barrow, who bought a small château—Château Courant—at Arcins, spent two years ferrying one relation to another trying to get a family consensus from some of his neighbours to exchange rows of vines so that they all could have continuous plots. Up to that time he had to go into his own vineyard with a chart to make sure he was not pruning someone else's vine.

Despite the great demand for fine claret there are many excellent vineyards at this moment where the proprietors are giving up the struggle and planting cabbages. They lack the means to make their own wine. They send in their grapes to the local co-operative where the wine is not necessarily very well made, where their grapes, which may well have been better than anyone else's, acquire total anonymity—indeed the only thing required of them is that they be ripe enough to give the required alcoholic strength. The growers' shares of the year's earnings come round years after the harvest—in fact, it is a disheartening business.

But the hunt for new names by the merchants who see the market for good and reasonably cheap claret expanding is a good sign. It may yet save many a good row of vines from replanting with cabbages.

*Soussans*　　　Soussans, the village which borders Margaux to the north, has three estates which are up to the Margaux standard: Châteaux La-Tour-de-Mons (a highly respected name), Paveil-de-Luze and La Bégorce-Zédé. They are allowed to use the appellation Margaux.

## Margaux

*Château Margaux*

Margaux is the last of the superlative, peerless communes of the Médoc, and perhaps the best known of all. Undoubtedly the fact that Château Margaux, its one first-growth, has the same name as the village has helped. Many people have confused the two and thought they were getting one of the world's greatest wines when they were really only getting a blended wine from the district.

It is the same story with Chambertin and Gevrey-Chambertin in Burgundy. The difficulty is to remember which of the two similar names is the star, and which the supporting cast. In fact, the price ought to make it clear enough. Château Margaux would always cost at least five times as much as plain Margaux.

Château Margaux is the most mansion-like of the first-growth châteaux. It presents a neoclassical façade to a fine avenue, and it has a park. The wine it makes is as unmistakable as the pediment and pillars, and very much more beautiful. Of all the first-growths, Margaux has the most ravishing scent; a flowery, fascinating bouquet. The wine is light and silky, but full of the quiet power of a great wine, not pungent and transitory but slowly moving through its stages of development, from hard and fine to soft and exquisitely delicate.

*Château Palmer*　　　Château Palmer next door, of all the other great names of Margaux, comes nearest to Château Margaux in quality and probably beats it in year-to-year consistency. This is a third-growth which should be a second, if not a first. Chateau Rausan-Ségla is a worthy second-growth; Rauzan-Gassies is more problematic. Then comes Château Lascombes, now the property of Bass Charrington Ltd, which was brought up to a very high standard by its former owner Alexis Lichine (and which has now been given the Médoc's most modern *chai*, almost Napa-valley style with a swimming pool). Lichine still owns the charming little Prieuré-Lichine and makes excellent wine there.

Châteaux Brane-Cantenac, Malescot, St-Exupéry and d'Issan might be singled out among the remaining Margaux *crus classés* for specially splendid wine in recent vintages. But the others remain great names from which very fine wine can be expected in good years. Chât-

*Arsac and Labarde*

eaux Kirwan, Marquis-d'Alesme-Becker, Cantenac-Brown, Durfort-Vivens, Marquis de Terme and Boyd-Cantenac are the *crus classés*.

A number of châteaux on the south side of Margaux and Cantenac (which are united under the name of Margaux) are also allowed to use the appellation Margaux. They lie in the communes of Arsac and Labarde, which themselves only have the appellation Haut-Médoc. Château Giscours at Labarde is the senior of these, followed by Château du Tertre at Arsac; both lie on (for the Médoc) a high ridge of ground. Between them comes the truly exceptional *cru exceptionnel* (one rank lower than a *cru classé*) Château Angludet. In any modern reappraisal Angludet would move up more than one rung.

Then over by the river to the east lie a charming pair of châteaux of growing reputation, Siran and Dauzac, both in Labarde and both owned by the owner of the great Pichon-Lalande.

## The rest of the Médoc

The rest of the Médoc has no other appellation than Haut-Médoc, despite the fact that it includes some superb growths and two famous communes, Ludon and Macau. Macau is the northern one of the two. It has one classified growth, a fifth which is now considered level with seconds or thirds, Cantemerle. It is a fine great building hidden by a lovely wood, in which you can well believe that the blackbirds of the name (which means blackbirds' song) sing with all their might. Cantemerle has less polish, perhaps, than the great Margaux wines, but the combined firmness and subtlety of claret of the highest class.

*Château Cantemerle*

*Ludon*
*Château La Lagune*

At Ludon there is also one classified growth, Château La Lagune. It has a very high reputation as a strong, solid and slow-maturing wine with a softness and scent which distinguish it. The château is small but fine, by tradition the work of Bordeaux's greatest architect, Louis, who designed the front of the Bordeaux theatre, one of the finest public buildings in France. The *chais* of La Lagune are also notable—modern and recently equipped. It is the nearest of the *crus classés* of the Médoc to Bordeaux, only about ten miles away, and welcomes visitors, which makes it perhaps better known that it would otherwise be without one of the magic names such as Margaux on its label. Among its neighbours is the irresistibly romantic moated fortress, Château d'Agassac, which sells its substantial wine mainly in the Low Countries. Châteaux Lafite-Canteloup, d'Arche, Ludon-Pomiés-Agassac and Nexon-Lemoyne are also *crus bourgeois* of some standing.

*Le Pian,*
*Parempuyre,*
*Blanquefort,*
*and Le Taillan*

There remain the relatively unimportant communes of Le Pian, Parempuyre and Blanquefort on the road to Bordeaux, and to the west, away from the Gironde, the commune of Le Taillan. At Le Pian, Château Sénéjac, at Parempuyre, Châteaux Parempuyre and Ségur and at Le Taillan, Château du Taillan, a Cruse property, are well known. Le Taillan is a very fine house with two façades of equal grandeur. It must be the only house in the world with a different name on each side, for one façade is used for the labels of its red wine, Taillan, the other is called La Dame Blanche on the labels of its white wine.

## Graves

Maurice Healy, an old Irish claret-lover and the author of *Stay Me with Flagons*, a book about his loves, made one of the most splendidly opaque remarks on the subject of wine when he described the difference between claret from the Médoc and from Graves. They are, he said, like matt and glossy prints of the same photograph. The matt ones are the Graves.

It comes as a surprise to most people to know that there is such a thing as red Graves, although the red is by far the best wine of the region, and constitutes over a quarter of its production. The word Graves, unqualified, commonly means white wine.

Graves starts at the very gates of Bordeaux. In fact, it is more true to say that Bordeaux is in Graves, and so is Bordeaux's airport, Mérignac. The noblest suburb of the city is now undoubtedly Pessac, for here, even before the little villas finally end, the road out of Bordeaux passes the gates of Château Haut-Brion. Although the merchants who devised the 1855 classification were not taking Graves into account, they could not ignore Haut-Brion. There was only one place for it—in the top four. Haut-Brion is a first-growth, but none of the other Graves châteaux are any kind of numbered growth at all. They are simply *crus classés*.

*Château Haut-Brion*

Château Haut-Brion is another American property. It belongs to Clarence Dillon, formerly the American Ambassador to France, now, as it were, France's ambassador to America. The kind of wine they make at Haut-Brion is very different from the first-growths of the Médoc. It seems more powerful and less clean-cut, full of flavour but needing a long time in bottle to bring out what eventually becomes a heavenly scent. I was once lucky enough to be at a dinner-party at the Mirabelle Restaurant in London when an Imperiale, a giant bottle holding eight and a half normal bottles, of Haut-Brion 1899 was opened. A fine plate of beef had just been put down in front of me. I forgot all about the beef: I shall never forget that wine. Its scent rose firmly to a peak like the pediment of the Parthenon. Below it were great depths of taste. It was pure delight of a kind which only the greatest of wines, or music, or poetry, or painting, can give.

*Château La Mission Haut-Brion*

Just across the road from Haut-Brion is Château La Mission Haut-Brion. Like Château Palmer in Margaux, La Mission is a direct challenge to its first-growth neighbour, occasionally surpassing it and never falling far behind. La Mission has a very fine second red wine, Château Latour Haut-Brion. Haut-Brion's second wine, Bahans, is less well known. Pessac's other great château is Pape-Clément, whose vineyards were first planted by the Bishop of Bordeaux who became Pope in the fourteenth century and moved the Papal headquarters (so great, one supposes, was his love of French wine) to Avignon. It is surprising that he did not move it to Bordeaux.

*Château Pape-Clément*

*Léognan*

The greater number of the best growths of Graves are in the communes of Léognan and Martillac, four miles south of Pessac in the typical sandy pine country in which growing vines is hard, unrelenting work and the rewards small. Yield is low and the wine relatively expensive. It has to be good to sell at all. At Léognan the great growths are Châteaux Haut-Bailly, Domaine de Chevalier (these two often among the very finest clarets of any district, both strong, consistent wines full of character) and Malartic-Lagravière, followed by Châteaux Carbonnieux, Fieuzal, La Louvière, Le Pape, Olivier, Larrivet-Haut-Brion. Many of these châteaux are equally famous for their white wine—a rare state of affairs. Graves is the only great wine-area in France where red and white vineyards are inextricably mixed.

*Martillac*

At Martillac, Châteaux Smith-Haut-Lafitte, Latour-Martillac and La Garde are the best growths. In the commune of Cadaujac next door the American-owned Château Bouscaut is thoroughly reliable.

There are few common everyday red Graves. As a class they are wines of strong character, even in their less good years (bad vintages are relatively rare in Graves), and ask to be used well, with simple roast meat or game. To me they are dinner-party wines. If the company is interested in wine it enjoys them for being unusual: if it is not, it enjoys them all the same.

## St-Emilion

Fashion swings back and forth from one end of the Bordeaux country to another. At one time no-one would hear of any wine except red Graves. Then it had to be Médoc. At the moment, the districts of St-Emilion and Pomerol are in high favour.

St-Emilion has more representatives on most wine-lists than any other Bordeaux district today. Perhaps this is not so surprising—it is the biggest. But Pomerol, which is the smallest of all the communes, has almost as many. The reason is partly that these wines need less time to mature than the great Médocs, and are good, though not at their best, after a mere four years or so. Partly it is their warmth of flavour. They are less dry and scented than the Médocs, more powerful, and with more of the savoury appeal of a burgundy. It is so often said that St-Emilion is the burgundy of Bordeaux that you might expect St-Emilions to taste like burgundy. They do not: they taste like claret, but claret moving towards burgundy—full, savoury and strong.

The slightly less temperate climate away from the coast has something to do with the difference, undoubtedly. But the main factors are the richer soil and the choice of grape varieties. The Cabernet Sauvignon, source of much of the Médoc's perfume and finesse (and also of its tannic hardness in youth) is little used here. The staple of St-Emilion and Pomerol is the Merlot, the relatively minor part of the Médoc blend. Merlot wine is softer, ages sooner, tends more to richness and sweetness.

The town of St-Emilion ranks after Beaune as the most interesting and attractive little wine-town in France. St-Emilion has vines in every nook and cranny. Whether you look up, down (for it is on a steep slope) or sideways, there is a vineyard in sight. The town fills the thin end of a wedge-like re-entrant in a hill of vines. Its cobbled streets and equally cobbled-looking rooftops, made of the Roman pattern of curved tiles, lead up to its astonishing old church which was cut out of the living rock of the hillside. I know of no other building like it. It has aisles, side-aisles, nave and chancel, the usual size but dug out, not built up—a church-shaped cave. Its belfry is built above it on what appears from above to be a platform of ordinary flat ground. It shares the view over the rooftops and the vines down to the Dordogne in the valley below with the town's best restaurant; one of the pleasantest terraces in France.

St-Emilion is about thirty miles east of Bordeaux, overlooking the Dordogne from the north. Its vineyards not only cover the hillside leading up to the town, but a wide plateau of high country behind. There is a distinction between the wines of the hill and those of the flat land. The hill-wines are known as Côtes-St-Emilion, the others as Graves- (meaning gravel) St-Emilion. A third area, Sables- (sand) St-Emilion at the foot of the hill by the river also makes wine, but of lesser quality. The terms are not used on labels—only in conversation.

## Côtes-St-Emilion
## Château Ausone

Côtes wines are the most full and generous, in the self-explanatory phrase of the wine-trade, of all clarets. Château Ausone is the most famous of them; though not necessarily, these days, the best. It is reputed to have been the estate and vineyard of the Roman poet Ausonius, who celebrated wine-growing both here and on the Moselle in the fourth century. If the story be true, it is one of Bordeaux's oldest vineyards. Its position under the brow of the hill, sheltered from the north wind and canted towards the sun, is more like Corton or one of the burgundy vineyards than the usual Bordeaux site. Still less typical of Bordeaux are its vast limestone cellars: the Côtes are honeycombed with these old quarries—the perfect place for storing wine. Ausone's neighbours, Châteaux Belair, Magdelaine, Canon and Beauséjour, Châteaux La Gaffelière below and Pavie opposite and Clos Fourtet almost in the town, with Château Trotte-vieille just the other side of it, are the most distinguished names of the Côtes. They were all classified as *premiers grand crus classés* in 1954.

The best known of the second rank, the *grand crus classés*, are Châteaux Chapelle-Madelaine, Curé-Bon-La-Madelaine, Grand-Pontet, Troplong-Mondot, Canon-La-Gaffelière, La Clotte, L'Angélus, Balestard-La-Tonnelle, Cap-de-Mourlin, Clos des Jacobins, Fonplégade—and there are a score of others.

At the bottom of the Côtes the land stretches away, level and sandy, to the river Dordogne. The substantial St-Emilion co-operative stands here. Its wine, St-Emilion-Royal, is generally reliable. But the founding fathers who allowed the appellation St-Emilion to this completely different terrain, the Sables, were honouring good grazing country rather than a classic wine area. One or two châteaux here, Monbousquet and Martinet in particular, make sound wine. But better is found in the hills east of St-Emilion which have no such grand title.

*Graves-St-Emilion*

The most famous name of St-Emilion, oddly enough, is only just in the district. The edge of its vineyard is the boundary of Pomerol.

*Château Cheval Blanc*

Château Cheval Blanc is usually mentioned in the same breath as Châteaux Lafite, Haut-Brion and Latour as one of the finest of all clarets. Occasionally it wins the distinction of being the best claret of all in a vintage, as it did in 1947. The wine of Cheval Blanc at its height—of which the 1947 was the classic example—is a wine of more power and solidity than the Médoc, even Mouton-Rothschild, ever achieves. At a dinner at Brooks's Club in London, where I first met it, I heard someone describe it as a monolithic wine, a single great upright pillar of polished stone, monumental, unyielding, perfect in proportion. He was right about the general effect but wrong, to me, about the stoniness. There is a velvet quality about it which is very different from cold stone. Above all, Cheval Blanc has more scent than most St-Emilions, almost the wonderful blossoming of perfume which we find in the first-growth Médocs.

This far corner of St-Emilion, which looks as though it should belong to Pomerol, is the Graves-St-Emilion district. It has far fewer estates than the Côtes, but some of the finest of all. After Cheval Blanc (which is a big vineyard—over eighty acres—in this district of small ones) come Châteaux Figeac (often a close second and another big property), Latour-Figeac and Latour-du-Pin-Figeac, Grand-Barrail-Lamarzelle-Figeac, La Dominique, Ripeau, Corbin, Croque-Michette . . . once you get going in St-Emilion (or Pomerol) it is hard to stop; so many small estates make wine of comparable quality. The best have something of the sweet and velvety quality of a Pomerol, with the power of flavour which is St-Emilion's special character.

The hinterland of St-Emilion, a broad undulating saddle of country between the Côtes and the little river Barbanne, its northern boundary, maintains a high and even standard, even if its château names are little known. Beyond the Barbanne, too, is wine-country—

though not the same monoculture of the vine—with considerable potential in the expanding market for claret. I have already said that the appellation St-Emilion might well have been withheld from the Dordogne valley with its sandy soil. But up here are hill-vineyards whose wine really deserves a good name. The law allows them to tack St-Emilion on to their own names of St-Georges, Montagne, Lussac, Puisseguin and Parsac. Edmund Penning-Rowsell has proposed the name St-Emilion Villages for them in the Burgundian manner. We should be seeing more and more good wine from them and their excellent co-operatives: St-Emilion at reasonable prices.

## Pomerol

Pomerol is the continuation of the plateau above St-Emilion to the north-west on the outskirts of the little market town of Libourne, which used to be the port for all St-Emilion and Pomerol wines before the road superseded the river and "shipping" came to mean diesel lorries. Libourne takes its name from Sir Roger de Leybourne, steward of Edward I of England, which gives it a sister-town, the little village of Leybourne in Kent where he had his castle.

There are many more châteaux crammed into the tiny commune of Pomerol than into any other, giving it the air of a suburb rather than the country. Everywhere you look there is a little villa, sometimes merely a big shed, proudly designated Château. Every acre of the gently undulating plateau seems to be covered with vines.

The best wines of Pomerol are those near the St-Emilion border, as the best wines of St-Emilion are those nearest Pomerol. The same patch of gravel mixed with clay which produces Château Cheval Blanc gives almost equal quality to Châteaux Petrus, Vieux-Château-Certan, Certan-de-May, La Conseillante, Petit-Village, L'Evangile, La-Fleur-Petrus, all in a group, and the flanking properties of Gazin to the east, Nenin to the west and Trotanoy to the north; these three are among the most substantial and best known of Pomerols if not in the absolute top-flight.

### Château Petrus

Château Petrus has a unique pre-eminence among Pomerols—especially as regards price. For the last decade or so it has regularly fetched as much as the first-growths of the Médoc and sometimes more. It is a relatively tiny vineyard, making only seventy-odd barrels as against Lafite's four hundred-odd. This is at least part of the reason. But more important, Petrus is a uniquely fruity wine: strong, rich, concentrated in flavour and powerfully sweet-scented—an eye-opener even to the least initiated millionaire . . . and (almost as important) even after the scant laying-down claret usually gets these days. Pomerol scarcely has a village worth the name, just a rather gaunt church among the vines and a slightly thicker crop of villas in mid-plateau. The good château names thicken on the ground again here: Clos l'Eglise, l'Eglise-Clinet and Domaine de l'Eglise, the church party; the eminent (if confusing) Latour-Pomerol; Le Gay, Rouget and La Grave-Trigant-de-Boisset. These are all first-class clarets, even if the quantities are small. But good properties are not confined to one area here. La Pointe, Clos René, Château l'Enclos reach over westwards into the suburbs of Libourne, the best among perhaps forty more thoroughly worthwhile properties.

Pomerol is very reliable, both as to the standard of its growths and the evenness of its vintages. In a poor year for most of Bordeaux, the Pomerols are often good, rather light and soft wines but with enough sweetness about them and not too much tannin. Pomerols rarely even start life as the sort of wine which makes you screw your face up. Their gentle qualities are probably what is making them so popular at the moment. They are very much the taste of France today, as well as of Britain and the United States. It is not hard to guess why; no-one wants to lay down wine for years any more, and Pomerol, of all the districts of Bordeaux, makes the wines which need least laying-down. This is not to say that they are like Beaujolais, which must be drunk as soon as you can lay your hands on it, by any means. But four or five years is a respectable age for a Pomerol, even of a good year—and for a poor year three or four may easily be enough. Their lasting properties are unaffected by this; fine Pomerols live as long as almost any wine.

## Other areas

Bordeaux has eight other red-wine areas, each closely defined by the laws of *Appellations Contrôlées*. None of them makes wine as fine as those I have described, but in each some good wine is to be found, and wine-merchants are spending more and more of their time outside the classical areas in finding it.

### Blaye

Opposite the Médoc across the Gironde the large district of Blaye, named after the pretty old fortified port in its centre, contains the smaller district of Bourg. There is a large production of white wines as well as red here, but the white is in general less good and less well known.

### Bourg

Bourgeais red wine is not unlike St-Emilion, though it is less fine; Blayais is not normally quite so good. There are far too many châteaux in both to list, and few really have names to remember. Two big estates in Bourg, Châteaux de Barbe and du Bousquet, are probably the most commonly seen. On the other hand, a wine-merchant might easily be able to recommend a very good wine he has been offered in Bordeaux. It is the Bordeaux trade's business to keep an eye out for bargains across the water.

### Néac and Lalande de Pomerol

### Côtes de Fronsac

Pomerol is surrounded on its north and west sides—the sides away from St-Emilion—with the communes of Néac, Lalande de Pomerol and Fronsac. The first two produce what might be called sub-Pomerols, less fine than the real thing, but cheaper. Château Bel-Air in Lalande de Pomerol is well known. The Côtes de Fronsac, with their superior central area, the Côtes de Canon-Fronsac, occupy the pretty hills west of Libourne in a bed of the Dordogne. Fronsac wine tends to be strong-flavoured like St-Emilion. A good Côtes de Fronsac, indeed, could easily be mistaken for one of St-Emilion's lesser growths. I have the impression that Fronsac wines have improved greatly since I first met them fifteen years ago. But I confess my research has been limited to those shipped to England—which are still surprisingly few for a district with such obvious potential. Châteaux Rouet, Canon, La Dauphine, Canon de Brem, Toumalin and Junayme are some of the best-known estates.

### Graves de Vayres

Opposite the south end of the Côtes de Fronsac is the district confusingly called Graves de Vayres, which has nothing to do with Graves, but takes its name, as the part of St-Emilion does, from its gravel soil. Its red wines have only the appellation "Bordeaux". Beyond St-Emilion and its satellites to the east the vines continue right up to the boundary of the *département* of the Gironde (where the appellation Bordeaux stops) and on into the next, Dordogne, where the appellation is Bergerac. The frontier districts have been little known even in France up to now. But prices are forcing us all to realize that a name may simply be an expensive luxury. When you further consider that this particular boundary is an old politico-religious one (the Catholics of Bordeaux excluding the Protestants of the hinterland from the benefits of being Bordelais), it is obviously worth keeping an open mind in judging the wine. There is some evidence of new interest in these areas in the recent creation of two new sub-appellations for the most easterly of the Bordeaux districts: Côtes de Castillon and Côtes de Francs. These are light red wines to drink young: not classic claret but very agreeable everyday wines.

*Ste-Foy-Bordeaux*
*Premières Côtes*
*de Bordeaux*

Far up the Dordogne beyond St-Emilion and Castillon on the south bank the district of Ste-Foy-Bordeaux makes both red and white wine. Finally, the long thin strip of the Premières Côtes de Bordeaux, right up the Garonne's east bank from Bordeaux to opposite Sauternes, is an appellation for red wines as well as white. Most of the red comes from the villages of Bassens, Ste-Eulalie, Yvrac, Carbon-Blanc, Lormont, Cenon, Floirac, Bouliac, Latresne, Camblanes, Quinsac and Cambes in the northern half of the area. A great deal of the wine is sold simply as Premières Côtes de Bordeaux. As such, it is cheap and good.

## When to drink claret

Claret has always been the Englishman's everyday wine, when he has had one. The reason, apart from the convenience of Bordeaux as a port for shipping to England, is that Bordeaux is the largest producer of good ordinary wine in the world. *Vin ordinaire* as the French understand it, poor-quality Mediterranean wine, is not to the English taste. It is not an inspiring drink. There is a move to sell it in England now, but I doubt if it will ever become the drink of the people. It is essentially dull, flat, and prone to penetrating, though faint, tastes of a kind which are foreign to clean, honest wine.

Even the most ordinary honest Bordeaux, on the other hand, is a clean, balanced and very straightforward wine. It is refreshing, comforting and slips down easily. It is not too strong, and whenever any particular character becomes apparent in it, it is pleasant and familiar.

As an everyday drink it goes with virtually everything. Like all red wines, it is at its best with meat, vegetables, cheese (the savoury part of a meal), and less good with fish and sweets. It is good in summer, even mixed with iced lemonade or soda-water, and in winter warmed in front of the fire. It should be treated freely as a basic ingredient: like water, in fact—drunk from tumblers, poured from a jug.

When one basic Bordeaux has become familiar in this way, its slightly superior cousins fall into place for special occasions. The little differences that make the similar, but better, wine you choose for a special dinner a more agreeable drink, with more in it to think about and enjoy than your daily wine, will come to be the basis of a really sound knowledge of claret. There is nothing more satisfying.

I think it is worth making a point, if you drink claret regularly, of drinking a really great claret occasionally—even if it is only once a year. Each time it is like a fresh revelation. Each time you will ask yourself how you could have forgotten that wine can do such wonderful things. There are some clarets in the world that are simply beautiful; there is no other word for them. They offer as much to the aesthetic sense as great music or great painting. If you ever come to the point of asking what all the fuss is about, why people talk so much about wine, that is the answer. Between the ordinary, which you do not bother to taste consciously before you swallow it, and the superb, which offers and suggests so many beautiful tastes that even after you have swallowed it the perfume lingers on your tongue and your lips, and you cannot bear to let it go . . . between these two comes the whole study of wine.

# The Red Wines of Burgundy

I have introduced Burgundy in the White Wine section of this book. The salient facts of its peculiar system of naming and blending wines and the difficulties in knowing exactly what you are getting are all there, and I shall not repeat them here. But it is important to read the Introduction to the section on Burgundy (page 84) before reading about red or white burgundy.

It is the custom to talk about Bordeaux and burgundy as though they were the opposite poles of red wine. Between them, the implication is, they cover everything that a red wine can be. Burgundy is popularly supposed to be fruity, dark, full-bodied and sweet; claret is supposed to be light, dry and delicate. The rest of the world's red wines are therefore divided into claret- or burgundy-types following these theoretical characteristics.

In fact, burgundy and claret both find themselves near the middle of the spectrum of red wine. There are much darker and fuller wines than burgundy, and drier and lighter wines than claret. Considering all the world's wines, burgundy and claret are seen to be not opposites but neighbours. They have in common the delicacy and balance that makes them the world's best red wines. Compared with the difference between them and almost any other red wines, they are twins.

When we discuss the difference between claret and burgundy, therefore, we are discussing subtleties. There is more similarity between claret and burgundy than, for example, between Australian burgundy-type wine and the real thing.

*The taste of burgundy*

When I begin to describe a wine there is always the same difficulty. It is impossible. You must taste burgundy—real burgundy—to learn what the burgundy taste is. Remarks in a vacuum about it being sweet and yet slightly reminiscent of green sap in perfume; full but penetrating in taste; more savoury than Bordeaux and yet at the same time slightly sweeter, are of no use. The answer to the question "What kind of wine is burgundy?" is that it is a very savoury, inviting wine, as tempting as good smells from the kitchen. When you find a good mature one, it is soft and sweet. Like a soft sweet face with a good bone structure, it is beautiful.

What burgundy is not, though it is often reputed to be, and sometimes fraudulently made to be, is something like an Australian tonic wine: rich, heavy, coarse, alcoholic, full of iron to build you up and keep out the cold.

Burgundy is the northernmost good red-wine district. It gets little sun and its wine suffers from, if anything, lack of alcohol. It is delicate —very rarely rich. The great burgundies in great vintages are famous for their big-bodied richness for this very reason. The rest of Burgundy makes smooth, savoury, balanced and beguiling wines like nowhere else on earth.

## Laying down burgundy

Whether red burgundy is quite as good as it used to be is a favourite debate among its drinkers today. In such a seller's market there are temptations. The grower must grow Pinot Noir vines, but the law has nothing to say about selected vine-stocks which give greater quantity at the expense of quality. Artificial fertilizers have been another factor in increasing production. Increased production inevitably means leaner, quicker-maturing wine.

The ideal burgundy is wine with enough "meat" in it to last in the bottle long enough to develop subtle secondary scents and flavours. The let-down of much of modern burgundy is that it fades away and loses its substance before the alchemy can take place. Great care is therefore needed in choosing burgundy to lay down today. In the following pages I shall mention the names of some of the growers known to me who aim at the old-fashioned style, long-maturing wine. But of course I cannot claim to know them all.

## The Côte d'Or

The northernmost district of Burgundy, Chablis, grows no red wine. Nearby Irancy, a village a few miles to the south, has a reputation for its *vin du pays*, Irancy Rouge, but it is not in the class of wine we expect to bear the great name of burgundy.

The Côte d'Or has a monopoly of the best red vineyards. From the start of its central slopes south of Dijon—for it really begins as some beautiful wooded hills to the north of the city—it has the great name

## The Côte de Nuits

of the Côte de Nuits. For thirty miles with only one break the narrow strip of vineyards along the middle slopes of the hill—never more than five hundred yards wide—produces what its growers, and about half the world beside, consider the finest red wine on earth. As soon as you leave Dijon on the road south to Beaune, the road which follows the Côtes all the way, the names begin to have a familiar ring. The first is

## Fixin

Fixin: famous, if not world-famous, for fine red wine. The second is Chambertin.

## Gevrey-Chambertin

The name of the village, in fact, is Gevrey-Chambértin. I have explained how the old single-barrelled village-names grafted on the more illustrious names of their best-known vineyards to identify themselves in a tricky market. The village of Gevrey was distinguished above all for one vineyard. Its name was Chambertin. The next field on the same level on the hill, going north, is called the Clos de Bèze. These names have been equal in reputation and quality for centuries. But the *grand cru* area of Gevrey-Chambertin, the biggest in Burgundy, contains seven other names besides: Charmes, Chapelle,

Griotte, Latricière, Ruchottes and Mazis. All these have the right to attach "Chambertin" after their individual names. (Or, of course, a grower can label the wine of one or more of them as "Gevrey-Chambertin Grand Cru".) Any names which appear on labels following that of Gevrey-Chambertin can be taken to be those of the *premiers crus*—confusingly enough, the second-growths. The best known of these are the Clos St-Jacques and Les Véroilles, whose owner, the Domaine de Varoilles (sic) is one of those who make wine of real staying-power in the traditional manner. It is hard to pick out growers' names in an area where so many make splendid wine, but those of Clair Daü, Drouhin-Laroze, Gelin, Rousseau, Camus mean almost as much today as the name of Gevrey-Chambertin. Those who look for truly grand Chambertin to lay down look above all to Clair Daü.

*Chambertin and Clos de Bèze*

Chambertin and Clos de Bèze are often called the greatest wines of the whole region. Even the simplest parish appellation of Gevrey-Chambertin, while not very restricting to the merchant (there are a thousand acres of vines in the parish), usually means a very good wine. Oddly enough, considering that this is the farthest north of fine red wines, and that for the Côtes of Burgundy the vineyards are on fairly flat ground, the wine here is the most robust, as the terminology goes, of all burgundies. It has tremendous strength of purpose, somehow; great staying-power and an almost oak-like solidity. Chambertin is the wine for moments of great decision, or great joints of beef on the bone and other things which you know are going to have plenty of flavour, character and savour of their own. Legend has it that Napoleon never took anything else with him on campaign. There was even Chambertin sold as "back from Moscow".

## Morey St-Denis

*Clos St-Denis*

The name of the next parish, Morey St-Denis, is not so well known. It has, indeed, added a vineyard name, that of Clos St-Denis, to its old short name of Morey. But it miscalculated. The Clos St-Denis is small, and not even the best in the parish. In short, the village is swamped by its great names. There are not many people who even know that the superlative vineyards of Clos de Tart, Bonnes Mares and Clos de la Roche are in Morey St-Denis at all. Of these, Bonnes Mares, I should add, has its greater part in the next parish of Chambolle-Musigny.

*Clos de Tart*

All these four vineyards are in Burgundy's top class. All are big strong wines, almost as big as Chambertin and as strong, though, as I think, with a little more grace and flexibility in them. Clos de Tart, particularly, which has the good fortune, rare among vineyards of Burgundy, to belong entirely to one man, Jean Mommessin, is a lovely soft, strong and savoury wine. It is capable of long life, and yet surprisingly ready to drink when quite young. Again these are wines for great feasts—as their prices, I fear, suggest. The other wine of Morey St-Denis, bearing the village name alone or followed by that of a *premier cru* (Clos de la Bussière is an excellent example) is not often seen abroad. If you do see it, on the other hand, you may be fairly certain that the wine-merchant has followed quality rather than fashion—for few people have heard of it.

## Chambolle-Musigny

Hard on the heels of Morey St-Denis, sharing the big vineyard of Bonnes Mares with it, comes the more famous Chambolle-Musigny. The *grand cru* of Chambolle-Musigny is Musigny, sometimes called Le Musigny to underline the point, but never called anything else.

The village is dominated by the biggest proprietor, Comte Georges de Vogüé, whose family also own the greater part of two of the biggest champagne-houses. In his superb, airy cellar, like the crypt of a great cathedral, rest the finest wines which are made here—and often, some say, in the whole of Burgundy. One *premier cru* here, with the lovely name of Les Amoureuses, is on the *grand cru* level. Another, Les Charmes, is not far off. De Vogüé goes one better and makes a *tête de cuvée* of the *tête de cuvée*, a special selection of the best of the best, which he calls Musigny Vieilles Vignes ("Old Vines"—those which give the finest fruit).

Musigny is a slightly more delicate wine than Chambertin. The soft savouriness of burgundy comes out in it more than in any other wine. It lingers and spreads in your mouth, making what French tasters call "the peacock's tail" with its bouquet of flavours and flavours-within-flavours.

Chambolle-Musigny, the blended wine of various vineyards within the village boundaries, is often one of the best of the burgundies which are almost universally stocked by wine-merchants. It varies, of course, enormously from shipper to shipper, for it is in the blending-vats of the shipper that it takes its final shape, but it is often less built up into a heavy-weight than most village-named wines which have undergone this treatment. It remains almost tender in character.

## Clos de Vougeot

The southern border of Chambolle-Musigny is the edge of the Clos de Vougeot, an enormous vineyard walled about with one great stone wall and dominated with the Burgundian countryside's one impressive building, used by the Burgundians as their symbol. Its foundation was the work of the Cistercian Order. Today it is the headquarters of the Order of the Chevaliers du Tastevin.

As a vineyard it has its faults. In fact it is not really one *climat* at all, but a whole *finage* (parish) of them. Its quality varies as much as the quality within any other parish. On the hill-slopes it is good—indeed superb. The top of the vineyard is right next to Musigny. On the flat land at the bottom of the hill it is no better than any such vineyard. The lowest part would rate perhaps as a *deuxième cru* if it were rated separately from the top. Thus the wine with the great name need not necessarily be great at all.

Clos de Vougeot is sometimes called the claret of Burgundy. It is markedly drier than most burgundies; the wine-merchants of the region, perhaps with tongue in cheek, call it feminine. The best of it has the most beautiful scent in Burgundy, with a faint suggestion of autumnal dankness about it which is typically burgundian. Joseph Drouhin and Drouhin-Laroze make this sort of wine.

## The Chevaliers du Tastevin

The Chevaliers du Tastevin are members of a body formed by the growers and merchants of Burgundy to promote the sales of their wine. It holds frequent dinners for as many as five or six hundred guests in the great hall of the old fortress-like building in the Clos de Vougeot. Recruitment for the order is carried on at a brisk rate. Each firm of *négociants* in Burgundy has to introduce ten new members a year in order to qualify for hiring the building for a dinner of its own. Members wear medieval-type red robes for the dinners. There is singing and a good deal of fulsome and often very funny praise for the wines of Burgundy in general and for those in the present glasses in particular. A good score of similar societies have sprung up to uphold the honour of the wines of their respective parts of France, but none carries it off with quite such style.

*Flagey-Echezeaux*

The name of the next village, Flagey-Echezeaux, is never used on wine-labels, although it is very much a wine-growing community. The village is in the valley, away from the best vineyards. Flagey has,

*Grands Echezeaux*

on the other hand, in the vineyards of Grands Echezeaux and Echezeaux on the south side of the top of the Clos de Vougeot, one of the best of all red burgundies, a wine definitely in the *grand cru* class. I imagine it is only kept off wine-lists—it is not often listed in Britain or the United States—by its sneeze-like name, which has the advantage of keeping the price down. Grands Echezeaux and Bonnes Mares are probably the two least known of the world's greatest wines.

Wine of the *premier cru* class from Echezeaux has the right to the name of Vosne-Romanée.

## *Vosne-Romanée*

The wine of the tiny vineyard of Romanée-Conti on the hill above the village of Vosne, marked with a crucifix and covering less than four and a half acres, fetches the highest price of any burgundy. It belongs to an estate known as the Domaine de la Romanée-Conti, which also owns the vineyard of La Tache, most of Richebourg and parts of Grands Echezeaux.

*Romanée-Conti*

André Simon once said that Romanée-Conti has something almost oriental about its fragrance. It is certainly spicy in a way which makes it, and the other wines made by the Domaine, immediately recognizable. There is something almost oriental, too, about a visit to the dank and crowded cellar which houses it: you feel you should leave your shoes at the door.

Whether or not the Domaine does something special in the making of its wine—there are whispers about adding a touch of brandy, or concentrating a small proportion of the unfermented juice—it gives it a stamp of sheer luxury which, combined with its amazing price, makes it quite irresistible to a large number of customers. The tiny courtyard and cellar, indeed, are always brimming over with American visitors, who put this with Montrachet as one of the sights of Burgundy to be seen. No doubt the whispers are the work of envious neighbours.

Vosne-Romanée has no less than five *grand cru* vineyards—none of them, it must be admitted, very big. Besides La Romanée-Conti they

*La Romanée-St-Vivant, La Romanée, La Tache and Le Richebourg*

are La Romanée-St-Vivant, the biggest, not quite such a perfumed and splendid wine; La Romanée, the smallest, perhaps a shade lighter; La Tache, which in truth is often better even than the most expensive; and Le Richebourg, which also has its supporters for the crown.

The second-rank wines of Vosne-Romanée must not be overlooked. They are labelled with the village-name as well as their own vineyard-names. La Grand Rue, a vineyard barely wider than a road running up the side of Romanée-Conti, Les Gaudichots, Les Suchots, Aux Malconsorts and Les Beaumonts are all well known, often exported and of very high quality. Vosne Romanée *tout court* is also often excellent; a middle-weight burgundy, a Sunday-lunch wine.

## *Nuits-St-Georges*

The town of Nuits-St-Georges brings us to the end of the Côte de Nuits, the hillside of Burgundy's best red wine. Nuits and Prémeaux next door, to the south, whose wines are sold as Nuits, are not the very greatest of burgundies, but they are typical, soft, savoury wines

*Les St-Georges*

with plenty of meat in them. If they lack anything it is scent. Les St-

Georges on the border of Prémeaux is the vineyard from which Nuits took its name. The best of the others are Aux Boudots, Aux Cras, La Richemone and Aux Murgers near Vosne-Romanée, and Les Cailles, Le Clos de la Maréchale, Le Clos des Corvees, Les Porrets, Les Pruliers and Les Vaucrains to the south. The total quantity of Nuits-St-Georges wine, owing to its merger with Prémeaux, is large for any one burgundian name: its share of the hillside is almost four miles long. It is also often "stretched" with cheaper, stronger wine. Genuine Nuits-St-Georges has nonetheless remained a rarity in Britain: it has been one of the most often faked of all burgundies.

It remains to be seen what the British will make of the real thing—and its real price—as the *Appellation Contrôlée* laws begin to bite.

## The Côte de Beaune

Corton, the northernmost vineyard of the Côte de Beaune, is the one which is said to approach most nearly to the wines of the Côte de Nuits in character and in quality. In general, wines from the Côte de Beaune, the southern one of Burgundy's two wonderful hillsides, are a little less highly regarded than the wines of Chambertin, Musigny and Romanée. Corton is the only one which is mentioned in the same breath.

While this holds true for the best wines of all, no doubt, it needs qualifying straight away. In the second class the Côte de Beaune wines hold their own with ease. They have the great advantage of quantity. Beaune has about two and a half thousand acres of vine; Pommard over one and a half; Volnay over a thousand. About half of these are planted with fine grapes for first-class wine. Chambolle-Musigny, which is typical of the Côte de Nuits, has less than two hundred acres.

Beaune, Volnay and Pommard have, therefore, made their name for supplying perhaps not the most wonderful wine the world has ever seen, but plenty of really admirable wine to drink regularly and often. Their wines mature sooner, taking perhaps five years on the average as against ten or so (depending on the grower) for the Côte de Nuits wines. They are lighter, though not light in the sense in which a claret is "lighter", than a burgundy. They are no drier or more acid. They just have less of the quality so happily known as "stuffing".

## Aloxe-Corton

After Nuits-St-Georges, again taking the same road south, there is a gap in the hills before the hill of Corton, rising above the village of Aloxe, which has embellished its name in the usual way. I have described how the hill is divided among white wines and red. I cannot honestly say that one is better than the other. It is probably the only great vineyard in the world of which this is true.

### Corton

Corton, which, like Chambertin and Montrachet, sometimes has the word Le added to its name to stress that it is the real thing and not one of its sisters or its cousins or its aunts that you are getting, shares the honours here with Corton-Clos-du-Roi, Corton-Renardes, and Corton-Bressandes. One shipper of high repute, Louis Latour, has a brand-name which sounds like another Corton vineyard—Corton-Grancey. In fact it is simply the name of his house, under which he sells some of his best Corton wine.

The village name, Aloxe-Corton, is one of the best known for shippers' blended red burgundy, partly because the villages on both sides also avail themselves of it. Of these, one, Ladoix-Serrigny, is never heard of under its own name; the other, Pernand-Vergelesses, sells the greater part of its red and white wines under the names of

### Ladoix-Serrigny
### Pernand-Vergelesses

Aloxe-Corton and Corton-Charlemagne (part of the great Charle-magne white-wine vineyard is in the parish), but also sells very good and largely neglected wine under its own mouthful of a name. Its best vineyard is called Ile des Vergelesses.

*Savigny-les-Beaune*

You would look for the vineyard called Aux Vergelesses, too, in Pernand, but you would not find it. It is in the next village to the south, Savigny-les-Beaune. Savigny adjoins the vineyards of Beaune itself on the north. Its wines are very like those of Beaune; rather pale in colour, light and soft in taste but with the background suggestion of strength which is always there in good burgundy. Their scent is if anything more fruit-like and less savoury than the scents of the Côte de Nuits wines. Strength and solidity, within reason, are at a premium in the Beaune and Savigny vineyards. They appear in good vintages but sometimes stay away in poor ones.

## Beaune

The town of Beaune, and its hospital, are the showplaces of Burgundy. Dijon is the old capital. There there are superb churches and the old Ducal palace. But Dijon has other interests; it is not in the thick of the wine-country. Beaune lives and breathes wine.

*The Hospices de Beaune*

The Hospices de Beaune, which is the local hospital, is the most re-markable and beautiful building in the whole world of wine. It sounds odd that it should be both a hospital and so wine-minded. It was a stroke of charitable genius by a fifteenth-century statesman. Nicolas Rolin, Chancellor to Duke Philip the Good of Burgundy, and his wife Guigonne de Salins founded the Hospices in 1443. They endowed it for its income with vineyards. Others followed suit, and to this day its expenses are paid out of the income of its vineyards, which are, on the whole, some of the very best of the Côte de Beaune.

At that time, although Dijon was the capital of Burgundy, its artistic and commercial centre was in its Flemish provinces. From Brussels Rolin fetched Rogier van der Weyden, the greatest Flemish painter of his day, to do an altar-piece for his new foundation. Van der Weyden's *Last Judgment* still hangs in an upper chamber.

The Hospices today is a remarkable mixture of ancient and modern. To enter its Gothic courtyard, with steep-pitched roofs of polychrome tiles like jesters' motley, with nurses in long religious habits and wimples, with its old elaborate wellhead of wrought iron, or to go into the kitchen, where great log fires make the copper pans beam and glow and where a smell of real old burgundian cooking puts aside all thoughts of steamed fish and sick-bed food, you would have no idea that operating theatres with all the devices of modern medicine share the same venerable walls.

Every November the market hall opposite the hospital is the scene of the auctions of its wine which decide its revenue for the next year. Merchants and wine-lovers come from all over the world to this re-markable event; an opportunity to buy some of Burgundy's best wine and to subscribe to an ancient charity at the same time.

The prices set at the Hospices auction are those which guide all dealings in the wine of that vintage in Burgundy. Hospices wines themselves tend to be expensive, not only because they are good but for charity's sake; all other burgundies have their more or less accepted relationships to the publicly decided Hospices prices. The weekend of the sale, therefore, sets off a busy week of dealing through-out the Burgundy countryside, as the *négociants*, the local wholesalers, go round to replenish their stocks.

Hospices de Beaune wines carry on their labels the name of the benefactor who gave the vineyard to the Hospital. They are known by these *cuvée* names rather than the names of their vineyards. There are twenty-two red and seven white (all the white except one are Meursaults). Of the red the best known are those in Beaune given by Nicolas Rolin and his wife themselves, which bear their names, and the Corton wines given by Charlotte Dumay and the unfortunately named Doctor Peste. Hospices wines appear on some of the best wine-lists in every country; there is every reason to buy one when you see it.

## The vineyards of Beaune

The vineyards of Beaune are large and vary from moderate to excellent. More different *climat* names are seen on Beaune bottles than on those of any other commune. The daunting list of *premiers crus* (there are no *grands*) of high repute includes Les Marconnets, Les Fèves, Les Bressandes, Les Grèves, Les Teurons, Aux Crus, Les Champs Pimonts, Le Clos des Mouches (where a little white is made as well as red), Clos-du-Roi, Les Cent-Vignes, Les Toussaints, Clos-de-la-Mousse, Les Avaux, Les Vignes-Franches, Les Epenottes. The Beaune *négociants* themselves own large parts of this grand sweep of vines, and add their private "Clos" names to some of their best wines. Jadot's Clos des Ursules and Bouchard Père's Vigne de l'Enfant Jésus are good examples.

I have said that Beaune tends to be rather pale and light in weight except in exceptional years. In the wines I have mentioned by their vineyards' names you can expect considerable character and the true burgundian savouriness. Wine labelled simply Beaune varies widely from merchant to merchant. He can find some very good wine to sell under that name, or he can use it as a way of selling something rather ordinary. In any case, wine labelled Beaune is slightly better than wine labelled simply Côte de Beaune. Beaune must come from Beaune; Côte de Beaune can come from anywhere between Aloxe-Corton and Santenay, from high or low ground. The difference in appellations is the same as that between, for example, Margaux and Haut-Médoc in Bordeaux.

## Côte de Beaune

## Appellations Contrôlées

The appellations of Burgundy cannot be grasped without a certain bafflement at first. Two other uses of the words Côte de Beaune have different legal meanings again, and must be mentioned. One is when the words are preceded by the name of a village, which is hyphenated to them (Santenay-Côte de Beaune, for example). This is that village's own appellation. It indicates that although the village is not all that well known, its wine is worth seeking out. The other is the label Côte de Beaune-Villages, which means that the wine is a blend of the wines of two or more of the lesser-known villages of the Côte—not Aloxe-Corton, Beaune, Pommard or Volnay.

## Côte de Beaune-Villages

The appellations in descending order for the Côte de Beaune are as follows. Best of all is one of the great vineyards which has its own appellation and needs no qualifications; for example, Corton. Second best are the *premiers crus*, which can either say, for example, Beaune Les Marconnets or Beaune-Marconnets. Third best would be simply Beaune. Then comes a village which needs -Côte de Beaune to reinforce it (for example, Santenay-Côte de Beaune). Then comes just plain Côte de Beaune. Finally, Côte de Beaune-Villages. Anything which fails to qualify for any of these names may yet get in one of the

*Hautes Côtes de Beaune*
*Vin Fin des Hautes*
*Côtes de Nuits*
*Bourgogne*
*Passe-Tout-Grains*
*Bourgogne Grand*
*Ordinaire*

lower ranges of appellations. The hills behind the great Côtes to the west have their own class, either Hautes Côtes de Beaune or Vin Fin des Hautes Côtes de Nuits (Hautes in this case meaning high in altitude, nothing else). Anything made anywhere in Burgundy of the right grapes—the classical Pinot—can call itself simply Bourgogne. Anything made from a third of the classical grapes and two-thirds of the common Gamay can call itself Bourgogne Passe-Tout-Grains. There is a bottom catch-all class: Bourgogne Grand Ordinaire, for low-strength wines which were at least made in Burgundy, and indeed often taste like it.

Labels are usually obliging enough to sort out for you which part of the name is the controlled appellation and repeat it underneath. Thus we have Corton, and then underneath *Appellation Corton Contrôlée*.

None of these regulations, incredibly enough, had any legal power at all in Britain up to 1974. A wine-merchant was entirely on trust; he could print *Appellation Contrôlée* on anything he liked. For this reason, people who are concerned about authenticity often prefer to buy wine which was bottled and labelled in France, where there would have been trouble in store for anyone who broke the rules. The other side of the coin is not such good news. For British wine-merchants used to buy genuine wines which for some reason (usually excess production) were denied the use of their own appellation. Wines without papers are obviously cheaper—so Britain was drinking good burgundy for less money than countries which applied the regulations.

Such a system put all the onus on the wine-merchant, of course. There were those who used it unscrupulously. But in all fairness there were a good number who could be trusted, rules or no rules.

## Pommard

At the southern limit of the vineyards of Beaune the road which has brought us past all the famous villages south of Dijon turns away from the Côte. To reach the next famous parishes of Pommard and Volnay you have to fork right along a side-road. To your left lies a vast flat vineyard, the source of a great deal of dull wine: the Pommard of corner-shops the world over. To your right on the rising ground both sides of the village of Pommard lie the *premiers crus*—the very opposite: limited in production and of superlative quality. Of all the parishes of the Côtes, Pommard is the one the man in the street thinks of first for a bargain bottle of something hearty. Paradoxically its real virtue is a clutch of ultra-conservative growers whose wines are rare treasures. Epenots and Rugiens are the names of Pommard's best *climats*. But the growers' names are the thing to watch for here. The Comte Armand (whose Epenots is spelt Epeneaux), Domaine de Courcel, the Hospices de Beaune (Cuvée Dames de la Charité) and the Clos de la Commaraine of Jaboulet-Vercherre are touchstone Pommards.

## Volnay

Volnay, the next parish, I must confess is my especial favourite. Volnay is the most delicate red burgundy: often, in my experience, a wine of real beauty. It has a pronounced scent—more than Beaune, certainly more than Pommard—and a way of being exquisitely fresh and lively without losing the richness of flavour which distinguishes good burgundy. It is not a surprise, when you taste it, that it is the last red burgundy before you come to the white wine country of Meursault and the Montrachets. I would not drink Volnay with any of the very rich and highly flavoured dishes of Burgundy—*Coq au Vin* or *Boeuf Bourguignon*—but with roast young lamb or a pheasant which has not been hung too long.

*Volnay Santenots*

The vineyards of Caillerets, Champans and Le Clos des Chênes are far and away the best known of Volnay. Volnay Santenots, which is also commonly seen, is in fact the name under which the red wine of the neighbouring village of Meursault is sold. Meursault is famous only for white wine. But Santenots is indistinguishable from Volnay and well deserves to profit from the name.

*Monthélie*

The same also applies to the wine of Monthélie, just round the corner of the hill overlooking Meursault. Monthélie's wine (almost all red) is like excellent Volnay. Indeed the Domaine Suremain at the Château de Monthélie makes some of the best wine of the district. Monthélie, however, has to struggle on without a well-known appellation to help sales—which makes it, of course, a name to look out for.

In Volnay itself the finest estate is that of the Marquis d'Angerville, which has, besides parcels of the famous *climats*, a Clos of its own—the Clos des Ducs. D'Angerville wines are old-style burgundy, developing gloriously in their maturity. But Volnay is never a wine to keep for very long: at ten years even the grandest is ripe.

Plain, unqualified Volnay is often not as light as it should be; shippers tend to reinforce it with something to give it more weight and colour. Wine with the name Volnay alone, in other words, will rarely justify so much enthusiasm. It costs remarkably little more, though, to buy a specified-vineyard wine which will immediately demonstrate what is meant by character.

*Chassagne-Montrachet*

Now the red-wine vineyards of Burgundy tail off. To the west, beyond Monthélie, Auxey-Duresses makes mostly white wine. To the south Meursault's red wine is sold as Volnay Santenots. Puligny-Montrachet makes virtually no red wine. Chassagne-Montrachet, on the other hand, has very important and excellent red-wine vineyards: Clos St-Jean, La Maltroie, La Boudriotte and Morgeot. It comes as a surprise to people who know the name of Montrachet only as a white wine. As in Meursault, the change from white to red comes in mid-village. South of the Montrachet vineyard there

*Clos St-Jean*

is a gap in the hill; then red wine begins. Clos St-Jean is often seen in England and is generally very good value. It is not, however, an extremely light Volnay-type wine, as you might expect. It has, oddly enough, a similarity to the bigger wines of the Côte de Nuits. It is full of flavour and well-scented, deep red and a slow developer, a slightly sweeter wine than most—all the things which should make it very popular.

*Santenay*

The last village of the Côte de Beaune is Santenay. It makes both red and white wines, but its red is better. Les Gravières, which goes on from the vineyard of Morgeot in Chassagne-Montrachet, is the best vineyard; Santenay-Gravières, indeed, is about the only Santenay you ever see in England. It is not so different from Chassagne-Montrachet; good and strong, with a tender softness about it. I remember having a Santenay-Gravières which made me think very differently, a thin poor wine, at a charming little restaurant called the Auberge du Camp Romain in the hills above Santenay. When I reported this to a *négociant* in Beaune he knew the wine straight away. "Ah, that was Monsieur Untel's wine," he said. "No wonder. He only planted those vines five years ago. You had his first wine from that plot." Where-upon he produced a wine to cancel out my bad impression of Santenay-Gravières—the big, tender wine that it should, and can, be.

## South Burgundy

There are three more famous outbreaks of vineyards in Burgundy after leaving the Côte de Beaune, the last hills of the Côte d'Or, going south. They are called the Côte Chalonnaise, Mâcon and Beaujolais.

Beaujolais is far and away the most popular and most important of the three. The demand for it is so great that all kinds of wines from near and far are used to stretch the supply. Switzerland or Paris alone would drink considerably more than the total production of the area if other wines were not called in to help.

*The Côte Chalonnaise*

The Côte Chalonnaise and Mâcon, though they produce wines which are often just as good, have never made it to this extent. Two Côte Chalonnaise wines are sometimes met on the kind of wine-list which looks for the best wine for the money rather than a popular name. They are called Givry and Mercurey. You might say they belong in the same class as Côte de Beaune-Villages—which means they can, on occasion, be splendid.

*Mâcon*

Mâcon's best wine is white: Pouilly-Fuissé. Mâcon Rouge is a good *vin du pays*, at least as good as most commercial Beaujolais, though not as good as really good Beaujolais, beside which it seems rather lifeless and dull. But then few wines are as lively and drinkable as Beaujolais.

## Beaujolais

It is only in the last ten years that anyone has taken Beaujolais seriously. As far as the wine-trade abroad was concerned Beaujolais was, until very recently, simply a pretty name to use for a blend of cheap (but not too cheap) red wine. Locally, in Lyons, and as far away as Paris, Beaujolais was drunk without ceremony as the best of all carafe wines. But the notion of a domaine-bottled Beaujolais would have been ridiculous.

Times have changed. Light wine has come into fashion; long cellaring and bottle-age have gone out. No wine stood to gain so much from the new fashion as Beaujolais. Beaujolais is not burgundy. It comes from a different grape, grown in a different countryside, made into wine with a different purpose. Its whole essence is lightness, youth, sweetness, amiability. If burgundy is stuffy and old-fashioned (it is not), Beaujolais is modern, liberated, fancy-free.

In the mid-sixties the old idea of Beaujolais as the poor man's Beaune began to be challenged. A few courageous shippers shipped the real thing, unblended. It was a revelation, and it started a cult.

Beaujolais then became two things, as far as the Anglo-Saxon world was concerned: the old red ink and this remarkable feather-weight, plummy, sweet and clean. The difficulty today is how to know which you are going to get before committing yourself to a bottle. The answer is not entirely simple.

*The countryside*

The appellation Beaujolais applies to a big area: sixty-odd parishes sprawled up and down the foothills of the Beaujolais mountains. It is some of France's least-known and loveliest country. The highlands, rising sometimes to three thousand feet, are wooded to the top. The forests of pine and chestnut tilt and tumble this way and that, following no ranges but thrusting up from meadows and brooks wherever they feel inclined. Cattle feed by the streams: otherwise there is little sign of life. The occasional village is pure Clochemerle.

*Beaujolais-Villages*

Beaujeu is the village in the foothills which has given its name to the district and its wine. Beaujeu and thirty-four others of the sixty constitute the area of the Beaujolais-Villages: what the Italians would call the *classico* zone. Of these elect (all in the north of Beaujolais) nine small districts in a block constitute the *crème de la crème* of the area. These are the *grands crus* Beaujolais with their own appellations: Moulin-à-Vent, Juliénas, Chénas, St-Amour, Fleurie, Chiroubles, Morgon, Brouilly and Côte de Brouilly.

To qualify for the name Beaujolais is easy: wine from any of the sixty parishes has only to reach 9 degrees of alcohol—which is not much—to do it. To be Beaujolais Supérieur is not hard either: one more degree and you're in. The wine is (or should be) very pale and light, with no body to speak of. In good years it is softly fruity; in bad thin and harsh. There is nothing to be gained by keeping this wine. It should all, ideally, be drunk up before the next harvest. Some of it is rushed through the vats like lightning to get it ready for sale by the first day the law allows: 15 November of its birth-year. This is the Beaujolais *en primeur* (the term is used for early spring vegetables too). It is the most fragile of wines. For a few weeks it keeps a sort of crude vigour which seems to come straight from the vine. At Christmas the *vin de l'année* is perfect; purply-pink, harsh, sweet, soft, sour all at the same time. But if there is any left at Easter you might as well throw it away.

*Beaujolais Supérieur*

*En primeur*

*Vin de l'année*

Nothing could be more different from the commercial mixture we used to know as Beaujolais in England, or come to that Holland, Switzerland or Germany. I have tasted the samples put out by a famous *négociant* in Beaujolais for a party of foreign buyers and found it impossible to look him in the eye. The wine was heavy, strong, sweet—even, I swear it, thick. Beaujolais growers, all but the best, have a weakness for sugar; they chaptalize up to (and no doubt beyond) the maximum allowed in good vintages as well as bad. But wine with no body can't take an extra dose of alcohol. It tastes hot and harsh, unless it is mixed with something fuller and rounder and sweeter . . . and so it goes on.

About a third of all Beaujolais comes from the northern part of the area with the appellation Beaujolais-Villages. To claim this appellation it must be of Supérieur strength, 10 degrees. But it is strength of character rather than alcohol which distinguishes Villages wines. They begin to have some of that body and vigour which ordinary Beaujolais lacks. They must still be bottled very young, before they start to tire and grow stale, but they last reasonably well in bottle. The wine of a good vintage grows rounder and more silky with a year's keeping.

*Quantity of production*

We are still talking of prodigious quantities of wine, even in this more restricted appellation. There are about forty thousand acres of vines in the Beaujolais. The yield allowed is about two thousand litres to the acre—half as much again as in the Côte d'Or. So there are something like eighty million litres of Beaujolais of all kinds in an average year, as against sixteen million litres of red wine from the whole of the Côte d'Or. By which token the price at least should stay relatively stable. And ten thousand of its forty thousand acres are in the nine *grands crus*.

*The character of Beaujolais*

I wish I could claim to know the characters of the *grands crus* better. There is a big step up from a Beaujolais-Villages to a Chiroubles or a Morgon. One is rarely disappointed with a *grand cru* Beaujolais from a reputable source. Yet at a blind tasting I have been at a loss to know a Fleurie from a Juliénas, or a Brouilly from a Côte de Brouilly. It is lack of application, I know; Beaujolais is not my regular drinking. I can pass on the received wisdom: that Moulin-à-Vent, Chénas and Morgon are the big ones which repay laying down for a surprising length of time; that Juliénas and St-Amour are fresh and vigorous; Fleurie and Chiroubles scented and silky; Brouilly and Côte de Brouilly rich and fruity. But to me they all have a great deal in common: at their best a sheer joyful smooth drinkableness which balks analysis. There is only one which in my experience stands apart, and that is Moulin-à-Vent.

It was a Moulin-à-Vent Château des Jacques 1959 which I had at the Chapon Fin at Thoissey near Pontanevaux in Beaujolais, with a glorious dish of *Volaille de Bresse aux morilles* (Bresse, of the famous chickens, is twenty miles away), followed by the delicious potato-flour pancakes, *crêpes Parmentier*. Lunch that day was cold Cavaillon melon, crayfish *à la nage*, the chicken in its cream sauce with morels, the *crêpes Parmentier* and *tartelettes aux framboises*, the raspberries sitting on that magic custard which makes two or three tartlets easy meat after enough food to last a weekend.

I was surprised to see that they proposed to serve the Moulin-à-Vent in the enormous glasses which are reserved for very special red wines. But they were perfectly right.

# The Rhône Valley

The Rhône is just beginning to come into its own on wine-lists, having been unjustly neglected for years. Often one vaguely named Côtes-du-Rhône, which might come from anywhere in a hundred-mile stretch of the Rhône valley, and an almost equally vague Châteauneuf-du-Pape are still its only representatives. Both are expected to be strong in alcohol and taste, dark in colour, and cheap.

A good deal of Rhône wine is like this. The Rhône leaves behind the delicacy of burgundy and Bordeaux. It is a wine of the south, where the sun fairly bakes the ground. The grapes ripen fully; the alcohol content is correspondingly high. Moreover the great grape of the Rhône, the Syrah, is one with a very dark colour, which gives the juice such a bite of bitterness that it is often mixed with a little white grape juice before the wine is made to soften it.

The result is a wine which needs a very long time to mature. If it is bottled young it will throw a deposit in the bottle almost like that of port. In the last century it was often offered as an alternative to port after dinner. Old Hermitage was reckoned, at thirty or forty years, a match for any wine on earth.

*Storage*   It is not made in quite this way now. Modern methods have cut down the time it takes to mature, but it still is rarely kept long enough. The oldest Rhône wine I have been able to find on any London wine-list is ten years old, and that is exceptional. No wine could so reward anyone who bought it while it was very young—and half the price of a comparable burgundy—and forgot about it for fifteen or twenty years. He would eventually have something priceless and unique, which he could send to auction or drink, or both. It would be soft, scented and so mouth-filling and warm in character that almost any other red wine would taste like red ink beside it.

*Côte Rôtie*

There are few names to remember in the Rhône valley, despite the fact that the vineyards stretch almost from Lyons to Avignon. Like the white wines, the reds are found in three principal places on the way. The first and (at any rate, by reputation) the best, just north of the vineyards of the great white Château Grillet at Condrieu, is the Côte Rôtie—the roasted hill. Its vineyards and production are both small but the wine is excellent; dark purple when it is young, browning slightly with age, heady, full of flavour and life, scented—more and more as it gets older—like lovely soft fruit. Curiously enough with age it becomes almost more like a big claret than burgundy: it acquires some of old claret's feather-light texture and sweetness.

Both sides of the river at the bend where Tain faces Tournon, thirty miles by road south of Côte Rôtie, make red wine. The west-bank appellation, St-Joseph, is an umbrella name for wine from a number of villages. It can be good, but it cannot be relied on like the Hermitage from opposite. The hill of Hermitage looks as though it was designed to give its front every minute of sunshine in the year; it faces south, rising above the river almost like the Rock of Gibraltar above the Straits.

*Hermitage*

Hermitage was called by Professor Saintsbury, the first man to write a book solely about the wine in his cellar, the manliest wine on earth. Dr Johnson was of the view that men should drink port (and boys claret). The juxtaposition of port with Hermitage again suggests its strength of character. But it is rarely old enough to show its character properly when it is offered to be drunk. If it were, it would be much more popular than it is.

*Crozes-Hermitage*

The village of Crozes-Hermitage lies just to the north of Hermitage proper. Its wine may not be sold as Hermitage, but Crozes-Hermitage is often seen. It is slightly cheaper; perhaps not reaching quite the same heights but an excellent substitute.

Game is usually suggested as the food for Hermitage and the other Rhône wines. Well-hung venison and wild boar, however, rarely come my way, and I prefer briefly hung game-birds with a lighter wine. To me the Rhône wines are for winter evenings when even the log fire and the candles leave a suspicion of chill in the dining-room. Then, whether it is liver and bacon or roast sirloin, cheese omelette or duck for dinner, they are fine.

*Cornas*

St-Joseph is the name used all the way down the west bank of the river to the village of Cornas, some six or seven miles. At Cornas a hill stands back from the river and the village. Its wine has not the qualities of Hermitage; it is rather dull beside the best of Rhône wines, clean but unsubtle; but it is often found as a speciality in the excellent restaurants of the area.

*Côtes-du-Rhône-Villages*

Côtes-du-Rhône is a general appellation for almost any Rhône wine. Over one hundred and twenty communes are entitled to it, which makes it on its own an unsatisfactory guide. With the extra word "-Villages", on the other hand, it becomes (like Beaujolais-Villages) a different matter. Less than one in ten of the Rhône communes are "-Villages". The great concentration of talent here is down in the southern Rhône area, sixty miles south of Hermitage, in the broad band of vineyards north of Avignon.

A number of these townships in this region whose names were unknown ten years ago are now giving us excellent wine, red, rosé and—surprisingly—white at very moderate prices.

*Chusclan*  The growers' co-operative at Chusclan is a typical example. It makes a substantial red, typical of the Rhône except in black durableness, a more-than-adequate rosé, a nicely gentle white and—significantly—a light red *en primeur*. *Primeur* wines for immediate drinking have long been known in the Rhône as *vins de café* (for drinking in cafés, not with coffee). But this is clearly aimed at the booming Beaujolais Nouveau market. With rather more alcohol and substance than the new Beaujolais, and rather less astrigency, Rhône *primeur* may easily become a craze in its own right.

*Château du Trignon*  The Château du Trignon at Sablet near Gigondas carries away as many gold medals as anyone in the neighbourhood, and is particularly interesting as an uninhibitedly experimental estate. The wine M Roux makes today (which is light and fruity, but admirably firm and long-lasting), others, one feels, will be making tomorrow.

*Lirac*  The Château de Segriès at Lirac is another good producer. Lirac has long been a mere poor relation to Tavel of the famous rosé. Now red and white Lirac make it a much more interesting proposition.

# Châteauneuf-du-Pape

Châteauneuf-du-Pape is far and away the most famous of the wines of the Rhône valley and Provence, for it is in both regions and both regions claim it.

The old castle, now in ruins, which gives it its name is a little way north of Avignon. The vineyards surround it and accompany the Rhône on its way for six or seven miles, stretching inland nearly to the old Roman city of Orange. Another ten miles or so inland lie the *Gigondas* vineyards of Gigondas. These should be considered part of the same complex; the Gigondas wine is very like its more famous neighbour.

Châteauneuf-du-Pape is unusual among French wines for being made of a large number of different kinds of grapes, some optional, some compulsory if the grower wants to keep his appellation. The wine they become is a by-word for strength, although alcoholically it is not necessarily any stronger than any other Rhône wine—it sometimes reaches 15 per cent.

What gives it its reputation more than its power to turn the head or buckle the knees is its warmth and strength of flavour. Without having the hard and almost overwhelming taste of young Hermitage it could almost hold its own with port for flavour, and yet it is not at all sweet.

Cheap Châteauneuf-du-Pape does not deserve this kind of praise—what cheap wine does?—but the best growths, which are becoming better and better known, mature relatively quickly, in say five or six years, into very satisfying and splendid wine. They are, however, no longer the bargain they once were.

Château Fortia, Chante Perdrix ("Partridge Song", if song is the word), the Domaine de la Nerthe, Château Rayas, Domaine de Mont-Redon and Château Vaudieu are some of these fine ones. Again, they are often described as the wine for game, but they should be drunk more often than this implies. If they were called the wine for steak they would have more of the use they deserve.

Châteauneuf-du-Pape is usually bottled in a sloping-shouldered burgundy-shape bottle. Some of the growers get carried away and use absurd rough-glass bottles which are supposed to look handmade, and as though they had been under the cobwebs for a century or two. If the wine were as old as the bottle looks it would be far too old. It is a publicity stunt and certainly detracts from the value for money of the package, including the wine. The wine inside may be good or bad, but it would be wiser to look for an ordinary bottle.

## Vins de Pays

*The Midi*

Up to now there has been very little reason to bother about the wine of the extreme south of France—the Midi. With few exceptions it has been grown simply as a commodity: *vin de consommation courante*. An old tradition of good, if not fine, wine-making in the hills round the coastal plain of the Languedoc died with phylloxera in the last century. After phylloxera all the replanting was with high-yielding vines of low quality. Moreover most of the planting was done on flat and fertile land which could never, with any vines, give wine as good as the Côtes or hillsides.

The exceptions to this rule, the hillsides that were replanted and have maintained a lead, if not a very great one, over the bulk of Midi wine, are a few in Provence and some fine stretches of country over *Minervois, Corbières* to the west, in the areas known as the Minervois, Corbières and *and Roussillon* Roussillon. Corbières and Roussillon are the lower hummocks and ridges of the slow build-up to the Pyrenees, inland of Narbonne and Perpignan. The Minervois, and the neighbouring St-Chinian, are comparable slopes leading up the Cevennes to the north. These four main areas usually managed to maintain a certain standard of strength and liveliness in the wine; enough to give them the *V.D.Q.S.* status.

Since the French parted with Algeria in the early sixties there has been a pressure on the Midi to improve its wine. No longer could it rely for colour, alcohol and body on cheap imports. More recently the rising prices of wine from the classical areas has given them another incentive. For all this they have not exactly leapt into action. It is only in the last three or four years that real moves have been made; they are still miles behind the comparable areas of California or Australia in technique and quality. But they are moving, and without any doubt we shall get to know their names and their wine very much better in the next ten years.

*New techniques*

The really vital move towards quality will be replanting with quality vines and settling for a smaller quantity. Experiments with the Syrah of the Rhône and the Cabernet of Bordeaux are already showing that there is nothing inherently wrong with Midi sunshine. In the meantime, though, there is a new technique (new to the area; something similar has always been done in Beaujolais) which is making a difference. They call it by the rather ambiguous name of *Maceration carbonique* *maceration carbonique*. What it means is dumping the whole bunches of grapes, stalks and all, without crushing, in a vat filled with carbon dioxide. Under these conditions, with no oxygen, the yeasts cannot begin normal fermentation. But a totally different form of fermentation starts up *inside* the unbroken grapes, extracting pigments and flavouring matter from the skins inwardly. The claim is that this extract is chemically different, and gastronomically superior, to that arrived at by normal fermentation from the start.

Fermentation finally bursts the skins and the juice, a lovely rich colour from the maceration, drops to the bottom of the vat. When the fermentation without air has gone as far as it will go (which is not far: up to about two per cent alcohol), the ruptured bunches are pressed, the press-wine mixed with what has collected in the bottom of the vat, and the lot fermented out together.

Maceration wines are still very much in the minority, and they have their detractors. I have found in them a freshness and fruitiness which are rare in the Midi, and a peculiar richness of smell and flavour I can only describe as malty—though the word conveys rather the wrong idea. They are good to drink with very little ageing, and what is more remarkable they seem to last well in the bottle, light as they are, and take on the complexity and the special smell of mature wine. Whether they are the final answer or not, however, they are an example of the sort of advance which will help to sell Midi wine. In a few years the differences between Corbières and Roussillon, and Minervois and St-Chinian, may be matters of gastronomic moment. In the meantime you should try any you see.

## Côtes de Provence

Things are more settled east of the Rhône in the hills behind the smart coast, from Marseilles to Nice. The area is broadly called the Côtes de Provence. Most of its wine is pink and white. Two or three estates make good red. Those at Bandol, just east of Marseilles on the coast and at Palette, inland, just east of Aix-en-Provence, are the best known. The outstanding Bandol wine is that of the Domaine Ott, which at eight years old can bear comparison with a more-than-adequate Bordeaux from, perhaps, the Côtes de Fronsac. There are two or three other Bandol wines exported: Domaine Tempier, which is made very light for a southern wine, and Château Pradeaux, which is allowed all its southern colour, strength and power, are two of the better known.

### Bandol

### Palette

The best-known wine of Palette is Château Simone. It is on every list in every restaurant in the area as the best wine of Provence. Round Aix the country is heavily wooded with pines. Where there are no pines there is a thick scrub of rosemary, thyme and savory. All these things are reputed to be discernible in the wine of Château Simone.

### Apt

In the sweeping red sandstone valleys of the inland Vaucluse the *vin du pays* is also good. The Château de Mille at Apt makes a very pleasant, rather thin red wine.

## The black wine of Cahors

The wine-merchant looking for value these days is being drawn more and more to the hinterland of Bordeaux. The classic wine name of the region is Cahors—a legend for "blackness", which is scarcely a fashionable characteristic today. Cahors has come of age recently, changed its wine-making style to something more contemporary and easier to drink, and been promoted from *V.D.Q.S.* to a full *Appellation Contrôlée*. Something has undoubtedly been lost in the process, but the something was not a commercial proposition: it was a quality which took many years in bottle to develop. Modern Cahors is not without personality: it is still solid, robust wine. Whether it can still be called a classic in its own right is open to question.

### Bergerac

Fewer claims are made for the red wines of the Dordogne, which, these days, virtually all travel under the name of Bergerac. Pécharmant is another appellation of the area, traditionally darker, harder and more like Cahors, but (I was told locally) now only a way of paying more for ordinary Bergerac. Not that there is anything wrong with Bergerac: there are full appellation Bordeaux wines with much less charm. Good Bergerac is eminently gulpable; well deserving of the name of claret. Bergerac in turn has its poor (or at least junior) relatives in the neighbouring *V.D.Q.S.* areas of the Côtes du Marmandais and the Côtes de Buzet. The tendency here is for wines to be thin, but a good vintage can provide the missing warmth. When it does they come well up to claret standard, too.

### The Loire

The Loire valley is more the land of white wine than of red. Its red wines are rare and consequently expensive. They have the fruitiness and distinctly grape-like taste of Beaujolais, though they are a little drier than young Beaujolais. The big difference is in the grapes from which they are made. Loire wines are made with the claret grape, the Cabernet. This gives them some of the tannin which conveys such full colour and long life to claret. They have the purple *robe* (the lovely French word for the colour of a wine), but not the bite which makes young Bordeaux difficult to like. At their best they can be thrillingly similar to a good Bordeaux of the lightest kind—perhaps a Margaux.

*Chinon and Bourgueil*
*Saumur-Champigny*

Chinon and Bourgueil, one on each side of the Loire, produce virtually identical red wine. Saumur-Champigny is a third red-wine appellation nearby, less renowned but worth investigating. Drunk young and cool their wines make a change from Beaujolais with some simple dish—a salad or a sumptuous *croque-monsieur*, the cheese, melted and bubbling, blending with the ham on a doorstep of succulent fried bread. But a good one should be aged, to acquire more finesse than Beaujolais ever could.

### Champagne

So precious is the production of the best villages of Champagne for the blends of sparkling wine that their grapes can hardly be spared for making anything else. The village of Bouzy, in the black-grape district, still makes a little red wine each year, chiefly for the families of the proprietors. Some is needed for mixing with white wine to tint pink champagne. A very little finds its way onto the market under the

*Bouzy Rouge*

delightful name of Bouzy Rouge.

It is capable of being one of the best red wines of France. In style it is like a very light and delicate burgundy, with all the finesse of one of the really good ones, with the addition of the peculiar fresh scent of champagne.

Bouzy will never become popular or be anything but hard to find. But it is a good card to have up your sleeve. I keep one bottle in my cellar. I have as much amusement wondering who I am going to open it for as I have in drinking it.

### The Jura

The Jura hillsides, the last gestures of the Alpine ranges in the direction of Burgundy, specialize in yellow and pink wines. Jura red has no great fame. The extraordinary enterprise of M Henri Maire of Arbois, however, has red wine to offer as well as the other colours. M Maire has made an industry out of the old small-time viticulture of the Jura. He has collected three-quarters of the production of the entire region into his own hands. The factory in a field which he has established near the old town of Arbois is like nothing else in France. Australians would recognize it from the great wineries of the Barossa valley. More than twenty different types of wine are processed there, from grape to despatch, complete with one of a range of gay and gaudy gifts tucked into the carton for good measure.

Maire has a way of giving his wines romantic names which makes it hard to find out exactly what they are. His range of labels is astonishing in its fertility of invention. Sub-history, sub-geography, sub-folklore are all represented. Among his red wines two of the best which have wide distribution, though they might possibly appear under different names in different parts of the world, are Marnebour, a soft, rather sweet and gentle wine, and Frédéric Barberousse, a stronger wine, like a rather bulky burgundy. The Barberousse is evidence that the hillsides of Arbois can make good red wine.

## Other areas

There are still a good number of *vins de pays* I have not mentioned, and probably many I have never heard of, scattered among the lonely hillsides of France. France is still an empty country by European standards. There are not many more than fifty million inhabitants; in England the same number fit into a country only a quarter of France's size. In many places cultivation is desultory and, for all we know, what could be a wonderful wine remains the local drinking of a few farmers and shopkeepers. There are wines which are almost legends—the famous *St-Pourçain-sur-Sioule*, for example, of the upper reaches of the Allier—a tributary of the Loire. You usually hear about these wines as you hear of the wines of Greece; they are the snatches of Elysium which somebody brings back from an enchanted holiday. If you ever find them anywhere but in their own land they are disappointing, and yet you cannot disbelieve the stories of their wonderful powers which generations of travellers have lovingly constructed. The Auvergne, the Basque country (Irouléguy is one of its odd, lilting names), the highlands around Vichy, the hills around Poitiers and the unvisited villages of Lorraine all have their wine-myths. Even Paris has its own wine—Suresnes—a by-word, in this case, for sourness.

*St-Pourçain-sur-Sioule*

In every case—except that of Paris—the answer is to ask for the *vin du pays*, or look under the entry on the wine-list, when you are in any region whose wine is not familiar from wine-lists at home. If it is unpleasant, as it sometimes is, you will not make the same mistake there again. But the chances are that you will have as good a wine as any in the house for very little money.

## North Africa

North Africa learnt to make wine from the French. But the special situation of wine in a dry country—Islam forbidding wine-drinking—has always been against it. Without a local demand, and with French imports demanding only the neutral wine, strong and dark for blending with the flimsy produce of the Midi—and farther north too, at times—quality wine-making was hardly a serious proposition. A good handful of Algerian vineyards did get as far as *V.D.Q.S.* status in the later years of French rule (which ended in 1962), but nothing approaching the research and investment that have made fine wine possible in California and Australia has ever taken place in North Africa.

Considering which, the wine North Africa makes today is not bad at all. To speak more particularly is difficult, because it tends to travel more or less anonymously. A few Moroccan brands have established themselves: the curious off-pink Gris de Boulaouane is one: Sidi Larbi, a middle-weight rather plain red, is another. On the face of it, Morocco, with its more temperate, Atlantic-influenced climate, should have the edge on Algeria. One is judging on very incomplete evidence, to be sure, but I find more substance and satisfaction in some of the Algerian wine shipped today than in the Moroccan.

*Morocco*

*Algeria*

I have read reports of the Algerian coastal-plain vineyards being grubbed up since the French market for their wine closed. I have not seen for myself, but if this is true, the Algerians seem to be abandoning the high-yield, low-quality strategy and concentrating on the hills, whence their better wines have always come. Such wines as I have tasted recently—clean, solid, vigorous and, I should guess, well worth ageing in the bottle for a year or two—are probably the *V.D.Q.S.* wines of French Imperial days. In any case at prices so modest one can afford to experiment. It would be foolish to leave North Africa out of one's hunt for good cheap wine.

*Corsica*     The same applies to Corsica—with the difference that here the wine-industry really only started when Algeria parted with France. Recently Corsicans have been found experimenting with alternatives to grapes for wine-making, which will not encourage anyone to try their wares. But Corsica has two *Appellations Contrôlées*, Patrimonio and Coteaux d'Ajaccio. There is obviously the serious intention of making good wine. I have not yet tasted one which has appealed to me particularly, but then I have not yet been to see for myself.

# Italian Red Wines

Renaissance is not too strong a word for what is happening to the Italian wine industry at the moment. Districts which used to make wine adequately are making it well, and districts which used to make it well are excelling themselves. Most of all is this true of red wine, which has always been Italy's trump card. Two parts of Italy can grow red wine which is in the international front rank. Piedmont in the north-west is one; Chianti is the other.

*Piedmont*     Piedmont is the Rhône valley, the Burgundy and the Champagne of Italy. Its sparkling Asti is the champagne. Its Grignolino and Dolcetto are the Beaujolais. Its Barolo and Gattinara are the great growths, its Barbaresco the second-growths, its Barbera the Côtes-du-Rhône. Nebbiolo is the good everyday wine and Freisa the sparkling red which even Burgundy cannot do without.

It is wrong, of course, to compare these with French wines. They are not like them, nor, like some wines which borrow plumage, do they desperately need the comparison. But Piedmont plays in Italy the role of all these areas in the life of France.

Piedmont is a large province. It stretches from the French border eastwards almost to Milan, south almost to the Italian Riviera and north, past Lake Maggiore, right up to the Simplon Pass in the Alps. Turin is its capital, the city of vermouth. Everywhere south and east of Turin, from Cuneo in the foothills of the Alpes Maritimes, thirty miles from France, to Novara, just south of Lake Maggiore, in an almost north-south line ninety miles long, the wine is Italy's best.

*The Alps*    The Alpine character of Piedmont needs stressing, because it is a factor, perhaps *the* factor, in the quality of Italy's best red wine. Although the Monferrato hills themselves are no Alps, the Barolo vineyards are still nearly two thousand feet above sea-level. More important, the Alps hem them in not only to the north, but to the south and west as well. This is not a Mediterranean climate. The upper slopes of Barolo can expect two months of snow a year. Conversely the summer reigns with untempered heat, leading into a truly Keatsian autumn: mists and mellow fruitfulness unabashed.

*Nebbiolo*    One great grape, the Nebbiolo, is as supreme in Piedmont as the Pinot is in Burgundy. Wine called just Nebbiolo, without any place-name, is good, often very good, light table wine. Nebbiolo from the district where the three towns of Alba, Asti and Alessandria are strung out along the river Tanaro is best. The great names here are Barolo and Barbaresco. The tendency of wine-names to begin with "Bar" is even more marked than that of towns to begin with "A". We still have to deal with Barbera and, to avoid further confusion, Bardolino, though it is a stranger in these parts.

*Barolo*    Barolo and Barbaresco are both village-names, available to small zones each comprising a handful of little settlements. They are the two classic Nebbiolo wines: the Barolo the bigger, fruitier and heavier of the two, coming from a higher, and at harvest time hotter, area; the Barbaresco, more rapidly affected by the autumn mists from the Tanaro, a similar but on the whole lighter, strictly speaking finer, wine. Barolo needs more age than Barbaresco. Three years in a huge oak cask is a statutory requirement, and another three in bottle is essential for even the beginnings of its potential to emerge. A formidable alcohol content is normal. When the cold weather stopped the 1970 vintage fermenting in November it had reached 13.5 degrees and still had considerable reserves of sugar. In March 1971 it started fermenting again and went on up to nearly 15 degrees. Barolo which fails to achieve 12 degrees may not even use the name, but has to call itself Nebbiolo d'Alba instead.

Old Barolo has an almost freakish amount of scent—a really rich and spicy blend of raspberries and dead leaves and mushrooms: impossible to analyze but enthralling to sniff, think about, and sniff again.

I'm sure I have not tasted the Barolo of all the best makers, but my list is already quite a long one. It includes the firms of Borgogno— promising name—Damilano and Guilio Mascarello in Barolo itself; Fontanafredda at Serralunga d'Alba; Franco Fiorina, Francesco Rinaldi and the Istituto Agrario Viticolo Enologico Statale at Alba; Cantina Terre del Barolo at Castiglione Falletto; Contratto at Canelli and Bersano at Nizza Monferrato. The same firms, in most cases, also offer the other wines of the region.

*Barbaresco*    Barbaresco is a less heavy, scented and impressive wine than Barolo. It has not the hardness to be softened down by time before it is at its best. For this reason it is often a safer wine to choose. Both come into what the Italians call the great roast wine category, meaning they are wines to drink with great roasts, or great wines to drink with roasts.

*Barbera*    Barbera is not the name of a village, although it would seem reasonable to suppose that it was a neighbour of Barbaresco. The Barbera is a grape. The wine has not the body or strength of flavour of Nebbiolo; it is good, not fine. It has a peculiar descant of sharpness above its substantial harmony of flavours which makes it extremely appetizing. In Turin I have had it with the amazing *fonduta*, a rich puddle of melted cheese and eggs and butter over which you shave slivers of the curious dank-tasting white truffle of Piedmont. It was a more than satisfying combination.

*Bardolino*

Bardolino, I should add here, because it is always being confused with the similar-sounding wines of Piedmont, is a wispily light red wine from the shore of Lake Garda near Verona.

*Dolcetto*

Dolcetto grapes are grown everywhere in the Langhe hills, where Barolo and Barbaresco are found. They make the Beaujolais of the area; light, sometimes slightly fruity red wine to be drunk very young.

*Grignolino*

There is some better and higher-strength wine made of the Grignolino, but it is hard to find.

The end of our line north towards Lake Maggiore is around Novara and Vercelli, in country more famous for its rice than its wine. The Nebbiolo is called the Spanna here. It produces a wine which, although its reputation is still to be made, is as good as Barolo. Gattinara and Ghemme are the two main producing areas which usually give the wine its name, although it is sometimes called just Vino Spanna. The firm of Antonio Vallana makes a superb Spanna wine; it has great colour even at ten years old, and the same spicy scent as Barolo.

*Gattinara and Ghemme*

*Vino Spanna*

Gattinara and Ghemme should specify that they are made from Spanna grapes. There is no regulation to say that they must be, as there is with Barolo. They are quite ordinary if they are not.

## Lombardy

The best wine of Lombardy, the next province going east, is from the extreme north, from a mere crack in the mounting Alps where the river Adda forces its way through and forms the narrow, spectacular Valtellina.

*Valtellina*

The north wall of the Valtellina is not unlike the north wall of that other valley, the Rhône in Switzerland, where the Alps give way to the power of water and allow the growing of vines. Above it is the Swiss border and, though there is no way of getting there except on foot, St-Moritz. Opposite it the south wall is no good for anything; it is so steep that it is in almost perpetual shadow.

In vineyards which appear, from down below on the flat valley floor, to be vertical, the wines of the Valtellina are grown. The best have the delightful names of Sassella, Grumello and Inferno. All are made from the great Nebbiolo grape, which here has yet another name, Chiavennasca, mixed with a little of two or three other varieties. Sassella, Grumello and Inferno are different parts of the valley between Sondrio and Chiuro. I asked Nino Negri, one of the principal and best producers of the valley, what was the difference between the three. "None," he said. "They're all the same." His habit is to take the best of whichever turns out best in a good year and keep it as his reserve for as long as six or seven years in wood before bottling, which suggests that it is an immensely hard, strong wine when it is made. After this time, and after three or four years in bottle, it has become another of Italy's very finest wines. It has all the body of Barolo with, I think, even more delicacy of flavour, if not quite so much scent. This superb wine he sells as Castel Chiuro, but there is very little of it.

*Sassella, Grumello and Inferno*

*Castel Chiuro*

The ordinary Infernos and the rest cannot be treated in this way.

Even so, they are generally four years old before they come on the market. They would benefit from more time to age, which they rarely get. They are good, rather hard and dark-coloured, strong and well-made wines.

*Sfursat*

The Valtellina has another speciality, which I must confess is not quite to my taste; a curious strong red wine called Sfursat. The grapes are left hanging up indoors until the January after the vintage to concentrate their sugar, a practice usually used for sweet wines. They are then made into wine by the usual methods for red table wine and allowed to ferment until the wine is dry and very strong. It has a curious intense flavour which I do not find appetizing, but which is highly thought of for drinking with the Sunday joint when there is time to sleep it off.

*Buttafuoco,*
*Sangue di Giuda*
*and Frecciarossa*

Southern Lombardy tries to outdo northern Lombardy in names. Memorable though Inferno may be, Buttafuoco (Spitfire), Sangue di Giuda (Judas' Blood) and Frecciarossa (Red Arrow) are evidently designed to spring to mind even more readily. The first two are traditional names of the red wines from the district of Oltrepo Pavese in the Po valley south of Pavia, the last a brand-name for a very pleasant and reliable light red wine from Casteggio in the same region. Frecciarossa describes itself on its label as a Château-bottled Vintage Claret. Perhaps if it had not gone quite so far in its claims it might have caused more confusion.

*Lambrusco di Sorbara*

One sparkling Lombardy red wine which has made a name for itself is called Lambrusco di Sorbara. Sorbara is just north of Modena, in flat unpromising country, which looks much more suited to the production of the Maseratis and Ferraris which are built there than to the growing of any very special wine.

It is not easy to make acquaintance with Lambrusco. Even at nearby Modena they tell you that it does not travel the dozen miles from the vineyards and keep its character. In the scruffy little café in Sorbara where I ordered it an incident happened which is all too typical of the Italian attitude to wine. The bottle they brought was labelled Lambrusco. In tiny writing underneath was a legend I did not understand until I had tasted it. The rich pink foam on it, and the extraordinarily unpleasant taste, were the work of a chemical which had been added. When I complained, the waitress whisked the bottle away without a word and came back with another, labelled Il Vero Lambrusco. The look she gave me said "If you wanted the real thing why didn't you ask for it?" The real thing was, in fact, delicious, as I had been led to expect. It might have been young Beaujolais with a dash of blackcurrant, put through a soda syphon. The only one I have had in England tasted terrible. The moral is that it is a mistake to take Italian wine too seriously. When it happens to be good, be thankful.

## The Veneto

The countryside of Verona must rank third, after Piedmont and Chianti, among Italy's regions for reliable and agreeable red wine. Its Bardolino we have touched on; a red wine which is barely more than a rosé: soft, gentle and pleasant. So gentle, in fact, that I have drunk it from a tumbler dipped into the top of a vat of week-old wine

*Valpolicella*

without any untoward effects. Valpolicella, its immediate neighbour, is more positive—but it is still an insinuating wine, light in colour, soft in texture, warning you only with a warm roundness of flavour that it is not kid's stuff.

The vineyards of Valpolicella are almost operatically pretty. They climb the hills to the north of Verona in a series of terraced valleys which seem to get into the background of every Venetian likeness of the Madonna. If you are ever lucky enough to be there in autumn you will see a landscape entirely wrought in copper and gold . . . and highly wrought; not wild but constrained, with villas at every turn in the road and only the vine ramping gleefully out of control.

At its western end the district of Valpolicella embraces the much smaller district of Soave, whose white wine has much the same qualities of warmth and gentleness. To the north the sub-district of Valpantena makes red wine very much like Valpolicella: I am told not quite so good. But it is at the eastern end of the hills facing Bardolino over the valley of the Adige (which flows parallel with Lake Garda as though nervous of being compromised by that body of water) that Valpolicella reaches its climax in the four communes of Fumane, Marano, Sant'Ambrogio and Negrar, the heart of Valpolicella Classico.

Tasting in the growers' cellars there I have seen a confusing variety of styles of wine. The traditional one, kept—by today's standards—rather too long in cask, is quite strong-flavoured and dry. Then there is an almost instant one: light, sweet and slightly fierce. Best of all there is a mature one, but matured in big glass jars rather than oak for two or three years. It keeps its clear cherry colour and develops a round, nutty flavour with its natural sweetness balanced by a distinctly bitter twist like almonds when you swallow. Tasted there, with grilled sausages and tongue from a little fire of vine-cuttings, and parmesan and white bread on the scrubbed table, it becomes one of the world's most appetizing wines. That bitter touch is a trademark of the wines of the Adige from the Tyrol southwards. You almost grow to need it if you spend any time there.

*Recioto and Amarone*

The growers also take endless trouble to make a kind of wine which to me is an aberration; their Recioto and Amarone which are pressed from grapes dried in the loft until the New Year. Recioto is (as Cyril Ray has pointed out) what the Germans would call an *Auslese*, a wine made from selected ripe grapes, in this case carefully dehydrated to concentrate their flavour. Recioto is dark red-brown and semi-sweet; Amarone is the same colour but more or less dry and pungently strong. When your host produces the prize bottle at the climax of dinner it is a nice test of diplomacy to see if you can get another glass of the light seductive Valpolicella instead.

Bolla, Bertani and Lamberti are three of the bigger houses of the area for Valpolicella and the other Verona wines. Allegrini is another whose wines I have particularly liked.

## Trentino-Alto Adige

The best red wines of the Trentino and the Alto Adige should be much better known in Britain and the United States than they are. Where the Adige cuts her valley southwards from Merano, leaving clean walls of granite hanging above the green valley-floor, the vine seems to have taken over everything. It laps like a tide against the cliffs and rolls in waves over the old rock-falls which give shape to the landscape. Every vine is trained up on to a lofty pergola, which makes the vineyards like endless burrowings in green earth, the roof held up by rows of props and the light filtering through a filigree of green and purple and gold leaves and heavy pendulous grapes.

The old road north from Rome and Florence to Germany over the Brenner Pass leads through this valley. At Bolzano, high up the valley, a magnificent Medici palace bears witness to the interests bankers had in this great trade-route over the mountains. Most of the wine of this country crosses these mountains today.

*Teroldego*

Teroldego is the red wine of the Trentino. It is made very light for local drinking—for it is the universal drink of Trento—but the best Teroldego, which is bottled, has considerable strength of alcohol and character.

*Lago di Caldaro*

The Alto Adige round Bolzano has two *D.O.C.* red wines: Lago di Caldaro (or in the German which is the language of the district and appears on most labels, Kalterersee) and Santa Maddalena. Lake Caldaro, a mere pond in comparison with the more celebrated lakes of northern Italy, lies just south of Bolzano, but its name is available to the wine of a large area without too many questions asked. The question I would ask, if it were offered to me, is "How sweet is it?" The Kalterersee I have had in a German dining-car was a pallid and treacly wine like an Italian attempt at a Rhine red *Auslese*. On the other hand, Caldaro I have had with an Italian label—and therefore presumably not so categorically designed for the German market—has been an adequate dark red wine, light in body but not unpleasant.

*Santa Maddalena*

Santa Maddalena is the more prestigious name. The smaller zone lies on the mountain slopes above the marshalling yard for the Alpine freight trains at Bolzano. The vines roast on a steep slope within sight, even in summer, of snow-capped Alps. The result is a red wine with plenty of colour and body, if no very special character.

*Lagrein*

The real character of the valley is the local grape called the Lagrein, which plays a minor role in the blend of the Caldaro and Maddalena, but which is mainly used on its own to make a quite unforgettable rosé of distinct personality. There is a monastery at Muri-Gries on the outskirts of Bolzano which makes a splendid Lagrein Dunkel (they use the German word for dark about it as though it were one of those thunderous Munich beers). The cellar-master, Father Gregor, scurries across the courtyard and down into his cavernous cellar under the booming of the vesper bell like a big squirrel who knows where the acorns are kept. The special character of Adige wine, the full ripeness matched with resounding bitterness as you swallow, is summed up in Lagrein. It is not the only good thing in the Father's cellar. His Malvasier was paler in colour than the Dunkel but even more solid and bitter. His Lagrein Rosato (or Kretzer in the dialect) was no ordinary rosé either.

*Imported varieties*

Alto Adige growers realize that their Alpine grapes are not to everyone's taste and experiment with imported vines to considerable effect. The Merlot of St-Emilion is grown here—and in most of north-eastern Italy—to make a very sound, if not fascinating, red wine. There is a little Pinot Noir, which seems, on the limited evidence I have seen, well worth pursuing. But better than either or anything else in the valleys is the Cabernet Sauvignon, which gives wine California would not be ashamed of. Strangely enough, though, even the Cabernet takes on the Adige character. Whether it is the soil or the Alpine air I don't know, but the trace of bitterness is there.

All the rest of north-east Italy is wine-country, more or less, but the red wine I have had from the eastern Veneto and Friuli has not been exciting. The Cabernet and the Merlot of Bordeaux are widely grown. Neither is particularly memorable; they taste rather thin. From Gori-

*Colfortin Rosso*

zia, the border of Yugoslavia, there is a pleasant wine called Colfortin Rosso, which reminded me of a light and rather sweet claret.

*Tuscany*

Not until after the Apennines, in Tuscany, do we meet another really good red wine. But this is Chianti, the best known of all Italian wines, the symbol of them all; the round flask in the straw jacket.

*Chianti*

Chianti is simply the red wine of the hills between Florence and Siena. It varies greatly from a light, rough, ordinary wine which is drunk before the next batch is made to a smooth and perfumed wine, not at all unlike a French one. The farmer continues to make his wine from the old, chaotic, mixed vineyards, which really means no vineyards at all, but a vine here and there among the olive-trees, cabbages, walnuts; whatever chance or fancy has given root in the fertile, sun-baked earth. The large estates clear and plough the land, roll away the great rocks which lie on the surface, drain hollows, decimate woodland and throw the ranks of vines from crest to crest. The farmer piles all his grapes, stalks, pips and skins, into a barrel to ferment, and then forgets about them. The proprietor of two valleys carefully measures proportions of this grape and that, sorts out the bad ones, strips off leaves and stalks and nurses every moment of the vine's progress. The contrast is familiar; there is no wine-country where some old farmers are not to be found doing things according to their old methods. But in Chianti it becomes pointed and plain. Both wines are equally Chianti. But they are as different as Midi red and Chambertin.

In the middle of the last century Barone Bettino Ricasoli (a man of the nineteenth century if ever there was one: Prime Minister of Italy, a collector, an architect and a devoted drinker of his own Chianti) experimented with the traditional methods of making Tuscan wine at his own estate.

*Brolio*

His castle, Brolio, the last outpost of Florentine territory on the Sienese border in the centuries when the two cities were never at peace, is in the heart of Chianti. From its high battlements the walls of Siena can be clearly seen. It had to withstand siege after siege. The Ricasolis have lived there for nine hundred years or more; nonetheless Barone Bettino was moved to rebuild the living-quarters of the castle in the red brick of Siena, leaving only the old battlements and towers which even nineteenth-century workmen could not pull down.

In the castle cellars he performed the experiments which established the classical formula for making Chianti. It is a very strange one.

*How Chianti is made*

Four kinds of grapes go into the blend. At first they ferment in the usual way together. But as the fermentation is dying down more of the same grapes, unfermented but slightly dried in the sun, are added —an operation called the *governo*. The fermentation starts again and continues very slowly, giving the wine, if it is drunk while it is still young, a slight prickle of fermentation—the slightest possible fizz— in the mouth. This is the characteristic Chianti which is so popular in the restaurants of Florence.

The best Chianti, however, is not drunk so soon. It is left to age for a formidable time—even as long as five or six years—in oak casks. When it is bottled it is ready to drink, unlike the French wines. It can be "governed" or not. If it is the extra fermentation works itself right out during this long time in the wood. The result is a perfect blending of the four grapes with something extra, a slightly roasted sort of richness, from the dried ones which were added. Such wines (with a minimum age of three years and 12.5 degrees of alcohol) as

*Reservas*

these are called Reservas. They are not found in the usual Chianti flask but in brown bottles of the narrow, high-shouldered Bordeaux shape. Formerly they appeared on the market at about eight years old; today, unfortunately, three or four years is a more typical age.

A good Reserva is second to no wine in Italy; it has all the qualities of a very fine one—scent, character and delicacy. Like the best Barolos, unfortunately, they are not often listed by wine-merchants. Barone Ricasoli's Brolio Reserva is probably the best distributed. It alone is enough to vindicate the name of Chianti from all the sour thin wines which have been perpetrated under it. The estates of the Marchesi Antinori (whose best wine is sold as Villa Antinori), Castello di Uzzano, Montepaldi, Bertolli, Marmoross Sergardi, Serristori-Macchiavelli and Badia a Coltibuono produce superb Chiantis within the Chianto Classico area. There must be many others I have not tasted.

*Other areas*

Outside the classical area there are others producing Chianti without quite the same control, and usually considered inferior in quality. Six areas are recognized: the Chianti dei Colli Aretini, Chianti Rufina (not to be confused with Ruffino, a shipper), Chianti dei Colli Fiorentini (the local wine of Florence, made best by the Frescobaldis at Nipozzano), dei Colli Pisani and dei Colli Senesi (of the Sienese hills). These wines are rarely treated as Reservas, but in their litre flasks in the restaurants of Florence and Siena they can be excellent.

At vintage time the game to be had in Tuscany is astonishingly varied and abundant. Little birds whose names I would rather not know succeed each other in endless variety to the table. At night in a little square in Siena, with the brick walls of palaces disappearing into the dark all round, and the flicker of a faint street-lamp giving a theatrical air to the scene, you can have dinner at a lonely table; the primitive charred little bodies of birds and a fat flask of Chianti from the Sienese hills.

*Brunello di Montalcino*

There is one other very little-known Tuscan wine which is not entitled to be called Chianti, but which is better than any except the very best Chiantis. It is made only at the village of Montalcino, near Siena, and takes the name of its grape, the Brunello. Brunello di Montalcino has more of the power and richness of a Barolo than of a Chianti. It has the cleanness and character of a very fine wine, strong but wonderfully delicate at the end. The firm of Biondi-Santi make it, and ten years is a good age for it. It makes a magnificent match for a partridge.

*Umbria*

Umbria's only famous wine is the white Orvieto. But in the last few years the diminutive *D.O.C.* of Rubesco di Torgiano, up in the hills between Perugia and Assisi, has been making a name for itself. Rubesco is not radically different from a Chianti Reserva, perhaps more claret-like—at any rate to be included among Italy's most serious red wines.

*Southern Italy*

None of the wines of the south can be mentioned in the same breath as the fine wine of Chianti or Piedmont. Most south Italian wine needs blending with something lighter to make it pleasant to those who are not used to it. Puglia, the heel of Italy, is the biggest wine maker of any of the provinces, but its wine is virtually unknown under any local name. It reaches the markets of the world as the body in a northern wine of a bad year, via the tankers which sail from Brindisi for the ports of the north.

*Puglia*

*Lachryma Christi*

On the way south, though, especially in Campania, around Mount Vesuvius, adequate red wine is produced. Red Lachryma Christi is made on the lava slopes of the mountain itself, or should be. Inland

*Taurasi*

from Vesuvius round Avellino, an unfrequented region, Taurasi red is well spoken of.

*Ravello Rosso*

On the Sorrento peninsula red wine is not so much in demand as white because of the weather, but Ravello Rosso is, if anything, the best of the three shades of wine made·on that lovely hill.

*Aglianico del Vulture*

South again, in the area of Potenza, the wine with the rather forbidding name of Aglianico del Vulture is typical of the more drinkable kind of southern wine. It is very strong (15 per cent alcohol, or half as strong again as French *vin ordinaire*). Aglianico has more scent than most of the wines and a flavour more interesting than the usual black bite of the far south.

## Sicily

Sicilian red wine has in the past had the same trouble as Puglian wine. It has, however, been quicker on the uptake and adapted to the modern world with some success. There is no dearth of dukes in Sicily to dignify the labels, which has helped to convince the sceptical public of its value in a competitive market. Italian restaurants now almost universally stock one or more of the estate reds of Sicily: Corvo (from near Palermo, very popular and sound, if not exciting), Regaleali, Etna, Val di Lupo are among them. I have not discovered any firm grounds for choosing one rather than another.

## Sardinia

The red wines of Sardinia are often made heavy and sweet. Oliena and Cannonau, which are two of the best known, have this fault. They are not, curiously enough, nearly as good as the heavy, dry, rather sherry-like, white Vernaccia. Common Sardinian red table wine, on the other hand, can be light and enjoyable. As a good carafe wine in Italian restaurants it has a considerable following.

# Spanish Red Wines

## Rioja

If I were asked what I think is the best value for money of any red wine in the world today—wine, that is, which is freely available—I would say Rioja, one of the old Reservas, wine fifteen or more years old, which is no harder to obtain than sherry, but which the majority of wine-merchants persist in ignoring.

The Rioja Reservas are like neither claret nor burgundy, nor any other French wine—and they do not claim to be. They have a style of their own; a very warm and smooth, velvety, very slightly roasted-tasting flavour. The lighter ones behave as a claret does after fifteen years or so—they begin to thin out a little, losing intensity and gaining delicacy. When the wine is good it grows fresher and sweeter with age.

The heavier ones stay stronger in flavour, but seem to radiate comfort and warmth like a roast chestnut. All have a subtle, fresh and somehow altogether Spanish smell.

They are certainly to be counted among the world's best red wines. Nothing except a traditional addiction to the wines of France prevents our using them as freely and as confidently as we do claret.

While the best old Reservas have little to lose by being compared with fine French wines, the cheap ordinary red Rioja has everything to gain from being compared with its opposite number in France. It is in every way a better and more satisfying everyday drink than French *vin ordinaire*. The French wine has been blended so much that not even age will redeem it, while the natural, cheaply made but honest wine of Rioja gains enormously from a year or two in bottle.

The Rioja district lies in the north of the kingdom of Castile, in territory which has from time to time changed hands between Castile and Navarre. The extraordinary little town of Najera in Rioja was at various times capital of both kingdoms, and keeps to this day some of the least-known monuments of medieval Spain, where the Moors were only seen fleetingly on their sorties from the south. The Moorish-inspired Gothic of the cloisters and the rock-hewn shrine of Najera are rarely visited. Like the whole of Rioja, they belong to the Spain not of oranges and mantillas but of cold steel and snowy passes.

*Haro*    Haro, the chief wine-town of Rioja, stands on a muddy bluff over the river Ebro, gazing north at a great wall of mountain, the Sierra of Cantabria. Even in hot summer clouds hang on the crest of these hills like a warning.

On a first acquaintance there is nothing much to it: three or four streets of steadfast old stone houses proudly displaying coats of arms as big as the front door; a handsome old church; a cardboard modern hotel. Over the bandstand in the square a stork planes with great self-satisfaction to his nest above the Café Suizo.

The Guide Michelin only mentions one establishment: the Restaurante Terete which it calls "typique". It is indeed. You edge between a butcher's-block and an ironing-board to reach the stairs. Upstairs ten-foot scrubbed pine tables and benches completely fill the room. On one a girl snips at a huge mound of purple lilac: the rest are bare as bones.

There is tunny-fish omelette and *cordero asado*, the sort of baked lamb which seems to be carved with an axe, its fat crinkled and brown. The salt, with bread the meat's only accompaniment, comes in a fat pink paper packet. The wine (this is where you learn that Rioja is extraordinary) is brought in a jug. It is in a different class from other Spanish wine: fruity, balanced, fresh, velvet-textured.

*The bodegas*    The great bodegas of Haro, at the foot of the hill, are a surprise after the modest little town. Not a scene of bright new paint, exactly, but of calm and shade and order on a grand scale. Big dusty gardens of alleys and oaks and box-hedges surround the shuttered houses. The wine, in casks, vats and bottles, fills barn after cavernous barn—the bodegas themselves. The whole Rioja industry is concentrated in these big bodegas. The law does not even allow small independent growers to export their wine as Rioja. Rioja names, therefore, are brand names (as in sherry) rather than the growers' names or the names of their properties as in Bordeaux.

*The vineyards*    The vineyards come right up to the walls of the bodegas. They are not like the orderly, staked-out vineyards of France. There are no wires or hedges of green vines. Each vine is a separate little bush, making its own way in the pale, stony, parched earth.

Some of the vineyards of Rioja are beautiful. In places they slant down from under brown rock bluffs to the row of poplars along the bank of the Ebro. Sometimes they cover a whole hill, looking from a distance like a spotted coverlet on a sleeper in bed. Sometimes they fill the spaces in orchard and woodland beside roads where the giant planes and poplars form stately avenues.

The whole region stretches for over sixty miles along the basin of the river Ebro and its tributaries, of which the Rio Oja is one. It is divided, chiefly on grounds of climate, into Rioja Alta and Rioja

# The Pleasure of the Table

"Wine is the pleasantest subject in the world to discuss. All its associations are with occasions when people are at their best: with relaxation, contentment, leisurely meals and the free flow of ideas."
**Above:** The late Ronald Avery, doyen of the English wine-trade, lunches on a buying trip at Pouilly-sur-Loire.

**Above:** Mme Louis Jadot of the famous Beaune firm of Louis Jadot discusses a bottle of burgundy with the firm's director, André Gagey.
**Left and right:** emblems of the variety of wine's pleasures, from a dry Ravello *bianco* with *fritto misto di mare* to a Boal Madeira with *patisserie*.
**Opposite:** in the grounds of the Château de Montmelas at Beaujeu in Beaujolais the Comtesse d'Harcourt presides at a long French summer lunch, the occasion when all the pleasures of the table reach their peak.

"The days are past when a noble lord could be congratulated on having consumed three bottles of port. When the nobleman in question was asked if it was true that he had drunk them all without assistance he replied 'Not quite. I had the help of a bottle of Madeira'."

Baja, upper and lower Rioja. The former, upstream at a greater altitude and with higher rainfall, gives the finer wine. Rioja Alavesa, the third and smaller part, is north of the Ebro in the province of Alava. As far as quality is concerned it can be considered part of Rioja Alta.

The history of Rioja as a wine region goes back to the Middle Ages. It must always have been one of Spain's best, the temperate climate would have seen to that. But its real break came in the 1870s, when phylloxera drove Bordeaux growers to look for new vineyard land. Rioja, today scarcely a day's journey from Bordeaux, was their first choice. The Bordeaux influence is still apparent in both the techniques of Rioja and its products—only the techniques are those of Bordeaux at the turn of the century, before changing tastes (and commercial pressure) led to wine being quickly fermented and quickly matured. Rioja's best reds still need, or at least get, twice as long in the barrel as modern Bordeaux. By modern standards the barrel-ageing is sometimes overdone, so that the flavour of the oak overlies the flavour of the wine. On the other hand, the flavour of oak and the light silky texture and dry finish that go with it are what Spaniards look for in their best wine—no doubt to intensify the contrast with the pungent produce of the rest of Spain.

The claret and burgundy bottles used by Rioja shippers for their reds are a fair indication of the difference between their lighter and heavier wines. On the whole the lighter kind in the claret bottles is the best of the area (and hence of Spain).

*The leading makers*  No single wine has general acceptance as the best of Rioja. The bodegas of the Marques de Riscal and the Marques de Murrieta are often quoted as the most illustrious. Marques de Riscal is the marque of the one, and Castillo Ygay the name for the best old wine of the other. But they are certainly matched in quality by some of the wines of the Companhia Vinicola del Norte España, C.V.N.E. (or Coonie to initiates). Their Viña Real Plata (silver) and Viña Real Oro (gold) are respectively lighter and more full-bodied, but both are excellent. The firm of Lopez Heredia in Haro with its brand Viña Tondonia is one of my favourites. The biggest bodega of all, Bodegas Bilbainas of Haro, has a good full dark wine called Viña Pomal and a first-class claret (it is fair to use this English word which well describes the style) called Viña Paceta.

I have come across very good wine from half a dozen more bodegas: La Rioja Alta, Bodegas Franco-Espanolas, Bodegas Palacio, Federico Paternina, Rioja Santiago, Bodegas del Romeral. But I am sure my list is not complete. Rioja has strict rules, and prosperous, competent, shippers. I can honestly say I have never had a bad bottle of Rioja, even if some have lacked the typical warmth and smoothness of the region.

*In search of other reds*  It would be good to think that there were excellent red wines lurking in other parts of Spain waiting to be discovered. I have set out on a journey with this very thought. I went to Madrid to consult the oracles, and I travelled as they directed. It was not a wasted journey, but nor did it alter my general impression that Rioja is the be-all and end-all of Spanish table wine. The only important exceptions are a handful of producers in Catalonia, and one estate—which I never reached—remote among the highlands of western Spain near Valladolid, the legendary Vega Sicilia.

*Vega Sicilia*  This last breaks all the rules. Its price justifies it being called the

Romanée-Conti of Spain. I have only tasted it once, at dinner in London with Jan Read, who describes the bodega fully in his book *The Wines of Spain and Portugal*. It was a huge wine; fleshy, well-structured, unmistakably strong yet well-balanced and subtle. I could have taken it for an exceptional Rioja, but for its strength.

*Panades*   The outstanding grower and shipper of Catalonia, apart from the specialist bodegas which make good sparkling wine, is Miguel Torres of Panades. Torres makes solid, dark wine, of a kind you might hope to find almost anywhere in Spain. The difference is that his pains-taking control of everything from the grape variety to the moment of bottling is very much the exception. His wine is consequently better, cleaner, more complex and complete. His red Sangredetoro is a wine of splendid substance and subtlety. A twelve-year-old bottle of his Tres Coronas is in the same sort of class as a very good Barolo.

*Valdepeñas*   The rest of Spain need not keep us. La Mancha, the great plain south-east of Madrid, is by far the biggest bulk-producer. Valdepeñas is the name given to most of its wine, which is made light for drinking young; the Beaujolais of Madrid, but without Beaujolais's charm, *Sangria* perfume and taste of the grape. The best thing to do with Valdepeñas is what everyone in Andalusia does in summer: serve it from a jug with ice and a squeeze of orange-juice, some sliced oranges and a handful of white sugar. Brandy or soda-water are added for more or less strength. The name of the drink is Sangria.

*Alicante and Tarragona*   Wine from Alicante and Tarragona is rarely shipped under its own name. The "Spanish Burgundy" of supermarkets probably contains a proportion, very likely mixed with Valdepeñas; the latter is over-light, the former too sweet and too strong. If there is another region *Navarre* to watch it is Navarre, south of the Pyrenees and east of Rioja. Traditionally Navarre wine has been remarkably heavy—Cariñena is a by-word for treacly red—but at least one bodega, that of Las Campanas, bottles well-balanced red wine.

## Portuguese Red Wines

The cheapness, the excellence and the unusual naming arrangements of Portuguese wine have been discussed in the White Wine section (page 137). Portugal's white wine is good, but her red is better. It is not easy to follow or find—and the tourist, sitting in the sun, often feels far more like a bottle of white wine than of red—but at its cheapest commercial level it is the competitor of the cheapest Rioja red from Spain, both in quality and value. Appearing simply as Dão or Serra-dayres red wine (its commonest form in Britain), it is one of the best buys for everyday, unceremonious drinking. Like the Rioja wine, it leaves French *vin ordinaire* far behind.

All Portuguese red wines have a quality which is found in the wine of Bordeaux—which is not to say that they are like claret—the quality of hardness when they are young, the result of thick dark grape-skins full of tannin. It is thought to be the influence of the Atlantic on the climate of the western half of France and all of Portugal, a level of humidity which encourages the skins to become thick. Certainly the red wines of western France, whether of the Loire valley, Bordeaux or the western part of the Massif Central, where the black wine of Cahors is made, have abundance of tannin in common with the red wines of Portugal. Black wine would indeed be a good description for

*Laying down*
Colares, which has the reputation of being Portugal's best red wine.

Hardness and blackness do not sound particularly attractive qualities. Commercially they are reckoned to be a dead loss. In a way they are good signs: they mean that the wine should last for years, eventually becoming (probably, if not certainly) very much better than a softer and paler wine ever could. But commerce would be rid of them if it were possible. In Portugal they are starting to mix some white grapes with the red to soften and subdue the wine from the beginning, as they do with the wine of the Côte Rôtie on the Rhône. In this way they can make a wine ready for the market in four years—still a long time—which previously would have taken six or eight. Even at twelve years, the age at which one of the Dão companies is currently selling its Reserva, the wine is very dark, pungent and seems young, still fairly kicking with life. Twenty or twenty-five years will probably see it at its best. Since these wines cost so very little they are the obvious ones to lay down in large quantities for anyone who has the space, to see eventual results that will obviously be quite out of proportion to the outlay.

## Dão

Dão is certainly the best known of the red-wine regions in Portugal. Its name presents a bit of a problem; "Dow", spoken in the nose as if you had a heavy cold, is about the nearest the English can get. Dão is the name of a river in the high country not far south of the Douro and well inland from the sea. The chief town of the area which has taken the river's name is Viseu (of which "Vishayoo" is a rough rendering).

*The countryside*
Dão is lovely country—rather like Provence. The soil is sand, and pine woods alternate with vineyards over monster, steep-sided sand-dunes, eventually tipping down suddenly to the rocky bed of the little river. There are few large, organized vineyards. You will come across a man with two small children and a dog, picking grapes off something like a washing-line in the middle of a wood, and eating as many, apparently, as they take home to press. The big companies of Viseu buy their grapes far and wide and make the wine under very modern conditions, but there is little indication of this in the hot scented pine woods above the town.

*Viseu*
Viseu is also provided with a cathedral and a very fine church in a style more subdued than most in Portugal, confronting each other across a magnificent square. An excellent hotel, named, like everything else in the town, after its most illustrious son, the painter Grão (The Great) Vasco, has very comfortable quarters, good food and the whole gamut of Dão wines. I have never come across a bad red Dão, either there or abroad.

## The Douro

The red wine of the port country of the Douro has no official standing, no demarcated area, as table wine. Nonetheless excellent red wines are made by modern methods. The port companies, among others, make them for their hospitable tables in Oporto. The famous Mateus Rosé has a little-known red stable-mate which is Douro wine, and remarkably soft and fine it is. Evel, the brand name of the Companhia Vinicola do Norte de Portugal, is said to be largely Douro red—though this is a more nervous, astringent wine. I have never tasted Ferreirinha, from the port-shipping house of Ferreira, but it is said to be quite exceptional.

*Vinho verde*
Officially speaking, *the* red wine of the north of Portugal is the red "green wine" of the Minho. In fact red *vinho verde* is more of a

curiosity than a pleasure. Very young, fizzy, cidery, and often cloudy —though admittedly fruity—red wine looks and tastes like some kind of a mistake to me.

*Colares*

Colares has, as I have said, the greatest reputation among Portuguese red wines. It is grown under unusual conditions, which gives it the distinction of being one of the very few vineyards of Europe which has never had the plague of phylloxera, and does not need to graft its vine-stock on to American roots. The vines are planted in deep sand; the only kind of earth inimical to the destructive beetle.

*The vineyards*

The vineyards of Colares are not, as they are often said to be, on the beach, but in the dune-country on top of low cliffs along the Atlantic, just west of Lisbon. Colares is the next village to Sintra, Byron's "Glorious Eden", where palaces are grouped about the green and misty mountain which used to lead up to the king. There never was such a case of mossy verdure. Here, rather as at San Francisco, the influence of the sea is felt in enriching and softening everything. To the north, brown farms stand parched on the plain, but where the hill of Sintra rises the sea-mists form, fertilizing the land until it stands out like an emerald on an old leather coat.

Down by the sea at Colares, and the row of tiny hamlets which grow its wine, the vine is a strange sight. It grows in little enclosures of piled stones like sheep-pens, two or three old gnarled bushes to the pen, straggling over the sand, weighed down with blue fruit. It is picked into tall baskets which fit snugly to the side of a donkey and covered over with sacks while the donkey picks his way over the sand and down the road to a farmyard, where the baskets are weighed and their fruit tipped into vast oak vats out in the open air to ferment.

Real Colares wine is made of one grape, the Ramisco, a small, blue, dusty looking grape which gives it great colour. Recently, farmers have been planting others which are easier to grow and make softer wine which can be drunk younger, but the new kind of Colares has no real distinction, none of the character which made its name. The grand old Palacio Seteais hotel at Sintra still had the 1931 Colares of Tavares & Rodrigues in 1970; it was a beautiful wine, like a strong, soft claret, still very dark in colour despite its age. Such wine is still being made, and still needs a good deal of maturing—though not necessarily for thirty-nine years—but it is not what you are given if you ask for Colares without qualification.

*Estremadura*

There are other red wines from farther north in Estremadura, but they are not geographically named or officially registered as coming from any particular district. In fact, it is work for a sleuth to discover where they do come from. Serradayres is one of these wines. The name is the property of the firm of Carvalho, Ribeiro and Ferreira. I believe the wine comes from Torres Vedras, where Wellesley had his famous lines. Their ordinary wine, labelled Serradayres, is very pleasant, fairly lightweight and a brilliant ruby colour. Their *garrafeira* (the word for special vintage)—I have had one twenty-five years old—would not disgrace one of the famous vineyards of France.

*Serradayres*

*Quality wines*

The brands of Alianca, Arealva, Fonseca, Messias, Palmela, Periquita, Quinta d'Aguieira are all known for their vintage wines—that is *reservas* or *garrafeiras*, wines which bear the date of the *colheita* or vintage. They must be thought of as the luxury versions of their ordinary wines, rather than vintages in the way French wines are known by the year they were made. There are no critical differences from year to year—the important thing is the wine's age. In my experience it is impossible to get a Portuguese red wine too old—though it is all too easy to get a white one in this condition.

It is important to distinguish these Portuguese shippers' wines, however, from brands created for export, which generally lack the rather old-fashioned distinction which is particularly Portuguese. The best way is to look for the shipper's name: brand names can be shifting sands. Apart from those I have mentioned, the houses of Borges and Irmao, J-M.de Fonseca, Imperial Vinicola, J. F. do Pinto Basto are all noteworthy. Their best wines are firm and solid—wines which give you the feeling, when they are young, that they are staining your teeth and tongue—ideal for casseroles and smoky roasts, strong cheese and plums. In their maturity they come into the polite company of cream sauces and tender cuts of meat with little flavour—the food of the international kind of hotel. I prefer the country way.

## Eastern European Red Wines

*Hungary*

The greater part of the wine made in the Austria-Hungary-Yugo-slavia wine-belt is white. The red wines of Austria are only of local interest. Vöslauer is the best known. Those of Hungary are less important than the white. Egri Bikaver (which means Bull's Blood of Eger) has a reputation for strength—which it deserves—and a warm, smooth style which makes it a good winter wine, the very thing for a casserole meal. A bottle of Egri Bikaver I once kept in my cellar until it was ten years old rewarded me handsomely, reminding me very much of a good, well-aged Chianti.

The traditional red-wine grape of Hungary is called the Kadarka. Its name on a bottle is normally an indication of a peculiarly Hungarian style of wine: a rather pale oversweet red. In Bull's Blood Kadarka is fortified with Bordeaux grapes to give it colour, substance and scent. More interesting than either, however, is the wine from the burgundian Pinot Noir which is coming from Vilanyi in the south of

*Vilanyi*

Hungary. Vilanyi Burgundi, as it is unassumingly called, is a strikingly fruity and well-made red; another that well repays laying down—perhaps more so than many new-style burgundies.

*Yugoslavia*

Yugoslavia also grows the Kadarka, but with a more export-minded wine industry the local grapes are giving way more and more to the international favourites: Cabernet, Merlot and Pinot Noir. The best-selling Yugoslav red wine abroad (in Germany, in fact) is a Pinot Noir under the name Amselfelder Spätburgunder. There are Cabernets with plenty of the characteristic smell and flavour—which becomes in time one of the easiest to recognize of any grape's. Merlots are less easy to identify. The common fault with all these wines tends to be sweetness.

*Dinjac and Postup*

The coast of Yugoslavia grows adequate red wine, again tending to sweetness, of which Dinjac and Postup are the best-known names. Both are made of a local grape, the Plavac. Tourists, who tend to stick to the coast rather than penetrate the country's rather formidable interior, are more likely to come across these than the superior wines intended for export.

*The Black Sea*   The red wines of the Black Sea wine-area have been available in the west for a good ten years now without making any very positive impression. Their biggest sales in Britain are in quasi-Austrian and other blends in which their identity is lost. Germany is their best western market, but here also they mostly sail under flags of convenience—in this case romantic quasi-names like Klosterkeller and Sonnenküste.

*Bulgaria*   Most of Bulgaria's red wines still come from her traditional native grapes: the Gamza (which may be the Hungarian Kadarka) and the Mavrud, respectively lighter and drier and heavier and sweeter. But she has also adopted the Cabernet and made some very acceptable wine with it. Its fault, which seems inevitable in any wine-country which has Russia as an important customer, is that she makes it sweet.

*Romania*   Romania probably has a higher proportion of exotic French vines than Bulgaria. The Franco-Romanian connection after all is old and strong. Her best native red wine is still made from the Babeaşca and other grapes: a dry, fresh and spicy wine of originality and charm. I have found her Cabernet less good: too sweet, again.

*The Soviet Union*   Mukuzani and Saperavi are the red wines of Georgia (their producers would be furious if they heard them called Russian wines—they even use Georgian script on their labels). Mukuzani is the drier, more strongly flavoured wine of the two. The red wine of Moldavia, which used to be a Romanian wine before the political rearrangement of this vine-prolific province, is called Negri de Purkar. It gives the impression that a generous shovelful of blackcurrants was added to the brew, is less sweet than most Russian wines, very scented and pleasantly light.

## Californian Red Wines

Many an experienced wine-lover, cornered into declaring his ultimate loyalties, has found himself choosing white burgundy as his first of white wines, and red Bordeaux as his first of reds. In this respect California herself has acted like an old hand. The wines her climate and soil have elected to make best of all are her own version of precisely these two. Chardonnay is her best white wine; Cabernet Sauvignon her best red.

Like any wine-country on the warm side of temperate, California is more at home with red wines than with white. Technology has vastly increased the possibilities with white wines. But with red they were there already.

Traditionally it is the wine-country just north of San Francisco Bay which is the red-wine area—the lush valleys of Napa and Sonoma. Today, in fact, red and white plantings are more or less evenly distributed over all the fine vineyards, north, south and east of the Bay, but it is still in the Napa valley, above all, that the finest red wines are found. The many wineries of the Napa valley consider themselves the best in the State, and certainly the finest Californian red wines I have tasted have come from Napa and the beautiful mountains round.

*The Napa valley*   Napa is an Indian word for plenty. The upper part of the Napa valley, where civilization barely seems to have penetrated, is a sort of earthly paradise, so fruitful and green, so sculpted from the hills for protection and privacy and peacefulness does it seem to be. The broad valley floor is planted for mile after mile with vines, interrupted only for a big stone winery building in a grove of gigantic oak trees, or a quiet white house with sprinklers hissing arcs of water on a green lawn. The hills on either side are covered mainly with oak, or pine, or sometimes the bushy manzanita with its blood-red limbs. Only occasionally has the high ground been cleared to make way for a ramp, or a mound, or an amphitheatre of vine plants, which stand each on its own, like trees in an orchard, not staked and wired into hedges as they are in France. There is evidence, nonetheless, that the hills may give the best wine. Certainly any European wine-grower would expect it to be so. It is only sad to think that what may drive the wine-maker to plant in the hills in California is the encroaching of housing subdivisions on his flat land.

## Cabernet Sauvignon

The great vine of Napa is the Cabernet Sauvignon. Some of the Napa Cabernets are in no way inferior to fine clarets, some of them are better than most clarets, and a few are almost as complex, subtle, scented and extraordinary as a first-growth claret of a fine vintage.

The same qualifications, however, apply to Californian red wine as to French: it is only the work of a fine and painstaking wine-maker which can ever come into this category—and his work will always be on a small scale. Furthermore, the wine needs time to mature just as French wine does. There is, therefore, a chronic shortage of the best Californian red wine in mature condition, and the greater part of it never reaches this condition at all. Only one or two wineries in the whole State keep the wine themselves until they really consider it ready to drink; the rest sell it shortly after it is bottled, as the French do. There is a difference, though, between the French and the Californian practice. Claret is bought from a château straight after bottling in the full knowledge that it is not ready to drink, and will not be ready for several years. A merchant buys it and either keeps it himself while it matures, or sells it to a customer who will keep it. The American public, though, expects its wineries to sell everything in the condition to be drunk immediately. They blame it on the winery, therefore, when it sells its Cabernets at three or four years old, saying (quite rightly) that they are not ready to drink. The market is therefore running on unaged wine, which has no prospect of being mature before it is drunk. Nor is there much prospect of it catching up with stocks of mature wine—for the demand is growing the whole time. The answer, I need hardly say, is for the customer to start a cellar, fill it with fine red wine and be patient.

*A superlative wine*

Of the small quantity of well-made Californian Cabernet which does reach maturity, then, this can be said: it is one of the finest red wines in the world. It is interesting to compare it with a great Médoc or St-Emilion, for the grape is the same, though the conditions of growing it are very different. What is more, California uses the great character-giving claret grape on its own, without blending, whereas red Bordeaux is all made with a quantity of Merlot and Malbec grapes to modify its extreme hardness and strength of character.

In California, therefore, you find wine which typifies the Cabernet more than claret does. It is the Cabernet which gives the spiciness, the cigar-box scent, the warmth and richness of claret, as well as the astringent, grimace-making hardness of its early years. In California these qualities come triumphantly forward. The wine does start hard

—though less unpleasantly so than in Bordeaux—but it finishes rich. The best of Napa valley Cabernets has wonderful warmth and fullness, through which its flavour comes with marvellous vividness.

If it lacks anything it is the sort of complexity of flavour which makes a great Bordeaux so endlessly worth tasting. One might hazard a guess that unrelenting varietal-mindedness has something to do with this. If Château Latour were made without its component 20 per cent of Merlot and Cabernet Franc who can doubt that it would be a less complex and subtle wine? Not, I hasten to add, that Californian vintners are committed to 100 per cent varietal wines. They are in a small minority. But the role of the secondary varieties is not yet defined in terms of the secondary flavours they can contribute. A Californian Cabernet is supposed to exhibit Cabernet character, not the character of a carefully thought-out blend.

*Outstanding wineries*

Would that I were in a position to list the California Cabernets in anything like an order of merit. I can mention some of the best examples I have drunk. But it is a woefully inadequate coverage of the field. The competition is very stiff indeed, with some of the best wines coming from new and tiny wineries which are (one would think) still wet behind the ears. It is obviously more prudent to stick to well-established classics, like Louis Martini's, Beaulieu's Special Reserve, or the immensely full-flavoured Cabernet of Joe Heitz, perhaps the most distinguished single wine-maker of the whole Napa valley.

*The Salinas valley*

Napa remains the heart of the Cabernet country. But it never had a monopoly, and even its lead in volume terms has disappeared in the vast new planting spree of the last few years.

The new area which has caused most excitement is considerably south of the classic Bay region, in a valley which has turned out to be like a climatic fault-line running inland and southwards from Monterey Bay. The first moves in this direction were made, almost in desperation, by wineries like Almaden which were being elbowed out of their home-ground by the southwards spread of the complex of Bay cities. On the face of it they were moving nearer to the desert, and could only expect hotter weather. But California's coastal climate has its own rules. The mouth of the Salinas valley acts (like the Golden Gate) as an entry point for cool ocean air. The planters found themselves with a problem they didn't expect: the near-gale off the Pacific as the day wore on and the land warmed up. Instead of concentrating on the sun they had to align their vine-rows to moderate the effects of this heat-tempering wind.

Grape-growing in the Salinas valley was started by migrating wineries; Almaden, Paul Masson, Wente Bros, and Mirassou in particular. But the lettuce-farmers who were there already were not slow to get the idea. Within less than a decade, starting from scratch, the new wine valley will have about as many acres of vineyards as the Côte d'Or; all of them "premium varietals"; quite a bit of the total Cabernet Sauvignon.

*Pinot Noir*

Oddly enough the great burgundy grape, the Pinot Noir, makes a comparatively undistinguished wine in California. It is still a premium wine—indeed possibly the next best after the Cabernet—but it never (or *very* rarely) approaches the quality of a fine burgundy in the way that a Cabernet draws near to Bordeaux. It makes, at best, a fairly light wine with a powerful and almost slightly fierce flavour. It is more like a light Rhône wine than a burgundy. Pinot Noirs, of course, vary from producer to producer as much as any wine—but none, I think, makes a really fine one. One, indeed, confessed to me that he thought his "burgundy", made with a blend of three or four grapes, more successful, and I agreed with him. It could be that one day California will develop a combination of grapes which will give this style of wine the interest it lacks at the moment. There is, after all, no virtue in slavishly sticking to one-variety wine-making for its own sake.

*Zinfandel*  Before all other grapes of any kind, however, in popularity and sheer quantity of production, California grows the Zinfandel, a kind unknown in Europe. Zinfandel is, as it were, California's own Beaujolais. Its price is low; it can be drunk young; it is seen everywhere. Like the best Beaujolais, too, the best Zinfandel gains distinction with age—though I personally doubt whether it improves enough to be worth the laying down.

Zinfandel has its devotees who find in it every virtue. To me it is an agreeable, light-coloured, slightly spicy wine, sometimes a little fiery, which I would never refuse; nor would I, on the other hand, ever serve it at a dinner party. As a lunch- or supper-time wine, to accompany cold meat or a stew, it is perfect.

*Gamay*  The Gamay of Beaujolais, in comparison with the Zinfandel, is little grown. The wine it makes (which is known as Gamay Noir) is of no great merit in California; it has none of the magic lightness of Beaujolais. Nonetheless it makes one of California's best rosés.

Several Italian grape-varieties are grown, chiefly by the Italian families who introduced them to the country. The most successful is *Barbera*  the Barbera of Piedmont, which makes as good a wine in California as it does in its native land; a strong wine, full of purple colour and flavour, but inclining to be sharp—ideal, in fact, for rich Italian food. Its fellow-countryman, the Grignolino, is also cultivated; though largely, it seems, for old time's sake.

The most successful innovation of the University of California's grape-breeding programme, which is aimed primarily at finding good grapes for table wine in very hot areas, has been the Ruby Cabernet, a cross between Cabernet Sauvignon and one of the classic vines of *vin ordinaire*, the Carignane. Enough of the character and flavour of the Cabernet has been kept to make a table wine of real individuality, while the Carignane parentage means huge crops happy *Ruby Cabernet*  in the heat. Paul Masson's Rubion is a Ruby Cabernet wine: its sweetness is the wine-maker's decision, not the grape's The reformation which is either due or actually in progress in the south of France (it is sometimes hard to tell which) should consider the Ruby Cabernet as a working compromise.

The great mistake in thinking of California wine, red or white but above all red, is to fall into the varietal trap. There is such obvious snob-appeal about varietals to a huge public still learning the ropes that any marketing-man is likely to be tempted. There is no absolute virtue in grape-names. Alsace wine is not better than Loire because it puts Riesling or Sylvaner on the label. Ultimately the best wine California produces, when the industry has had another century or two to shake down, may well be a blended wine without a varietal name. For that matter some of the best wine she produces today may lurk under the unfashionable title of Burgundy, or just plain old Mountain Red.

# Other Red Wines

*Australia*

One of the very best bottles of red wine I have ever drunk was a twenty-year-old Rutherglen red, without so much as a label. I drank it at home, so there was no question of the mood of the moment, the Victorian sunshine, overpowering my judgement. It was on the same giant scale, in both scent and savour, as the great Pomerol Château Petrus in one of its richest vintages. More than anything else that bottle confirmed my view that Australia can make some of the world's greatest red wine.

It is no fantasy, however, that most (if not all) of Australia's best wine stays in Australia. Quantities are small, and knowledgeable Australians plentiful. The Australian wines listed at the Australian Wine Centre in London, or appearing in Safeway supermarkets in California, are good standard commercial wines, fairly priced. But they stand in relation to Australia's best as a *négociant*'s Gevrey-Chambertin does to a grower's Chambertin. It is a hard decision for Australia to take: whether to put her best wines on the international market, have them recognized for what they are, and pay twice as much for them; or continue to drink them, and let the world go on in ignorance.

Red wine comes more naturally to Australia than white: it did not have to wait for modern methods to reach perfection. If anything, indeed, modern methods threaten to compromise its ultimate quality.

*Coonawarra*

From early times Australians seemed to have a knack of finding pockets of exceptional soil for vines. There could hardly be a better illustration of the importance of the right soil than Australia's best red-wine vineyard. Two hundred and fifty miles south of Adelaide, near the south-west coast of South Australia, the terrain is completely flat. There are wind-blown farms, sheep, and huge stands of bright green Monterey pines growing at breakneck speed to be made into newspapers. In the middle of nowhere (or more precisely, between Hollis and Mt. Gambier) there is an abrupt deposit of a most unusual fertile red earth. Below it lies a few yards of pure chalk, and then a great reservoir of water. The soil is only three feet deep and a mile wide by nine miles long. But already it is recognized as one of the world's most distinguished vineyards: Coonawarra.

Coonawarra benefits from its far-south climate as well as its soil. Its wines have what the trade calls "elegance" even while they are young. To this extent they are untypical of Australian reds. "A bloody kangaroo" is how one (very good) South Australian Cabernet was described to me. The term "sweaty saddle" is accepted as a *mot juste* for the peculiar character of the Hunter valley reds. It is easy to be frightened off by this he-man talk, suggesting wines of high octane and little else. But this would be a pity, since when you come to taste them this is rarely the case.

*Cabernet and Shiraz*

Two of the red-wine vines the Australians have planted have done them proud. The Bordeaux Cabernet (which they pronounce *Carb*enet) and the Shiraz of the Rhône (often called Hermitage) are both so successful that neither can be called better than the other. The best wineries make varietal wines from both, most of them in several different places, and either blend them or sell them separately as their judgment dictates.

*The Hunter valley*

As a very general rule one can say that the Hunter valley, the quality area of New South Wales, makes big and robust red wines:

huge, almost-sweet, Hermitage; strong tough Cabernet. A typical Hunter Burgundy (Lindeman's, for example) is soft-textured, long-flavoured, sweet and spicy. The terms claret and burgundy are used in the obvious way for blends—though with so little agreement about their meaning that one wine has been known to win both the claret and burgundy classes at a local show. Among the profusion of Hunter wineries the names most often heard are McWilliams' Mount Pleasant, Drayton's Bellevue, Penfold's Dalwood, and Elliot's, Tyrell's and Tulloch's. One newer one, too, must come into any such list: Lake's Folly, the property of a Sydney surgeon with a consuming passion for Cabernet which seems to communicate itself even to his grapes.

*South Australia*      Compared with Hunter wines, the reds of South Australia (which are the huge majority: South Australia makes more wine than all the other States put together) have a more French-style balance. The best South Australian Hermitage is supple and deep flavoured but nerved with acidity like a good Bordeaux. Cabernet, curiously enough, is less like Bordeaux than Hermitage. Unblended it can be rather over-bearing; many wine-makers prefer it blended with Shiraz or a lesser grape. A Barossa Cabernet and Malbec blend from Penfold's re-minded me fleetingly of a Pauillac. But these impressions are far from complete—or even consistent.

*The Barossa valley*      The Barossa valley, Clare, Southern Vales and Langhorne Creek are all part of the South Australian complex centred on Adelaide. Adelaide itself has vineyards on its suburban slopes—including the illustrious Grange vineyard of Penfold's at Magill. Clare is the nor-thernmost and hottest of these districts. Its red wine is mainly Shiraz of great power. Barossa with its German background has traditionally concentrated more on white wine. But its growers have taken to Cabernet with conspicuous success. Seppelt's were among the first, followed by Buring's Gramp's, Kaiser Stuhl (the co-operative), Tolley, Scott and Tolley, Penfold's Kalimna and others. Of those I have tasted (which is only a sketchy sampling), the Kaiser Stuhl wines have been the tenderest and softest, the Tolley, Scott and Tolley wines the most tremendous and characterful. Shiraz does not seem as popular as Cabernet in the Barossa valley.

The Southern Vales and Langhorne Creek lie close to Adelaide on the south. Hardy's Reynella, Seaview, Metala, Stonyfell and d'Aren-berg are the main wineries in this long-established district. Cabernet and Shiraz are both grown, and often blended, to give typical South Australian reds: wines of substance and balance with a distinctive saltiness of scent and savour which is one of the most attractive Aus-tralian characteristics. It was here that the bloody kangaroo came from.

Coonawarra also grows both Cabernet and Shiraz, but here their wines are not so often blended. In a curious way their French roles are reversed: Shiraz tends to make the drier and more graceful Coona-warra wine; Cabernet the stronger, more pungent, richer, more "burgundian". Much depends, of course, on the wine-maker. But in Coonawarra there are not so many to choose from. Rouge Homme (belonging to Lindeman's), the ubiquitous Penfold's, Wynn's and Mildara are the (relatively) big ones. Eric Brand's Laira is a lonely little estate, for all the world like a little Pomerol château lost in the unend-ing levels of South Australia, with only a few poplars for company.

*Other areas*      Between the Hunter valley and South Australia the vine is scattered almost, it seems, at random. I have mentioned Rutherglen, in north Victoria, whose vineyard is only a tiny remnant of its pre-phylloxera glory. My lonely Rutherglen red was sublimely good. Rutherglen today, however, is almost entirely a dessert-wine area.

Château Tahbilk, north of Melbourne, is another remnant—though one kept very much alive by an energetic proprietor who makes good solid Cabernet, as well as Riesling and Marsanne for white wine.

Great Western, near Ballarat, is another; in this case thriving on its modern "champagne"-industry, as well as being a source of Seppelt's good commercial claret (Moyston) and burgundy (Chalambar). Such districts go on making wine because their results are so good. Quantity is easier to obtain elsewhere. The really big vineyards are in the irrigation areas, where cultivation is easy and production can be boosted, literally, by turning on a tap. There are good light red wines made by some of the big firms in these most unclassical vineyards. But one comes across some comic "varietals" from local companies. In one Griffith winery I had a "Carbenet" which reeked of, of all things, Muscat.

## South Africa

In South Africa very much the same range of red-wine grapes are grown as in Australia. The star performers are the Cabernet of Bordeaux and the Shiraz or Syrah of the Rhône, which is also known as the Hermitage. The Pinot of Burgundy has been crossed with the Hermitage to give a very successful new grape unknown elsewhere—the Pinotage.

The Cabernet in South Africa does not make the light claret-type wine you would expect from its ancestry. Here, as in Australia, Cabernet wines are the strong-flavoured, dark, winter-weight ones. Most firms produce one wine like this and another, lighter, more claret-like, often their Hermitage. The best known of the lighter kind in Britain are Château Libertas from Stellenbosch and Muratie Claret, and, of the heavier, Roodeberg.

Von Carlowitz's Carlonet, Nedeberg Cabernet and Rustenberg Claret are names only known to me, unfortunately, by hearsay. These and others sound excellent, even if they do not evoke quite the same enthusiasm in visitors to South Africa as the Australian red wines do in visitors to Australia.

In South Africa these wines are wonderfully cheap—the Hermitages rather cheaper than the Cabernets—and clearly should be everybody's daily drinking. Table-wine consumption is rising steadily; undoubtedly the day will come when South Africa will be a real wine-country, when wine will be her national drink as well as the best produce of her soil. This state of affairs seems to be necessary, though, for the establishing of the sort of supreme craftsmanship in which France at the moment leads the world.

## Chile

Chile, despite being so far away, is at present one of the best suppliers of cheap table wines in the world. Wine-making is apparently little organized for commercial purposes, but strictly supervised by the government. Prices are very low and standards are very high—the ideal arrangement from everybody's point of view except that of the Chilean farmer.

*Aconcagua*
The Aconcagua plains to the north of Santiago, the capital, which lies in the middle of the country, and the Maipo foothills of the Andes south of the capital are the best wine-areas. "In the *caveaux* of certain wine-vaults", according to an article I have from the firm of Wagner

Stein in Chile, "there are respectful bottles of evoking Romanée." About the Aconcagua area it says: "From San Felipe to Calera, along the wide course of the Aconcagua river, running from east to west, on the south banks, an echelon series of picturesque sheltered coves of slopes can be seen descending in display from the chain of hills which separates Santiago from the provinces of Valparaiso and Aconcagua. In this location, full of natural beauty, Pinot stocks produce a marvellous wine. Its colour is brilliant; its flavour unctuous and mild, having a mild fragrance of distinction which its generous vinosity hardly covers."

*Maipo*    A similar state of affairs is found south of Santiago, where the Maipo river also runs east-west (from the Andes to the sea), offering its north-facing banks for good wine-production. The sub-soil here is gravel and the Cabernet is grown with the Merlot, as it is in Bordeaux. The wines from the Maipo apparently need most age and are considered Chile's best.

The names of grapes are used for most of the wines which are exported, and red wines predominate. The Cabernet gives a very pleasant, full-coloured, softish and dry wine which at half the price of any red Bordeaux in Britain must be counted one of the world's great bargains. I have bottled a hogshead of it at home for daily drinking and enjoyed every bottle. Among white wines the Riesling has the highest reputation. Although at the moment the range available is so narrow that little can usefully be said about it, there are authorities who think that Chile is potentially one of the world's great wine-countries, and could one day produce wines as superlative as those of France and Germany.

*Argentina*    The only other South American country whose wine is at all widely exported is Argentina. She is among the world's biggest wine-makers, for an enormous domestic market, but she has only recently started looking for opportunities abroad. Wine-growing is on an industrialized scale on the plains of Mendoza, on the same latitude as Aconcagua in Chile, but with a much drier climate. Very modern methods are used to make extremely sound wine. But so far there is no evidence of any wine up to Chilean standards.

# After-Dinner Wines

It is not just convention that puts the sweet things last in a meal. Sugar discourages appetite; its effect is to make you feel satisfied. The after-dinner wines are those which, for one reason or another, still have a lot of grape-sugar left in them. Their lusciousness, in relatively small doses, is the best end of all to a meal.

For the same reason—that they stave off appetite—they make an ideal snack when there is no meal coming. The mid-morning glass of wine and a biscuit, much talked about in magazines, but, I fear, little practised for fear of the effects of the alcohol, should be one of these sweet ones. Madeira and Madeira cake used to be the thing. I prefer tawny port or cream sherry and digestive biscuits. The sweet after-dinner wines are also good before a meal if you do not find that they spoil your appetite. The French, after all, always drink sweet aperitifs, nor do their appetites seem any the worse for it.

*Stopping fermentation* — Spare sugar left over in wine when the fermentation has come to an end is not something which normally happens naturally. In most cases the sugar will go on fermenting until it is all converted into alcohol. But it is not difficult to discourage the yeast from going on with the fermentation process simply by filtering it out of the wine with a micro-filter, which is what they do in Germany, or by artificially increasing either the alcohol level or the concentration of sugar to an abnormally high level. After-dinner wines are all made in one of these three ways. They vary as much as any other class of wine. Their only common factor is that they are intensely sweet. At one end of the scale you have the sweet wine of Sauternes, whose sugar is naturally concentrated by a form of rot in the overripe grapes. At the other end you have port, whose sugar is held in the wine by a massive dose of brandy, which stops the fermentation.

Most of the sweet wines come from the hottest wine-countries, where very ripe grapes are more common. Yet, curiously enough, what some people consider to be the most exquisite sweet wine of all, and certainly the most expensive, comes from Germany, the coldest wine-growing country.

The German wines which come into this category, like the Sauternes, are only the best of their districts. To most people hock and Sauternes mean table wines—sweetish, but not syrupy. Only the best wine of the best vineyards in the best years achieves this special condition in which the juice is concentrated and the sugar outlasts the process of fermentation.

*The sweet course*
Whether you drink a sweet wine with a sweet course or fresh fruit, or leave it until the plates have been cleared away, is a matter of taste. I like Sauternes with a peach, or even a creamy *bombe*. Fine sweet hock, on the other hand, I prefer on its own.

Madeira goes superbly well with such things as a raspberry tart or a very rich praliné confection. Chocolate, on the other hand, is one of the few things which spoils the taste of most wines.

Port does not go so well with the sweet course. Its best partner is cheese. If the port is very good an apple, particularly a Cox's Orange Pippin, is excellent with it. There is an old saying in the port trade that you should "buy on an apple and sell on cheese"; apple, in other words, brings out any weaknesses in the wine; cheese hides them. But if you are confident in your port with apples and nuts it makes a splendid end to a very Christmassy kind of meal.

*Temperature*
The same serving principle applies to sweet wines as to all others: the white ones are better cold, the red at room temperature. But in after-dinner wines there enters a third class which can only be described as brown. These are the muscatels, Malagas, Marsala and Madeiras, all sweet and strong and all, to my mind, better served stone-cold. If you should happen on one of the very rare great Madeiras, a vintage wine of the last century—and they do still exist on several merchants' lists—it might be better to serve it at room temperature. But modern Madeira profits by half an hour in the refrigerator.

You will never need as much of a sweet after-dinner wine as you will of a table wine. The days are past when a noble lord could be congratulated on having consumed three bottles of port. When the nobleman in question was asked if it was true that he had drunk them all without assistance he replied, "Not quite. I had the help of a bottle of Madeira."

# Port

It was the British who invented port. It was somewhere between a desperate measure and a brilliant scheme for making the wine of Portugal palatable. The invention took place at the beginning of the eighteenth century, when the wines of France were excluded from England as a wartime measure.

If port were made as any other red wine is made it would be strong, dark red, very dry and rather unpleasant. What character it had would never emerge from the strong black taste, and it would die unlamented. It would be a table wine for those who had no better. And such it was.

*Origins*

It was the brilliant notion of some (we imagine) British wine-shipper, who had gone out to Portugal to take advantage of the favourable trade position, to change all this. He deserves credit just as Dom Pérignon does for champagne. His scheme was to take advantage of all the rich sugar in the grapes which was fermenting away to make over-strong wine. To stop it fermenting and keep the wine sweet (for the English, he knew, have always been sweet-toothed), he added brandy. And, after a time, he had port.

The principle of the making of port is as simple as that. In the high Douro valley, among the mountains of inland Portugal, red wine is made. Great care is taken to see that it takes as much colour from the skins as possible. It starts fermenting in the usual way; but as the fermentation reaches a half-way stage, and the wine, though weak in alcohol, is still full of unfermented sugar, the grower adds brandy. The proportions are about one of brandy to four and a half of wine.

The mixture is too strong for the yeast to work in; it is asphyxiated by the concentration of alcohol. But the sugar is still there. That mixture of brandy and wine, full of alcohol and sugar, is port. It was just what the people of England wanted.

*Ageing*

The trouble with port is that it has to be old. Wine that has been made in this—to say the least—unusual way takes a long time to settle down. A mixture of brandy and wine is just a mixture of brandy and wine for a long time. It does not marry, so to speak, overnight.

Not only is the fermentation brought to a stop by the brandy, but all the natural ageing processes of wine are slowed down and held up. If the resulting wine is treated as red wines usually are—given two years in a cask and then bottled—it takes at least ten or fifteen years to be ready or even pleasant to drink.

Vintage port is that wine, and has that trouble. Eventually it is the best port of all; in the meanwhile there is nothing to do but wait. But most port cannot be treated like that. It would not be so wonderful in the end as to be worth it, so it is left to age in wood.

*Ruby*

Port which has been aged in barrels and not bottled until it is judged ready to drink is called either Ruby or Tawny. Ruby is young and still full of colour, rich, a little harsh sometimes, and the cheapest port there is. Tawny has spent perhaps ten or fifteen years in wood, until it has faded to the colour its name suggests. Wine ages much faster in a barrel than in a bottle. The change that takes place in the taste in that time is greater than in a vintage port of the same age. It loses some of its body, dries out a little, but gains greatly in smoothness and in scent. A very old tawny is to most people the most delicious of all ports, and the most versatile. It is almost as good before dinner, especially in winter, as after it. The smoothness and nuttiness of its flavour are incomparable.

*Tawny*

Both ruby and tawny are blended wines, which is to say that the wine is not all of one age or from one place. The port-shipper, like the sherry-shipper, is concerned with continuity in his brands. He mixes, therefore, old and newer wine, sweeter and drier, from his stocks to make the wine he requires. He will have several brands of both ruby and tawny, ranging from a wine of about the price of the cheapest Spanish sherry to a very old and fine one, often called Director's, at about twice the price.

A "vintage"

Only in years when everything has gone well with the vines, the weather has been perfect and the fermentation exactly right do the port-shippers "declare a vintage". In some years, perhaps three times in a decade, they are unanimous. In others one is luckier than his rivals and declares a vintage alone. There are no rules. It is up to the individual shipper.

When the port of a year is declared to be "vintage" it is kept aside from the rest. The various wines of that year are blended together and given two years' rest in Portugal. Then they are bottled, still inky, purple and pungent, in very dark glass bottles. In the old days no label was put on the bottle. The vintage year was sometimes stencilled on, the shipper's name was branded on the cork, otherwise it was anonymous. It had one distinguishing mark: a splash of white paint on one shoulder. Wherever it lies in a bin or on a shelf this mark or, today, the label, must stay at the top. It shows where the heavy crust of sediment will form—on the side of the bottle opposite to it.

The wine comes on the market as soon as it is bottled, and it is one that the merchants never have any difficulty in selling. It is almost all bought at once to be laid down.

Wine-merchants keep a small stock of matured vintage port, which means wine anything from twenty to forty years old, which they will sell to customers who want their port in a hurry. If you want to drink it straight away they will suggest that they decant it for you in their cellars into a clean bottle, so that you can pour it easily when you get it home.

The disadvantage in buying vintage port when it is mature is that all the sediment caused by the settling down and ageing of the wine, which in most wines would have been the dregs in a barrel, is still in the bottle. The port has thrown a crust, as it is called; a dirty-looking veil which clings tenuously to the side of the bottle as long as it is not disturbed. But if the bottle is stood in a carton, dumped into a delivery van and hauled out again at the other end, this deposit detaches itself and mixes with the wine, making it murky and unpleasant. All is not lost; you can give it time to settle down and then filter the wine through muslin. But it is a nuisance. It is much better either to have your own port laid down at home, so that you can decant it without stirring it up, or buy it when you need it and get the merchant to decant it the same day.

Laying down port

Most vintage port is sold young to be laid down by the eventual drinker. It means having a cellar, or something like it. It also means having a permanent home, which not everybody has. Clubs and restaurants therefore take a large proportion of it nowadays. If you do buy vintage port when it is first offered (two or three years after the vintage), you will get it at a very reasonable price, and one which will always rise steadily. From the point of view of pure investment, in fact, port is one of the safest wines you can buy.

The devotees of vintage port will swear that no other wine in the world compares with it for fragrance, fatness, delicacy and strength. I cannot say that it has ever given me as much pleasure as a great claret or burgundy, but I know what they mean: it has depth.

*Late-bottled vintage*

Some port-shippers offer late-bottled vintage port as a compromise for people who prefer vintage to tawny but have no space for laying it down. By bottling it late, not at two years but anything from six to ten, they avoid the heavy deposit on the sides of the bottle which vintage port throws while it is still young. That part of the development takes place in the barrel, as it does with tawny. The wine is vintage in the sense that it comes from one good year and is not a blend, but its development has started as it would if it were to be a "wood" port. It is speeded up so that it will be ready to drink at ten or fifteen years. It can safely be treated like a bottle of ordinary wine with no fear of shaking up a deposit. In taste it is always a little light for a vintage port.

## The Douro

Vines like mountains. There are many claimants to being the most spectacular vineyards in the world. The vine-covered slopes are steep on the Rhine and the Moselle, steeper still in Switzerland, more beautiful where the peninsula of Sorrento tilts headlong into the sea. But no sight can compare with the first sight of the Douro.

To come on it suddenly, as you do if you approach it from Spain, through Bragança and the lovely quiet country of Tras-os-Montes, where the valleys are green and the hills and the haycocks pure gold, has something like the impact of a first sight of the Grand Canyon. Without warning the land falls away, in range after range of escarpments and re-entrants, for thousands of feet. In the dim distance, far below, the river winds among rocks. On every side, like a sapper's nightmare, terraces repeat patterns of endless fortifications in endless curves and eddies of grey-brown stone.

The countryside should really be desert. For six months of the year there is not a drop of rain. The valley walls are granite, solid rock. But through some miracle what should be a dust-bowl is a market garden. The best oranges, vegetables, olives, corks and vines in the whole of Portugal grow in prodigal profusion from end to end of this valley.

As you descend from the ridge the air begins to be sweet with the scent of cedar and gum, the silver olive and the green vine alternate and mingle. *Quintas*, the big white farmhouses, and dusty villages full of donkeys and children begin to thicken as the road winds down. Each bend reveals more terraces and more vines; the scene seems to be composed entirely of granite and grapes—even the props at the ends of the rows are grey stakes of slaty rock.

In the bottom of the valley it is hotter than higher up. The vintage starts earlier. Already by mid-September picking parties are out in the fields. The river is shrunk to a grey drain among the boulders, a mere fifty yards wide instead of the three hundred yards of foam and torn trees of its winter spate. (Or so it has been in every vintage up to today. But things are changing: dams are raising the water level.)

## A quinta

The Quinta da Roeda, which belongs to the firm of Crofts, the oldest of all the English firms in the port-trade, lies near the river, on a two-hundred-foot bluff, just upstream from the village of Pinhao. It is typical of the estates of the high Douro.

Here the road up the valley ends. Henceforward, the railway and the river are the only means of communication. To reach the higher villages by car you have to drive back out of the valley, along the ridge and down into it again. Thus it takes twenty-five miles to travel five as the crow flies.

The *quinta* might be the bungalow on an Indian tea estate. It is single-storied, with a high-pitched red roof and a verandah all round. Sprinklers work all day to keep the garden of grass and acacia trees green. A spring in the fold of the hill under the house runs under arbours of vines and pears in a little musical water-garden.

The house is surrounded by its vineyards and olive groves. Above and below it on the hill are the outbuildings where the wine is made. One group of white houses, on a platform of dust, is where the staff live and the pickers eat and sleep at vintage-time. There are stables, donkeys and a cow, pigs and hens and ducks all living in the shade of olive trees. There is a large dimly lit kitchen where the thorns crackle under a pot of vintage soup, and a flower-garden where roses and dahlias grow like weeds.

On the level below the house stands the *lagar*, a long white building, taller than most in the area. This shelters the pressing and the fermentation. Terraced on a lower level, but under the same roof, are the great oak barrels to contain the new wine.

## The harvest

The vintage is still a ceremony, a ritual and a time of rejoicing in the Douro. Life is very primitive in the high hill-villages where the workers live. It is no exaggeration to say that their superstitions extend to witch-doctors to this day. Picking-parties at vintage-time come to the Douro valley from miles around. Each band of thirty or forty peasants brings its musicians with it; always a drum, an accordion, sometimes a pipe as well. They march as many as thirty miles over the hills as vintage-time approaches, old men and young girls, old women and boys, their possessions in bundles on their heads.

Each day as they go out to work the musicians lead the way with their monotonously jaunty tune. They go everywhere in procession, and do everything to the sound of music. After nightfall, as the men work in the *lagares*, the women and girls dance together to the tunes they have heard in the fields all day.

## Making the wine

This is a time of transition in the Douro, as it is in so many wine-districts. The old method of making wine is still common, but the biggest and best producers are rapidly going over to new techniques which radically alter the whole appearance of the vintage.

The old method consisted of bringing the grapes down to the *lagares* and tipping them into huge stone troughs, in which, late in the evening, they were trodden hour after hour by teams of bare-foot men and boys.

In the low, lantern-lit *lagares*, heady and sweet with the fumes of fermentation and loud with the choruses of traditional songs, the men linked arms and trod, thigh-deep, the purple mass. The endless pounding of feet and the warmth of the human flesh extracted every drop of colour from the skins and set the fermentation going. The wine fermented in the *lagares* until it was run off through a sluice into the waiting barrels, already a quarter full of brandy.

The new method dispenses with the treading altogether. The grapes arrive on mules' and men's backs from the fields and are fed straight into machines, which crush them and remove the stalks. From there they are pumped up into tall concrete vats, which may take as long as two days to fill. During this time the must is kept cool and the fermentation cannot begin. When the vat is full a cover is put on, and it is not long before enough heat is generated inside to start it going.

The gas given off by the fermentation operates a churning system, driving the must up a pipe on to the top of the vat, from where it drops back to the bottom. The circulation of the wine under its own power by this method has the same effect as the treading: it extracts all the colour from the skins.

When the wine has reached the correct halfway stage of fermentation (which is when it is about 8 per cent alcohol), it is run off from the vats into the waiting barrels in the traditional way.

In the villages the old method is used by the farmers. Large *quintas*, the properties of the shippers, use the new technique. Any bottle of port will contain some wine made by both these two methods. The shippers make only a small proportion of the wine they need. The rest they buy, often under long-standing contracts, from the farmers who make it for them.

## Oporto

The Douro valley itself and its side-valleys high above the tributary river Corgo are the place for the best port. From here it is fifty or sixty miles down to Oporto, the city which gives the wine its name. The legal definition of port is "wine which has been shipped over the bar of Oporto", which means that until the wine has left its own country it is not really port. This shows the influence of the export trade, for in Portugal port is hardly drunk at all.

It is not actually in Oporto, but over the bridge on the other side of the Douro, that the shippers have their lodges—the vast establishments where they age and blend their wine.

## Down the river

They bring the new wine down the river in the spring to the lodge where it will stay for perhaps two years if it is a vintage port, or twenty or thirty if it is to become tawny. The journey down the river used to be made on the beautiful boats, the *barcos rabelos*, which now swing idly at anchor by the quays; for the railway has taken their place. The journey down the Douro in the spring, when the river was running fast, was a dangerous and exciting experience. The long Viking-style ships with square sails and six oarsmen standing at long sweeps in the bows would carry a dozen great pipes of wine. In some of the gorges where the river narrows to a single tumbling channel the rapids drop ten or fifteen feet in one great smooth rush of water. The boatmen had to get the *barco*'s head straight on for the fall. Then it was like going down in a lift with a great fountain of spray at the bottom. There are still some of the smaller boats on the river, but the day when they were the only way of getting the wine down from the high country is past, as are the early days when the shippers had to ride over the mountains to visit the vineyards. There is still a tradition of the hard living which used to go with port, something of the feeling that "up the Douro" is an adventure. But the railway came, and the boatmen had blotted their book by drinking the wine and topping-up the casks with river water.

## The lodges

The lodges of Vilanova de Gaia, the wine-suburb over the river from Oporto, have something of the atmosphere of the sherry bodegas of Spain. There are the long, half-dark barns, in which shafts of light saunter all day across the old unshaven beams, the rows and rows of casks, the rich smell of hundreds of thousands of gallons of wine maturing in oak. And yet the bodegas are pure Spain, lofty and white-walled, slightly forbidding, while the lodges seem to have no particularly Portuguese character. They might almost be part of an

English brewery. Most of the shippers' names, too, are completely British: Cockburn, Taylor, Graham, Croft, Sandeman, Dow, MacKenzie, Offley, Warre, Delaforce.

The process of tasting and blending never stops. The white-coated managers have to maintain a constant, unchanging supply of at least half a dozen different kinds and prices of port. The blender's art is to maintain quality and value, and to establish consistency and order, in all the hundreds of slightly different pipes of wine which come down from the hills.

Nearly all port is shipped overseas in pipes to be bottled in Britain, or France, or wherever it is going. (In the last few years France has been the first country ever to buy more port than Britain.)

*Ritual*

Port used to have its ritual place at table, at the end of dinner, when the ladies went off to discuss whatever ladies discuss in the drawing-room and the men remained behind in the dining-room. They closed their ranks, moving up to the end of the table near their host, basking—it is easy to believe—in the feeling of relief at not having to alternate the conversation to left and right any more. The host waited importantly until the butler had got everything except candles and glasses off the table, and had put the decanters down beside him. Then he poured himself a glass, and sipped, and looked smug, and handed the decanter to the man on his left.

The port went round, cigars followed it, and everybody had the comfortable feeling of being involved in a timeless rite. However, it has turned out to be less timeless than they thought.

*When to drink port*

Even at dinner-parties today most people get up and move into the other room together. And by the time you have left the table, shifted your ground, resettled and been given a cup of coffee, the magic moment for port seems to have gone. A glass of brandy goes better with the coffee. Somehow the decanter going round without the polished mahogany and the gleam of candlesticks seems wrong.

Perhaps my sensitivity to the nuances of appropriateness is inflated: I hope so. There is no reason why you should not enjoy a vintage port as much in a comfortable chair as beside a dining-table. And there are the wonderful tawnies, which many people enjoy more than vintage port. Their lightness and smoothness makes them excellent after coffee—a thousand times better than gaudy, syrupy liqueurs.

*Port-type wines*

The law in Britain prevents the name of port from being used for any wine which is not grown in Portugal. It is the only wine-name which is protected by statute in Britain. Wine from Australia or South Africa which wants to give the impression that it is of a similar type is occasionally called port-type, but more often the words Ruby and Tawny are used. They have become almost a part of the name of port.

*Australia*

In *Wine in Australia*, Walter James says: "Port joins sweet sherry and muscat to form the terrible trinity of the Australian wine trade." The bulk of the sweet wines made in Australia are carelessly and quickly made for an undiscriminating market. To be fair, though, I must add that most of the best wineries make a superior port-type wine with great care, and in some cases, conspicuous success. Penfold's "Grandfather" is, though intensely sweet in a way port is not, one of the most remarkable tawnies I have ever tasted. What Australian "ports" seem so far unable to achieve is the delicacy of flavour of the real thing. Walter James quotes Mr Tom Seabrook, himself a senior Australian

*South Africa*

wine-maker, as saying that Australian port-types can never get rid of a heavy suggestion of sugar, even in old age.

South African tawnies, as a whole, approach nearer to the Portuguese, although they always seem to have a raisin flavour which is totally absent from port. Some of the light tawnies are so light that it is hard to believe that, like port, they are made from red grapes—certainly the skins are not mixed with the juice during fermentation to obtain the darkest possible colour, as they are in Portugal. It is a short-cut to an old-looking wine, of course, to make it light to start with instead of making it dark and then giving it time to fade.

The Shiraz grape from the Rhône valley, which is also very popular in Australia, is used to make a sweet, dark, after-dinner wine called Hermitage in South Africa. It has considerable character, a slightly raisin-like taste with a suggestion of bitterness.

André Simon once brought back with him from South Africa a bottle of a 1944 vintage port-type South African wine which was astonishing; I believe very few people would have known it was not port. A senior shipper drank it with him and was utterly baffled. Admittedly it was a rare and uncommercial case, but it indicates that wonderful wine could be made if there was a demand for the finest quality. There was a time, after all, when all Europe vied for bottles of Constantia sweet wine from the Cape. For a short while it was the most expensive and most highly prized wine in the world. Faking soon spoilt the market for it, but it is more evidence that there is no reason why South Africa should not make superb wine.

*California*

Californian wine-makers have no inhibitions about calling their wine port, any more than about calling it sherry or champagne. The problems which beset Australian port apply to most Californian port, but the exceptions, where skilful wine-making makes a very fine after-dinner wine, are more marked. The wine with perhaps the most preposterous bottle I have ever seen, made of pink glass in the shape of a heart, was a very good Californian port-type from Paul Masson. Ficklin of Madera is the most highly esteemed Californian wine-maker in this field, particularly for his varietal Tinta Madeira wine.

# Madeira

Historically Madeira has gone back and forth across the scene from before dinner to after dinner and back again to before it. Those who are passionate about it—and they are many—will drink it joyfully at any time. To most people it is rather an unknown quantity. They think that it is going to be very sweet and then are surprised that it is not. Or they think that it is going to be dry and get a shock when they find that it is quite sweet. The truth is that there are Madeiras of all kinds to suit every taste.

The character which is common to all the wine of Madeira is, first of all, a slightly burnt, smoky and caramel taste, subtle and running deep through the wine. Second, it is a slight sharpness. It is never pure honey, but has a delicate edge of acidity which it never loses. It keeps this balance between lusciousness and austerity beautifully. There is something very satisfying in the first scent of Madeira, a scent as fat and smooth as butter, being followed by the tang of smoke. It is a wine which keeps on surprising you and calling back your attention to the variety of sensations in a single glass.

The after-dinner Madeiras—though all kinds are possible after-dinner drinks—are above all Boal (or Bual) and Malmsey, the sweeter two of the four which are offered. Occasionally old bottles bear the name of other grapes, notably the Terrantez, the Tinta and the Bastardo or even, very occasionally, place-names, such as Cama de Lobos or Campanario. The Tinta and the Bastardo are still grown, and their wine still goes into the blends of Madeira, but their names no longer appear. Only the four noble varieties of Sercial, Verdelho, Bual and Malmsey are now thought good enough to have their names mentioned.

*Malmsey*      Malmsey was the first and most famous of Madeiras. The name of the grape comes from the town of Monemvasia in the Peloponnese in Greece, whence it came with the traditional name of Malvasia, eventually to be called Malmsey.

It is one of history's curious coincidences (Osbert Lancaster points it out in *Classical Landscape with Figures*) that the Duke of Clarence, whose title was derived from Glarentsa, was drowned in a butt of Malmsey—by courtesy, rumour has it, of Richard III. Glarentsa and Monemvasia are both towns in the same wild corner of Greece.

Malmsey has always been the rarest and most precious of Madeiras, the most difficult grape to grow and the most luscious, most sweet and most perfumed of the wines. It is usually darker in colour, more syrupy in consistency and much fuller in flavour than the other Madeiras. I can imagine anyone enjoying any other Madeira before a meal, but Malmsey is certainly an after-dinner wine. It is comparable with port and cream sherry. Although at the age when they are usually drunk the differences between these wines are very marked, it is extraordinary how age develops the qualities they have in common. I have occasionally tasted a fifty-year-old cream sherry, for example, and been sure that it was Madeira.

*Boal*      Boal grapes make a paler, more golden wine with a softer, more gentle quality. It has more of the smoke and less of the honey than Malmsey. Both are equally good with or after the coffee following dinner. They are also wonderful, though rarely drunk, with a creamy sweet dish, or cake, or even raspberries and cream.

# Other Strong Sweet Wines

The after-dinner wines department seems sometimes to be a home for lost causes, for wines which have burnt themselves out with a brief blaze of glory—often as far back as Victorian England—and which now linger on the shelves of off-licences because no-one has the heart for the deathblow.

Worst of all, they are regarded as cooking-wines. We see a Madeira sauce almost as often as we see Madeira itself. Marsala is a complete stranger except in the froth of *zabaglione*. And as for poor Malaga, where do we see it at all?

Madeira is the most healthy of the three today, and has a growing number of admirers. It is not the wine it was when it preceded all others at every dinner-table in the United States, England and even France, but it is very much alive and kicking.

But Marsala, invented by the British as an alternative to sherry at the end of the eighteenth century, had its moment when Nelson ordered five hundred butts of it for the fleet, grew to extreme popularity in mid-nineteenth century, but even by the end of the century was hanging around in decanters on suburban sideboards hoping for a happy release.

As for Malaga, once proudly engraved on silver decanter-labels as Mountain, it is no longer even listed—as Marsala still is for cooking—by wine-merchants.

The wines, however, continue to be made for their reduced circulations, and are none the worse for age. There is unlikely ever to be a great renaissance of Malaga or Marsala, but they are both worth tasting and bearing in mind for some moment when you want something different. The fact that they are unfashionable makes them very good value for money. The finest Virgin Marsala costs the same, for example, as a second-rate sherry—and is as good a drink, from the point of view of quality, as a first-rate one.

## Marsala

Marsala has a taste not unlike old sherry, with some of the caramel flavour of Madeira. Many things about the conditions of its making are the same. John Woodhouse, the Englishman who invented it, seems to have learnt a great deal from the makers of sherry and of Madeira. The process he adopted for making the wines of western Sicily suitable for the English market has obvious ancestors in these older wines.

The town of Marsala is no-one's idea of heaven. It lies in flat, poor country on the west coast of Sicily, in the district with a bad reputation for violence and squalor. Partinico, one of the grape-growing towns, has an old name for undesirability. In Latin its name was Pars Iniqua, which might be translated "The Dump".

Woodhouse, however, saw that it could be made to produce a rival to sherry. The principle he adopted for making wine was to cook some of the grape-juice, fortify another part of it to stop it fermenting and keep it sweet, and to add various proportions of these cooked or sweet wines, as the Spanish add sweetening or colouring wine to sherry, to the local rather ordinary but very strong white. While the wine was therefore naturally dry like sherry, it could be made to any degree of sweetness. Today it comes in three categories. The first is

*Virgin*

Virgin, which is the best quality, the most expensive and least sweetened (it can be like an old oloroso sherry—dry, nuttily scented and deep-flavoured). A second quality is sometimes known as Garibaldi, after the hero's landing at Marsala, and is sometimes called Colli (Hill wine). A third is Italia, which is usually kept for cooking. Colli, as it is made by the firm of Ingham Whittaker, the second of the three Marsala companies, is a much more toasted wine, with a scent which reminds me distinctly of a good beef broth. It is considerably sweeter than Virgin, but is still not very sweet. It is, incidentally, far superior to sherry as an additive to clear soups and consommé. A drop of it in clear chicken soup is marvellous. Alternatively, Virgin Marsala is a very good wine to drink with the soup—another thing for which I think Marsala is really better than the better-known sherry.

Woodhouse developed the system of making Marsala; Ingham, who settled there just after the success of selling stores of the wine to the Royal Navy, had a great influence on the farmers' ancient methods of making wine and growing grapes. Florio was the third man to set up a firm there. All three firms now belong to the same company as Cinzano, but they continue to market their own individual brands under their own names.

They have another popular wine, *Marsala al'uovo*, a sweet Marsala mixed with eggs and bottled as a sticky yellow mixture. A similar thing used to be done, apparently, with sherry-sack in Shakespeare's day. Like Falstaff, I can do without "pullet-sperm in my brewage".

## *Malaga*

Malaga has a similar constitution but a longer history. It is made partly with the Pedro Ximenez grape, which is used for sweetening sherry. At one time it and sherry were equally known as sack; indeed, for a time "Malligo sack" prevailed. But it has dropped back for want of variety, delicacy and all the qualities which make sherry great.

The port of Malaga is not far from Gibraltar, going eastwards along the coast of Spain—in the opposite direction from Jerez. Its speciality today is a comparatively low-strength fortified and partly cooked wine, either sweet or semi-sweet, made of Pedro Ximenez and Muscatel grapes, either dark gold or brown in colour. It is about half the price of a good port. The finest Malaga, which is known as Lagrima, is not—as far as I know—shipped abroad. No Malaga is common now in the English-speaking world, though it deserves attention—very much more so than the Tarragona wine which is popular, and which tastes as though it were made from raisins.

## *Commandaria*

Commandaria is the Marsala of Cyprus: the distinctive, original strong wine. But whereas Marsala was invented less than two hundred years ago, Commandaria takes its name from the district of Cyprus governed by the Knights of the Temple, who bought their land from Richard Coeur de Lion in 1191. It is probably at least a thousand years old, in methods if not in name. To this day in the mountain villages which are most famous for their Commandaria—Kalokhorio, Zoopiyi and Yerasa—some of the farmers use methods of such hoary antiquity for ageing their wine—burying it in earthenware jars in the ground—that little seems to have changed since the days of Homer.

### *Keo*

This, however, is not the Commandaria which is exported. Keo, the Cyprus wine company which is said to buy half the entire wine production of the island, has very different methods. At Limassol, where they have their plant, concrete vats rather than amphorae are used. Commandaria has become, whatever it used to be in heroic times, a rather characterless dark sweet wine; Cyprus's speciality, but no longer its best product. No doubt farmers in the hills could produce a goblet of something very different, but the Commandaria which is sold in Britain has cheapness as its main recommendation.

## *Cream sherry*

The sweetest kinds of sherry, the creams and browns, are not often used as after-dinner drinks. Advertisements have been trying to persuade Americans to drink cream sherry with coffee. To me it is a case of not having the sherry with the coffee but after—or before—it. The two tastes do not go together.

Lingerers over the nuts following a meal would find sweet sherry, or old unsweetened olorosos if they can find them, good alternatives to port. They are much more often drunk, however, despite the advice of the wine-trade, as aperitifs by people who do not like, or have not tried, dry sherry.

### *Empire wines*

I will not take up the cudgel again here about non-Spanish sherries, but merely note that there are more sweet than dry among them, that Cyprus produces a lot of sherry in this category, and that it is in this category that all the British "wines" come, if they come anywhere in this book. They are principally drunk, like the sweet wines, rubies and tawnies of Australia and South Africa, to keep out the cold, rather than for their taste.

*British "wines"*

I have been glad of one, too, as the wind sent a chisel of sleet down Market Street in Manchester and the door of a wine-bar stood open beside me. The ruby from the wood in a "dock" ("samples" are half the size and half the price) went perfectly with the Hogarthian scene; the whole of the centre of the room was taken up with crates and cartons, the walls were lined with small milds and sample rubies in hats and caps, the door kept opening and the sleet kept adding to the puddles on the floor. The fiery strength of the wine made sense.

# Light Sweet Wines

One way or another, to produce a sweet wine, the wine-maker has to make the sheer quantity of sugar in the juice overcome the ferments which want to change it into alcohol. With fortified wine the sugar is retained by dosing the ferments with brandy. But there is another method which concentrates the juice in the grape, lowering the proportion of water in the sugar-and-water mixture of the grape juice. The ferments will then be overpowered because there is so much sugar, just as they are in jam.

In hot countries the concentrating is often done by hanging the grapes up to dry or spreading them out in the sun. Whether in sun or in shadow, they start to turn into raisins. When they have reached the right state of dryness they are pressed and fermented.

In humid countries and the north this cannot be done. The grapes will not dry properly off the vines. But there is a kind of rot which afflicts them under certain conditions which has something like the same effect.

*Pourriture noble*

The unpleasant-looking fungus which is so useful to the wine-grower is called "the noble rot". In German it is *Edelfaul*, in French *pourriture noble*, in learned Latin *Botrytis cinerea*. It happens in years with sunny, misty autumns in Sauternes, in Germany, in Hungary and occasionally elsewhere. If the grapes are left late on the vines until they are overripe a sinister-looking growth begins to appear on their skins. It cracks them open and lives on the juice, while the sugar content of the grape gets higher and higher. By the time they are picked they are as sweet as honey, with all their elements, all the traces of acids and oils and minerals which give them their flavour and scent, concentrated into a quintessence of ripe grape-juice. From these shrivelled berries the wine is made.

Such wine is intensely sweet and extremely aromatic. All its qualities have been intensified. The work of making it is very laborious, because the grapes do not shrivel conveniently at the same time. Pickers have to go round the vineyard again and again, taking only the grapes that have reached the right stage of apparent dereliction. Fritz Hallgarten, in *Rhineland Wineland*, reports a case where it took a hundred workers two weeks to gather enough fruit from seven and a half acres of vineyard to make three hundred litres of juice. The record sweetness ever attained by a wine like this in Germany was in the 1920 Steinberger from the Rheingau, which contained well over a pound of sugar in each bottle.

The German word for wine made like this is *Trockenbeerenauslese*, which means a selection of dried (*trocken*) berries (*Beeren*). A less extreme use of the same technique, picking the grapes individually off the bunches but not waiting until they have reached quite the same shrivelled stage makes wine called *Beerenauslese*.

The French wines in this category are the best growths, known by château names, in Sauternes and the next-door commune of Barsac.

The Hungarian wine is Tokay.

## The hallmark of quality

There is far more difference between Château d'Yquem and plain Sauternes than there is between Château Lafite and plain Pauillac. Château Lafite is the same sort of wine as Pauillac, only much better. Château d'Yquem is a completely different thing from plain Sauternes. The ordinary grower of Sauternes cannot afford continually to send his pickers round the vineyard; he has to gather all his grapes at once. He waits until they are very ripe, with, he hopes, a certain amount of *pourriture noble*, then he picks and presses everything together. The wine will be sweetish but not sweet enough. It will not arrive naturally at the point where alcohol and sugar together prevent the fermentation from going any further. It has to be stopped artificially with sulphur, which stuns the yeasts. So it has neither the strength nor the sweetness of the great growths. It is hardly, in fact, an after-dinner wine at all but a table wine, a sweet alternative to white Graves. As such, it is very popular. But this wine and the superb châteaux which cluster round Yquem, like planets round the sun, should not be confused.

## Sauternes

Sauternes is the southernmost of the areas which make up the vast complex of Bordeaux. For Bordeaux it is hilly. Compared with the Graves district it is tiny. It reaches down from its low hills to the Garonne just where the river, flowing westwards from the mountains towards the sea, takes a turn to the north and heads up towards Bordeaux. If it has any centre it is the sleepy town of Langon, which lies just outside it. Langon has quite a respectable square, where plane trees have been thickly planted to keep the sun off, but it barely winks at you as you go through.

## Château Yquem

The universal place of pilgrimage in Sauternes is Château Yquem, whose labels, for some reason, call it Château d'Yquem. The chateau is one of the most impressive in all Bordeaux. It is what everyone hopes a château will be like, for it is one of the few which is a castle. The Middle Ages planted it soberly on its hilltop. The seventeenth century made it habitable—though by no means luxurious—and the twentieth century has perfected the symmetry of the rows of vines which march up the hill to it in an unbroken procession.

At Yquem every stage of wine-making is carried out with the loving care that goes into the manufacture of a Rolls-Royce. It is said to be the only place where all the wine-making machinery, without exception, is made of wood—even the intricate moving parts of presses—so that no metal ever comes in contact with the wine, in case it should affect its taste. They make what they firmly believe to be the best sweet drink in the world, and there are very few who would deny their claim. No trouble is too much for it. As a result even in poor years—though not in disastrous ones, when no wine is sold under the château's name—the wine they make is an astonishing mixture of richness and freshness. It is so rich as to feel almost like cream in your mouth, but strangely uncloying—its scent and flavour are so intense that they call you back to sniff and sip again.

The late Marquis de Lur Saluces, the proprietor of Yquem and one of the most distinguished figures of Bordeaux, held that his wine was good with several kinds of food. He drank it with *foie gras*. He once made me drink it with lobster. I am obviously not in a position to say that he was wrong. To me, though, it is still the wine to sip after—or indeed before—all others, quite by itself, not even with a peach or some grapes, as many people suggest. Its balance is perfect: why add the acidity which even a perfect peach cannot avoid? A wine like this is so much better than any mere fruit.

*Barsac*
*Château Climens*
*Château Coutet*

Yquem is certainly the summit of Sauternes, but it is no reason to ignore the flanks of the mountain. At times the neighbouring châteaux draw near to it in every quality of richness. The names of Châteaux Climens and Coutet are the most familiar in Britain of the rest of Sauternes, although strictly speaking they are Barsacs—that is wine of the commune of Barsac next door to Sauternes to the north. Barsac wines have the right to call themselves either Barsac or Sauternes as they see fit. The difference between the two is almost imperceptible. Perhaps Barsac is just a little less rich and sweet, with a little less of the softness of texture brought about by the glycerine which is a component of Sauternes in good years. But a Sauternes of a poor year is certainly drier than a Barsac of a good one.

Climens is often a slightly fatter and less delicate wine than Coutet, but both maintain standards which are second only to Yquem—and yet they fetch only a third of the price. Châteaux Doisy-Védrines and Doisy-Daëne are important Barsacs of the second rank. Châteaux Nairac, Broustet, Suau and Piada are less known but worth looking out for.

Sauternes itself is a district of four villages, which are all equally entitled to the name Sauternes, just as Barsac is. These are the village of Sauternes itself, Bommes, Fargues and Preignac. One cannot say that any of these is better than the others, except in so far as it is in Sauternes itself that Château Yquem stands.

Besides Yquem in Sauternes there are Châteaux Guiraud and Filhot, Château d'Arche, Château Lamothe and Château Raymond-Lafon. The first two are often among the best wines of the district. Both, like Yquem itself, produce a dry white as well, and Guiraud even a red, Pavillon Rouge.

*Bommes*

The best growths of Bommes are Châteaux Rayne-Vigneau, Lafaurie-Peyraguey (another very impressive castle), Rabaud-Pro-

*Château Rayne-Vigneau*

mis, Rabaud-Sigalas and La Tour Blanche, which is run as a school for wine-makers. An extraordinary thing happened in 1925 at Château Rayne-Vigneau. According to Professor J. R. Roger's *The Wines of Bordeaux*:

> The fortunate owner, the Vicomte de Roton, who had already made his name as a man of letters and a talented artist, announced to the learned world his discovery of a great quantity of gems in his vineyard. Before long more than twelve thousand stones had been gathered, some of them quite beautiful enough to stand comparison with the best of their kind from Brazil, Peru, Madagascar and Arizona. There were agates, opals, sapphires, amethysts, chalcedony, jasper, onyx, sardonyx, cornelian. More than two thousand of these jewels have been cut and are to be seen in M. de Roton's collection. "Cornelians in melting colours side by side with Hungarian opals, their iridescent fire flickering in the moonlight beam of white sapphires. After the boreal brilliance of cold chalcedony, deep amethyst and sardonyx, the tawny flame of topaz and the flickering brightness of uncut stones reflect the sunset sky."

Nobody has been able to explain how the stones came to be in the soil of Rayne-Vigneau and only there. Its name, however, is one to remember as one of the best in Sauternes.

*Preignac*

Château Suduiraut is the one really great name in Preignac. In the last few years, in such vintages as 1967 and 1970, Suduiraut has made some of the most sumptuously sweet wine of Sauternes. The Château de Malle at Preignac is perhaps the most beautiful building of the countryside. For centuries it has been in a branch of the Lur-Saluces family, the Bournazels. It is one of the prettiest of the small châteaux of France; a low quiet building with two wings ended by round towers, the wings enclosing a court. Its garden and its rooms seem to stand as the seventeenth century left them. I cannot imagine that it is ever anything but autumn at Malle. Everything is the colour of walnuts: the shutters, the furniture, the leaves and the moss on the statues.

*Fargues*

Fargues, again, has one name which is equal to anything except Yquem (whose vineyard it touches), Château Rieussec, a particular favourite of mine and a wine I have long thought was one of life's bargains. I can hardly begrudge the proprietors the recent doubling of its still modest price. Château Romer and Château de Fargues are also occasionally seen.

*Ste-Croix-du-Mont*

The area producing Sauternes-type wines does not end here. Immediately opposite Sauternes on the other side of the river the districts of Ste-Croix-du-Mont and, next door to it, Loupiac produce magnificent sweet wines in good years. Named growths from these districts are not often seen, but they are usually amazing value. I once found in an auction some bottles of old Ste-Croix-du-Mont which were indistinguishable from a fine Sauternes. On the other hand there are few good châteaux which can be relied on, or names which you can expect to see on lists, so it is always rather a matter of buying a pig in a poke. Château de Tastes is one of the few exceptions.

*Loupiac*

Loupiac is in a similar position, also having its own *Appellation Contrôlée* but not often being seen abroad; both lie within the larger area of Premières Côtes de Bordeaux, which stretches all the way along the eastern bank of the Garonne from the bend by Sauternes to opposite the city of Bordeaux itself. The names of one or two of the Premières Côtes villages are occasionally mentioned on lists, although they have no appellations of their own. Capian, Cadillac, Langoiran are sometimes seen. But Premières Côtes white wines are more comparable with Graves than with Sauternes.

*Cérons*        Finally, north of Sauternes and Barsac lies the district of Cérons, which comes between Sauternes and Graves in character, never being as sweet as a good Sauternes, but always being among the sweetest of Graves. In any case, only in exceptional years does it become an after-dinner wine. The communes of Podensac and Illats are included in the name of Cérons, though I have seen both listed under their own names. All three—Cérons, Podensac and Illats—have the right to call themselves Graves, just as Barsac, Bommes and the rest have the right to call themselves Sauternes. As their names are seldom seen on wine-labels, I imagine that they often take advantage of this.

*Monbazillac*        Although it is outside the Bordeaux area altogether, the sweet golden wine of Monbazillac, near Bergerac, fifty miles up the valley of the Dordogne from Bordeaux, has a close affinity to Sauternes. In it the flavour of Muscat, which in Sauternes is entirely subdued (although a form of Muscat grape, the Muscadelle, is used in small quantities) comes forward a little more. Monbazillac is by no means a Muscat wine, but it is enriched by a hint of the musky scent and flavour. The famous hotel Le Cromagnon at Les Eyzies, in the higher Dordogne where the cliffs are honeycombed with the cave lodgings of prehistoric man, has (or had a few years ago) a collection of old Monbazillacs going back some thirty or forty years. Some were dark gold, some almost brown, but nearly all showed that the wine which is merely agreeable when it is young can become very fine with time. There is so little demand for Monbazillac that growers may have stocks of wine as much as ten years old: never the case nowadays in fashionable areas.

*When to drink Sauternes*        Sauternes has this much in common with red Bordeaux; the better it is, the longer it will last and even improve in bottle, and the more there is to gain by keeping it. Château d'Yquem is kept for three years in wood anyway, because the fermentation takes such a long time to finish, so it never appears on the market until the fourth or fifth year after the vintage. At this time it is ready to drink—in a sense. It is superb, but it will get better. It is a lovely straw-gold at this age, very strong and vital, intense and penetrating in flavour. With age the gold will deepen, eventually it will be tinged with brown, but, long before this happens and before there is a hint of brown, it will change to the gold of a rich old ring. The scent will seem to embrace even more flowers and spices. It is, in short, well worth keeping good Sauternes for anything up to twenty years—indeed you can hardly keep it too long. If two alternative good vintages are offered to you, take the older one.

*Temperature*        The greatest pundits of Bordeaux are in favour of serving Sauternes very cold—the better and sweeter, the colder. Château d'Yquem they serve at a couple of degrees below the others. I hate to take issue with those who have far more experience in these matters than me, but I hold the opposite view. The better your white wine, the less you need to chill it. I would drink Château d'Yquem at the same temperature as its peer, Montrachet—very cool. If it is so cold as to mist the glass it mists its own majesty. This is simple to test. Put a bottle in the refrigerator until it is really cold. Pour out a glass. Smell the scent of the wine; taste it. Then wait and warm it a little with your hand. As it comes back to cellar-temperature its intensity and balance return. All its qualities emerge. To me to ice Yquem is to waste it. If you have a poor or ordinary Sauternes, on the other hand, the way to disguise the fact is to serve it at Martini-temperature.

*The deep-freeze treatment*

Having said that, and still believing it, I must add a footnote about a most unusual idea. At dinner at Château Mouton-Rothschild the Baron Philippe served Yquem 1916 in a decanter which had been put in the deep-freeze. The wine actually had ice-floes in it. Strictly speaking this was a Sauternes which *was* too old, the colour was really brown. But the shock of deep-freezing combined with the exposure to air in the decanter had given it some of its old vitality—or so it seemed. In any case it was very good, if a bit like a sorbet. Ronald Avery has also suggested reviving old German wines with a severe chilling followed by "splashing them about a bit" by pouring them from a height. In fact I always pour white wines, young or old, from a height to get some air into them.

*Imitations*

The name of Sauternes is taken in vain everywhere. It is often misspelt by its borrowers "Sauterne", which has the advantage that it helps to identify the imitation from the real thing. In general usage in Australia, Spain and many other places it can simply be taken to mean the sweeter of the local white wines, the drier being called Chablis. There is no justification for this. The product rarely bears the remotest resemblance to Sauternes. It may have merits of its own, in which case its makers are illogical in claiming for it the merits of something else.

## Sweet German wines

The most expensive wines which ever come on to the market in the ordinary way of business, not counting auctions of old cellars and great rarities, are the sweet German wines. They often reach two or three times the price of Château d'Yquem.

The reason for this is partly their rarity, for they can only ever be made in very small quantities, and partly the fantastic cost of the sort of operation I have described, where a hundred workers are engaged for two weeks to gather enough grapes for three hundred litres.

Wines are made like this only on the very best estates, where the owner knows that the result will be well worth the trouble, and only in good years. It is a common practice for the grapes from the different parts of the vineyard, picked on different days, to be kept apart, if there are enough of them, right through every stage of the making process, so that the buyer can choose from which cask, made at which stage of the picking, he wants his wine. Normally the price rises with the cask-numbers, as the grapes become riper and riper.

As a general rule, it is safe to say that the sweeter a German wine is, the better it is, always supposing that the sweetness is natural. The struggle is always towards riper grapes and sweeter wine. Thus the best of all Germany's wines are made by this method which lifts them clear into another range of sweetness altogether, and makes them after-dinner, rather than table, wines.

Wines as precious as these, I need hardly say, are never drunk with food, but sipped and sniffed with hushed reverence—at any time, not necessarily after dinner at all. The ideal occasion would be a sunny morning or warm evening on one of those legendary terraces overlooking the Rhine or Moselle vineyards, with a vine-trellis overhead, or, as some eighteenth-century gentleman remarked, out of a golden goblet in one's gazebo. In any case, they are strictly wine for wine's sake. They are not even strong in alcohol. The very sweetest often have half the usual percentage. But the intensity of flavour in each sip makes them slow and serious drinking all the same.

I will not go round the hills and valleys of Germany again telling of the wonderful late-gathered wines which are made on the Moselle and its tributaries, the Saar and the Ruwer, in the Rheingau (perhaps best of all), Rheinhessen and the Palatinate. It is such a mark of prestige to have made a *Trockenbeerenauslese* that every grower, given the chance of a fine autumn, will try to leave some grapes in the hope of their overripening.

In good years any fine wines from the *Spätlese* (just plain late-gathered) category onwards, including *Auslese* (selected), *Beerenauslese* (selected grapes) and *Trockenbeerenauslese* (selected shrivelled grapes) wines will be so sweet as to be better on their own than with food. One final category exists, more as a curiosity—for the German wine-growers love showing off—than as a commercial proposition. It is called *Eiswein* (ice-wine), which is wine made from grapes in which the juice has been frozen by the night-frost on the vines. They have to be picked very early in the morning and taken to the press-house while they are still frozen. The harvest for wine like this has been as late as the beginning of January. St-Nikolaus wine is made on or about St-Nikolaus' Day (6 December), Sylvester wine on New Year's Eve: there used to be pious names like these for wines made on almost any date in December or later. But the new laws have swept them all away.

*Eiswein*

These wines have been made much more in recent years than before. Since 1965 in fact they have almost become a craze. They have great intensity of flavour, but not the lovely velvety quality of a *Trockenbeerenauslese*, at least in my experience. Perhaps the ones I have tasted have been far too young.

Such wines as these cannot be kept too long. Age cannot harm them. Very old ones are, of course, extreme rarities because the cost of laying them down makes everyone except a German steel magnate recoil. The 1949s which still exist are superlatively good now. No wine comes so near honey and flowers, without honey's fierceness.

*Tokay*

Tokay belongs in history as the favourite dessert wine of a world which thought dessert wine the *summum bonum* of gastronomy: above all the Hapsburg court of the Holy Roman Empire, the Russian Imperial court and the nobility of Russia and Poland. It was the wine-merchants of Warsaw who had the biggest and oldest stocks of Tokay up to this century: the great house of Fukier had 1606 Tokay when it was destroyed.

There was Tokay of various qualities and ages and degrees of sweetness—and there was, in a class apart, Tokay Eszencia. The secret of Tokay lies in this quasi-mystical fluid. It should really be translated as Quintessence.

Tokay lies in easternmost Hungary, near the Russian border, on the river Bodrog. The Bodrog is to Tokay what the Garonne is to Sauternes and the Rhine to Schloss Johannisberg: the source of the mists of autumn which encourage the noble rot. Just crushed and made into wine in the usual way, as in Sauternes and Germany, nobly rotten grapes give exceptional and extraordinary quality. But the Hungarians have a characteristically theatrical way of going further. What they do is simply to pile the Tokay grapes on a grating or a sieve. What their own weight squeezes out of themselves is Tokay Eszencia.

*Eszencia*

Eszencia contains so much sugar that it is very reluctant to ferment at all. I have two half-litres of it in my cellar—and I may say I had to go to Tokay and be very polite to the boss to get them—and neither of them has started to ferment noticeably yet, although one is now over six years old.

Eventually, the theory goes, this most remarkable grape-juice does become wine of a sort: very low in alcohol, sweet and concentrated in flavour. It is this wine which has always been held to have the power of bringing men back from the dead; or at least death's door. There are innumerable tales of Magyar or Polish nobles or bishops on the point of giving up the ghost when somebody hastens to the hushed bedside with a flask of Eszencia. Hardly has the elixir moistened the greying lips when we find his lordship up and playing golf. I mentioned my little hoard to the life insurance company, thinking that they might reduce my premium on the strength of it. Their answer, I may say, just shows how far the commercial motive has clouded men's view of what is great and noble.

Whether any Eszencia finds its way to the Kremlin these days I could not discover. But clearly such a super-aristocrat of wines has no place in a Communist state. What they do with it now, sensibly enough, is to use it for blending with and improving their standard sweet wines.

*Aszu*

Tokay today is a mixture of strong white wine with a very sweet one—the sweet made from botrytis-infected grapes and added in certain set proportions to make different grades of the final product. The most luxurious Tokay sold is all *aszu* (the word for the sweet wine); the plain everyday one has none. Szamorodni, as it is called, is a good aperitif rather than a dessert wine.

*Szamorodni*

The intermediate degrees of sweetness are indicated by the number of measures of *aszu* added to the base wine. The measure is a seven-gallon tub called a *puttonyo*; the barrel, a *gonci*, holds thirty-five gallons. Five-*puttonyos* Tokay is therefore all *aszu* (since five sevens are thirty-five); four-*puttonyos* (or *putts*) has seven gallons of *szamorodni*, and so on. All Tokay—except plain Szamorodni—has a little neck-label showing the number of *puttonyos*, so that you know how sweet you can expect it to be. The bottles, incidentally, only hold half a litre (or two-thirds the content of an ordinary wine bottle). They are not cheap.

*The town*

Tokay itself is probably the least visited of all the world's famous wine-towns. Its position forty miles from the Soviet border may have something to do with this. It feels remote enough—with the sort of memorable stillness of a small provincial town in a Chekhov play. The centre of its social life is the incongruously grand Halasczarda (or fish restaurant), backing, like all one side of the main street, on the broad poplar-fringed Bodrog river. Above the gables opposite can be seen, from the window tables, the wavy crest of a hill of vines. In the gloom inside you will eat hot, substantial, peppery dishes: soup with the rich fresh-water fish of Hungary, the pontj; bulky noodles with smoky bacon and sour cream cheese; flaking pastries like something in an Eastern bazaar; coffee as good as in Budapest.

*Furmint*

The ordinary house wine is not Tokay, or not strictly the sort of Tokay you came to taste. It is the Furmint of the district; the table wine made of just one of the Tokay grapes—but that the one which epitomizes Hungarian originality; a grape of pungent fruitiness and searching astringency. Furmint is, you might say, the starting point of Tokay. Into the vat with it go smaller quantities of two other grapes, the Harslevelu (or lime-leaf grape) and a Hungarian form of the Muscat.

The wine-maker's problem with any sweet wine is always how to make it stable, so that refermentation does not make it arrive at its destination fizzing. Anciently in Tokay the stabilization was done with brandy, as it still is in the making of port. The modern method, though, is to pasteurize the wine by raising it to a high temperature for a short time to kill any remaining yeasts. I have no positive proof, but I suspect that the trace of toffee in the taste of modern Tokay may come from the pasteurization—that in other words the classical wine of Hapsburg and Romanoff was a shade different.

The notes I made tasting a wide range of Tokays in the State cellars bring the whole thing back to me vividly. They are what you might call small-bore tunnels; men of any stature keep brushing their heads on the mildewed roof. Candles are the only light: each visitor takes a long-handled candlestick and plunges into the stygian labyrinth, up and down ramps and stony ladders, past endless files of diminutive barrels: the *gonci* are only a little over knee high. Here and there at the far end of a gallery you will see a conspiratorial group, heads and shoulders crouching in the flickering light, as cellarmen taste or manoeuvre a barrel. There are no cellars in the world like them for the feeling of being in the bowels of the earth; the analogy with a gold-mine is irresistible—particularly when you come to the little circular cave of a tasting-room and taste the golden wine.

The oldest wines I tasted on this occasion were not the very sweetest quality; nonetheless the 1937 four-*puttonyos aszu* was like a lovely old bottle of Château d'Yquem, silky and lingering. It had been in bottle for at least fifteen years. Unfortunately it is open to doubt whether modern pasteurized Tokay would benefit by laying down.

*Temperature*  It is a mistake, I think, to chill Tokay too much before serving it. There are some who like their Sauternes to make the glass fairly sweat with cold. They would presumably do the same to Tokay. Both, I think, lose some of their scent and flavour if they are really cold. Cool, the temperature of a deep well, is best. They should not be anything of a shock to your mouth, but come into it as easily and refreshingly as spring water. Then you should slowly chew Tokay while the flavour of a Hungarian autumn, of long golden days drawing into night-frosts, of the first snow on the hills, seeps into you.

# The Muscat Family

Of all the varieties of grapes which are made into wine there is one family which stands apart as unmistakable to everybody. It is the Muscat. As a grape it is familiar as the tastiest of hot-house varieties. It is used for wine all over the Mediterranean—in Spain, Italy, Africa, Greece and all the islands—and in Portugal, Russia and California.

The Muscat apparently gets its name from the Italian *moscato*, which means smelling of musk. Musk is the scent with which deer attract their mates, a secretion which is collected and used in making perfume. It occurs in many aromatic melons, apples and pears, and even roses, besides grapes. They all have the same haunting, sweet quality which is called musky.

Muscat wine is called Moscato, Muscatel, Muscadel or Muscadine.

I suppose it changes as much as any other wine from place to place, though the scent they all have in common is so overpowering that it is difficult to say more than whether it is sweeter or drier, stronger or less strong, more or less delicate, better or worse. The best Muscats come from Portugal, the south of France, the islands round Sicily and Australia.

*Setúbal*

Portugal makes one of the best of all: a fortified one, dark and strong, called Setúbal.

Setúbal is just south of Lisbon. To reach it from Lisbon you now go across the Tagus by a suspension bridge, one of the longest in the world, whereas previously it was an all-too-short trip in a little steamer among the big-sailed fishing boats, with the hills and churches of Lisbon growing smaller and smaller over the water. Another twenty miles, up and over the Arrabida mountains, brings you to Setúbal. It is largely a manufacturing town now. Its vineyards lie along the Lisbon road and the road west to the fishing port of Sesimbra.

Setúbal's reputation rests on its sweet, heavy wine, the port of the Muscat world—an extraordinary concentration of grape flavour, the very essence of aromatic hot-house grapes.

It is golden brown wine, presented in very fine, rather stumpy bottles with brilliant blue labels. It is not difficult to find it ten or fifteen years old—the older the better. As far as I know, it never stops improving. Like Madeira, Setúbal was sometimes sent as ballast in ships for the sake of the improvement which movement and tropical heat would cause. *Torneviagem* (back from a journey) Setúbal is rare now, but a few very ancient bottles do exist, and are exquisitely fine. Age stops the wine from being so syrupy as it is in youth, and develops amazingly subtle, almost geranium-like scents under the ever-present raisin scent of Muscat.

Setúbal is a fortified wine. The sugar is retained in it by the same method as it is in port. Extra scent is derived from the skins of the grapes after the pressing—for in the Muscat grape even the skin is scented—by soaking skins in the wine for a while after it has been made. Certainly no other wine captures so much of that magic aroma so clearly.

Setúbal is at its best with a plain, rather sweet cake. It is probably one of the very best wines to be almost totally unknown in Britain. It is considerably less expensive than the best cream sherries. Both the quality and the character which could make it immensely popular are there.

*Frontignan*

The most famous of France's many Muscats is that of Frontignan, from the Mediterranean coast not far north of the Pyrenees. It is usually sold under the name of Frontignac.

There is a special variety of the Muscat grown at Frontignan, which gives the wine more delicacy than most, but it is intensely sweet; one glass is as much as most people can drink. It is slightly fortified, enough to bring it up to 15 per cent of alcohol, which puts it into the official category of *vins de liqueur*—the same as port. In fact, it is considerably less strong than port.

*Lunel and Rivesaltes*

Lunel and Rivesaltes also make very similar wines, but famous as these are, none of them can compare in delicacy with an almost unknown Muscat made just north of Châteauneuf-du-Pape, at the

*Beaumes-de-Venise*

curiously named little town of Beaumes-de-Venise. Muscat de

Beaumes-de-Venise is unfortified, and hence far less strong. It brings something of the balance of a Loire wine, gentle and tentative, to the Muscat flavour. Its aroma is much less blatant and more intriguing, but, sad to say, it is very rare.

### Pantelleria

The Sicilian and island Muscats are very raisin-like. They are all made from more or less sun-dried grapes in which the sugar is concentrated to the power of treacle. Perhaps the most famous of all comes from the tiny island of Pantelleria.

#### Syracuse

Syracuse and Noto in Sicily are also both famous for moscatos. That of Syracuse is the oldest of which there is any record. It was first made in 700 B.C., when Rome was still a group of tiny villages. Syracuse is like that. No place I know so gives me the feeling of having been there since the beginning of time. In spirit it is still a metropolis, the greatest city of the Greek world, although it has long since shrunk to the size of a small port. It once had ten inhabitants for every one there is today. And the wine they drank—one of the few wines we can be fairly sure has not changed out of all recognition since ancient times—was moscato.

#### Noto

Noto could not be more different from Syracuse, although it is only a few miles away. It is a strange little miniature Rome, a city composed entirely of a few enormous, forbidding, Baroque buildings, whose high embattled walls break only for a gesticulating frontispiece —the end of the church, for they are convents and monasteries. But Noto's moscato is indistinguishable from that of Syracuse. Paganism and Christianity evidently found common ground in the wine to drink after dinner.

### The Crimea

The Crimea is a strange place to find another really fine Muscat—but not so strange as it seems. According to Edward Hyams, in *Dionysus*, his fascinating history of the vine, it was in the sixth century B.C. that the Greeks established the first vineyards in the Crimea. What is more likely than that they took cuttings of the same vine, their favourite, which is supposed to have come from Byblia in Thrace, to their colony in Syracuse and their trading post in the Crimea? That vine appears to have been the moscato. I have only tasted one Crimean Muscat, that of Massandra, which is sold in England. It is certainly one of the smoothest, most delicate and best—very sweet, rather like a Frontignac, but, I think, better.

### Other Muscats

The Muscat had one of its greatest triumphs in yet another of the history-book wines which are made no more—the legendary Constantia of the Cape. Constantia is said to have been made of the brown Muscat. But it faded from view in the middle of the last century.

#### Constantia

#### Australia

Curiously enough that was just the time when Australia was planting its vineyards. Australia-bound ships put in at the Cape for provisions. So it is perfectly possible that some of Australia's Muscat vines are descendants of those of Constantia.

It seems more than possible, in fact: it seems very likely when you taste the best modern Muscats of Australia. The northern Victorian region of Rutherglen, late in the last century Australia's biggest vineyard, produces a wine of immense distinction under the unpromising name of Morris's Liqueur Muscat. I find it easy to believe that a wine so intense in flavour was the favourite of First Empire Europe.

#### California

California has some original ideas about the Muscat. The best is making it into a very light, pale, very sweet wine at relatively low strength. The Christian Brothers' Château La Salle is the best-known example. The fancy bottle and the low price give little indication of what a good wine it is. It should be served very cold, even from a deep-freeze, after dinner on a hot summer evening—with strawberries.

The other manifestations of the Muscat as a grape for fine wine come into other parts of this book. It makes the excellent sparkling wine of Asti in Italy, and—I think its only performance in a really dry wine—the delicate Muscat of Alsace. It plays a minor role in the making of Sauternes, and is found all over Italy under the *nom de guerre* of Aleatico.

## Passiti

The third traditional method of making the wine sweet, which involves neither adding brandy nor long drawn-out late harvesting, nor the modern practice of filtration, is used in Italy, Switzerland, and to some extent in France and Spain. The general word for the wine it makes in Italy is *vino passito*, or sometimes *vino santo*. The method is to pick the grapes when they are ripe and hang them up in bunches in a dry place to shrivel and become raisins before pressing them.

Almost every part of Italy uses this method for some wine. Many of the moscatos, and their close relation the Aleaticos (a red Muscat grape) are made like this. Caluso in Piedmont, Sfursat in Lombardy and the best known of them, the *vinsanti* of Tuscany, are *passiti*.

All are sweet and have the natural flavour of the grape intensified and slightly overladen with the rather different taste of the raisin. As the local after-dinner wine they are worth trying when you are in Italy. They are usually much better than the local liqueurs.

*Vins de paille*     In Switzerland similar wines are found under the generic name of *vin flétri*; in France they are called *vins de paille* (*paille* means straw). The grapes are traditionally laid out on straw mats either in the sun or indoors throughout the winter to dry out.

The best-known *vin de paille* is made in the Jura. Grange aux Ceps is the brand-name of the most widely distributed one. Again, it is the thing to drink after dinner if you are in the neighbourhood; each wine-district has some speciality which it keeps to itself. It is always worth enquiring for novelties.

## Sparkling Wines after Dinner

Champagne never used to be drunk at any time other than after dinner. It became known, as soon as the industry of Reims and Epernay began to expand at the beginning of the nineteenth century, as the drink for balls, for supper-parties, for everything that started late and went on all night. It was never thought of as an aperitif, for the idea of drinking before the meal or of meeting just for drinks had not arrived.

*Sweet champagne*     The champagne which, in Dickens' words, took its place "amongst feathers, gauze, lace, embroidery, ribbons, white satin shoes and eau de cologne" as "one of the elegant extras of life . . . which a cavalier might appropriately offer at propitious intervals to his danceress", was a sweet wine. It was heavily sugared in the final stages of its manufacture. The Russians, particularly, who were one of the first really big markets for champagne, liked it syrupy. It is said that they even laced it with Chartreuse—as I suspect, not because they liked the mixture but to make the slipper so sticky that their mistress could not get it off again.

Sweet champagne went right out of favour at the beginning of this century. It was not snobbishness, as many people think, which made dry champagne fashionable—indeed one British statesman is reputed to have said that anyone who claimed to like dry champagne was an unmitigated liar—but the discovery that all the best qualities of the wine, its scent and freshness, its liveliness and its way of making the drinker lively, are much more marked when it has not been sugared. Sweet champagne is still made, and has its proper place. It is a common form of celebration to end dinner with a high note, with a bottle of champagne with the ices, *bombe*, gâteau, fruit-salad, Baked Alaska or *soufflé surprise*. Dry champagne tastes pitifully thin and sour with a sweet rich dish. But sweet champagne is perfect.

No champagne is labelled sweet. One or two brands call their sweet version Rich, others call it *demi-sec* (half-dry) or even *sec* (dry). Even *sec* is sweet compared with the usual dry champagne, which is labelled *brut*.

*Asti Spumante*

The end of dinner is also a very good moment for Asti Spumante, the Italian equivalent of champagne which is always more or less sweet. Its honeyed, musky quality is perhaps better with fruit or ices than with any other dish. I would go further and say that if you are having Asti (or any sweet sparkling wine) for a drinking-party at any time, the biscuits to serve with it are not the usual cocktail canapés, cheese-straws and olives, but little macaroons, sweet wafers, dates and almonds.

# Recent vintages
# and when to drink them

This chart gives an idea of the kind of wine to
expect from each area in each vintage, and how
long, at a rough estimate, it will take to reach
its best. Where two figures are given in the
When to Drink column they refer to the cheapest
and the most expensive wines of the vintage.
The latter take longer to mature. Expect exceptions
to these generalizations, particularly when the
wine has had a long sea journey. In the United
States European wines are often found to age
more quickly, and be ready a year or two earlier,
than in Europe.

## White Bordeaux

| | | GRAVES | SAUTERNES |
|---|---|---|---|
| 1991 | some good Sauternes; small, high quality Graves harvest | now-1997 | 1995-2005 |
| 1990 | classic Sauternes; excellent, balanced Graves | now-1997 | 1995-2010 |
| 1989 | Graves rich and heady; a great vintage for Sauternes | now-1996 | 1994-2010 |
| 1988 | an excellent vintage | now-1995 | now-2010 |
| 1987 | Graves good but no good Sauternes | now-1994 | never |
| 1986 | delicious Graves; classic Sauternes | now-1994 | now-2000 |
| 1985 | heatwave vintage: careful selection needed | now-1995 | now-2000 |
| 1984 | some good Sauternes, fresh charming dry wines | now | now-2000 |
| 1983 | an excellent Sauternes year; equally good for white Graves | now | now-2000 |
| 1982 | Sauternes good, not great; some fine Graves to drink early | now | now-1995 |
| 1981 | fine Sauternes, ditto Graves | now | now-1996 |
| 1980 | Graves very poor, Sauternes remarkably good | now | now-1994 |

## Rhine

| 1991 | a good vintage | now-2005 |
|---|---|---|
| 1990 | excellent with high acidity levels | now-2010 |
| 1989 | classic vintage | now-2010 |
| 1988 | good or very good | now-2005 |
| 1987 | variable, no great wines | now-1998 |
| 1986 | some good balanced wines | now |
| 1985 | small crop, good quality | now-1997 |
| 1984 | ordinary | now |
| 1983 | generally excellent, more stylish than sumptuous | now-1995 |
| 1982 | oceans of wet wine | now |

## Moselle

| 1991 | small crop but good quality | now-2000 |
|---|---|---|
| 1990 | superb | 1993-2005 |
| 1989 | superb | now-2005 |
| 1988 | a fine vintage | now-2005 |
| 1987 | adequate, some lively wines | now-1993 |
| 1986 | fair, good to keep | now-1997 |
| 1985 | Small crop, good quality | now-1995 |
| 1984 | Firm, adequate | now |
| 1983 | best vintage since 1976; lovely balance | now-1995 |
| 1982 | wishy-washy; adequate | now |
| 1981 | some sprightly wines; satisfactory | now |

## White Burgundy

| 1991 | ripe but diluted by vintage rain | now-2000 |
|---|---|---|
| 1990 | well balanced and elegant | now-2000 |
| 1989 | uneven but some very good wines | now-1998 |
| 1988 | classic fresh-tasting, golden wines | now-1998 |
| 1987 | disappointing with some exceptions | now-1994 |
| 1986 | graceful, charming wines | now-1996 |
| 1985 | ripe, full wines | 1987-1995 |
| 1984 | fresh, flowery | now-1994 |
| 1983 | powerful rich wines, not all in balance. Superb Chablis. | now-1996 |
| 1981 | fine lively wines | now |

## Champagne Vintage Years

1990, 1989, 1988, 1986, 1985, 1982, 1981, 1979, 1976, 1975, 1973, 1971, 1970, 1969, 1966

## Alsace

| 1991 | good, crisp, useful vintage | now-2000 |
|---|---|---|
| 1990 | superb rich, round wines | now-2000 |
| 1989 | superb, maybe up to 1976 standard | now-2000 |
| 1988 | outstanding vintage of late harvest wines | now-1995 |
| 1987 | variable, some Eiswein | now |
| 1986 | useful, refreshing wines | now |
| 1985 | comparable to 1983 | 1987-2000 |
| 1984 | fresh, for early drinking | now |
| 1983 | outstanding in every way | now-1996 |

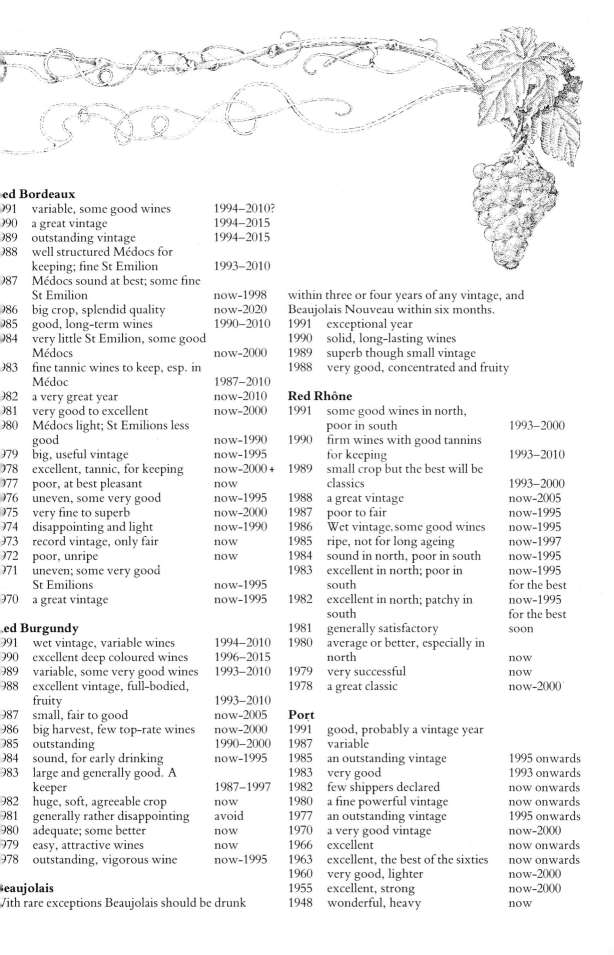

## Red Bordeaux

| | | |
|---|---|---|
| 1991 | variable, some good wines | 1994–2010? |
| 1990 | a great vintage | 1994–2015 |
| 1989 | outstanding vintage | 1994–2015 |
| 1988 | well structured Médocs for keeping; fine St Emilion | 1993–2010 |
| 1987 | Médocs sound at best; some fine St Emilion | now-1998 |
| 1986 | big crop, splendid quality | now-2020 |
| 1985 | good, long-term wines | 1990–2010 |
| 1984 | very little St Emilion, some good Médocs | now-2000 |
| 1983 | fine tannic wines to keep, esp. in Médoc | 1987–2010 |
| 1982 | a very great year | now-2010 |
| 1981 | very good to excellent | now-2000 |
| 1980 | Médocs light; St Emilions less good | now-1990 |
| 1979 | big, useful vintage | now-1995 |
| 1978 | excellent, tannic, for keeping | now-2000 + |
| 1977 | poor, at best pleasant | now |
| 1976 | uneven, some very good | now-1995 |
| 1975 | very fine to superb | now-2000 |
| 1974 | disappointing and light | now-1990 |
| 1973 | record vintage, only fair | now |
| 1972 | poor, unripe | now |
| 1971 | uneven; some very good St Emilions | now-1995 |
| 1970 | a great vintage | now-1995 |

## Red Burgundy

| | | |
|---|---|---|
| 1991 | wet vintage, variable wines | 1994–2010 |
| 1990 | excellent deep coloured wines | 1996–2015 |
| 1989 | variable, some very good wines | 1993–2010 |
| 1988 | excellent vintage, full-bodied, fruity | 1993–2010 |
| 1987 | small, fair to good | now-2005 |
| 1986 | big harvest, few top-rate wines | now-2000 |
| 1985 | outstanding | 1990–2000 |
| 1984 | sound, for early drinking | now-1995 |
| 1983 | large and generally good. A keeper | 1987–1997 |
| 1982 | huge, soft, agreeable crop | now |
| 1981 | generally rather disappointing | avoid |
| 1980 | adequate; some better | now |
| 1979 | easy, attractive wines | now |
| 1978 | outstanding, vigorous wine | now-1995 |

## Beaujolais

With rare exceptions Beaujolais should be drunk within three or four years of any vintage, and Beaujolais Nouveau within six months.

| | |
|---|---|
| 1991 | exceptional year |
| 1990 | solid, long-lasting wines |
| 1989 | superb though small vintage |
| 1988 | very good, concentrated and fruity |

## Red Rhône

| | | |
|---|---|---|
| 1991 | some good wines in north, poor in south | 1993–2000 |
| 1990 | firm wines with good tannins for keeping | 1993–2010 |
| 1989 | small crop but the best will be classics | 1993–2000 |
| 1988 | a great vintage | now-2005 |
| 1987 | poor to fair | now-1995 |
| 1986 | Wet vintage, some good wines | now-1995 |
| 1985 | ripe, not for long ageing | now-1997 |
| 1984 | sound in north, poor in south | now-1995 |
| 1983 | excellent in north; poor in south | now-1995 for the best |
| 1982 | excellent in north; patchy in south | now-1995 for the best |
| 1981 | generally satisfactory | soon |
| 1980 | average or better, especially in north | now |
| 1979 | very successful | now |
| 1978 | a great classic | now-2000 |

## Port

| | | |
|---|---|---|
| 1991 | good, probably a vintage year | |
| 1987 | variable | |
| 1985 | an outstanding vintage | 1995 onwards |
| 1983 | very good | 1993 onwards |
| 1982 | few shippers declared | now onwards |
| 1980 | a fine powerful vintage | now onwards |
| 1977 | an outstanding vintage | 1995 onwards |
| 1970 | a very good vintage | now-2000 |
| 1966 | excellent | now onwards |
| 1963 | excellent, the best of the sixties | now onwards |
| 1960 | very good, lighter | now-2000 |
| 1955 | excellent, strong | now-2000 |
| 1948 | wonderful, heavy | now |

# Index

Figures in bold type indicate where the main information on the subject will be found. All château-names appear under Châteaux.

## A

*Abboccato* 134
Abruzzi **135**
Absinthe 81
Abymes 106
Achille Fould 178
Achkarrenner 111
Achleiten 145
Aconcagua **228**
Adda, river 209
Adelaide 158, 226, 227
Adriatic 164
Aegean 160
Afonso III 78
Africa, North 74, **206**, 250
Africa, South *see* South Africa
After-dinner wines 35, 57, **230–54**. *See also under* Port, Madeira, Sauternes, etc.
Ageing wine 17, 20, **25–9**, 31, 35, 52, 54 (sherry), 68 (champagne), 70, 83 (white wines), 94 (white burgundy), 97 (white Bordeaux), 105 (white Rhône), 138, 139 (*vinho verde*), 186 (Pomerol), 193 (red burgundy), 199 (Beaujolais), 201 (Hermitage), 202 (Châteauneuf-du-Pape), 210 (Valtellina), 213 (Chianti), 216 (Rioja), 219 (Portuguese), 220 (Colares), 223 (Californian reds), 232–3 (port), 239, 241 (Commandaria), 246 (sweet white), 247, 248 (Eszenia Tokay), 249
Age of Inflation 18
Aglianico del Vulture **215**
Aguieira, Quinta d' 140, 220
Ahr 122
Aigle 144
*Aioli* 162
Aix-en-Provence 106, 204
Alaska, Baked 254
Alava 217
Alavesa, Rioja 217
Alba 208
Alba, Istituto Enologico of 208
Alban hills 133
Albano 134
Alcobaça 137
Alcohol 11, 54, 79, 141, 203, 230, 232, 249
Alcoholic strength 11, 52 (sherry), 58, 79, 81 (aperitifs), 89 (Chablis), 97 (Graves), 103 (Alsace), 106, 112, 115 (German wines), 138 (*vinho verde*), 154 (Californian), 159 (South Africa), 164 (Ravello), 167

(red wine), 172 (Bordeaux), 199 (Beaujolais), 202 (Châteauneuf-du-Pape), 213 (Chianti), 215 (southern Italian), 232 (port), 247 (sweet German), 251 (Frontignac)
Aleatico 130, 253
Alella **141**
Alessandria 208
Alexander valley 153
Algarve 140
Algeria 147, 203, 206
Alianca 220
Alicante 142, 160, 218
Aligoté 96
Allegrini 211
Allegro 140
Allier, river 206
Almada 140
Almaden 75, 154, 224
Almonds 254
Aloxe 90, 193
Aloxe-Corton **193–5**
Alpes Maritimes 208
Alps, the 132, 146, 208, 209, 212
Alsace 43, 44, 47, **102–4**, 111, 126, 132, 146, 155, 163 (rosé), 253
Alsheim 125
Alto Adige 130, **132**, **211**
Alvariño 142
Alvarinho Cepa Velha 139
Alves, J. C. 139
*Amabile* 134
Amarone 211
Americano (cocktail) 80
American vines 15, 76, 220
America, North. *See* U.S.A., California, etc.
America, South **228–9**
Amer Picon **81**
Amigne 143
Amontillado 21, 52, 54, **56**, 58
Amoroso **56**
Amoureuses, Les (Chambolle-Musigny) 191
Amphorae 241
Amselfelder Spätburgunder 221
Anapa Riesling 150
Ancona 135
Andalusia 49, 58, 218
Andes, the 228
Angerville, Marquis d' 197
Angostura bitters 81
Angove's 157
Anheuser 126
Anjou **102** (white), **162** (rosé)
Antinori 133
Antinori, Marchesi 214
Apennines, the 213
Aperitifs 35, **46–81**, 239, 241, 253
Aperitifs, patent 81
Apetlon 145
Apitif 55
*Appellation Contrôlée* **21–2** (origins and working), 73, 130 (equivalent to in Italy), **172** (Bordeaux), 186

(Bordeaux), **196** (Burgundy), 202 (Châteauneuf-du-Pape), 204, 207, 245 (white Bordeaux)
Apremont 106
Apt 204
Aquitaine, Queen Eleanor of 16
Aragon 141
Arbia, river 133
Arbois 78, 108 (white), **163** (rosé), 205 (red), 206
Arcachon 99
Arcins 179
Arealva 140, 220
Argentina 150, **229**
Arizona 245
Armand, Comte 196
Armenia 149
Arrabida mountains 251
Arsac **181**
Artichokes 42, 80
Artificial fermentation 230
Arvine 143
Aschrott 124
Asprinio 136
Assisi 214
Assmanshausen 122
Asti 208
Asti Spumante **73–4**, 131, 207, **254**
*Aszu* **249**
Atlantic 159, 218, 220
Aubance, river 102
Auberge du Camp Romain 197
Aude, river 107
Ausonius 183
*Aus eigenem Lesegut* 116
*Auslese* **115–16**, 128, 212, 248
Ausonius 126
Australia 12, 14, 21, 30, 45, 48, **59** (sherry), **156–8** (white wines), 158 (Australian wine in Britain), **165** (rosé), 205, **226–8** (red), **237** (port-type), 238, 251, 252
Australian Wine Centre, the 226
Austria 108, 132, 143, **144–6**, 164, 222
Autostrada del Sole 134
Auvergne 206
Auxerre 89
Auxey-Duresses **91** (white), **197** (red)
Avaux, Les (Beaune) 195
Aveleda 138
Avellino 215
Avelsbach 118
Avelsbacher Hammerstein 118
Avensan 179
Avery, Ronald 92, 247
Avery's of Bristol 55
Avignon 105, 182, 201, 202
Avize 65
Avize Blanc de Blancs 70
Avocado pears 42
Ay 65, 66, 67
Ayala 69
Ayl 117

## B

B.O.B. (Buyer's Own Brand champagne) 69
Babeaşca (grape variety) 2
*Bacalhau* 140
Bacharach 121
Badacsonyi **147**
Bad Dürkheim 127
Baden 111, 113, 146
Baden-Baden 111
Baden-Württemberg 164
Bad Kreuznach **125**
Bad Vöslau 146
Bahans 182
Baiken (Rauenthaler) 124
Balaton, Lake **147**
Balkans, the 149
Ballarat 228
Banda Dorada 142
Bandol **106**, **204**
Barbanne, river 184
Barbaresco 207, **208**
Barbera 130, 207, 225 (California)
Barberani and Cortoni 13
Barberousse, Frédéric 206
Barcelona 141
*Barcos rabelos* 236
Bardolino **210**
Bari 164
Barolo 130, **208**, 218
Barolo Chinato 80, 208
Barossa valley 158, 165, 22
Barrow, Nicholas 179
Barsac **244**, 246
Barton, Ronald 178
Bas-Médoc **173**
Basque country, the 206
Bass Charrington 180
Bassens 187
Bassermann-Jordan, von 1
Bastardo 239
Bastei 126
Bâtard-Montrachet **93**
Béarn **107**
Beaujeu 85, 199
Beaujolais 26, 28, 35, 47, 8 96, 165 (rosé), 165, **198– 200**, 201, 207, 210, 218,
Beaujolais blanc 96
Beaujolais Supérieur **199**
Beaujolais-Villages 199, 20
Beaulieu Winery 154, 224
Beaumont, de 176
Beaumes-de-Venise **251**
Beaumonts, Les (Vosne-Romanée) 192
Beaune 18, 85, **90**, 92 (whi 118, 183, 189, **193–6** (re
Beaune, Hospices de **194**
Beausite-Haut-Vignoble 1
Beef **44**, 201 (sirloin)
*Beerenauslese* 115, 128, 243 **248**
Belgrade 148
Bellevue 227
Bellingham 159
Belvedere Hotel, Ravello 164
*Bereich* 112, 113, 114, 1 125, 126
Bereich Johannisberg 114, 121, 122

Berenson, Bernard 10
Bergerac 99, 186, **204**, 246
Bergzabern 127
Bernese Oberland 143
Bernkastel 112, **119–20**
Bernkasteler Badstube 114
Bernkasteler Doktor 91,
  **119**, 125
Bernkasteler Graben 114
Bernkasteler Kurfürstlay 114
Berry 101
Bersano 208
Bertani 211
Bertolli 214
Berzaberner Kloster
  Liebfrauenberg 127
Bessarabia 149
Bessarat de Bellefon 69
Beycheville 178
Beyer 104
Bianco (vermouth) 79
Bianco dei Colli Euganei **131**
Biancolella 136
Bienvenues-Bâtard-
  Montrachet, Les 93
Bilbainas, Bodegas 142, 217
Billigheim 127
Bingen **125**
Bingen Hole, the 121
Biondi-Santi 214
Birds (game) **45**
Birkweiler 127
Biscay, Bay of 100, 141, 168
Bischöfliches Konvikt 118
Bischöfliches Priesterseminar
  118
Bitters 80, 81
Blackcurrants 106 (liqueur
  made from, in Burgundy),
  222
Blackfriars 106, 112
Black Sea, the **149** (white
  wines), **222** (red wines)
Black wine of Cahors **204**,
  218
Blagny 91
Blanc de blancs (champagne)
  **65**, 69
Blanc de blancs de Béarn 107
Blanc de blancs de Limoux
  107
Blanc de blancs de Provence
  106
Blanc Fumé 100
Blanchots, Les (Chablis) 88
Blandy 77
Blanquefort 174, **181**
Blanquette 158
Blanquette de Limoux **73**
Blayais **186**
Blaye 17, 179, **186**
Blending **53** (sherry), **63**
  (champagne), 87 (bur-
  gundy), 115 (Germany),
  236 (port)
Blois 101
Blue Nun 112
Boal (Bual) 77, **239**
Bocksbeutel 128
Bockstein (Ockfen) 117
Bodega **51**, 216
Bodenheim 125

Bodrog, river 248
*Boeuf Bourguignon* 197
Bolla 131, 211
Bollinger 65, 69
Bologna 132
Bolzano 132, 211
Bommes **244**, 246
Bonn 122
Bonnes Mares 190, 192
Bonnezeaux **102**
Bookmark 157
Boordy vineyard 165
Bordeaux 16 (English
  possession of), 16 (England
  loses), 16 (Medieval wine
  fleet to), 17 (Scottish
  advantages in), 18 (Golden
  Age), 19, 20 (decline in
  quality of), 22, 24, 28
  (drunk too young), 30,
  43 (on picnics), 61, 73
  (sparkling), 94, **96–9** (dry
  white), 134, 153, **163** (rosé),
  167, **168–88** (red), 169
  (vineyards), 171 (classifica-
  tion and growths defined),
  172 (*Appellations Contrôlées*
  in and communes of), 195,
  200, 204, 213, 222, 224,
  226, **243–7** (sweet white).
  *See also under various
  districts*
"Bordeaux Bible" 177
Bordeaux, Bishop of (Pope
  Clement) 182
Bordeaux, city of **168**, 174,
  187
Bordeaux, Classification of,
  in 1855 20, **171**, 175, 182,
  in 1932 **171**, in 1973 **172**
Bordeaux, Supérieur 172
*Bordeaux, The Wines of* 176,
  245
Borges and Irmao 221
Borgogno 208
Boston 169
*Botrytis cinerea* 242, 249
Bottière, La 178
Bottle 68 (champagne), 104
  (Alsace), 111 (German),
  200 (Châteauneuf-du-
  Pape), 213 (Chianti), 218
  (Steinwein)
Bottle, evolution of the 26
Bottle, maturing in the 25–8
Bottle-sickness 35
Bouchard Père et Fils 93, 195
Boudots, Aux (Nuits-St-
  Georges) 193
Boudriotte, La (Chassagne-
  Montrachet) 197
Bougros (Chablis) 88
*Bouillabaisse* 106
Bouliac 187
Bourgueil 205
Bourgogne 84, **196**. *See also
  under Burgundy*
Bourg **186**
Bourgogne Grand Ordinaire
  **196**
Bournazel 245
Bouzy Rouge **205**

Bragança 234
Brains 45
Branco Seco 140 (Especial)
Brand, Eric 227
*Brandade de morue* 162
Brand-named wines 35, 55
  (sherry), 59 (Australian
  "sherry"), 69–70 (cham-
  pagne), 72, 77 (Madeira),
  79–81 (aperitifs), 106 (the
  Rhône valley), 114, 135,
  136, 140 (Portuguese white
  wines), 157, 161 (rosés),
  209–10 (Italian red wines),
  215, 222 (the Black Sea),
  228 (South Africa)
Brandy 12 (fortifying with),
  64 (and champagne), 79,
  218, 231, 232, 235 (and
  making port)
Bratenhöfchen (Bernkasteler)
  114, 119
Brauneberg **119**
Braunfels, Wiltinger 117
Brazil 245
Bremen 169
Brenner Pass 211
Brescia 131
Bressandes, Les 193 (Corton),
  195 (Beaune)
Bresse 85, 200
Briare 89
Brillante 142
Brindisi 214
Brisbane 158
Bristol 56, 169
Bristol Cream 56
Bristol Dry 55
Bristol Fino 55
Bristol Milk 56
Britain, wine in **15–20**, 28,
  31, 42, 48, **54–7** (sherry),
  60 (British "wine"), 72, 75,
  76, 80, 88, 97, 108, 110,
  137, 140, 147, 158, 164,
  168, 200, 211, 215, 218,
  222, 232, 237 (port), 239,
  241–2 (Empire wines)
British "wine" 48, 60, 75, 242
Brittany 20, 100
Brolio 133 (white), 213 (red)
Brooks's Club 184
Brouilly 199
Brown sherry 54, 57
Brücken 125
Brugière, M 176
Brunello di Montalcino 214
Brussels 194
*Brut* **64**, 75, 254
Bucelas **139**
Buck's Fizz 75
Budapest 148
Bué 101
Bühl, von 127
Bulgaria **149–50** (white),
  **222** (red)
Bull's Blood 148, 221
*Bundesweinprämierung* 116
Burgundy 14 (emergence of
  character of), 19, 20, 21,
  22 (domaine-bottling), 24,
  26, 28, 29, 30 (vintages),

32, 35, 44 (and salmon), 47,
  **72–3** (sparkling), **84–96**
  (white), **84–8** (general
  introduction), **88–96**
  (village by village survey),
  106, 152, 162 (rosé), 167,
  172, **188–200** (red), 200,
  204, 207, 223, 226
Burgundy, classification of **87**
Burgundy, Dukedom of 84,
  194
Burgundy, Hearty 152
Burgundy, South **198–200**
  (red)
Buring 227
Bürklin-Wolf 127
Busby, James 13
Buttafuoco 210
Buyer's Own Brand (B.O.B.)
  69
Byblia 252
Byron, Lord 15 (quoted), 220
Byrrh 79, **81**

C
C.V.N.E. (Companhia
  Vinicola del Norte
  España) 142, 217
Cabernet Sauvignon (grape
  variety) 152, 162, 183, 203,
  205, 212, 221, 222, **223**
  (California), 225, 226, 229
Cadaujac 182
Cadillac 246
Cadiz 48
Cahors, Black wine of **204**,
  218
Cailleret-Dessus 85
Caillerets, Les (Volnay) 41
  (with food), 197
Cailles, Les (Nuits-St-
  Georges) 193
Cake, sweet 251
Caldaro, Lake 212
Calera 229
California 14 (origins of wine
  in), 18 (and Prohibition),
  19, 24, 30, 35, 45, 48, **60**
  (sherry), **75** (sparkling), 77,
  **150–6** (white), 164 (rosé),
  206, **222–5** (reds), 238
  (port), 250, **252** (Muscat)
California, University of 151,
  225
California, University of
  (Dept. of Viticulture and
  Enology) 151
Calvet 93
Caluso 253
Cama de Lobos 239
Camargues 107
Cambes 187
Camblanes 187
Campanario 239
Campanas, Las 218
Campania **136**
Campari 79, **81**
Campo Grande 140
Camus 190
Canary Islands 48
Canelli 208

Cane-sugar 12, 77
Cannonau 215
Cantabrian Sierra, the 141, 216
Canteloup 175
Cantenac **181**
*Cantina sociale* 130
*Capataz* 51
Cap Corse **81**
Cape, the 14, 58, 76, 159, 238, 252. *See also under* South Africa
Capian 246
Capon 45
*Carafe* 40
Carafe wine 33, 36, 89, 131, 141, 144, 163, 200, 218, 225
Caraman Chimay, Princesse de 63
Carbon-Blanc 187
Carcassonne 73
Carcavelos 139
Carelle-sous-la-Chapelle 85
Carignane (grape variety) 225
Cariñena 218
Carlonet 228
Carlowitz, von 228
Carpano 80
Carrots 42
Carruades de Château Lafite 176
Caruso family 136
Carvalho 220
Casa Juan 56
Casal Avelada 138
Casal Garcia 138, 139
Casal Mendes 138, 139
Cask, maturing in the 25, 232
Casserole 221
Cassin, Mme 80
Cassis 106
Casteggio 210
Castel Chiuro 209
Castel Gandolfo 134
Castellane, de 69
Castelli dei Jesi, Verdicchio dei 133
Castello di Uzzano 214
Castiglione Falletto 208
Castile 141, 216
Castillo Ygay 217
Castillon 187
Castillon, battle of 16
Castillon-la-Bataille 80
Castle Pomal 218
Catalonia 75, 141, 217
Catania 136
Caucasus, the 149
Cavaillon melon 200
Caviar (Portuguese wine) 140
Cazes, M (mayor of Pauillac) 177
Cellar, ideal conditions in 34
Cendré de Novembre 163
Cenon 187
Cent-Vignes, Les (Beaune) 195
Cérons **246**
Cevennes 203
Cézanne 162
Chabannes, Comtesse de 98
Chablais 144

Chablis 21 (and fraud), 43 (with oysters), 44, 85, **88–9**, 95, 99, 117, 120, 152, 189
Chacolí 142
Chagny 94
*Chai* 98, **169**, 178, 179
Chaintré 95
Chalambar 228
Chalone 154
Chalon-sur-Sâone 94
Chambertin 45, 85, 86, 180, **189–90**, 193
Chambéry **79**
Chambéryzette 79
Chambolle 86
Chambolle-Musigny **190–1**, 193
Champagne 11, 14 (emergence of character), 21, 23, 24, 36, 43, **60–71**, 61 (effects of the taste of), 61 (region), 62 (still), 64 (*remuage*), 64 (dégorgement), 64 (*dosage*), 65 (vineyards), 66 (vintage), 66 (pressing), 66–7 (*cuvée*), 67 (non-vintage), 67 (vintage), 68 (ageing), 69 (buying), 70 (serving with food and consumption figures), 70 (rosé), 71 (glasses for), 71 (quantity to serve), 71–5 (imitators and competitors), 156 (American version), 205 (red), 253 (sweet)
Champagne method 62–5, 71–3
Champagne, Avenue du (Epernay) 62
Champans (Volnay) 197
Champanski 150
Champs Pimonts, Les (Beaune) 195
Chante Alouette 106
Chante Perdrix 202
Chantemerle 106
Chapelle-Chambertin 189
Chappellet 155
Chaptal, M 12
Chaptalization **12**
Chardonnay (grape variety) 44, 96, 152, 153, 154, 222. *See also* Pinot Chardonnay
Charentes, Pineau des 79
Charles II, King of England 17
Charmes, Les (Chambolle-Musigny) 191
Charmes, Les (Meursault) 91
Charmolüe, Mme 174
Charollais 85
Chartreuse 254
Chassagne-Montrachet 86 (white), **197** (red)
Chasselas 158
Château **169** (in Bordeaux), 185
Château-bottling **22**, 171
Château-Chalon **78**
Châteauneuf-du-Pape 45, **105** (white), 162, 200, **202** (red), 251

CHATEAUX
Ch. d'Agassac 181
Ch. Andron Blanquet 175
Ch. Angludet 181
Ch. Anseillan 177
Ch. d'Arche 181, 244
Ch. Ausone 183
Ch. Balestard-La-Tonnelle 184
Ch. de Barbe 186
Ch. Baret 97
Ch. Batailley 177
Ch. Beauséjour (St-Emilion) 184
Ch. Beauséjour (St-Estèphe) 175
Ch. Beausite 175
Ch. Belair (St-Emilion) 184
Ch. Bel-Air (Lalande de Pomerol) 186
Ch. Belgrave (St-Laurent) 179
Ch. Bellegrave (Pauillac) 177
Ch. Bel-Orme-Tronquoy-de-Lalande 174
Ch. Beychevelle 178
Ch. Bontemps-Dubarry 179
Ch. Bouscaut 97 (white), 182 (red)
Ch. du Bousquet 186
Ch. Boyd-Cantenac 181
Ch. Branaire-Ducru 178
Ch. Brane-Cantenac 180
Ch. de la Brède 98
Ch. du Breuil 175
Ch. Broustet 244
Ch. Calon-Ségur 175
Ch. Canon 184, 186
Ch. Canon de Brem 186
Ch. Canon-la-Gaffelière 184
Ch. Cantemerle 181
Ch. Cantenac-Brown 181
Ch. Capbern 175
Ch. Cap-de-Mourlin 184
Ch. Carbonnieux 97 (white), 182 (red)
Ch. de la Cassemichère 100
Ch. du Castera 173
Ch. Certan-de-May 185
Ch. Chappelle-Madelaine 184
Ch. Chasse-Spleen 179
Ch. Cheval-Blanc **184**, 185
Ch. Citran 179
Ch. Clarke 179
Ch. Clerc-Milon-Mondon 177
Ch. Climens **244**
Ch. Corbin 184
Ch. Cos d'Estournel **174**
Ch. Cos-Labory 175
Ch. Coufran 174
Ch. Couhins 97
Ch. Courant 179
Ch. Coutet 244
Ch. Croizet-Bages 177
Ch. Croque-Michette 184
Ch. Curé-Bon-La-Madelaine 184
Ch. Dauzac 181
Ch. Doisy-Daënes 244
Ch. Doisy-Védrines 244
Ch. Ducru-Beaucaillou 177, 178

Ch. Duhart-Milon 177
Ch. Duplessis 179
Ch. Durfort-Vivens 181
Ch. Dutruch-Grand-Poujeaux 179
Ch. de Fargues 245
Ch. Fieuzal 182
Ch. Figeac 184
Ch. Filhot 244
Ch. Fonbadet 177
Ch. Fonpiqueyre 175
Ch. Fonplégade 184
Ch. Fontpetite 175
Ch. Fortia 202
Ch. Fourcas-Dupré 179
Ch. Fourcas-Hosten 179
Ch. de la Galissonnière 100
Ch. Gazin 185
Ch. Giscours 181
Ch. Glana 179
Ch. Gloria 179
Ch. Grand-Barrail-Lamarzelle-Figeac 184
Ch. Grand-Pontet 184
Ch. Grand-Puy-Ducasse 17
Ch. Grand-Puy-Lacoste 17
Ch. Grand-St-Julien 179
Ch. Gressier-Grand-Poujea 179
Ch. Grillet **105**
Ch. Gruaud-Larose **178**
Ch. Guiraud 244
Ch. Haut-Bages-Averous 1
Ch. Haut-Bages-Liberal 17
Ch. Haut-Bages-Monpelou 177
Ch. Haut-Bailly 182
Ch. Haut-Batailley 177
Ch. Haut-Brion 17, 30, **98** (white), 171, **182** (red), 1
Ch. Houissant 175
Ch. d'Issan 180
Ch. Junayme 186
Ch. Kirwan 181
Ch. La Bégource-Zédé 180
Ch. La Closerie-Grand-Poujeaux 179
Ch. La Clotte 184
Ch. La Conseillante 185
Ch. La Couronne 177
Ch. La Dame Blanche 98, 1
Ch. La Dauphine 186
Ch. La Dominique 184
Ch. Ladouys 175
Ch. Lafaurie-Peyraguey 24
Ch. Lafite 18 (1797 vintage), 31 (1949 and 1953 vintages), 109, 158, 172 (*Appellation Contrôlée* of) 174, **175–6**, 177, 184, 243
Ch. Lafite-Canteloupe 181
Ch. La-Fleur-Petrus 185
Ch. Lafon-Rochet 175
Ch. La Gaffelière 184
Ch. La Garde 182
Ch. Lagrange 178
Ch. La Grave-Trignant-de-Boisset 185
Ch. La Haye 175
Ch. La Lagune **181**
Ch. de Lalamarque 179
Ch. La Louvière 182

Ch. La Mission Haut-Brion 30, 182
Ch. Lamothe 175, 244
Ch. Lanessan 179
Ch. L'Angélus 184
Ch. Langoa-Barton 178
Ch. La Noë 100
Ch. La Pointe 185
Ch. Larose Trintaudon 179
Ch. Larrivaux 175
Ch. Larrivet-Haut-Brion 182
Ch. La Salle 253
Ch. Latour 152, 172, 175, **176**, 184, 224
Ch. La Tour Blanche 244
Ch. La Tour Carnet 179
Ch. La Tour-de-By 173
Ch. La-Tour-de-Mons 180
Ch. Latour-du-Pin-Figeac 184
Ch. Latour-Figeac 184
Ch. Latour Haut-Brion 182
Ch. La Tour-Milon 177
Ch. La Tour-Pibran 177
Ch. Latour-Pomerol 185
Ch. Laujac 173
Ch. Laville Haut-Brion 97
Ch. Le Boscq 175
Ch. Le Gay 185
Ch. L'Eglise-Clinet 185
Ch. L'Enclos 185
Ch. Léoville-Barton 178
Ch. Léoville-Las-Cases 178
Ch. Léoville-Poyferré 178
Ch. Le Pape 182
Ch. Le Roc 175
Ch. Les Ormes de Pez 175
Ch. L'Evangile 185
Ch. Libertas 228
Ch. Liversan 175
Ch. Loudenne 98 (white), 173 (red)
Ch. Ludon-Pomiés-Agassac 181
Ch. Lynch-Bages **177**
Ch. Lynch-Moussas 177
Ch. MacCarthy-Moula 175
Ch. Magdelaine 184
Ch. Malartic-Lagravière 182
Ch. Malescasse 179
Ch. Malescot 180
Ch. de Malle 245
Ch. Marbuzet 175
Ch. Margaux 98 (Pavillon Blanc), 173, 179, **180**
Ch. Marquis-d'Alesme-Becker 181
Ch. Marquis de Terme 181
Ch. Martinet 184
Ch. Maucaillou 179
Ch. Médoc 178, 179
Ch. Meyney 175
Ch. de Mille 204
Ch. Monbousquet 184
Ch. de Monthélie 197
Ch. Montrose **174**
Ch. Morin 175
Ch. Moulin-de-la-Rose 179
Ch. Moulis 179
Ch. Mouton-Baron-Phillippe 177
Ch. Mouton-Cadet **177**

Ch. Mouton-Rothschild 172, **176–7**, 184, 247
Ch. Nairac 244
Ch. Nenin 185
Ch. Nexon-Lemoyne 181
Ch. du Nozet 101
Ch. Olivier 97 (white), 182 (red)
Ch. des Ormes 179
Ch. Palmer **180**, 182
Ch. Pape-Clément 182
Ch. Parempuyre 181
Ch. Patache d'Aux 173
Ch. Paveil-de-Luze 180
Ch. Pavie 184
Ch. Pedesclaux 177
Ch. Petit-Village 185
Ch. Petrus **185**, 226
Ch. Peyrabon 175
Ch. de Pez 174
Ch. Phélan-Ségur 174
Ch. Piada 244
Ch. Pibran 177
Ch. Pichon-Lalande 181
Ch. Pichon Longueville-Baron 177
Ch. Pichon Longueville-Lalande **177**
Ch. Pierre-Bibian 179
Ch. Pomeys 179
Ch. Pomys 175
Ch. Pontet-Canet 177
Ch. Pradeaux 204
Ch. Preignac 244
Ch. Prieuré-Lichine 180
Ch. Rabaud-Promis 244
Ch. Rabaud-Sigalas 244
Ch. Ramage-la-Batisse 175
Ch. Rausan-Ségla 180
Ch. Rauzan-Gassies 180
Ch. Rayas 202
Ch. Raymond-Lafon 244
Ch. Rayne-Vigneau **244**, 245
Ch. Rieussec 245
Ch. Ripeau 184
Ch. Romer 245
Ch. Rouet 186
Ch. Rouget 185
Ch. St-Exupéry 180
Ch. St-Pierre-Bontemps 178
Ch. St-Pierre-Sevaistre 178
Ch. de Segriès 202
Ch. Ségur 181
Ch. Semeillan 179
Ch. Sénéjac 181
Ch. Simone 106 (white), 204 (red)
Ch. Siran 181
Ch. Smith-Haut-Lafitte 97, 182
Ch. Suau 244
Ch. Suduiraut 245
Ch. Tahbilk 228
Ch. du Taillan 181
Ch. de Tastes 245
Ch. de Tertre 181
Ch. Toumalin 186
Ch. du Trignan **202**
Ch. Tronquoy-Lalande 175
Ch. Troplong-Mondot 184
Ch. Trottevieille 184

Ch. Vaudieu 202
Ch. Verdignan 174
Ch. Vieux-Château-Certan 185
Ch. Villegeorge 179
Ch. de Viré 94
Ch. d'Yquem (Yquem) 29, 33, 92, 146, **243–4**, 246, 247
Cheese 45, 57, 209, 221, 231
Cheilly **94**
Chekhov 249
Chénas 199
Chenin Blanc (grape variety) 102, **155**
Chevaliers du Tastevin 191
Chevaliers-Montrachet **92–3**
Chianti 24, 43, **133** (white), 207, 210, **213–14** (red), 213 (how Chianti is made), 221
Chianti Classico 131, 133, 214
Chianti dei Colli Aretini 214
Chianti dei Colli Fiorentini 214
Chianti dei Colli Pisani 214
Chianti dei Colli Senesi 214
Chianti Rufina 214
Chiaretto del Garda **163**
Chiavennasca 209
Chicago 39
Chicken **45**, 94, 162
Chile **228–9**
China 19
Chinese dry white wine **78**
Chinon **205**
Chipiona 53
Chiroubles 199
Chiuro 209
Chocolate 231
Choosing wine **32–8**, 33 (in a wine shop), 36 (in a restaurant)
Christian Brothers 155, 253
Christie's 19
Christmas 231
Church, the 13
Church lands, (secularization of) 13
Churchill, Sir Winston 62
Chusclan 202
Ciclopi 136
Cinqueterre **131**
Cinzano **80**, 240
Cissac 175, 179
Cistercians 191
Clair Daü 190
Clairette de Die **72**
Clape, La 107
Clapham, Sir John 16
Clarence, Duke of 239
Claret 16 (origin of English taste for), 17, 26, 28–9 (age to drink), 35, 44 (with beef and lamb), 47, 91, 94, 97, 157, 163, 167, **168–88**, 201, 205, 215, 218, 223, 233. *See also* Bordeaux, red
*Classical Landscape with Figures* 239
Classification of wines *See under* Bordeaux, burgundy, sherry, etc.

*Clavelin* 78
Cléray, Domaine du 100
Clicquot, the widow **63**
*Climats* 86, 191, 196, 197
Clochemerle 198
"Clone" 87
Clos des Abbayes (Dézaley) 144
Clos des Amandiers (Riquewihr) 104
Clos de Bèze 189, 190
Clos de la Bussière 190
Clos du Chapitre 94
Clos des Chênes (Volnay) 41, 197
Clos de la Commaraine (Pommard) 196
Clos des Corvees 193
Clos des Ducs 197
Clos Fourtet 184
Clos des Jacobins 184
Clos de la Maréchale (Nuits-St-Georges) 193
Clos des Mouches (Beaune) 195
Clos-de-la-Mousse (Beaune) 195
Clos René 185
Clos-du-Roi (Corton) 193, 195
Clos de Tart (Morey-St-Denis) **190**
Clos des Ursules 195
Clos de Vougeot 86, **90** (white), 123, **191–2**
Clos Fourtet 184
Clos, Les (Chablis) 88
Clos l'Eglise 185
Clos St-Denis (Morey-St-Denis) **190**
Clos Ste-Hune 104
Clos St-Jacques (Gevrey-Chambertin) 190
Clos St-Jean (Chassagne-Montrachet) **197**
Coast Range, the 152
Cockburn 237
Cocks and Feret 174, 177
Codorniu 75
Coffee 237, 241
Cognac 24
Colares 139, 219, **220**
*Colheita* 220
Colli (Marsala) 240
Colmar 103
Colombard (grape variety) 155
Colonna 134
Coltibuono, Badia a 214
Comblanchien 90
Commandaria 59, **241**
"Commercial" wines (German) **111**
Commonwealth 19
Communes of Bordeaux 172
Companhia Vinicola del Norte España 142, 217
Companhia Vinicola do Norte de Portugal 219
*Concise Economic History of Britain* 16

Concord (grape variety) 156
Condrieu **105**, 201
Conegliano 131
Consommé 240
*Consorzi* 131
Constance, Lake 111
Constantia 27 (maturing time), 159, 238, 252
*Consumo* 23
Contratto 208
Cooking-wine 240
Coonawarra 158, **226**, 227
Co-operative (at St-Estèphe) 175. *See also* Cantina Sociale *and* Winzerwein
*Copita* 55
*Coq au vin* 45, 197
*Coq au vin jaune* 45
Corbières 204
*Cordero asado* 216
Cordial 81
Cordier 178
Cordoba 56
Corgo, river 236
Corked wine 38
Corks 17, 22, **26**, 64
Corkscrews 26, **39**, 40
Cornas **201**
Coronata 131
Corsica 133, 207
Cortese **131**
Corton 85, **90** (white), 184, **193** (red), 195, 196
Corton-Bressandes 193
Corton-Charlemagne 31, 85, **90**, 92, 194
Corton-Clos-du-Roi 193
Corton-Grancey 193
Corton-Renardes 193
Corvo 136, 215
Cossart Gordon 77
Côte, La 144
Côte Chalonnaise **94** (white), 198
Côte de Beaune **90–4** (white), **194–8** (red)
Côte de Beaune-Villages 195, 198
Côte des Blancs 65
Côte de Brouilly 199, 200
Côte de Nuits **89–90** (white), 163, **189–93** (red), 195
Côte d'Or 85, 89, **189**, 224
Côte Rotie **201**, 219
Coteaux d'Ajaccio 207
Coteaux de la Loire 102
Coteaux du Layon 102
Côtes de Buzet 205
Côtes de Castillon 187
Côtes de Canon-Fronsac 186
Côtes de Francs 187
Côtes de Fronsac 172, **186**, 204
Côtes de Lubéron **107**
Côtes de Provence **106** (white), 162 (rosé), **204** (red)
Côtes du Marmandais 205
Côtes-du-Rhône 43, 106, 200, 202
Côtes-du-Rhône-Villages 106
Côtes-St-Emilion 183

Courtiers 170
Cradle, how to use a wine 40
Cramant 70
Cras, Aux (Nuits-St-Georges) 193
Crayfish *à la nage* 200
Cream sherry 52, 54, **56**, 230, **241**, 251
*Crémant* 70
*Crêpes Parmentier* 200
Crépy 106
*Criadera* 52
Crimea 149, **252**
Criots-Bâtard-Montrachet 93
Cristal 70
Crofts 234, 237
*Croque-monsieur* 205
Crown of Crowns 112
Crozes-Hermitage **105**, 106, **201**
*Cru artisan* 171
*Cru bourgeois* 171, 173, 174, 177, 178, 179, 181
*Cru bourgeois supérieur* 171
*Cru classé* 172, 174, 177, 180, 181, 182
*Cru exceptionel* 171, 181
*Cru paysan* 171
Crus, Aux (Beaune) 195
Cruse, House of 177, 181
Crust on port 233
Cucumbers 42
Cuneo 208
Cussac **179**
*Cuve close* 73, 75
*Cuvée* 66
Cuvée Dames de la Charité 196
*Cuvée privée* 95
Cyclops 95
Cynar 80
Cyprus 48, **59** (sherry), **160** (white wines), 241 (Commandaria)


D

D.O.C. *(Denominazione di origine controllata)* 130, 131, 212, 214
Dalmatian coast 149
Dalwood 227
Damilano 208
Danube 144, 148
Dão **139–40** (white), **219** (red)
Dates 254
Davis, near Sacramento 151
Daubenheim 125
Daubhaus 125
Dautenpflänzer 126
Debro 148
De Castellane 69
*Dégorgement* 64, 75
Deidesheim 127
Deidesheimer Hofstück 128
Deidesheimer Hohenmorgen 128
Deinhard & Co. 112, 119
Delaforce 237
Delbeck 69
*Demi-sec* 64, 254

*Denominazione controllata e garantita* 131
*Denominazione di origine controllata* 130, 131, 212, 214
*Denominazione semplici* 130
Deutelsberg (Hallgartener) 123
*Deutsches Export Weinsiegel* 116
Deutz & Geldermann 69
*Deuxième cru* 191
De Vogüé 191
Dezaley 144
Dézize **94**
Dhron 119
Diamant Bleu 70
Dickens, Charles 253
Die, Clairette de **72**
*Diebetiker-Weinsiegel* 116
Dienheim 125
Digestion, wine as an aid to 19
Digestive biscuits 230
Dijon 189, 194, 196
Dillon, Clarence 182
Dimiat 149
Dinjac **221**
*Dionysus* 16, 252
Director's port 233
Discount for quantity 34
"Dock" Glass 242
Doktor (Bernkasteler) 119, 120, 125
Dolcetto (grape variety) 207, **209**
Dolin 79
Dolomites 132
*Dom* 118
Dom Ruinart 70
Domaine-bottling 22–3, **88**, 100
Domaine de Chevalier 98 (white), 182 (red)
Domaine de Courcel 196
Domaine de l'Eglise 185
Domaine de Mont-Redon 202
Domaine de la Nerthe 202
Domaine de Varoilles 190
Domaine du Cléray 100
Domaine Ott 204
Domaine Suremain 197
Domaine Tempier 204
Domdechaney (Hockheimer) 124
Domestica 160
Dom Pérignon **62**, 232
Dom Pérignon (Moët et Chandon) 69
Domprobst (Graacher) 120
Domtal, Niersteiner 124
Dopff 104
Dopff & Irion 104
Dordogne, river 80, 99, 168, 174, 183, 184, 185, **204**, 246
Dorin 144
*Dosage* **64**
Douro, river (in Spanish, Duero) 24, 139, **140** (white), **219** (red), **232–4** (port)
Dow 237

Drake, Sir Francis 48
Drayton's 227
Drouhin, Joseph 191
Drouhin-Laroze 191
Dry (sherry) **55**
Dry Fly 55
Dry Sack 55
Dryness and sweetness **83**
Dublin 168
Dubonnet **81**
Duke of Wellington 139
Dumas, Alexandre 93
Dumay, Charlotte 195
Durance, river 106
Durkheimer-Fuerberg 128
Dürnstein 145


E

E.E.C. 22
Eastern Europe *See* Europe, Eastern
East India sherry 57
Eau-de-vie 66, 80
Ebro, river 141, 216, 217
Echezeaux 192
*Edelfaul* 242
*Edelzwicker* 104
Eden 138
Eden Valley 158
Edenkoben 127
Edinburgh 168
Edward I, King of England
Eel, smoked 43
Eger 148
Eggs **43**, 241
Egon-Müller 117
*Egrappoir* 170
Egri Bikaver 221
Egypt, ancient 13
Ehrenfels, Schloss 121
Ehrmann's 27
*Einzellage* **114**, 119, 120, 12
*Eiswein* 248
Eitelsbach 118
Eitelsbacher Karthäuserhofberg 118
Elba, Isle of **133**
Eleanor of Aquitaine, Quee 16
Elizabetha 55
Elliot's 227
Eltville 121, **123**, 124
Eltz, Count 123
Emerald Riesling (grape variety) **155**
Emilia-Romagna **132**
Empire wines 241
*En primeur* 26, **199** (Beaujolais), 202
*Encyclopaedia of Wine* 60
England, wine-growing in 15, 16
Enkirch 121
Entre-Deux-Mers **99**, 169
Epenots (Pommard) 196
Epenottes, Les (Beaune) 19
Epernay 62, 66, 71, 253
Epernon, Duc d' 178
Erbach 121, **123**
Erden 121
Ermida 140

ntebringer, Johannisberger
 122
zeugerabfüllung 115, 116
scalope de veau à la tante Nini
 89
scenzia **249**
schbach 127
schbacher Herrlich 127
scherndorf 128
spumoso 75
st Est Est 130, **135**
state-bottling (California)
 153
state-bottling (Germany)
 22, 110, 116
storil 139, 140
Estournelle 174
stremadura **220**
stufas 76, 77
tna, Mount 136, 215
uganean hills 133
urope, Eastern 19, **146–50**
 (white), 146–8 (Hungary),
 148–9 (Yugoslavia), 149–50
 (the Black Sea), **164** (rosé),
 **221–2** (red), 248–50
 (Tokay)
vel 219
xcise duty 18, 60
zerjo, Mori 148

alernum **134**
alkenberg 119
allacy, Scenic 131
aller 104
alstaff, Sir John 48, 241
ederal State, the German, as
 proprietors of vineyards
 116
elsenberg 125
endant 143
endant de Sion 143
eria (at Jerez) **49**
ermentation **11–12, 50**
 (sherry), 62 (champagne),
 66, 73, 83, 159, **170**
 (Bordeaux), 203 (maceration
 carbonique), 213 (Chianti),
 **230–1**, 232 (port), 236,
 242, 243
ermentation, tumultuous 50
ernet Branca **81**
errara 131
errari (motor car) 210
erreira 219
erreirinha 219
èves, Les (Beaune) 195
iltering vintage port before
 drinking 233
inage 191
ine wine defined 24
inger Lakes 156 (red), 165
 (rosé)
ino (sherry) 21, **51–2, 55**, 56,
 57, 58
iorina, Franco 208
irst-growth, meaning of **171**
ish 41, **43–4**, 95, 100
ixin **189**
lagey-Echezeaux 192

Flambeau d'Alsace 104
Fleurie 199
Floirac 187
Flor **51–2**, 58, 59, 78
Florence 133, 211, 213, 214
Florio 240
Foie gras 103, 244
Folle Blanche (grape variety)
 155
Fonduta 209
Fonseca, José-Maria 140, 220,
 221
Fontanafredda 208
Food with wine **35–6**, 36 (in
 a restaurant), **41–5**, 57
 (with sherry), 70 (with
 champagne), 94 (with
 white burgundy), 100
 (with Muscadet), 103 (with
 Alsace wines), 105 (with
 Rhône wine), 110 (with
 German wines), 128 (with
 Steinwein), 138 (with vinho
 verde), 161–2 (with rosé),
 166 (with red wines), 187
 (with claret), 190 (with
 Chambertin), 197 (with
 Volnay), 200 (with
 Beaujolais), 209 (with
 Italian wine), 214 (with
 Chianti), 221 (with
 Portuguese red wine), 230,
 231 (with sweet wines),
 237 (with port), 239 (with
 Madeira), 244 (with
 Château d'Yquem), 249
 (with Tokay), 254 (with
 sweet sparkling wine)
Forastera 136
Formal dinners **41–2**
Forst 127
Forster Jesuitgarten 127
Forster Mariengarten 128
Forster Schnepfenflüg 128
Fortification 11, 12, 53
 (sherry), **77** (Madeira), 159
 (South African laws about),
 232 (port), 251 (Setúbal)
Fortified wine **11–12**, 78.
 See also under port, sherry,
 etc.
Forts de Latour, Les 176
Fourchaume, La (Chablis) 88
Fournier, Charles 156
"Foxiness" 156
France 10 (treading of
 grapes) 12–13 (origins of
 wine-growing in), 14
 (establishment of regional
 types in), 15 (phylloxera
 in), 16 (English possessions
 in), 16–17 (Anglo-French
 relations strained), 18
 (attitude to wine of), 19
 (wine consumption
 figures), 21–2 (laws of
 Appellation Contrôlée in),
 23 (vin ordinaire and vin de
 pays), 24 (great wine in),
 27 (vin de l'annee in), 29
 (taste in white wine of),
 34 (lack of cellars in),

60–73 (sparkling wines of),
 71 (champagne consump-
 tion in), **79–81** (aperitifs
 in), **82–108** (white table
 wines of), 109 (wine laws
 of France and Germany
 compared), 130 (wine-
 industries of France and
 Italy compared), 151
 (California and France
 compared), **161–3** (rosé
 wines of), **167–207** (red
 wines of), 215 (cheap wines
 of France and Spain
 compared), 218 (cheap
 wines of France and
 Portugal compared), 223
 (France and California
 compared), 237 (port
 drinking in), **242–7** (light
 sweet wines of), 251
 (Muscat wines of), 253
 (vin de paille in), 253
 (sweet sparkling wine of).
 See also under regional
 names
France, the south of **106–7**,
 **203–4**, 251
Franco-Espanolas, Bodegas
 217
Franco-Prussian War 103
Franconia 111, **128**
Frank, Dr Konstantin **156**
Franschhoek 159
Franzia 152
Frascati **133–4**, 135
Fraud **21**
Frecciarossa **210**
Frédéric Barberousse 206
Freemark Abbey 154
Freiburg 111
Freisa 207
French Revolution, the
 168
Frescobaldis 214
Fresno 151
Freundstück 128
Frexenet 75
Friedrich of Prussia, Prince
 123
Friedrich Wilhelm
 Gymnasium 118
Friuli 131, **132**, 212
Frizzante 136
Froccs 147
Froissart's Chronicle 16
Fronsac 186
Frontignac **251**
Frontignan **251**
Frost 30, 248
Fruit, fresh 45, 231, 253
Fruit salad 45
Fruska Gora, mountains 148
Fry, Christopher 177
Fugger, Bishop 135
Fuissé 95
Fuissé, Château de 95
Fukier 248
Full, old pale (sherry) 54
Fumane 211
Fumé Blanc 155
Furmint 147, **249**

**G**
Gaeiras 140
Gaillac **107**
Galicia 141
Gallo, E. & J., of Modesto
 152
Gamay (grape variety) 165,
 196, 225
Gamay Noir (grape variety)
 225
Game **45**, 201, 202, 214
Gamza (grape variety) 222
Gancia 74
Gard (département) 107
Garda, Lake 131, 132, 163,
 209, 211
Garibaldi 240
Garonne, river 99, 168, 169
 187, 243
Garrafeira 140, 220
Garvey 55
Gattinara 207, **209**
Gaudichots, les (Vosne-
 Romanée) 192
Gavi 131
Gebiet 113
Gebietsweinprämierung 116
Gehrn (Rauenthaler) 124
Geisenheim 121, **122**
Gelin 190
"Generic" names 152
Geneva, Lake of 143, 144
Genevrières, Les (Meursault)
 91
Genoa 131
George (Australian sherry) 59
Georgia 150, 222
Georgics, Virgil's 134
Gérant 169
Germany 12 (addition of
 sugar to wine), 13 (origins
 of wine in), 19, 20 (decline
 in quality of wine), 22,
 23–4 (wine terms), 27 (very
 old German wine), 31
 (German and English taste
 compared), 74 (sparkling
 wines), **108–28** (white
 wines), 110 (German wine
 with food), 111 ("commer-
 cial" wine of), 112 (wine-
 growing conditions in),
 **113–16** (wine-laws and
 labels of), 143, 145, 146,
 147 (comparison with
 Hungarian wine), 151
 (comparison with
 Californian wine), 159
 (comparison with South
 African wine), **164** (rosé),
 166 (red), 221, 231, 242,
 **247–8** (sweet wines of)
Gerumpel, Rechbächel and
 (Wachenheimer) 127
Gevrey 86, 189
Gevrey-Chambertin 36, 86,
 180, **189–90**, 226
Gewürztraminer (grape
 variety) **104**
 (Alsace), 127, **155**
 (California), 156
Ghemme **209**

Gibraltar 48, 241
Gigondas **202**
Gilbeys 173
Gilly 86
Gilly-les-Vougeot 86
Gimmeldinger Meerspinne 128
Gironde (*département*) 169, 186
Gironde, river 173, 186
Givry 94, 198
Gladstone, W.E. 18, 173
Glarentsa 239
Glasses **38–9** (best shape of),
  57 (sherry), 71 (champagne)
Glycerine 244
Göcklingen 127
Göcklinger K.L. 127
Goldbachel, Wachenheimer
  127
Golden Age of wine **18**, 20
Golden Guinea 72
Golden (sherry) 54, **56**
Goldtröpfchen (Piesporter)
  119
Golfe de Lyon 107
Gonzales Byass 51, 55
"Good" wine defined **23–4**
Goose 45, 103
*Gonci* 249
Gorizia 212
Gout de terroir 132
Goutte d'Or, La (Meursault)
  91
*Governo* 213
Graach 119, **120**
Graacher Himmelreich 120
Graben 114
Graben, Bernkasteler 114
Grafenberg (Kiedricher) 123
Grafting of vines 15
Grainhubel (Deidesheimer)
  127
Graham 237
Gramp's 157, 227
Grand Canyon 234
*Grand cru* 87, 88, 89, 172, 190,
  191, 192, 199
*Grand cru classé* 172, 184
*Grand cru* defined 87, 89
Grand Siècle 70
*Grand vin d'Alsace* 104
Grande, La Rue (Vosne-
  Romanée) 192
Grandfather, Penfold's 237
Grandjo 140
Grands Echezeaux 192
Grange aux Ceps 253
Grange Hermitage, Penfold's
  157
Grão Vasco (Portuguese
  painter) 219
Grape varieties, *See names*,
  Riesling, etc.
Grapefruit 42
Grape-sugar 10, 12, 242, 243
Graves 44, 47, **97–8** (white),
  169, 171, **181–2** (red), 186,
  243, 246
Graves de Vayres 186
Graves-St-Emilion 183
Graves Supérieures 97
Gravières, Les (Santenay) 197
Great Western (New York

"champagne") 156, 227
Great Western, winery 228
Great wine 20, **23–4** (defined),
  187
Greece 13 (ancient), 48, 81
  (aperitif of), **160** (white
  wines of), 206, 239, 250,
  252
Green Label, Deinhard's 112
Gregor, Father 212
Grenache 165
Grenouilles, Les (Chablis) 88
Grèves, Les (Beaune) 195
Grey Riesling (grape variety)
  155
Griffith 157
Griffith winery 228
Grignolino (grape variety)
  207, **209**, 225
Grinzing 144
Griotte (and Chambertin) 190
Gris de Boulaouane 206
Grk 149
Gros Plant (grape variety) **100**
*Grosslage* 113, 114, 117, 118,
  119, 120, 121, 122, 123,
  124, 127, 128
*Grottas* 134
Grottaferrata 134
Grouse 45
Grozden 149
Grumello **209**
Grüner Veltliner 144
Guadalete, river 48
Guadalquivir, river 55
Guide Michelin 216
Guigonne de Salins 194
Guild 152
Guinea-fowl 45
Gumpoldskirchen **145**, 146
Gun-flint 101
Guntersblum 125
Gunterslay 119
Gurdjani 150

**H**

Haardt Mts 126
Habisham, Mr 77
Hail 30
Halasczarda 249
Halasz, Zoltan 148
Half-bottles, usefulness of 36
Hallgarten 121, **123**
Hallgarten, Fritz 242
Hallgarten's Blackfriars 112
Ham, wines to drink with **44**,
  94
Hambach 127
*Hamlet* 24
Hammondsport 156
Hanns Christoff Wein,
  Deinhard's 112
Hanzell winery 154
Hapsburg court 248, 250
Hardy's 227
Haro **216–17**
Harslevelu 147, 148, 250
Hasensprung, Winkeler 122
Hattenheim 121, **123**
Haut-Médoc 172, 173, **174**,
  181, 195

Haute-Savoie 106
Hautes Côtes de Beaune 196
Hautes Côtes de Nuits, Vin
  Fin des 196
Hautvillers, Abbey of 62
Healy, Maurice 181
Hearty Burgundy 152
Heidelberg 111
Heidsieck, Charles 69
Heidsieck Dry Monopole 69
Heidsieck Monopole's
  Diamant Bleu 70
Heiligenberg 123
Heitz, Joe 224
Heitz winery 154
Henriot 69
Henriques & Henriques 77
Henry II, King of England 16
*Henry V* 84
Henry the Navigator, Prince
  76
Hérault (*département*) 107
Hermannsberg 126
Hermannshöhle
  (Niedehausen) 126
Hermitage **105** (white), 106,
  200, **201** (red)
Hermitage (Australian) 226
Hermitage (South African)
  228, 238
Hermitage (Swiss) 143
Herrenberger, Krup and 117
Hesse, State of 124
*Heurige* 144
Himmelreich (Graacher) 120
Himmelreich (Zeltinger) 120
Hipping (Niersteiner) 124
Hirondelle 146
Ho Bryan 17
Hockheim 110, **124**
Hock 24, 44, **110**, 124, 231.
  *See also*, Rhine wine
Hogarth 242
Hohenmorgen
  (Deidesheimer) 128
Hollis 226
Hook of Holland, the 169
*Hors d'oeuvre* **42**
Hospices de Beaune **194**, 195
Hot-house grapes 250
Hugel 104
Humagne 143
Hungary 24, 44, 47, 145,
  **146–8** (white), **164** (rosé),
  **221** (red), 242, **248–50**
  (Tokay)
Hunsrück 125
Hunter Burgundy 227
Hunter valley 157, 226
Hutte (Serriges) 114
Hyams, Edward 16, 252
Hyères 106

**I**

Ice-buckets 38
Ice-cream 45, 254
Ice-wine (*Eiswein*) 248
Ihringer 111
Ilbesheim 127
Ile des Vergelesses 194
Illats 246

Imperial Vinicola 221
Inferno **209**
Ingham Whittaker 240
Inocente vineyard (sherry)
Inocente, Valdespino's 55
Investment, wine as 20, 23
  248
Iphofen 128
Irancy 189
Irouléguy 206
Irroy 69
Ischia **136**
Islam 160, 206
Israel **160–1** (rosé)
Italia (Marsala) 240
Italian Swiss Colony 152
Italy 10 (grapes trodden in
  13 (the vine comes to),
  21 (wine laws in), 23 (w
  pasteurized in), 24 (grea
  wines made in), 35, 44,
  **73–4** (sparkling wines of
  **79–81** (aperitifs and
  vermouths of), **129–36**
  (white wines of), 130
  (French and Italian wine
  compared), 143, **163–4**
  (rosé), **207–15** (red wine
  of), 225 (Italian-style wi
  made in California), 250
  (Moscato), 252, 253
  (*passiti*), 254 (Asti
  Spumante)

**J**

Jadot 195
James, Walter 237
Jasnières **102**
Jerez de la Frontera 24, **48–**
  50, 51, 53, 56, 58, 59, 24
Jesuitgarten (Forster) 127
Johannisberg 114, 121, **122**
Johannisberg Riesling (gra
  variety) (California) 154
Johannisberg, Schloss **122**,
  124, 248
Johannisberg (South Africa
  159
Johannisberg (Swiss) 143
Johnson, Dr Samuel 201
Josephshof (Graacher) 120
Josmeyer 104
Juffer, Brauneberger 119
Jug wine 151
Juliénas 199, 200
Juliusspital, the 128
Jungfer (Hallgartener) 123
Jura 45, 78, 85, **107–8** (whi
  155, **163** (rosé), **205–6** (re
  253
Jurançon **107**
Justina 140

**K**

K.W.V. Kooperativ
  Wijnbouwers Vereenigi
  59, 159
*Kabinett* 115
Kadarka 221, 222
Kahlenberg 125, 144

Kaiser Stuhl winery 158, 165, 227
Kaiserstuhl **111**
Kalimna, Penfold's 227
Kalkhofen 128
Kallstadt 127
Kallstadter Kobnert 128
Kalokhorio 241
Kalterersee 212
Kapela 148
Karthäuserhofberg, Eitelsbacher 118
Kasel 118
Kayserberg-Kientzheim 104
Keknyelu 148
Keo **241**
Kerner (grape variety) 127
Kesselstatt, von 120
Kesten 119
Keuka, Lake 156
Kiedrich 121, **123**
Kinheim 121
Kirchenstück 124, 127
Kitterlé, Schlumberger's 104
Kloster Eberbach **123**
Kloster Liebfrauenberg 127
Klosterberg 117
Klosterkeller 222
Klusserather St Michael 118
Knights of the Temple 241
Koblenz 111
Kobnert, Kallstadter 128
Königin Viktoria Berg (Hockheimer) 124
*Konsumwein* 23, 111
Koran, the 160
Korbel winery 75
Korcula 149
Kremlin, the 249
Krems 145
Kreuz (Oppenheimer) 125
Kreuznach **125**, 126
Kriter 73
Kröv 121
Krug 65, 69, 95
Krug, Charles 154, 155
Kues 119
Kupfergrübe (Schloss-böckelheim) 125
Kupp (Ayler) 117

**L**
Labarde 181
Lachenheimer Schenkenbohl 125
Lachryma Christi 130, **136** (white), **214** (red)
La Clape 107
Ladoix-Serrigny 193
*Lagar* 49, 50, 235
*Lagen* 114
Lagoa **78**, 140
Lago di Caldaro **212**
Lagrein **212**
Lagrein Dunkel 212
Lagrein Rosato **164**, 212
Lagrima 241
Laguiche, Marquis de 93
La Ina, Pedro Domecq's 55

Laira, Eric Brand's 227
Lake Caldaro 212
Lake's Folly 227
La Lagune 181
Lalande de Pomerol **186**
La Mancha 142, 218
Lamarque **179**
Lamb 41, **44**, 197
Lamberti 211
Lambrusco di Sorbara 132, **210**
Lamothe 175
Lancaster, Osbert 239
Lancers (Portuguese rosé) 164
Landshut (ruined castle) 119
Langenbach 112
Langenlonsheim 126
Langenstück 124
Langhe hills, the 209
Langhorne Creek 227
Langoiran 246
Langon 243
Langoustine 100
Lanson 69
La Rioja Alta 217
La Riva 55
*Last Judgment*, Van der Weyden's 194
Late-bottled vintage (port) 234
Latour-Martillac 97
Latresne 187
Latricière (Chambertin) 190
Laubenheim 126
Lauerburg estate 119
Lausanne 143, 144
Lavaux **144**
Laws relating to wine 21, 237. *See also under Appellation Contrôlée*
Lay 119
Laying-down wine 27, 33 (financial advantage), **34** (cellar conditions needed), 185, 200, **219**, **233** (port), 248
Layon 155
Layon, Coteaux de **102**
Leacock 77
Leanyka (grape variety) 148
Le Cromagnon (hotel) 246
Leinhohle (Deidesheimer) 128
Leinsweiler 127
Leith 169
Lemon 42
Lenchan (Oestricher) 123
Léognan 97, **182**
Le Pian 181
Les Eyzies 246
Le Taillan **181**
*Levante*, the 49
Lexia, McWilliams's 157
Leybourne 185
Leyburne, Sir Roger de 185
Lezirão 140
Libourne 185
Lichine, Alexis 180
Liebfrauenkirche 112
Liebfrauenstiftswein 112
Liebfraumilch 24, **111**, **112**, 124, 147, 149
Light sweet wines **242–50**

Liguria **131**
Lillet 79, **81**
Limassol 241
Limousin oak 154
Limoux, Blanquette de **73**, 107 (blanc de blancs)
Lindeman's 165, 227
Lindos 160
Liqueurs 237, 252
Liquor, hard 46
Lirac **202**
Lisbon 139, 220, 251
Listan (grape variety) 50
Listel 107
Listrac 172, **179**
Liver 45, 201
Livermore valley 153, 154
Lobster 36, 100, 244
Lodges, port **236**
Loir, river 102
Loire, river 102, 206
Loire, Coteaux de la 102
Loire wines 47, 61, **72** (sparkling), **99–102** (white), 153, **162** (rosé), **205** (red), 218, 252
Lombardy 163, **209–10** (red), 253
London 19 (wine-trade in), 27, 75, 144, 157, 171, 218
Longuicher Probstberg 118
Lopez Heredia 142, 217
Lorch 122
Lormont 187
Lorraine 206
Los Angeles 150
Louis XIV, King of France 17
Louis XVI, King of France 168
Louis Roederer 69
Loupiac 99, 245
Lourmarin 107
Low Countries 181
Lubéron, Côtes de **107**
Ludon **181**
Ludwig, King of Bavaria 27
Lump (Escherndorfer) 128
Lunel **251**
Lupo, Val di 136, 215
Lur Saluces, Marquis de 244
Lussac 185
Lutomer 148, 149
Luxembourg 110, 116
Lyons 26, **85**, 198

**M**
Macaroons 254
Macau 181
Macedonia **149**
*Maceration carbonique* 203
MacKenzie 237
McWilliams 157, 227
Mâcon 85, **94**, **198**
Mâcon Blanc **94**
Mâcon Supérieur **94**
Madagascar 245
Maddalena 212
Madeira 17, 27, 43, 46, **75–7**, 230, 231, **238–9**
Madrid 142, 217, 218
Maggiore, Lake 208, 209
Magill 227

Magyar 164 (wine brand), 249
Main, river 27, 110, 111, 124, 128
Mainz 121, 124
Maipo, Chile 228, 229
Maikammer 127
Mailberg 145
Maire, Henri 205
*Maisons (de Champagne)* 62
*Maître de chai* 169
Malaga 231, 240, **241**
Malartic-Lagravière 97, 182
Malbec 223
Malconsorts, Aux (Vosne-Romanée) 192
Malligo sack 241
Malmsey 26, 48, 57, 76, 77, **239**
Maltroie, La (Chassagne-Montrachet) 197
Malvasia 239
Malvasier 212
Malvoisie (Swiss) 143
Manchester 242
Manhattan (cocktail) 80
Mannberg (Hattenheimer) 123
Manzanilla **55–6**, 57
Marano 211
*Marc* 66, 170
Marcobrunn (Erbacher) 123
Marconnets, Les (Beaune) 195
Margaux 173, **180–1**, 195, 205
Marino 134
Market Street, Manchester 242
Markobrunn (Erbacher) 123
Marmoross Sergardi 214
Marne, river 61, 62, 63
Marnebour 206
Marsala 43, 231, 239, **240–1**
*Marsala al'uovo* 241
Marsannay **163**
Marsanne (grape variety) 143, 158 (Rhône), 228
Marseilles 106, 162, 204
Martillac **183**
Martin, Henri 179
Martini, dry 79
Martini, Louis 154, 224
Martinsthal 124
Marx, Karl 118
Maryland **165**
Mascarello, Guilio 208
Maserati (motor car) 210
Massandra 252
Massif Central 218
Masson, Paul 75, 154, 224, 225, 238
Mastroberardino 136
Mataró 141
Mateus Rosé 140, 164, 219
Mattheisbildchen 114, 119
Maturing, artificial 20
Maturing, the process of **25–8**. *See also under Ageing wine*
Matuschka-Greiffenclau, Count 122
Mavrud (grape variety) 222
Maximin Grünhaus 118

Mazis (Chambertin) 190
McKenzie, Barry 158
Meat, wine with **44**
Medici 212
Medicinal benefits of wine 19
Mediterranean 44 (fish of),
    48, 74, 105, 208, 250
Mediterranean, white wines
    of the eastern **160**
Médoc 16, **98** (white wines),
    169, 171, **173–82** (red
    wines), 183, 184, 185, 186,
    223
Melbourne 228
Melon 42
Mendocino 151
Mendoza 229
Merano 132
Mercier 69
Mercurey **94** (white), 198
    (red)
Mérignac 82
Merlot (grape variety) 183,
    212, 221, 223, 224
Mertesdorf 118
Messias 220
Metala 227
*Méthode champenoise* 62–5, 72,
    73, 75
Mettenheim 125
Metternich, Prince 122
Meursault 85, 90, **91**, 96,
    195, 197
Micro-climates **31**
Middle Ages, the **16**, 26, 217,
    243
Middle Moselle **118–20**
Midi **203**, 206, 213
Milan 80 (and origin of
    Punt e Mes), 132, 207
Mildara 59, 227
Milk (sherry) **56**
Minervois **203**
Minho 138, 140, 219
Ministry of Food, the 56
Mint sauce 44
Mirabelle Restaurant,
    London 182
Mirassou 155, 224
*Mis en bouteilles à la propriété*
    23
*Mis en bouteilles au château*
    22
*Mise au(du) domaine* 23
*Mise en bouteille au domaine*
    23
*Mise en bouteille dans nos caves*
    23
Misket (grape variety) 150
Mitans, Les 85
Mitford, Nancy 29
Mittelhaardt **126–7**
Mittelheim 121, 122
Mobilette 91
Modena 132
Möet & Chandon 69
Moldavia 149, 222
Mommessin, Jean 190
Monbazillac **246**
Monção 142
Monção, Vinhos de 139
Mondavi, Robert 155

Monferrato hills 208
Monemvasia 239
Moniga 163
Moniga del Garda 163
Mont Damnés, Les (Sancerre)
    101
Montagne 185
Montagny **94**
Montalcino, Brunello di **214**
Montée de Tonnerre
    (Chablis) 88
Montefiascone 135
Montepaldi 214
Monteporzio Catone 134
Monterey Bay 152, 224
Montesquieu 98
Monthélie 197
Montilla 56, **57–8**
Montlouis **102**
Montrachet 29, 85, 87, 90,
    **91–4** (white), 93 (and
    food), 192, 193, 197 (red),
    246 (how to serve)
Montreux 143
Monts de Milieu 88
Moors in Spain 48, 216
Mor **148**
Morey-St-Denis 90 (white),
    **190** (red)
Morgon 199
Morgeot (Chassagne-
    Montrachet) 197
Morocco **206**
Morris's Liqueur Muscat 252
Morvan 85
*Moscato* 250
Moscato (grape variety) 130,
    250, 253
Moscow 190
Mosel-Saar-Ruwer 113
Moselblümchen 112
Moselle 19, 24, 43, 44, **74**
    (sparkling), 91, **101–11**,
    112, 113, **116–17**, **118–21**,
    148, 234, 247
Moselle, sparkling 74
Moser, Lenz **145**, 146
*Mosto* 50
Moulin-à-Vent 199, 200
Moulin des Carruades 176
Moulis 172, **179**
Mount Gambier 226
Moussec **75**
*Mousseux* 70
Mouton-Cadet *See* Châteaux
    Mouton-Cadet
Moyston 228
Mukuzani 222
Müller-Thurgau (grape
    variety) 121, 124, 127
Mumm 69
Münster-Sarmsheim 126
Munsterer 126
Muratie Claret 228
Mure 104
Murfatlar 149
Murgers, Aux (Nuits-St-
    Georges) 193
Muri-Gries 212
Murio-muscat (grape variety)
    127
Murrieta, Marques de 217

Murrumbidgee 157
Muscadel 250
Muscadelle (grape variety)
    246
Muscadet 26, 43 (with *hors
    d'oeuvre*), 44, **100**
Muscadine 250
Muscat (grape variety) 74,
    **104** (d'Alsace), 128, 246,
    **250–3**
Muscat Ottonel 149
Muscatel 45, 231, 241, 250
Musigny 86, 90 (white),
    **191–2** (red), 193
Musk 250
Mussels 100
Muted wine 78, 102

**N**
Nackenheim **124**
Nahe, river 111, **125–6**
Najera 216
Nantes 99, 100
Napa valley 151, 180, **222–3**,
    224
Naples 134, 136
Napoleon 13, 123, 190
    (campaigning with
    Chambertin)
Narbonne 203
Navarre 141, 216, 218
Néac 186
Nebbiolo (grape variety) 130,
    207, 208
Neckar, river 111
Nedeberg 159, 228
Neef 121
*Négociant* 170, 171, 191, 194,
    195, 199, 226
Negrar 211
Negri de Purkar 222
Negri, Nino 163, 209
Nelson, Lord 239
Nenin 185
Neuchâtel 143, 164
Neumagen 121
Neusiedler *See* 145
Neustadt 126
Nevers oak, used in making
    barrels 154
New Orleans 169
New South Wales 157, 226
New World, the **14–21**. *See
    also under* Australia,
    California, etc.
New York 19, 27, 28
New York State 75
    (sparkling), 150, **156**
    (white), **165** (rosé)
Nice 204
Nieder-walluf 124
Niederhausen **126**
Nierstein **124**
Niersteiner Domtal 124
Niersteiner Gutes Domtal 124
Nipozzano 214
Nizza Monferrato 208
Noble rot 142, 156, **242**
Noilly Prat **79**
Nomenclature of wine **20–1**,
    **23–4**, **85–8** (Burgundy),

109, **113–14**, 153. *See also
    under* Appellation
    Contrôlée
Nonnenberg 120, 124
Nonnenberg Wehlener 120
Non-vintage champagne **67**,
North Africa 23, 60, 74, **200**,
    250
Noto **252**
Novara 208, 209
Nuits, Côte de **89–90**
Nuits-St-Georges 22, 85,
    **89–90** (white), **192–3** (red)
Nüssbrunnen (Hattenheim)
    123
Nüssdorf 144
Nuts 57, 231, 241

**O**
Oberemmel 117
Oberotweiler 111
Ober-walluf 124
Ockfen 117
Odysseus 136
Oechsle scale in German
    classification 109, 112, **115**
Oeil de Perdrix 72, 161
Oestrich 121, **123**
Offley 237
Oja, river 216
Old Full Pale (sherry) 54, 56
Oliena 215
Olive oil, used as a stopper 2
Olives 254
Oloroso 21, 49, 51, **52**, 53,
    240, 241
Oltrepo Pavese 210
Omelette, wines with 43, 20
Oporto 138, 219, **236**
Oppenheim 124, 127
Orange, France 202
Orange (fruit) 42
Ordinary wine defined **23**
Oregon 150
Orfevi 133
Orléans 101
Orvieto 24, **134** (white), 149
    214 (red)
Ouzo **81**
Oxygen 25
Oysters **43**, 99, 100

**P**
P.X. *See* Pedro Ximenez
Paarl 159
Paarlsack 59
Pabstmann 124
Paceta, Viña 217
Pacific Ocean 224
Paella **43**
Palacio, Bodegas 217
Palacio Seteais Hotel 220
Palatinate 110, **126–8**, 248
Palermo 136, 215
Palette **204**
*Palma* 51
Palmela 220
Palo Cortado **52**
Palomino (grape variety) 49,
    58, 158

nades **141**, **218**
ndo 55
ntelleria **252**
pal palace 136
ris 26, 85, 89, 91, 101, 144, 171, 198, 206
rempuyre **181**
rma 132
rmesan 45
rtinico 240
rs Iniqua 240
rsac (St-Emilion) 185
rtridge 45, 214
sse-Tout-Grains **196**
assito (vino passito) 253
asta **43**
asteur, Louis 12
asteurization of wine, 23, 35, 135
astis **81**
atache d'Aux 173
âté **42**
âté de foie gras 103
atent aperitifs 79, **81**
aternina, Federico 217
atrimonio 207
au 107
auillac 172, 173, **175–80**, 243
aulinshofberg (Kestener) 119
avia **131**, 210 (Pavese district)
axarete 54
eaches 45, 102, 138, 231, 244
ears 45, 138
écharmant 204
edro Domecq 55
edro Ximenez (grape variety) **54**, 58, 241
eloponnese Islands 239
elure d'oignan 161
endeli 160
enfold's 157, 227, 237
enning-Rowsell, Sir Edmund 185
epys, Samuel 17
erelada 75
eriquita 220
erla 149
ernand-Vergelesses **193**
ernod 79, **81**
erpignan 203
errier Jouet 69
errières, Les (Meursault) 91
ersia, ancient 13
eru 245
erugia 214
essac 97, 182 (red)
este, Dr 195
etit Chablis **88**
etermichl 145
etrurbani 135
ettenthal 124
ewsey Vale 158
falz 126. See also Palatinate
farrgut St Michael 120
heasant 41, 197
hilip the Good, Duke of Burgundy 194
hylloxera **14**, 15, 18, 21, 76, 203, 217, 220
iacenza 132
ichon-Lalande 181

Picnics 43, 163
Piedmont 130, **131** (white), 207–8, 214, 225, 253
Piesport **119**
Piesporter Michelsberg 119
Pineau des Charentes **79**
Pinhao 234
Pink champagne 70, 205
Pinotage (grape variety) 228
Pinot Blanc (grape variety) 127, 132, 155
Pinot Chardonnay (grape variety) 149, 152, **153**, 154
Pinot Grigio (grape variety) 132
Pinot Gris (grape variety) **104**, 132
Pinot Noir (grape variety) 101, 104, 133, 149, 152, 189, 196, 212, 221, 224 (California), 229 (Chile)
Pinto Bisto, J. F. do 221
Piper Heidsieck 69
Pizza **43**
Planalto 140
Plavac 221
Pleasant Valley Wine Company 156
Plettenberg, von 126
Po, valley 132, 210
Podensac 246
Poitiers 206
Poland 147, 248
Pol Roger 62, 69
Pomal, Viña 217
Pomerol **172**, 183, 184, **185–6**, 226
Pommard 85, 86, 193, 196
Pommery & Greno 69, 70
Pontanevaux 200
Po, river 132
Pork **44**, 102
Porrets, Les (Nuits-St-Georges) 193
Port 11, **17**, 19, 21, 46, 75, **77** (white), 200, 231, **231–8**, 239, 251
Port, vintage 32, 34, 233, 234
Port-type wines 237–8
Portici 136
Portofino 131
Portugal 10, 17, 21, 23, 24, 35, 45, 47, 76, 78, 108, **137–40** (white), 142, 147, 159, 165 (rosé), **218–21** (red), 250, 251. See also under Port
Poruzot, Le (Meursault) 91
Postup **221**
Potenza 136, 215
Pouilly-Fuissé 85, **95–6**, 100
Pouilly-Fumé 85, **100–1**, 108
Pouilly-Loché **96**
Pouilly-sur-loire 100
Pouilly-Vinzelles **96**
Poulsard 163
Pourriture noble 242, 243
Prädikatswein 115
Praliné 231
Prawns 43
Préignac 244, **245**
Preiss Zimmer 104

Prémaux 193
Premier cru (Burgundy) **87**, 195, 196
Premières Côtes de Bordeaux 169, **245–6**
Pressing **10**, 50, 243
Preuses, Les (Chablis) 88
Price of wine 18, 20, 28, **32**, 190, 205
Prohibition 18, 150
Prosecco **131**
Provence 13, 72, 105, **106**, **162**, 202, 203, 219
Provence, Côtes de 106 (white), **162** (rosé), 204 (red)
Pruliers, Les (Nuits-St-Georges) 193
Prüm, the Family 120
Prussia, Prince Friedrich of 123
Pucelles, Les 93
Puerto de Santa Maria 48
Puglia **214**, 215
Puisseguin 185
Puligny 93
Puligny-Montrachet 92, **93**, 94, 197
Punt e Mes **80**
Pupitres 64, 68
Pusterla (of Brescia) 131
Puttonyos 249
Pyramide Restaurant 105
Pyrenees, the 168, 203, 218, 251

**Q**
Quail 45
Qualitätswein bestimmter Anbaugebeite 115
Qualitätswein mit prädikat 115
Quality, control of by law 21
Quantity to serve 71 (champagne), 251 (after dinner)
Quarts de Chaume **102**
Queltaler Hock 157
Quiche Lorraine 43
Quick-maturing wines **26**
Quincy 100
Quinine aperitifs **80**
Quinsac 187
Quinta **234**
Quinta d'Aguieira 220
Quinta da Barão 139
Quinta da Roeda 234

**R**
R.D. See récemment dégorgé
Radishes 42
Rainwater **77**
Ramage-la-Batisse 175
Ramisco (grape variety) 220
Randersacker 128
Ranina Radgona Spätlese 149
Raspberries 45, 200, 239
Ratafia **79**
Rauenthal 121, **124**
Ravello **136**, 164, 215
Ravello Rosso **215**

Ray, Cyril 136, 211
Rayas, O. 51
Read, Jan 218
Realeza 140
Récemment dégorgé 70
Rechbächel 127
Recioto **211**
Red table wines 25 (maturing of), **28**, 37–8, 39 (serving of), **166–229**. See under regional names
Refrigeration 151, 159
Regaleali 136, 215
Regency Dry 55
Reggio 132
Rehbach (Niersteiner) 124
Reil 121
Reims 61, 64, 71, 101, 253
Reims, Mountain of 14, 65
Reinhartshausen, Schloss 123
Remoissenet, M 92
Remuage **64**, 75
Renault, Emile 95
Renmark 157
Renski (Rhine) Riesling 148
Reserva **140** (Portuguese) 213 (Chianti), 214, 215 (Rioja), 219 (Dão), 220
Réserve exceptionnelle 103, 104
Restaurants, wine in 32, **36–8** (choosing and sending back), 215, 216, 220
Retsina 160
Reuilly 100, 101
Reynella, Hardy's 227
Rheingau 110, 113, 116, 120, **121–4**, 125, 128, 243, 248
Rheinhessen 113, **124–5**, 126, 248
Rhenish 17, 110
Rhine, river 24, 27, 103, 108, **110**, 111, 117, 121, 122, 123, 124, 125, 126, 127, 128, 143, 234
Rhine Riesling (grape variety) 145, 154, 158
Rhine wine 24, 41, **110**, 112, 121, 143, 152, 164, 247. See also under districts, Alsace, Palatinate, Rheingau, etc.
Rhineland Wineland 243
Rhodes, island of **160**
Rhodt 127
Rhodter Ordensgut 127
Rhône, river **105–7**, 144, 158 (grapes of), 162, **200–2**, 203 (grapes of), 204, 209, 219, 226 (grapes of), 228, 238
Rhône valley, wines of 35, 72 (sparkling), **105–7** (white), **200–2** (red), 207, 219
Ricard **81**
Ricasoli, Barone Bettino 133, 212, 214
Rice 43, 209
Rich (champagne) 254
Richard Coeur de Lion 241
Richard III, King of England 239

Richebourg **192**
Richemone, La (Nuits-St-Georges) 192
Rickmansworth 75
Riesling (grape variety) **104** (Alsace), 111, 120 (Moselle), 127, 128, 132, 144, 145, 147 (Balaton), 150 (Yugoslav), 154 (Johannisberg), **158**, **159** (South Africa), 225
Riesling (wine) 47, **104**, 147, 150, 154, 159, 229 (Chile)
Rinaldi, Francesco 208
Ring, the Great 118
Rioja 75, **141–2** (white), **215–17** (red), 216 (food with), 218
Riquewihr **103**, 104
Riscal, Marques de 217
Risotto 43
Rivera **164**
Riviera, Italian 207
Rivesaltes **251**
*Robe* 205
Röhrendorf 145
Roche-aux-Moines, La- **102**
Rochepot, La 91
Roeda, Quinta da 234
Roederer, Louis 69, 70
Roger, Professor J.R., author of *The Wines of Bordeaux* 176, 245
Rolin, Nicholas 194, 195
Rolls-Royce 244
Romanée 85, 86, 192, 229
Romanée-Conti 42 (1858), 91, **192–3**, 218
Romanée-Conti, Domaine de la 93
Romanée, La **192**
Romanée-St-Vivant, La **192**
Romania **149** (white), 150, **222** (red)
Romanoff 250
Romans, the ancient 13
Rome 18, 133, 134, 135, 164, 211, 252
Romera, Bodegas del 217
Roodeberg 228
Roquefort 45
*Rosato* **164**
Rose Pauillac, La 178
Rosé wine 23, 26 (as quick-maturing wines), 35, 37, 43 (on a picnic), 70, 72 (sparkling), **161–5**, 202, 212, 219, 225
Rosenberg 117, 124
*Rosso* (vermouth) 79
Rothenberg (Nackenheimer) 124
Rothenberg (Rauenthaler) 124
Rothschild, Baron Phillippe de 177, 247
Rothschild, Elie de 31
Rothschild family 175
Rotlay 118
Roton, Vicomte de 245
Rouge Homme, Lindeman's 227

Rousseau 190
Roussillon **203**
*Routiers* 174
Roux, M 202
Rowland Flat 158
Royal Navy, the 240
Rubesco di Torgiano 214
Rubion 225
Ruby port 35, **232**, 233, 237
Ruchottes (Chambertin) 190
Rüdesheim **121**, 122, 125
Rüdesheimer Berg 31, 121
Rüdesheimer Berg Schlossberg 121
Rüdesheimer Burgweg 122
Ruffino 214
Rufina, Chianti 214
Rugiens (Pommard) 196
Ruinart 69, 70
Ruländer (grape variety) 127
Rully **94**
Rum 66, 77
Ruppertsberg 127
Russia 63, 149, 150 (white), **222** (red), 248, 249 (and Tokay today), 252 (after-dinner wines), 253 (Russian tastes). *See also* Soviet Union
Russian Imperial court 248
Russian Information Service 150
Russian Republic 149, 150
Rust 145
Rustenberg 228
Ruster Ausbruch 145
Rutherford, Miles 77
Rutherglen 157, 226, 227, 228, 252
Ruwer, river 111, 117, **118**, 248
Ruzica 164

S
Saar, river 111, **117–18**, 248
Saarburg 117
Sables-St-Emilion 183, 184
Sables, Vins de 107
Sablet 202
Sack 17 (as replacement for claret), 48, 241
Sackträger (Oppenheimer) 125
Sacramento 151
St-Amour 199
St-Amour-Bellevue 96
St-Bris-le-Vineux **89**
St-Chinian 203
Ste-Croix-du-Mont 99, 245
St-Emilion 169, 171 (and 1855 classification), 172, **183–5**, 186, 212, 223
St-Emilion-Royal 184
St-Estèphe 172, 173, **174–5**, 179
Ste-Eulalie 187
Ste-Foy-Bordeaux 187
St-Georges, Les (Nuits-St-Georges) **192–3**
St-Joseph 201
St-Julien 172, 173, **178–9**

St-Laurent 179
St-Martin 127
St-Moritz 209
St-Nikolaus wine 248
St-Péray **72**
St-Pourçain-sur-Sioule **206**
St-Raphaël **81**
St-Saphorin 144
St-Sauveur **175**
St-Seurin-de-Cadourne **174**
St-Tropez 106
St-Véran 96
St-Vérand 96
Saintsbury, Professor George 42, 201
Salad 43, 205
Salaparuta, Duca di 136
Salinas valley 152, **224**
Salmon **44**, 133
Salmon, smoked **43**
Salomon, Fritz 145
Samos, island of **160**
Sampigny-les-Maranges **94**
"Sample" glass 242
San Benito County 153
San Felipe 229
San Francisco 150, 151, 220, 222
San Joaquin 151
San Matteo 133
San Patricio 55
San Sadurni de Noya 141
San Sebastian 75
Sancerre 85, 98, 99, **100–1**, 155
Sandeman's 55 (sherry), 237 (port)
Sandgrub (Kiedricher) 123
Sangiovese 130
Sangredetoro 218
Sangria **218**
Sangue di Giuda **210**
Sanguinhal 140
Sanlucar de Barrameda 48, **55**
Santa Christina 133
Santa Clara County 153
Santa Maddalena **212**
Sant'Ambrogio 211
Santenay 86, **197**
Santenay-Côte de Beaune (*appellation*) 195
Santenay-Gravières 197
Santenots, Les (Volnay) 197
Santiago 228
Sâone, river 85, 94
Saperavi 222
Sardinia 78, 129, **215**
Sassella **209**
Saumur **72**, 155
Saumur-Champigny 205
Sausage 45
Sauterne (California) 152, 247
Sauternes 19, 29, 41, 82, 83, 88, 97, 103 (with rich food), 142 (Spain), 155 (California), 169 (red), 171 (and 1855 classification), 187, 230, 242, **243–7**, 248, 253
Sauvignon (grape variety) 89, 98, 101, 132, 152, 154, 155
Sauvignon Blanc (grape

variety) 101, 132, 152 (California), **154**, 159
Savannah, Georgia 77
Sava, river 148
Savennières **102**
Scala, Giuseppe 136
Scandiano **132**
Scandinavia 147
Scharlachberg (Bingen) 12
Scharzberg, Wiltinger 117
Scharzhofberg, Wiltinger 1
*Schaumwein* 74
Scheurebe (grape variety) 127, 128
Schillerwein 164
Schloss Ehrenfels 121
Schloss Johannisberg **122**, 124, 248
Schloss Kauzenberg 125
Schloss Reinhartshausen 12
Schloss Saarfelser 117
Schloss Vogelsang 117
Schloss Vollrads 91, **122**
Schlossberg, Rüdesheimer Berg 121
Schlossböckelheim **125**, 12€
Schluck 145
Schlumberger 104
Schonbörn, Count von 123
Schönhell (Hallgartener) 12
Schoonmaker, Frank 60
Schramsberg 75
Schubert, von (family) 118
Schwarzer Katz 121
Schweigener Guttenberg 1:
Scotch 66
Scotland (as importer of claret) 17
Scott and Tolley 227
Seabrook, Tom 237
Seafood. *See* fish, etc.
Seaview winery 227
*Sec* 64, 254
*Secco* 134
Secondary fermentation **68** (champagne), 73, 230–1 (stopping)
Sediment **39**, 64 (champagn 233 (port)
Seitz factory 126
Sekt 74, 75, 111, 117
Semeillan 179
Semillon (grape variety) 98, 152, **155**, 158
Seppelt's 156, 165, 227, 228
Serbia **148**
Sercial **77**
Serein, river 88
Serradayres 140 (white), 21¹ **220** (red)
Serrador 140
Serralunga d'Alba 208
Serrig 117
Serristori-Macchiavelli 214
Serving wine **38–41**, 57 (sherry), **70** (champagne) 231 (after-dinner wines)
Sesimbra 251
Seteais, Palacio, hotel at Sintra 220

túbal **251**
ville 48
vre-et-Maine (*département*)
  100
yssel **72** (sparkling), 106
  (still)
ursat **210**, 253
akespeare 27, 84 (quoted),
  110, 241 (quoted)
antung 78
ellfish 43, 133, 138
erris-sack 48, 241
erry 12 (fortification of),
  19, 21, 35, 43, 47, **48–60**,
  48 (the name sherry),
  49–50 (vineyards and the
  vintage), 50 (treading and
  pressing), 50–51 (fermentation and classification),
  51 (flors and finos), 53 (the
  Solera system), 53 (blending), 55 (the meaning of
  label terms), 57 (serving
  sherry), 57 (decanters and
  glasses), **58–60** ("sherry"
  from other countries), 75,
  81, 141, 232, 238, 239, 240,
  **241** (cream sherry)
erry Kina **80**
ips, medieval, tonnage of 16
iraz (grape variety) **226**,
  227, 228, 238
chel 99, 112
cily 48, **136** (white), **215**
  (red), 240 (Marsala), 251,
  252
di Larbi 206
ena 133, 213, 214
evering 144
mon, André 71, 192, 238
mplon Pass, the 208
ntra 220
ion 143
ran 181
tges 141
kate 100
ivova 150
ovenia **148**
moked eel 43, 57
moked fish 43, 57
nipe 45
nobbery, wine 10, 28, 254
oave 43 (with food), 129,
  **131** (white), 135, 211
oave Classico 131
obel 59
ofia 150
olar 140
ole 44, 89, 100
ole Deauvillaise 44
olera system **53**, 59
olutré **95–6**
omlo **148**
ommeliers **37–8**
ondrio 209
onnenküste 222
onnenuhr 120
onnenuhr, Wehlener 120
onoma valley 151, 152, 153,
  222
orbara, Lambrusco di 210
orrento 136, 215, 234

Sotheby's 19
*Soufflé surprise* 254
Soup 43, 240
Soussans **180**
South Africa 14, 19, 24, 27
  (and slow-maturing wines),
  48, **58–9** (sherry), 78, 150,
  **159** (white), **228** (red),
  237–8 (port-type wine),
  242, 252
South America **228–9**
South Australia 157, 226, **227**
South of France. *See* France
Southern Vales 227
Soviet Union 149, **150**
  (white), **222** (red), 249
Spain 10, 21 (Spanish
  "Chablis"), 35, 43, 45,
  **48–58** (sherry), **75**
  (sparkling wine), **141–2**
  (white), 147, **215–18** (red),
  233, 236 (Malaga), 247,
  250, 253. *See also under*
  Sherry, Rioja, etc.
Spanna 209
Sparkling wines **11** (making
  of), 23, **60–71** (champagne),
  **71–2** (France), **73–4** (Italy),
  **74** (Germany), **75** (Spain),
  **75** (California), 75 (British),
  140, 164, 207, 210
  (Lambrusco di Sorbara),
  219, 253–4 (after-dinner
  wines)
*Spätlese* 115, 116, 158, 159,
  248
Spirits **46**, 66
Spritzig, Seppelt's 165
*Spumante* 73, 74, 254
State Domain, the German
  122, 123, 126
*Stay Me with Flagons*,
  Maurice Healy's 181
Steak 202
Steen (South African grape
  variety) 58, 159
Steen (wine) 159
Stein 145
Steinberg **123**, 126, 243
Steinberger Kabinet 91
Steingarten, Gramp's 158
Steinmacher 124
Steinwein 27 (1540 vintage),
  **128**
Stellenbosch 159, 228
Stilton 45
Stony Hill winery 154
Stonyfell 227
Storage of wine, conditions
  for 34
Strawberries 45, 253
Strength, alcoholic. *See*
  Alcoholic strength
Suchots, Les (Vosne-
  Romanée) 192
Südbahn 146
Südliche Weinstrasse 126
Sugar 10 (addition to wine),
  11, 12, 47 (and suppression
  of appetite), 81, 111, 113,
  115, 116, 159, 230, 231, 232
Suizo Café 216

Sulphur 83 (addition to wine
  to stop fermentation), 97,
  102, 134, 138
*Sur lie* 100
*Sur pointe* 68
*Sur souche*, effect on price by
  buying 170
Suresnes 206
Surrey 48
*Süss-reserve* 12, 113, 116
Suze **81**
Sweet course, the 45, 231, 254
Sweetbreads 44
Switzerland 61, 94, 105, 108,
  **143–4** (white), **164** (rosé),
  199, 209, 234, 253 (*vin
  flétri*)
Sydney 157, 158
Sylvaner (grape variety) **104**
  (Alsace), 124, 127, 128
  (Steinwein), 132, 143, 144,
  149, 150, 155 (California),
  225
Sylvester wine 248
Syracuse **252**
Syrah (grape variety) 200,
  203, 228
Szamorodni **249**
Szurkebarat 147

**T**
Table wine **11** (making of),
  **47** (as an aperitif), **82–161**
  (white), 82–3 (introduc-
  tion), 84–96 (burgundy),
  96–9 (Bordeaux), 99–102
  (Loire), 102–4 (Alsace),
  105–8 (Rhône valley),
  108–28 (Germany), 129–36
  (Italy), 137–40 (Portugal),
  141–2 (Spain), 143–6
  (Switzerland and Austria),
  146–50 (Eastern European),
  150–56 (Californian), 156–9
  (Australia), 159 (South
  Africa), **161–5** (rosé),
  **166–229** (red), 166–7
  (introduction), 168–88
  (Bordeaux), 188–200
  (burgundy), 200–3 (Rhône
  valley), 203–7 (*vins de
  pays*), 207–15 (Italy),
  215–18 (Spain), 218–21
  (Portugal), 221–2 (Eastern
  European), 222–5 (other
  reds), 226–9 (other
  reds)
Tache, La **192**
*Tafelwein* 115, 130
Tagus, river 137, 251
Tain 105, 201
Taittinger 69, 70
Talbot, Marshall 16
Tanaro, river 208
Tannin 25, 154, **166**, 205, 218
*Tapas* 55
Tarn, river 107
Tarragona 141, 142, 218, 241
Tartaric acid (crystals of as
  sediment) 39

*Tartelettes aux framboises* 200
*Tastevin* 95
Taunus mountains 121
Taurasi **215**
Tavares & Rodriguez 220
Tavel **162**, 165, 202
Tawny port 35, **77**, **232**, 237,
  238
Taylor 237
*Teinturiers* 83
Temperature for serving
  wine 34, **71** (champagne),
  231 (after-dinner wines),
  **246–7** (Sauternes), 250
  (Tokay)
Tempier, Domaine 204
Terete Restaurant, Haro 216
Terlaner **132**
Termeno 130, 132
Teroldego (grape variety)
  130, **212**
Terrantez 239
*Tête de cuvée* 69
  (champagne), 191
Teurons, Les (Beaune) 195
Thanisch, Dr 119
Thénard, Baron 93
Thermalpen 146
Thrace 160, 252
Ticino 143
Tiergarten 118
Tigermilk (Ranina Radgona
  Spätlese) 149
*Tinajas* 58
Tinta 239
Tinta Madeira 238
Tio Pepe, Gonzalez Byass's
  55
Tirnave 149
Tocai (grape variety) 132
Tokaji *See* Tokay
Tokay 45 (with food), **146**,
  147, 243, **248–50**
Tokay d'Alsace 104, 132
Tolley, Scott and Tolley 227
Tomato salad 42
*Torneviagem* 251
Tongue 45
Tonic-water 80
Torres 141
Torres, Miguel 218
Torres Vedras 220
Toucy 89
Touraine 72 (sparkling),
  **101–2** (white), 155
Touraine Sauvignon 102
*Tournedos* 36
Tournon 105, 201
Toussaints, Les (Beaune) 195
Traben-Trarbach 121
Traisen 126
Traminer (grape variety) 103,
  104, 128, 132, 144, 149,
  157, 158
Tras-os-Montes 234
Travelling, wines improved
  by 76, 190, 251
Travelling, wines spoilt by
  19, 139, 144
Treading 10, 50 (sherry),
  235 (port)
Trebbia, river 132

Trebbiano (grape variety) 130, **132**, 135
Trent, Council of 74
Trentino **132** (white), **211–12** (red)
Trento 74, 212
Treppchen (Piesporter) 119
Tres Coronas 218
Tres Cunhas 140
Tres Palmas, La Rira's 55
Treviso 131
Trier 18, **117–18**
Trierer Hammerstein 118
Trierer Römerlay 118
Trimbach 104
Tripe 45
Trittenheim 119
Trockenbeerenauslese 115, 116, 128, 146, 156, 243, 248
Trousseau (grape variety) 163
Trout 44, 110, 133
Truffles, white (Italian) 209
Tsinandali 150
Tulbagh 159
Tulloch's 227
Tun 16
Turbot 100
Turin 73, 79, 208, 209
Turkey (the bird) 45
Tuscany **133** (white), **213–14** (red), 253 (vinsanto)
Twee Yongegezellen 159
Tyrol, Italian 74 (white), 163 (rosé), 208
Tyrrell's 227

**U**

U.S.A. 18–19, 37, 39, 46, 60 (Californian "sherry"), 71, 75 (sparkling), 77, 88 (insistence on domaine- or château-bottled wines), 91, 139, **150–6** (white), 163, 164, 165 (rosé), 170, 211, **222–5** (red), 239. See also California
Ullage 170
Umbria 133, **134–5** (white), **214** (red)
Underberg **81**
Ungstein 127
United Kingdom. See Britain
Ürzig 120
Ürziger Schwarzlay 120

**V**

V.D.Q.S. (vins délimités de qualité supérieure) 22, 115, 203, 204, 205, 206, 207
Val di Lupo 136, 215
Valdepeñas 142 (white), **218** (red)
Valdespino 55
Valencia 142
Valladolid 217
Vallana, Antonio 209
Valmur (Chablis) 88
Valpantena 211
Valparaiso 229

Valpolicella 131, **210–11** (red)
Valpolicella Classico 211
Valtellina 209, 210
Van der Weyden, Roger 194
Vanillin 154
Var (departement) 106
"Varietal" names 152 (California), 158 (Australia), 224
Vaucluse 204
Vaucrains, Les (Nuits-St-Georges) 193
Vaud 143
Vaudésir (Chablis) 88
Vaulorent (Chablis) 88
Veal **44**, 94
Vega Sicilia 217
Velletri 134
Veneto **131–2**, **210–11**
Venice 131
Venison **44**, 126, 201
Venusbuckel 127
Vercelli 209
Verdelho **77**, 239
Verdicchio (grape variety) 133, **135**
Verdiso (grape variety) 132
Verduzzo (grape variety) 132
Vereingte Hospitien 118
Vergelesses, Aux (Savigny-les-Beaune) 194
Vergelesses, Ile de (Pernand-Vergelesses) 194
Vergisson 95
Vermentino 131
Vermouth 47, **79–81**, 208
Vernaccia 78, 215
Vero Lambrusco, Il 210
Verona 131, 209, 210, 211
Vertheuil **175**
Verzenay 67
Vesuvius, Mount 136, 214
Veuve Clicquot **63–4**, 69
Veuve Laurent Perrier 69
Vevey 143
Vichy 206
Victoria, Australia 157, 227, 252
Victoria, Queen 110 (her favourite wine), 124 (wine named after)
Vienna 143, **144**, 145
Vienne 105
Vigne de l'Enfant Jésus, Bouchard Père's 195
Vignes-Franches, Les (Beaune) 195
Vilafrancha de Panades 141
Vilanova de Gaia 236
Vilanyi **221**
Vila Real 140
Vin blanc cassis 106
Vin blanc de Cassis 106
Vin de consommation courante 203
Vin de garde 162
Vin de goutte 170
Vin de l'année 27, 100, **199** (Beaujolais)
Vin de liqueur 251

Vin de noyer, recipe for 80
Vin de paille 107, 253
Vin de (du) pays **23**, 43, 100, 189, 198, **203–7**
Vin de presse 170
Vin du glacier 143
Vin d'une nuit 27
Vin Fin de Hautes Côtes de Nuits 196
Vin flétri 253
Vin gris 78, 163, 206
Vin jaune 78, 107
Vin ordinaire **23**, 37, 96, 103, 106, 108, 137, 151, 167, 187, 215, 218, 225
Vin rosé **23**, 26 (as quick-maturing wines), 35, 37, 43 (on a picnic), 70, 72 (sparkling), 79, 97, **161–5**, 202, 212, 219, 225
Viña Paceta 217
Viña Pomal 217
Viña Réal Oro 217
Viña Réal Plata 217
Viña Sol 141
Viña Tondonia 142, 217
Vincent, Marcel 95
Vincent, St, patron saint of wine 95
Vinegar 26, 42
Vinho maduro **139–40**, 219
Vinho verde 26, 47, 116, 137, **138–9**, 140, 142, 144, **219**
Vinifera Wine Cellars 156
Vinland 156
Vino corriente **23**, 141
Vino de color **54**
Vino de pasto **57**
Vino passito 253
Vino santo (vinsanto) 253
Vino Spanna **209**
Vins de café 202
Vins délimités de qualité supérieure (V.D.Q.S.) 22, 115, 203, 204, 205, 206, 207
Vintage charts **23**, 30, 31. See also pages 256–7
Vintage, declare a 32, 67 (champagne), 233 (port)
Vintage of the century (1959) 31
Vintage port. See Port, vintage
Vintage, the 32, **49–50** (sherry), 66 (champagne), 138, **170** (Bordeaux), 232, **235** (port), 242, 243 (Sauternes), 247–8 (German), 249 (Tokay)
Vintages **29–32** (reasons for individuality), 38, 152
Viognier (grape variety) 105
Viré 94
Virgin (Marsala) **240**
Viseu 219
Visp 143
Visperterminen **143**
Viticulture and Enology, Department of (University of California) 151
Vitis Vinifera 13, 156
Vogelsang, Serrig 117

Vogüé, Count Georges de 191
Volaille de Bresse aux morille 200
Vollrads, Schloss 91, **122**
Volnay 41, 85, 86, 193, 195, **196–7**
Volnay Caillerets 41, 197
Volnay Champans 197
Volnay Clos des Chênes 41, 197
Volnay Santenots **197**
Vosges, the **103**, 126
Vöslaüer 221
Vosne 86, 192
Vosne-Romanée 86, **192**, 193
Vougeot 86
Vouvray **72** (sparkling), 10: (white), 102

**W**

Wachau, the **145**
Wachenheim 127
Wachenheimer Goldbächel 127
Wagner Stein 228–9
Waldrach 118
Walluf 121
Walnut leaves 80
Warre 237
Warsaw 248
Washington 150
Wasseros (Kiedricher) 123
Waterloo, battle of 63
Wawern 117
Weather 29, 30 (importance of), 31 (micro-climates), 111
Wehlen 119, **120**
Wehlener Sonnenuhr 120
Weinbaugebeit 113
Weinstube 150
Weinviertel 145
Weissburgunder 127
Weisserkirchen 145
Wellesley, Sir Arthur 220
Welsh Riesling (grape variety) 148
Wente Brothers 154, 224
Werner 124
Weyden, Roger van der 19
White Pinot 155
White Riesling (grape variety) **154**
White table wines 26, **29** (maturing of), 40 (decanting of), 41 (temperature to serve), 43 (with food), 44, 47 (as aperitifs), **82–16** See also under regional and other names
Widmers 156, 165
Wiesbaden 124
Wild boar 126, 201
Williams and Humbert 55
Wilson and Valdespino. See Valdespino
Wiltingen 117
Wiltinger Braunfels 117
Wiltinger Scharzberg 117

ine **9–41** (general introduction), 10-13 (making of), 13 (as a civilizing influence), 18–19 (as a luxury or necessity, also increase of consumption in Great Britain and U.S.A.), 19 (consumption in France, Great Britain and U.S.A.), 19 (medical benefits), 20 (future trends of), 20-3 (nomenclature) 21–2 (legislation about), 25 (life-cycle of), 25-9 (effects of time on), 35 (for immediate drinking), 35–6 (for special occasions), 38-9 (glasses for), 39 (preparation of), 41-5 (wine and food combinations—*see also under* Food), 42 (enemies of). *See also under colours, regional names, etc.*

Wine-bar, a 242
Wine-basket (or cradle) 37, 40
*Wine in Australia*, Walter James's 237
Wine-lists 29, 33, 36, 200
Wine-merchant, choice of a 29, 32, 33
Wine School (Neustadt) 127
Wine-shop, in a **33–4**
Wine-trade, the 16 (medieval), 17 (during the seventeenth century), **19**, 33, 35, 53, 167, 194, 196, 215
Wine-waiters 37
*Wines of Bordeaux, The,* Professor J. R. Roger's 176, 245
*Wines of Spain and Portugal,* Jan Read's 218
Winkel 121, **122**
Wintrich 114, 119

Winzenheim 126
*Winzergenossenschaft* 126, 145
*Winzerverein* 126
Wolkonski, Prince Serge Alexandrovitch 63
Wood, port maturing in. *See* Ruby and Tawny
Woodhouse, John 240
Worms 112, 126
Wulfen (Rauenthaler) 124
Württemberg **111**
Würzburg 27, 128
Würzgarten 120, 123
Wynn's 227

**X**
*Xampan* 75, 141

**Y**
Yalumba 59, 158
Yeast 11, 50, 83, 230

Yerasa 241
Ygay, Castillo 217
Yugoslavia 47, 146, **148–9** (white), **164** (rosé), 212, **221** (red)
Yvorne 144
Yvrac 187

**Z**
*Zabaglione* 239
Zell 121
Zeller Schwartz Katz 121
Zeltingen **120**
Zeltinger 120
Zeltinger-Rachtig 120
Zermatt 143
Zilavka (grape variety) 149
Zinfandel (grape variety) **225**
Zoopiyi 241
Zurich 143
*Zwicker* 104

# Acknowledgments

The Publishers gratefully acknowledge the assistance of the following in providing photographs

*The Work of the Vineyard*
Pictor, Guy Gravett, Susan Griggs/Adam Woolfitt, Grants of St James's, Bob Estall, Grants of St James's, Tony Stone Associates, Daily Telegraph/Patrick Thurston, Agence Top/J N Reichel

*The Work of the Cellar*
Agence Top/J N Reichel, Peter Titmus, Agence Top/A Valtat, Guy Gravett, Agence Top/J N Reichel, Hugh Johnson, Grants of St James's, Grants of St James's, Agence Top/J N Reichel, Spectrum

*The Work of the Wine-Trade*
Grants of St James's, Daily Telegraph/Graham Finlayson, Daily Telegraph/Graham Finlayson, Daily Telegraph/Graham Finlayson, Daily Telegraph/Graham Finlayson, Hugh Johnson, Daily Telegraph, Guy Gravett, Hugh Johnson, Agence Top/J N Reichel

*The Pleasures of the Table*
Hugh Johnson, Grants of St James's, Hugh Johnson, Hugh Johnson, Susan Griggs/Michel Boys, Tony Stone Associates.